Exegesis in the Making

Exegesis in the Making

Postcolonialism and New Testament Studies

By
Anna Runesson

BRILL

LEIDEN • BOSTON

This paperback was originally published in hardback as Volume 103 in the series *Biblical Interpretation Series*.

The Library of Congress has cataloged the hardcover edition as follows:

Runesson, Anna.
  Exegesis in the making : postcolonialism and New Testament studies / by Anna Runesson.
    p. cm. — (Biblical interpretation series, ISSN 0928-0731 ; v. 103)
  Includes bibliographical references (p.   ) and index.
  ISBN 978-90-04-18836-5 (hardback : alk. paper) 1. Bible. N.T.—Postcolonial criticism. I. Title.

  BS2379.7.R85 2011
  225.6—dc22
                                                                                2010036400

ISBN 978-90-04-39326-4 (paperback, 2019)
ISBN 978-90-04-18836-5 (hardback, 2011)
ISBN 978-90-04-19034-4 (e-book, 2011)

Copyright 2011 by Koninklijke Brill NV, Leiden, The Netherlands.
Koninklijke Brill NV incorporates the imprints Brill, Brill Hes & De Graaf, Brill Nijhoff, Brill Rodopi, Brill Sense, Hotei Publishing, mentis Verlag, Verlag Ferdinand Schöningh and Wilhelm Fink Verlag.
All rights reserved. No part of this publication may be reproduced, translated, stored in a retrieval system, or transmitted in any form or by any means, electronic, mechanical, photocopying, recording or otherwise, without prior written permission from the publisher.
Authorization to photocopy items for internal or personal use is granted by Koninklijke Brill NV provided that the appropriate fees are paid directly to The Copyright Clearance Center, 222 Rosewood Drive, Suite 910, Danvers, MA 01923, USA. Fees are subject to change.

This book is printed on acid-free paper and produced in a sustainable manner.

In loving memory of my father
Göran Gyllenör

CONTENTS

List of Illustrations xi
Preface xiii
Acknowledgements xvii
Abbreviations xix

Chapter One   Introduction 1

PART ONE

THE THEORETICAL LOCATION AND CONTRIBUTION
OF POSTCOLONIAL NEW TESTAMENT STUDIES

Chapter Two   Introduction 7
2.1   Procedure 7
2.2   Postcolonial Studies: Some Initial Remarks 9

Chapter Three   The Theoretical Location of Postcolonial
Studies 17
3.1   The Postcolonial Phenomenon: A Presentation and a
      Definition 17
      3.1.1   Excursus: Who is a Postcolonial Scholar? 30
3.2   Perspectives and Methods 32
      3.2.1   Episteme: What is Reality? 33
      3.2.2   Deconstruction—a Theory and a Method 39
3.3   Postcolonial Studies and New Testament Exegesis 40
3.4   Summary 48

Chapter Four   Deconstructing Western Biblical Studies 51
4.1   Introduction 51
4.2   Exegesis in a Nutshell: A Short Presentation of its
      History 53
      4.2.1   Defining Exegesis 53
      4.2.2   The Historical Critical Discourse 55
      4.2.3   Summary 57
4.3   Postcolonial Critique of Traditional Historical Critical
      Discourse 58

	4.3.1	General Critique of Historical Critical Discourse	59
		4.3.1.1 Positivism and 'Objectivism'	61
		4.3.1.2 The Nature and Intention of the Biblical Text	64
	4.3.2	Specific Critique of Historical Critical Discourse	67
		4.3.2.1 Orientalism and the Portrayal of 'the Other'	68
		4.3.2.2 Hegemony and Truth Claims	71
		4.3.2.3 Relevance as a Critical Problem	77
	4.3.3	Kwok and the Quest for the Historical Jesus: A Test Case	82
4.3	Summary		87

Chapter Five Constructing Postcolonial Biblical Analysis 89
5.1 Redefining Exegesis: Introducing Postcolonial Approaches 89
5.2 Category One: Postcolonial Analysis within the Historical Critical Paradigm 91
    5.2.1 Tracing Colonial Elements and Abuses in New Testament Texts 94
    5.2.2 Mapping Colonial Spread of Western Biblical Criticism 97
    5.2.3 Translating the Bible in an Indian Context 99
    5.2.4 Inter-Textual Comparisons 102
    5.2.5 Mapping Historical Contacts: The Ancient World Beyond the Euphrates 105
5.3 Category Two: Postcolonial Methodological Approaches Beyond Western Historical Critical Discourses 107
    5.3.1 Dhvani Exegesis 108
    5.3.2 Dalit Exegesis 113
    5.3.3 Minjung Exegesis 115
    5.3.4 Postcolonial Imagination 118
5.4 Summary 123

Chapter Six Summary and Conclusion: Postcolonialism and the Search for "Authentic Exegesis" 127

CONTENTS ix

PART TWO

POSTCOLONIAL READINGS

Chapter Seven   Introduction 135

Chapter Eight   Postcolonial Analysis, History, and
Hermeneutics 141
   8.1 Musa W. Dube (University of Botswana). Consuming a
Colonial Cultural Bomb: Translating *Badimo* Into
'Demons' in the Setswana Bible (Matthew 8.28–34;
15.22; 10.8) 141
   8.2 Khiok-Khng Yeo (Garrett-Evangelical Seminary, USA/
Beijing University, China). The Rhetorical Hermeneutic
of 1 Corinthians 8 and Chinese Ancestor Worship 168
   8.3 Gregory David Wiebe (McMaster University, Canada).
The Demonic Phenomena of Mark's "Legion":
Evaluating Postcolonial Understandings of Demon
Possession 186

Chapter Nine   Postcolonial Approaches Beyond Western
Historical Critical Discourses 213
   9.1 George M. Soares-Prabhu (De Nobili College in Pune,
India [†1995]). And There Was a Great Calm:
A 'Dhvani' Reading of the Stilling of the Storm
(Mk 4:35–41) 213
   9.2 George Zachariah (Gurukul Lutheran Theological
College, Chennai, India). The Parable of the not so
Prodigal Daughters: A Postcolonial Dalit Womanist
Reading 225

Bibliography 235

Author and Subject Index 249

LIST OF ILLUSTRATIONS

Figure 1   Illustration of the postcolonial phenomenon   23
Figure 2   Inter-discursive similarities and inter-epistemic
           developments   37
Figure 3   *Svensk teologisk kvartalskrift*, United Theological
           College, Bangalore, 2003   99
Figure 4   The relationship between dhvani of attribution,
           vastu-dhvani, alamkara dhvani, and rasa-dhvani   110
Figure 5   The relationship between perspectives and methods
           in postcolonial exegesis   124
Figure 6   Understanding and Illustrating the Mizoram
           incident   131

PREFACE

Visiting Toronto's China Town or Indian Bazaar, strolling in downtown Hong Kong, or riding a rickshaw through Bangalore in India will leave no one in doubt regarding the level of globalisation in the world today, or the speed at which this development is travelling. Cultures meet, merge and/or clash; regardless whether we are conscious about what happens or not, it affects us all. Traditional ideas about who 'the Other' is are constantly challenged.

Historically, the North Star has guided us to the four cardinal points East, West, South, and North—a fact easy enough to learn in elementary school. However, adding a political aspect to the geographical makes it harder to use the compass, a fact directly connected to Western colonisation. Beginning in the 15th century and culminating in the late 19th and early 20th century, the cardinal points were gradually transformed into classifications where 'the West' and parts of 'the North' became the 'centre,' and 'the East' and 'the South' were defined as the 'periphery.'

Subsequently, through the process of colonisation, new political 'Wests' were created. Australia and New Zealand, far to the Southeast from a European perspective, politically became parts of the Western hemisphere. Canada and the USA have emerged as even more 'West' than Europe itself, whereas Central and South America, longitudinally just as much West of Europe as North America, have found themselves politically and economically marginalised, excluded from inclusion in 'the West.' In the South, we find equally or even more marginalised Africa. Complicating matters, the status of Japan, and more recently, Singapore, Thailand and China, is being renegotiated in Western discourses, filling the term 'East' with new political and economic content from a European and North American perspective.

Whatever the geographical definition, East, West, South, and North are today inextricably intertwined through colonisation, migration, and different forms of globalisations, creating what is today referred to as a *postcolonial world*.

The present book is a result of this situation. Academia, and more narrowly New Testament exegesis, is also part of our postcolonial world: my aim is to define in what way.

In this study I will focus on New Testament interpretation in a global context as moulded in the tensions between the West and the Two-Thirds World. My interest in these questions began during extensive travels in Asia, the Middle East, Africa, and North and Central America in the 1990s. The consequences of the modern colonial enterprise, in all their complexities, became for me a flesh-and-blood reality. As has increasingly become clear through the vast amount of scholarly literature on the topic published in recent years, these complexities reach into the heart of the academic world too.

Numerous people have, in different ways, been of great inspiration and help as this study took form. Only a few can be mentioned here, but I am grateful to all. I would like to thank Aasulv Lande, who initially suggested that this would be a fruitful area to explore; he was indeed right. The advice of Birger Olsson and Bengt Holmberg has been invaluable from beginning to end. For their kindness and critical comments I am deeply appreciative. I would also like to express my sincere thanks to the late David Kerr. David had generously agreed to write the preface to the book, but passed away before being able to do so.

Fernando Segovia supported the project from the beginning; for his help and kindness I am very grateful. Thanks are also due to Jayne Svennungsson, who read and commented on the discussion of Derrida.

Parts of my work were done in Bangalore, India. I am thankful to Tord Fornberg, Uppsala, for helping me to establish contacts in India, and to Joseph Pathrapankal, then at Dharmaram Vidya Kshetram (DVK). Thanks also to Joseph Muthuraj of the United Theological College (UTC). For financial support during my stay in India over several months in 2002 and 2003, I am grateful to *The Swedish Foundation for International Cooperation in Research and Higher Education* (STINT). Thanks also to *Crafoordska Stiftelsen* for several grants and financial support, both in relation to my stay in India and for technical equipment.

Halfway through the book I moved with my family from Lund, Sweden to Hamilton, Canada. I am grateful to faculty and staff at the Religious Studies Department at McMaster University for their friendship and kind support. I am also grateful to Marlene Powers at Redeemer College, Ancaster, for checking the English in PART ONE and to Gregory Wiebe, at McMaster University for his careful reading of the manuscript. Any errors still remaining are, of course, my own responsibility. Thanks are also due to Liesbeth Hugenholtz at Brill Academic Publishers for her patience and valuable help as this book emerged in its final form.

The last preparations before publication were made in Jerusalem during a year of leave of absence from my work as pastor of the Swedish Lutheran Church in Toronto 2009-2010. Special thanks are due to École biblique et archéologique française de Jérusalem and Hebrew University for generously allowing me to use their excellent libraries.

We are all moulded in various ways in specific social, cultural and religious matrices, from the moment we are born until the day we die. My father, Rev. Göran Gyllenör (1944–2009), always played an important role for me as I grew up, with his strong focus on those less fortunate, the poor, the destitute and those whose voices are not heard by the powerful. He was and continues to be a constant inspiration. It is with deep gratitude that I dedicate this book to him.

Finally, I would like to express my warmest gratitude and love to my fellow traveller through life—my husband Anders. His wise insights in questions regarding emancipation and justice in combination with a deep sensitivity to cultures and methodological/perspectival exegetical approaches created that truly stimulating scholarly atmosphere—even around the dinner table!—without which this book would never have seen the light of day. Thank you my dear, and thanks also to our wonderful children Rebecca, Noah, and Rachel.

Anna Runesson
Jerusalem, the Armenian Quarter
of the Old City
March 2010

ACKNOWLEDGEMENTS

For permission to reprint previously published articles appearing in PART TWO I am grateful to SAGE Publications, USA, Brill Academic Publishers, the Netherlands, Asian Women's Resource Centre for Culture and Theology, Sri Lanka, and St. Thomas Apostolic Seminary, Kottayam, India. The texts of the articles have been modified in terms of format to fit the current publication (*the SBL Handbook of Style*). Also, the New Testament passages interpreted in respective article have been added in Greek and English before the texts in order to facilitate for the reader.

ABBREVIATIONS

Whenever works have been abbreviated I have followed *The SBL Handbook of Style: For Ancient Near Eastern, Biblical, and Early Christian Studies.* Edited by Patrick H. Alexander, John F. Kutsko, James D. Ernest, Shirly A. Decker-Lucke, and for the Society of Biblical Literature David L. Pedersen. Peabody: Hendrickson, 1999.

AIC	African Independent Churches
AJT	Asia Journal of Theology
BiBh	Bible Bhashyam
BNTC	Black's New Testament Commentary
ICC	International Critical Commentary
ISPCK	Indian Society for Promoting Christian Knowledge
JAAR	Journal of the American Academy of Religion
JES	Journal of Ecumenical Studies
JFSR	Journal of Feminist Studies in Religion
JLE	Journal of Lutheran Ethics
JSNT	Journal for the Study of The New Testament
NBCLC	The National Biblical Catechetical and Liturgical Centre
RelS	Religious Studies
SBL	Society of Biblical Literature
SBLDS	Society of Biblical Literature Dissertation Series
SJT	Scottish Journal of Theology
SP	Sacra Pagina
TDNT	Theological Dictionary of the New Testament

CHAPTER ONE

INTRODUCTION

Early one evening, the inhabitants of a small village in Mizoram in northern India gathered together at the village-square. A fire was lit, and the flames reached up towards the darkening evening skies. People were talking intensely with each other, upset, it seemed, about something that had just transpired in their midst. The pastor of the Presbyterian congregation stepped forward, carrying a package that had been sent to the church from England. It was a book, a doctoral thesis in biblical studies, written by one of the young and gifted members of the community. Some years ago, they and their pastor had decided that this young man should be sent to the West to be thoroughly educated in theology and biblical studies. The pastor took the book out of the package and threw it on the fire.

Within minutes, hundreds of pages of discussion and thinking, years of the young man's labour in a foreign country, went up in smoke and merged into the nothingness of the silent night. The fire was meant to erase this product of historical critical scholarship so intensely foreign to the cultural and religious situation and life of the community. The research was perceived as deeply irrelevant, to the point of being offensive. People were disappointed, very disappointed. When the young man found out what had transpired, he decided to stay in the socio-political and cultural milieu in which his thinking had been formed: England.[1]

Many questions arise from this story. Why did this happen? Why were people so upset? And why was the young man sent to a different culture to study in the first place? How are we to explain this violent

---

[1] In February 2003, a Presbyterian student at the United Theological College in Bangalore told me the story, here somewhat dramatised by myself, about the burning of the book. The student, who did not approve of this reception of Western scholarship in his home village, noted to me that the main concern in the village was that the study they disapproved of tended to reject and/or explain away most of the biblical stories, on the basis of them being myth. Myth, however, according to the UTC student, is a vital part of the Christian religious tradition among his people, and to reject its religious significance is tantamount to heresy and perceived as an attack against their faith.

clash of academic and religious cultures? What developments led up to and made possible a situation in which books are considered so important that they trigger such powerful reactions?

We live in a postcolonial world. This means that the postcolonial phenomenon, or 'postcoloniality,' in one way or another affects the everyday lives of almost all human beings in the world today. The term 'postcoloniality' may be defined broadly as the entire outcome of and reactions to a colonial situation.[2] The most obvious and visible effect of this reality is the imbalance between richer and poorer countries with regard to health care and economic growth—an imbalance that in large part finds its origins in the modern colonial period. New Testament exegesis, as a scholarly discipline, is also part of postcoloniality since its epistemological foundations were established about the same time as the modern colonial project began to take form.

During this period, New Testament studies and colonialism influenced each other in a variety of ways, as we shall see below. Most effects of colonialism have been and are negative, not to say disastrous, in terms of oppression and economic and cultural exploitation. It should not be forgotten, however, that there are attempts, currently, to use some of the outcomes of the colonial enterprise in positive ways in order to avert catastrophic developments, such as climate change. Such consequences are also directly connected to past colonial activities resulting in intensified contacts between different parts of the world, including common decision-making about environmental and human rights issues.

In this book, I use postcoloniality as an analytic-descriptive term. It refers to a reality that is open to a wide variety of analyses, such as the study of literature written during the modern colonial era; investigations into the environmental effects of colonialism; historical studies of colonial situations other than the modern; analyses of the Western—mostly North American—movie industry and its neocolonial approaches to the rest of the world. The areas of investigation are innumerable.

Because of the complexity of the concept of postcoloniality, both regarding definitions and concrete real-life expressions, it is important to approach the phenomenon from a broad perspective. Only in this way will it be possible to consider the many aspects of the episteme to

---

[2] For discussion and a definition, see 3.1.

which postcoloniality belongs and upon which it depends for its existence. This will, as we shall see, facilitate the analysis of the varied phenomena permeated by the effects of postcoloniality, as well as indicate how such phenomena are related more specifically to biblical studies.

In brief, the current situation in postcolonial biblical scholarship is complex, sometimes even contradictory, and often hard to grasp. There seems to be little consensus theoretically, methodologically, and terminologically. To what do we refer when we speak of postcolonial New Testament interpretation? What are the cohesive forces keeping the field together, making it possible to identify specific scholarly interpretations as postcolonial? The aim of the present book is to bring clarity to these questions, suggest a frame within which to understand this new and growing academic field, and exemplify interpretive mechanisms and methodologies by including a selection of postcolonial studies focusing on specific New Testament passages.

We shall proceed as follows. In PART ONE, "The Theoretical Location and Contribution of Postcolonial New Testament Studies," we shall define, categorise, and situate the *specific* (postcoloniality in New Testament exegesis) within the *general* (postcoloniality in the world today). Chapter three, entitled "The Theoretical Location of Postcolonial Studies," will focus on presenting and defining postcoloniality, including postcolonialism, in order to use it as a tool for analysing the dimension of power within academia. In the same chapter, we shall also discuss the definition of the above-mentioned concept of episteme and its use as an analytical tool for understanding perceived realities, such as postcoloniality and, by extension, the contextual aspects of reading biblical texts. These basic discussions will set the frame for the analysis of the shape and function of postcoloniality within New Testament exegesis.

Chapter four, "Deconstructing Western Biblical Studies," focuses on presenting and analysing postcolonial criticism of traditional Western exegesis. While chapter four is aimed at presenting the deconstructive element in postcolonialism, chapter five, "Constructing Postcolonial Biblical Analysis," is a discussion of new perspectives and methods that have evolved over the past 30 years. In chapter six, we shall briefly summarise the main results of PART ONE and say a few words on possible future developments of biblical exegesis, locally and globally.

In PART TWO, "Postcolonial Readings," five studies will exemplify postcolonial biblical interpretations, giving concretion to the theoretical discussion in PART ONE. These articles have been divided into two categories. The first category, *Postcolonial Analysis, History, and Hermeneutics* (chapter eight), deals with Postcolonial analysis, which utilises historical critical methodology but takes it hermeneutically in new directions. Musa W. Dube's "Consuming a Colonial Cultural Bomb: Translating Badimo into 'Demons' in the Setswana Bible (Matthew 8.28–34; 15.22; 10.8)" deals with the problem of translation in a postcolonial context. Khiok-Khng Yeo, contrary to traditional exegesis, shows how Paul's rhetoric may be understood as opening for intercultural diversity in "The Rhetorical Hermeneutic of 1 Corinthians 8 and Chinese Ancestor Worship." Finally, "The Demonic Phenomena of Mark's "Legion": Evaluating Postcolonial Understandings of Demon Possession," by Gregory David Wiebe, puts the spotlight on postcolonial exegesis itself, problematising modern assumptions about and explanations of demon possession.

The second category, *Postcolonial Approaches Beyond Western Historical Critical Discourses* (chapter nine), focuses on interpretations that go beyond traditional historical critical interpretations. The first article, by George M. Soares-Prabhu, "And There Was a Great Calm: A 'Dhvani' Reading of the Stilling of the Storm (Mk 4:35–41)," compares a traditional Western understanding of the Markan passage with the perspective that emerges when the Indian Sanskrit method of dhvani is applied. The second text, "The Parable of the not so Prodigal Daughters: A Postcolonial Dalit Womanist Reading," by George Zachariah, redirects our attention to problematic aspects of a well-known text, with implications for our understanding of both the biblical author and modern readers.

As will be discussed in PART ONE, all categorisations have shortcomings; there are no neat borders between the studies of PART TWO. I hope, however, that both the selection of articles and the way they are presented here will facilitate, not least for newcomers to the field, the navigation and appreciation of the diversity of postcolonial interpretation. The articles selected also serve as examples of the theoretical discussion of PART ONE, where a similar categorisation is used.

It is my hope that this two-part structure, with overarching theoretical analysis and specific approaches applied to New Testament passages, will serve the main purpose of the book, that is, to bring clarity to a critical and growing field within New Testament studies.

PART ONE

THE THEORETICAL LOCATION AND CONTRIBUTION OF
POSTCOLONIAL NEW TESTAMENT STUDIES

CHAPTER TWO

INTRODUCTION

The main purpose of PART ONE is to understand postcolonial New Testament exegesis in the wider theoretical context of postcoloniality, with special consideration of the relationship between postcolonial perspectives and Western historical critical discourses.

This purpose is realised by asking three overarching questions that will be addressed in the study. *First*, what is the theoretical location of postcolonial biblical exegesis, i.e., where does postcolonial biblical exegesis belong theoretically within the wider scholarly field? *Second*, what exactly is the postcolonial deconstructive critique of 'mainstream' exegesis? *Third*, what can we say about the constructive contributions of postcolonial biblical studies so far?

These three questions are subdivided into several more detailed problems that we shall address:

What is postcolonial exegesis? Is it a science or an ideological criticism from a confessional perspective, or something in between? What is the position of 'objectivity' in postcolonial theory and how is it played out in exegetical textual studies? How does postcolonial exegesis relate to 'traditional' biblical studies? What shape does its critique of Western exegesis take? Is it consistent? What is the relationship between deconstructive and constructive elements in postcolonial exegetical approaches? What is the relationship between hegemony and truth claims in academia according to postcolonial scholarship, and how is this argued to affect the global academic society? What is the relevance of exegesis according to postcolonial exegetes, and what is the position of relevance in postcolonial theory more generally?

These and similar questions will help us to map and analyse the variety of approaches that are commonly labelled postcolonial biblical studies.

2.1 Procedure

To answer immediately one of the questions above, most scholars working with postcolonial theories do not admit the possibility of meta-perspectives because of the researcher's dependence on the context, historical and present, in which s/he[1] is living. A meta-perspective is often defined as creating or achieving distance between the scholar and the subject studied in terms of the scholar's personal interests. Since this definition of meta-perspective often, but not always, goes hand in hand with claims of objectivity, postcolonial scholars frequently position themselves as opposed to the possibility of working from a meta-perspective.[2]

Defining meta-perspective in this way, and noting my own embeddedness in my lived context (a white, middle-aged, Swedish woman, living as a 'hybrid'[3] in the Swedish 'diaspora'[4] in postcolonial Canada and Jerusalem), this seems a legitimate basic point of departure. Consequently, on the one hand, I find it impossible to analyse postcolonial biblical exegesis from an 'outside' meta-perspective. On the other hand, the task I have set before me in this study is not to produce a postcolonial analysis from 'within.' I have chosen a third way to proceed, understanding postcolonialism within the postcoloniality of our time via a discussion of the theoretical location of all exegesis.

Building on Michel Foucault, the present study discusses the theoretical location in which we all do exegesis with the help of the theory of episteme. Before this discussion can take place I must give a more

---

[1] The present study uses language that strives towards gender-neutrality. Referring to men and women collectively by merging the pronouns 'she and he' into 's/he' achieves an emphasis on equality between sexes. Unfortunately, we lack a convenient term merging 'her and his.' However, by reversing the traditional order in which these words are listed, the importance of challenging y/our thinking is emphasised.

[2] We may here compare this with basic approaches within anthropology. Early anthropological assumption was that the scholar doing fieldwork was able to 'view' and 'observe' events in the culture studied from a meta-perspective and then report them 'objectively.' Today this view is abandoned. Anthropologists are encouraged to partake in the event through 'participant observation,' since partaking adds to knowledge; indeed, since it is not possible to observe without affecting the observed, participant observation is methodologically more sound. For a discussion of aspects of historical research, see also Anders Runesson, "Vägar till det förflutna" in *Jesus och de första kristna: Inledning till Nya testamentet* (ed. Dieter Mitternacht and Anders Runesson; Verbum: Stockholm, 2006), 42–54.

[3] For an explanation of the concept of 'hybrid,' see section 3.1.

[4] Diaspora usually, in our field, refers to Jews living outside Israel. For a definition on the Jewish diaspora see Kwok Pui-lan, *Postcolonial Imagination and Feminist Theology* (Louisville: Westminster John Knox Press, 2005), 45. See also Kwok's definition of diaspora within postcolonial studies; in the same study she argues for a definition of diaspora as the physical movement of people beyond their original homelands due to colonisation, past or present. However, it seems better to understand the phenomenon of diaspora within the more general concept of postcoloniality. See further below.

general introduction to postcolonial studies. The discipline of New Testament exegesis will be approached from a variety of perspectives, with special focus on its historical origins, current forms, and its functions in a global setting. Then follows a careful analysis of postcolonial critique of New Testament exegesis, in particular its historical critical methods.

After tearing down comes re-construction: the final chapter will map some important postcolonial exegetical approaches in order to understand the exegetical future as envisioned by postcolonial scholars. As we shall see, while being diverse and sometimes contradictory, postcolonial approaches may be sorted broadly within two general categories. Such categorisation facilitates understanding of the approaches themselves and at the same time sheds light on the relationship between postcolonialism and Western traditional exegetical methods.

Before we can proceed with these tasks we need to introduce some of the main components and definitions of postcolonialism in order to set the stage for the more in-depth discussion of the phenomenon in chapter three.

2.2 Postcolonial Studies: Some Initial Remarks

> Post-colonial literary theory is an umbrella term that covers a multitude of literary practices and concerns of diverse races, empires, colonies, geographical centres, times and genres. One of its defining characteristics is that it emphasises the pervasiveness of imperialism and relates imperial expansion, impact, and response to certain literary practices and practitioners.[5]

These introductory words about postcolonial literary studies by Musa Dube indicate the broad character of the field. However, as we will see in section 3.1 below, postcolonial studies may be defined even more open-endedly, taking the discussion beyond literary practices.

In her description Dube states that writers are influenced by the pervasiveness of imperialism, and so defines one of the main characteristics of postcolonial studies. Dube touches on an important component in the development of different methods and perspectives generally—namely the importance of contexts for the scholar as an incentive for developing, using, or changing scholarly methods and

---

[5] Musa W. Dube, "Post-Colonial Biblical Interpretations," *Dictionary of Biblical Interpretation*, 2: 299.

perspectives. Therefore, the beginnings and developments of, or the changes in, scholarly methods and perspectives should be understood within the general context of interaction between academia and society.[6] Such shifts in methodological approaches are often preceded by circumstances that are hard to isolate and date. Nevertheless, certain achievements with regard to methodological development distinguish themselves as more significant than others and become landmarks by which people navigate.

One such landmark is Edward Said's book *Orientalism*, which was published as a contribution to the field of literary studies in 1978.[7] Many scholars have understood this study as the formal start of a criticism whose roots go back several years before Said wrote.[8] With inspiration from constructive theories developed by Foucault, Said argues that 'the Orient,' as a concept, is not a place or a reality but rather a theoretical construction. Ideas about 'the Orient' were formulated in Western countries (or the so-called 'Occident'), beginning during the modern colonial period.

This construction of 'the Orient' is termed 'Orientalism' by Said. 'Orientalism' is, in other words, a construction of 'the Other' living in the part of the world that is designated 'the Orient.' Therefore, in the process of constructing 'the Orient,' the self-designated centre (the Western world) was itself constructed. What differs between the two constructed entities is of course that definitions of 'the West' are made in positive terms while definitions of 'the Orient,' 'the Other,' are usually less appreciative. The same phenomenon is well known in gender studies where the construction of the male gender is dependent on the construction of the female gender as 'weaker.' To exaggerate some-

---

[6] For a closer examination of this topic, see the discussion on episteme below, section 3.2.1. For a discussion of interaction between academia and society, see Anna Runesson, "Feministisk exegetik: En undersökning av dess vetenskapliga värde belyst utifrån den feministiska teologin och exemplifierad genom feministisk historisk rekonstruktion och feministisk retorisk analys av 1 Kor 11:2–16" (Honours Thesis, Lund Univerity, 1995).

[7] Edward Said was Professor of English and Comparative Literature at Columbia University. He died in September 2003. His most well-known books are, *Orientalism* (New York: Vintage Books, 2003); *The World, the Text, and the Critic* (Cambridge: Harvard University Press, 1983); *Culture and Imperialism* (London: Vintage, 1994); and *Humanism and Democratic Criticism* (Columbia Themes in Philosophy; New York: Columbia University Press, 2004).

[8] Fernando F. Segovia, "Mapping the Postcolonial Optic in Biblical Criticism: Meaning and Scope" in *Postcolonial Biblical Criticism: Interdisciplinary Intersections* (ed. Stephen D. Moore and Fernando F. Segovia; London: T&T Clark, 2005), 26–27.

what, females are traditionally said to be fragile, sensitive, intuitive, and in need of protection (they do not always know what is best for themselves). Males, on the other hand, are strong, think logically, are intelligent and protective.

Interestingly, similar constructions of differences are to be found in descriptions of colonised peoples and colonisers. The colonised are often described as weak, lazy, sensitive, intuitive, superstitious, and in need of protection (and education). The colonisers, on the other hand, are described as strong, they think logically, they are intelligent, have a (superior) belief in the Christ, and see their mission as protecting and 'saving' the colonised. A Swedish example of such characterisations of differences may be found in John Magnusson's description of the Brazilian population in 1948. Magnusson, a missionary in the area, writes, "Brazil has a particularly heterogeneous population, just as most of the other South American republics. The great mixture of races creates a people with bad physics, and a weak character. However, among the descendants of European immigrants you often find pure raced families—good, hard-working farmers."[9]

Because of Western ethnocentric orientalism, the centre ('the West') became even stronger and the periphery ('the Orient') was weakened by its construction as the opposite of 'the West.' A classic example of orientalism is found in Rudyard Kipling's *The Jungle Book*, where he presents India as, to put it mildly, undeveloped, and England, needless to say, as civilised. In this well-known book we read about the Indian boy Mowgli, who was raised by wolves in the jungles of India. One day he comes in contact with 'civilisation,' (which is of course the English colonial presence in India), and he begins to turn 'human' again, which means that he morphs into an Englishman.

However, even though he succeeds in learning the English language and English manners, he is not allowed to marry the English lady he is in love with. Kipling's words "East is East and West is West and ne'er

---

[9] John Magnusson, "Örebro Missionsförenings mission i Brasilien" in *Missionen i bild* (ed. G. Lindeberg; Stockholm: AB Svenska Journalens Förlag, 1948), 321 (my translation). For further examples, see Musa W. Dube, "Postcoloniality, Feminist Spaces, and Religion" in *Postcolonialism, Feminism and Religious Discourse* (ed. Laura E. Donaldson and Kwok Pui-lan; New York: Routledge, 2002), 104. Because of the close relationship of postcolonial studies to other ideologically oriented approaches that are also based on reflection about unequal relationships of power (like feminist criticism, liberation criticism, minority criticism, and queer criticism), Segovia argues that postcolonial studies should not be done in isolation from but in dialogue with these other ideological approaches, Segovia, "Mapping the Postcolonial Optic," 23.

the twain shall meet" are meant to say that the differences between the peoples are so huge that it is impossible for them to ever match, despite changes on the surface. Mowgli remains animal-like even though he is taught English 'civilised' manners. Kipling's message is clear enough: there is an unbridgeable difference between 'the Orient' and England in the sense that England is 'civilised,' while 'the Orient' is not and never will be—in other words the Orient can never win and is always to remain inferior.[10]

Another example of orientalism may be found in the movie *Annie* that hit the screens in 1981. In this movie we find a man called Punjab who is the servant of the billionaire, Mr Warbucks. Punjab is mysterious and magical and he can make things like flowers and toys fly around in the room. What is interesting is that Punjab does not have a proper name, but is named after a state in India, Punjab. Even more awkward is the fact that he wears a turban and is obviously a Sikh, even though he, in the end of the movie, quotes Buddha. The mix of Sikhism and Buddhism in a person named after an Indian federal state and who, moreover, has magical powers (!) mirrors an orientalistic view of that particular character.

Examples of orientalism are not only found in books and movies, but also in our everyday lives, not least in daily newspapers. In the Canadian newspaper *The Hamilton Spectator* we find an article about how "five indigenous tribes" survived the tsunami disaster on the Indian archipelago of Andaman and Nicobar Islands. The heading reads, "Instincts may have saved isolated tribes." In the article, the environmentalist and lawyer Ashish Roy stated that the reason why the tribes fled from the beaches long before the tsunami hit the shore was because of their "instincts" and their "sixth sense." The orientalistic element consists in Roy's mystifying of these peoples, talking about them in terms typically used when describing animals (instinct) or spiritual mediums (sixth sense). It is true that Roy acknowledges that their rescue probably was due to their long experience and deep knowledge of the nature and environment in which they live as nomads.

---

[10] Rudyard Kipling, *The Jungle Book* (London: Macmillan, 1907). Kipling's story about Mowgli mirrors what in postcolonial studies is called hybridity (see further below). Hybridity is one of the outcomes of a colonial project, deriving from the colonial power's "need to 'civilise' its 'others,' and to fix them into perpetual 'otherness.'" Ania Loomba, *Colonialism/Postcolonialism* (London: Routledge, 1998), 173. Hybridity in this context refers to the tension created by this 'otherness' as it affects the individual living in the cross section of indigenous and colonial culture.

However, Roy's conclusion is not that these people survived because of their knowledge and logical thinking.[11]

The list can be made longer. Even though Said's work mainly focuses on the Middle East, orientalism as a concept has been applied to a wider range of situations. Zhaoming Qian, for example, argues for such a wider application of "orientalism." The concept may be used in a way that includes any countries affected by colonisation and the ideological-imperialistic constructs that follow with it—in Qian's case China.[12] R. S. Sugirtharajah uses 'orientalism' in his description of 'the Orientalist Mode' as a colonial reading practice applied in the search for India's history. This mode was "the cultural policy advocated by colonialists as a way of promoting and reviving India's ancient linguistic, philosophical, and religious heritage."[13]

Since Said's book was published, discussions of the concept of the 'Orient' have resulted in further theories about neo-colonialism, post-colonialism, and postcoloniality.[14] Some of the important—and well-known—contributions to this development of postcolonial studies include: *The Empire Writes Back: Theory and Practice in Post-Colonial Literatures*, by Bill Ashcroft, Gareth Griffiths, and Helen Tiffin,[15] *Colonialism/Postcolonialism*, by Ania Loomba[16], and *Colonial Discourse and Post-Colonial Theory: A Reader*, edited by Patrick Williams and Laura Chrisman.[17] These studies provide an excellent introduction to

---

[11] Neelesh Misra, "Instincts May have Saved Isolated Tribes," *The Hamilton Spectator*, Canada/World (January 5, 2005): A9.
[12] Zhaoming Qian, *Orientalism and Modernism: The Legacy of China in Pound and Williams* (Durham and London: Duke University Press, 1995), 1–2.
[13] R. S. Sugirtharajah, "From Orientalist to Post-Colonial: Notes on Reading Practices," *AJT* 10 (1996): 20–27, 21. For example, the use of the 'Orientalist Mode' had a great part in the construction of 'Hinduism' as an umbrella term for the different religions of India.
[14] These concepts will be dealt with in section 3.1 below.
[15] Bill Ashcroft, Gareth Griffith, and Helen Tiffin, *The Empire Writes Back: Theory and Practice in Post-Colonial Literatures* (London: Routledge, 1989). Other often quoted studies by the same authors are Bill Ashcroft, *Post-Colonial Transformation* (London: Routledge, 2001), Bill Ashcroft, Gareth Griffith, and Helen Tiffin, *The Postcolonial Studies Reader* (London: Routledge and Kegan Paul, 1995), and Bill Ashcroft, Gareth Griffith, and Helen Tiffin, *Post-Colonial Studies: The Key Concepts* (London: Routledge, 2002).
[16] Loomba, *Colonialism/Postcolonialism*. See also her study, *Shakespeare, Race, and Colonialism* (Oxford: Oxford University Press, 2002).
[17] Patrick Williams and Laura Chrisman, eds., *Colonial Discourse and Post-Colonial Theory: A Reader* (New York: Columbia University Press, 1994). See also, Peter Childs and Patrick Williams, *An Introduction to Post-Colonial Theory* (London: Prentice Hall,

postcolonial studies from a broad perspective; still, however, within the field of Comparative Literature.

Due to the close relationship between postcolonialism and research done in areas focusing on marginalised people and events,[18] there have appeared several contributions that combine the postcolonial approach with areas such as gender studies,[19] queer studies,[20] liberation theology,[21] cultural studies,[22] economics,[23] and questions about the meaning and impact of globalisation.[24]

This diversity and the emphasis on local contexts warn against any sweeping statements.[25] The term 'localism,' used by Feroza Jussawalla and Reed Way Dasenbrock in their book *Interviews with Writers of the Post-Colonial World*, is useful in this regard. In their study they argue for "using critical criteria derived from the region or locale itself to understand and judge the literature of that region."[26] Postcolonial

---

1997), and the more recent, Ania Loomba et al., eds., *Postcolonial Studies and Beyond* (Durham: Duke University Press, 2005).

[18] Concepts like 'margins' and 'periphery' might be seen as constructions, which are part of the designing of a 'centre.' When speaking about 'margins' we automatically 'marginalise' people that are not necessarily in the margins other than in the construction itself. However, since the construction of 'the margins' is not only a drawing-board product but has real flesh-and-blood implications, I will, in this study, use words like 'margin,' 'marginalise,' and 'periphery.'

[19] See for example, Gayatri Chakravorty Spivak, "Diasporas Old and New: Women in the Transnational World," *Textual Practice* (1996): 245–69, Mrinalini Sebastian, "Reading Archives from a Postcolonial Feminist Perspective: 'Native' Bible Women and the Missionary Ideal," *JFSR* 19:1 (2003): 5–25, Anne McClintock, *Imperial Leather: Race, Gender, and Sexuality in the Colonial Contest* (London: Routledge, 1995), Kwok Pui-lan, *Introducing Asian Feminist Theology*, vol. 4. (Introductions in Feminist Theology; Sheffield: Sheffield Academic, 2000), and Laura E. Donaldson and Kwok Pui-lan, eds., *Postcolonialism, Feminism, and Religious Discourse* (New York: Routledge, 2002).

[20] John C. Hawley, ed., *Postcolonial and Queer Theories: Intersections and Essays* (Westport: Greenwood Press, 2001).

[21] Leonardo B. Boff, *Global Civilization: Challenges to Society and to Christianity* (Cross Cultural Theologies; London: Equinox Publications, 2005) and Ivan Petrella, *The Future of Liberation Theology: An Argument and Manifesto* (Aldershot: Ashgate, 2004).

[22] Diana Brydon, ed., *Postcolonialism: Critical Concepts in Literary and Cultural Studies* (London: Routledge, 2000) and Gunew Sneja, *Haunted Nations: the Colonial Dimensions of Multiculturalisms* (Transformations; London: Routledge, 2004).

[23] O. Zein-Elbdin Eiman and S. Charusheela, eds., *Postcolonialism Meets Economics* (Economics as Social Theory; London: Routledge, 2003).

[24] Mario Blaser, Harvey A. Freit, and Glenn McRae, eds., *In the Way of Development: Indigenous Peoples, Life Projects and Globalization* (London: Zed Books, 2004).

[25] See Childs and Williams, *Post-Colonial Theory*, 23, n. 1.

[26] Feroza Jussawalla and Reed Way Dasenbrock, eds., *Interviews with Writers of the Post-Colonial World* (Jackson: University Press of Mississippi, 1992), 3–23. See also Hawley, ed., *Postcolonial and Queer*, x, where Hawley points out different local definitions of same-sex relations in different countries and cultures. We have to look at the different locations in order to do local-based definitions.

studies, one could say, work reciprocally in two directions, analysing the local in the global and the global in the local.

Despite the importance of the previously mentioned studies, any discussion of postcolonialism would be remiss not to mention the work of two theoretical trailblazers in this field: Homi Bhabha[27] and Gayatri Chakravorty Spivak.[28] Said, Bhabha, and Spivak have become the foundational trio within postcolonial studies, and their work is referred to frequently. All three have been influenced by postmodern philosophy, especially the poststructuralist philosophy of Foucault and Derrida.

In Bhabha's analyses of how postcoloniality has affected people he uses theories from semiotics and psychoanalysis. Terminology associated with Bhabha includes *mimicry, ambivalence,* and *hybridity*.[29] Spivak on the other hand has a more articulated philosophical approach. She criticises the overarching structures in Western academia and the way they construct 'the Other.' Terms associated with her work are *subaltern, ethical responsibility/ethical singularity, strategic essentialism*.[30]

---

[27] Homi Bhabha is the Chester D. Tripp Distinguished Service Professor in English Language and Literature at the University of Chicago. His most known works are, "The Commitment to Theory," *New Formations* 5 (1988): 5-23; "Of Mimicry and Man: The Ambivalence of Colonial Discourse" in *Modern Literary Theory* (ed. Philip Rice and Patricia Waugh; London: Edward Arnold, 1989), 234-41; and *The Location of Culture* (London: Routledge, 1994).

[28] Gayatri Chakravorty Spivak is the Avalon Foundation Professor in the Humanities at Columbia University. Her best known works are, *In Other Worlds: Essays in Cultural Politics* (New York: Routledge, 1988); *Outside in the Teaching Machine* (London: Routledge, 1993); "Can the Subaltern Speak?" in *Colonial Discourse and Post-Colonial Theory* (ed. Patrick Williams and Laura Chrisman; New York: Colombia University Press, 1994), 66-111; "Moving Devi," *Cultural Critique* (2001): 120-63; *Conversations* (Oxford: Blackwell Publishers, 2004); *Death of a Discipline* (The Wellek Library Lectures in Critical Theory; New York: Columbia University Press, 2003) and *Of Derrida* (Oxford: Blackwell Publishers, 2006). See also, Donna Landry and Gerald MacLean, eds., *The Spivak Reader* (London: Routledge, 1996).

[29] *Mimicry* describes "a strategy of colonial power/knowledge emblematic of a desire for an approved, revised Other," i.e., an attempt to form 'the Other' in the image of the centre, but still not making it identical to the centre. *Ambivalence* is derived from Freud's terminology marking the tension between the sexual instinct and the death instinct. Bhabha uses the term to mark the tension in the colonial discourse between "deride and desire," which is related to both "identification and disavowal." Childs and Williams, *Post-Colonial Theory*, 124-25, 129. For a definition of *hybridity*, see section 3.1.

[30] The term *subaltern* is found in her well-known and controversial article "Can the Subaltern Speak?" In this article, Spivak concludes that the subaltern cannot speak: not because they are without voice, but simply because the subaltern is a constructed group—and thus have no voice, since they do not exist. The *ethical responsibility/ ethical singularity* is the responsibility of making room for 'the Other' to exist. This existence is dependent on relationships and these relationships always go back to the individual, which is why Spivak uses the term ethical singularity. *Strategic essentialism*

All three of these authors have a common aim that unites them, namely to show how knowledge is interwoven with hegemony and how this epistemological hegemony has been used in the colonial endeavour. In their analysis, Foucault's theory of episteme is sometimes used as a tool, but in a vague way and not as a hermeneutical key to understanding what is involved in the phenomenon of postcoloniality. It is my contention that a consistent use of the theory of episteme will facilitate an understanding not only of postcolonial exegesis but also of exegesis generally.

We shall now turn to the question of the theoretical location of postcolonial biblical exegesis.

---

is a result of Spivak's reaction against essentialism, since it implies an uncritical development. Spivak works deconstructively, searching for the processes in which "truths are produced." To work with strategic essentialism is to search for truths in history that change the present. Gayatri Chakravorty Spivak, (http://www.english.emory.edu/Bahri/Spivak.html, 2003 [cited 6 May 2005]).

CHAPTER THREE

THE THEORETICAL LOCATION OF POSTCOLONIAL STUDIES

No academic discipline comes from nowhere. This is especially noticeable for a field like postcolonial studies and other subjects in the so-called 'margins.' Consequently, in order to do any analytical work at all it is important to understand the foundations of the discipline. Therefore, before focusing on postcolonial critique of modern biblical studies and its contributions to the field, it is necessary to analyse the theoretical location of the field.[1] By theoretical location I understand the discipline's locus within its episteme. In order to trace and define this locus it is important to understand in which episteme, and where in the episteme, the discipline belongs. Only then may the overarching theoretical origins and foundations of the field be found.

We shall begin this 'epistemic search' with a discussion of the postcolonial phenomenon. Then we shall proceed to define some important terms used to describe the postcolonial phenomenon. Finally, a definition of the episteme will be given followed by the localisation of New Testament exegesis within the realities in which postcolonial studies exist.

3.1 The Postcolonial Phenomenon: A Presentation and a Definition

Postcolonial studies are often thought of as being complex and difficult, lacking a clear consensus regarding its definition.[2] One of the few ideas that seems to be acceptable to most scholars is that a phenomenon exists that causes reactions and consequences, a phenomenon that

---

[1] The question of locating postcolonial studies has been debated in many studies, cf. Loomba, *Colonialism/Postcolonialism*, 1–103, Ashcroft, Griffith, and Tiffin, *The Empire Writes Back*, 1–13, Bhabha, *The Location of Culture*, 1–39, and Segovia, "Mapping the Postcolonial Optic," 23–78.

[2] For an introduction to terminological problems in postcolonial studies, see Robert J. C. Young, *Postcolonialism: An Historical Introduction* (Oxford: Blackwell, 2001), 13–69.

has its roots in a colonial situation.³ What it should be called and how it should be defined are still under debate.⁴ It is therefore necessary to give an introductory discussion and presentation of the definition that will be used in the present study.

The simplest definition of what is usually called 'postcolonialism' understands the phenomenon as having its beginnings after a colonial period has ended. With this definition, the word 'post' is emphasised and 'colonialism' is defined as a situation in which a geographical or political entity is ruled by a coloniser during a limited time period. The problem with this definition is that it implies an understanding of the period following the withdrawal of the colonial power as one of independence without enslaving foreign influences. The former colonised country would become *non*-colonised when the colonisers have left.

This might be true if we consider a colonisation as a military act only—but the term 'postcolonial' is usually applied to refer to more complex aspects of a hegemonic political and epistemic situation than such a one-sided definition would allow for.⁵ Ashcroft, Griffiths, and Tiffin write:

> We use the term 'post-colonial,' however, to cover all the culture affected by the imperial process from the moment of colonization to the present day.⁶

Defining the term in this way, a postcolonial situation describes a state of being, during and after a colonial enterprise has taken place. In

---

³ Terry DeHay, *What is Postcolonial Studies?* (http://www.sou.edu/English/IDTC/Issues/postcol/postdef.htm, 2004 [cited 8 October 2004]).

⁴ For an excellent discussion, see Stuart Hall, "When was 'the Post-Colonial'? Thinking at the Limit" in *Postcolonialism: Critical Concepts in Literary and Cultural Studies*, vol 1 (ed. Diana Brydon; London: Routledge, 2000), 237–57; repr. from *The Post-Colonial Question: Common Skies, Divided Horizons* (eds. Iain Chambers and Lidia Curti; London: Routledge, 1996). See also Segovia, "Mapping the Postcolonial Optic," 64ff., Loomba, *Colonialism/Postcolonialism*, xi. Vijay Mishra and Bob Hodge, "What is Post(-)colonialism?" *Textual Practice* 5:3 (1991): 399–414.

⁵ See Hall, "When was 'the Post-Colonial'?" 245. Hall states that "the 'post-colonial' references something more than direct rule over certain areas of the world by the imperial powers. I think it is signifying the whole process of expansion, exploration, conquest, colonisation and imperial hegemonisation which constituted the 'outer face,' the constitutive outside, of European and then Western capitalist modernity after 1492." Hall's definition of postcolonialism is broad; he considers it to be a global phenomenon and emphasises that the postcolonial reality does not necessarily have to be in the "*same way*" everywhere, which does not mean that the postcolonial reality is not "*in any way*" (241). For further discussion, see Laura. E. Donaldson, "Postcolonialism and Biblical Reading: An Introduction," *Semeia* 75:3 (1996): 1–14, 3.

⁶ Ashcroft, Griffith, and Tiffin, *The Empire Writes Back*, 2.

this sense, a postcolonial phenomenon, by necessity, takes different forms in different situations, depending on the cultural context. More importantly, a postcolonial phenomenon does not merely refer to a certain situation in a specific country—it is about the reactions and the consequences resulting from colonial oppression, and the effects this oppression has in the world at large.

In one sense, it is possible today to consider almost all humans and cultures to be postcolonial because of the global influence of the modern colonial period.[7] However, it is important to keep in mind the different contexts in which people experience the effects of postcoloniality within such a global postcolonial setting. Some individuals and groups are conscious about their postcolonial status and some are not. Consequently, a postcolonial situation may be understood by some as referring to the situation in which former colonised people exist; however, they would not consider themselves part of a postcolonial reality. It is easily forgotten, though, that the West[8] often benefits from the economic aspects of the postcolonial situation. In other words, most of the bricks with which the West has been constructed have their clay from the modern colonial era. This means that people in the West also live in a postcolonial situation, marked by the effects of colonialism, although not as victims.

---

[7] 84.6 percent of the land surface of the globe was under colonial influence during the 1930s. Loomba, *Colonialism/Postcolonialism*, xiii.

[8] In the definition of 'the West,' four areas need consideration, namely, *history, geography, culture*, and *politics*. Australia and New Zealand may be defined as Western countries, even though they are not located in the part of the world that we geographically define as 'the West.' This is so because the Western lifestyle has come to dominate these societies, a lifestyle that had its start during Britain's exportation of prisoners to these areas during the 18th century. For example, Australia's national day, January 26, commemorates the day when Britain put its flag on Australia's soil in 1788. The national day is therefore not connected to the native aboriginal people and their history but to Britain and Britain's (colonial) history. On the other hand, Australia and New Zealand can also be excluded from the definition of 'the West,' since the native population, the Aborigines and the Maoris, are peoples that have been subordinated by the West. This aspect of the national identity of Australia and New Zealand is, therefore, not possible to define as 'the West,' while other aspects are. The situation is the same regarding the First Nations and Inuit in North America, as well as for the Sami population in Sweden, Norway, Finland, and Russia. Therefore, the definition of 'the West' in the present study is based on the historical, cultural, and political sphere of influence, in which New Testament exegesis had its origins and early development as a scholarly discipline. Geographical aspects are thus less important in this regard. 'The West,' therefore, refers to the Western parts of Europe, North America (i.e., the USA and Canada), Australia, and New Zealand.

Colonisation includes mobility of culture and people, which is important to consider when analysing postcoloniality. Bhabha describes the effects that this mobility has had by introducing the concept of 'hybridity.' The expectations, transformations, adaptations, and marginalisation that occur, both during and after a specific colonial enterprise, create what Bhabha calls hybridity.[9]

According to Bhabha, hybridity is what happens with a person living in the cross section between countries and cultures, which results in a merging of two cultures into one body. However, hybridity is not only a reality for people that live in a colonial situation but also for all who are living in these cross sections. This includes people all over the world, regardless of whether they belong to the margins of the Two-Thirds World[10] or to the privileged societies in the West. The difference between a 'hybrid' person in the Two-Thirds World and a 'hybrid' person in the West is that the former is often in a disadvantaged position. The 'hybrid' person in the West, on the other hand, is

---

[9] Bhabha, *Location of Culture*, 112, 207-9. See also Childs and Williams, *Post-Colonial Theory*, 133-37.

[10] There is an ongoing discussion of how to designate the part of the world that is commonly called 'the Third World.' Sugirtharajah and Virginia Fabella argue that 'the Third World' is an accurate term. They state that the term 'the Third World' shows the "helplessness or vulnerability" that people still experience: 'the Third World' mirrors this situation better than, e.g., 'the Two-Thirds World' does. The term 'Two-Thirds World,' according to Sugirtharajah and Fabella only indicates the quantity and not the quality of those living in, what they call, 'the Third World.' R. S. Sugirtharajah, *Postcolonial Reconfigurations: An Alternative Way of Reading the Bible and Doing Theology* (London: SCM Press, 2003), 1, Virginia Fabella and R. S. Sugirtharajah, eds., *Dictionary of Third World Theologies* (Maryknoll, New York: Orbis Books, 2000), xxi-xxii. Nevertheless, in the present study the term 'Two-Thirds World' will be used, for two reasons. First, as Said has shown, the naming of others always implies value judgements, which have after-effects (e.g., to portray people as lazy and helpless cement these characteristics as part of the identity of these people in the eyes of those labelling them). This speaks against the term 'the Third World,' since it indicates (permanent) marginalisation. Second, 'the Two-Thirds World' indicates the strength of a majority and as such may eventually be what brings about change in global relations, just as the salt march of Gandhi showed the strength of an overwhelming majority. To continue to *designate* the majority with a term indicating marginality is, literally, to *keep* them in the margins. Therefore, the present study will use the term 'Two-Thirds World.' However, just as Sugirtharajah and Fabella state, the locations of 'the Third World' and the 'First World' (or perhaps we should say 'the One-Third World'?) are intertwined: "…there is already a Third World in the First World, just as there is a First World in the Third World." Fabella and Sugirtharajah, eds., *Dictionary of Third World Theologies*, xxii. What they mean is that the categories of 'first' and 'third' are not only a question of geography, but also a question of marginalisation and class distinction *within* countries.

in a position where s/he often partakes, consciously or unconsciously, in a system privileging her/himself at the expense of the 'other.'

Hybridity for those in the 'margins' is mostly shaped by a negative colonial influence, while the Western hybridity is a hybridity that is nurtured by the advantages of, historically, having been in a superior position. Both kinds of hybridities often include a certain amount of self-denial and self-alienation.[11] For hybrids in the margins this may imply a denial of ones cultural and national background, so that they risk becoming alienated from their own heritage. For hybrids in the centre, on the other hand, this may result in denial of and alienation from the responsibility that follows from being in a privileged position.

When describing postcoloniality it is important always to have in mind that it is not possible to identify *a single* colonial period as the point of departure for the discussion since the definition depends on which country is in focus and what kind of colonialism is at hand.[12] This is especially important within a historical discipline such as New Testament exegesis. Colonialism does not necessarily mean British colonialism during the 19th century. Other colonial enterprises have, of course, occurred in the world (e.g., the Alexandrian Empire during the 4th century B.C.E.[13] and Genghis Khan's colonial enterprise in the 13th century C.E.).[14] Consequently, the problem of defining a colonial empire is that it may include more than just one country's military domination over another. A colonial power may also be characterised as an agent of a certain culture or worldview that proceeds from a political centre to areas defined by this centre as marginal during a certain period in history.

---

[11] Childs and Williams, *Post-Colonial Theory*, 50. See also Frantz Fanon, *Black Skin. White Masks* (New York: Grove Press, 1967). Here Fanon does a psychoanalytic analysis of what happens to black individuals in a white postcolonial setting.

[12] For example, in *The Empire Writes Back*, Ashcroft, Griffiths, and Tiffin, are focusing on postcoloniality "during and after the period of European imperial domination…" Ashcroft, Griffiths, and Tiffin, *The Empire Writes Back*, 2.

[13] The Gregorian Calendar is an example of hegemonic-related changes imposed on colonised nations. Since the colonial enterprise began, Western chronology has been made globally authoritative in most areas of society, e.g., in trade and academy. In an effort to deconstruct the religious-imperialistic element of the Western calendar, the designations B.C.E. and C.E. have replaced B.C. and A.D. in most academic contexts. Thus, the confessional element of the calendar is diminished; however, it should not be forgotten that we are still using a western calendar, which is part of the postcoloniality.

[14] Loomba, *Colonialism/Postcolonialism*, 2.

Due to the difficulties involved in defining the postcolonial phenomenon, different terms have been used to describe it—*postcolonialism, neocolonialism*, and *postcoloniality*. The discussion is still going on and today some scholars are leaning towards abandoning the term 'postcolonial' in favour of 'globalism.'[15] Leela Gandhi, as well as Spivak, argues in favour of the term 'postcoloniality' as the continuation of colonialism.[16] She is not clear in her definition of this concept apart from the fact that she prefers the term postcoloniality to the term postcolonialism. However, there are many advantages in keeping both terms and letting them refer to different phenomena.

The distinction between postcolonialism and postcoloniality is helpful, since it makes it possible to talk about the effects of colonialism in a broader sense, without the theoretical apparatus developed by certain scholars. This distinction will therefore provide a basic point of departure for the definitions used in the present study. The following chart summarises and relates some important terms to one another.

Following Loomba, *colonisation* refers to a "conquest and control of other people's land and goods."[17] Such an enterprise can be political as well as economic, or both. A political colonisation refers to a concrete occupation of a territory or nation using military force. It has a clear beginning and a clear end. An economic colonisation, however, is when a 'colonisation' occurs within a capitalistic system. The latter is often referred to as economic 'imperialism.'[18]

This means that a colonisation may extend beyond the use of military force and focus on other factors that keep a country bound to the hegemonic centre. For example, the expansion of multinational companies,[19] export of a specific lifestyle, Western academic

---

[15] See, e.g., Vilashini Cooppan, "The Ruins of Empire: The National and Global Politics of America's Return to Rome" in *Postcolonial Studies and Beyond* (eds. Ania Loomba et al.; Durham: Duke University Press, 2005), 80–87. Sugirtharajah is certainly correct in stating that the roots of current globalisation go "back to colonial history and it is a legacy of European colonialism and modernity." R. S. Sugirtharajah, *Postcolonial Criticism and Biblical Interpretation* (New York: Oxford University Press, 2002), 30. In this sense the term 'globalism' should be seen as an outcome of the colonial enterprise and therefore under the postcolonial umbrella.

[16] Gayatri Chakravorty Spivak, "Neocolonialism and the Secret Agent of Knowledge," *Oxford Literary Review* 13:1–2 (1991): 220–51, 224.

[17] Loomba, *Colonialism/Postcolonialism*, 2.

[18] Loomba, *Colonialism/Postcolonialism*, 6.

[19] One example of negative effects of multinational companies: Fifteen years ago multinational companies, such as Coca-Cola, were excluded from marketing their soft drinks in India. Only local soft drinks like Thumbs Up, Mirinda and a few others were

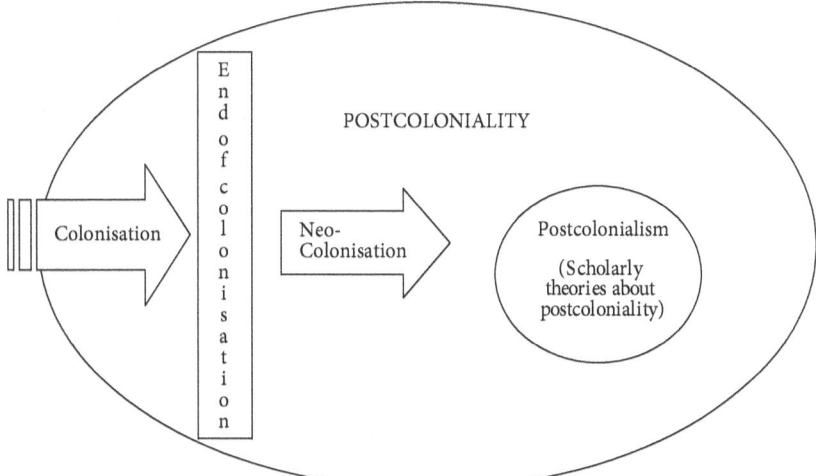

Figure 1. Illustration of the postcolonial phenomenon.

epistemology,[20] or the Western movie industry—all of these very different phenomena may be understood as aspects of a colonisation. However, the interest of a colonial power lies not in the 'colonised' country itself, but in the hegemonic and economical gains and benefits the colonial relation brings with it. In other words, the 'colonial' centre will in this way gain hegemonic power in order for it to benefit economically.

The act of colonisation, either political or economic, as shown in figure one, is the beginning of a state of postcoloniality. The seeds of the consequences and reactions that eventually will occur are sown during the very first contact between coloniser and colonised. The consequences of the process are not lagging behind, but occur simultaneously and immediately with the arrival and presence of the colonial

---

available. When the ban on foreign companies was lifted other brands entered the market. Coca-Cola then bought most of the Indian soft drink companies. Today the variety of soft drinks in India is slightly larger than it was fifteen years ago. You can still buy Thumbs up and Mirinda. However, the difference is that, what now seems to be a greater variety in choice of soft drinks is, in fact, rather a restriction of choice in terms of producers: any soft drink you buy will support one single company, namely Coca-Cola.

[20] Scholarly methods used within New Testament studies are part of an epistemological colonialism and neocolonialism. Having their roots in Western rationalistic enlightenment, such methods belong to the episteme-embedded discourses that were part of (the cultural aspects of) the colonial enterprise.

power. This means that the consequences of and reactions to the colonisation constitute the postcolonial phenomenon—or, in other words, *the postcoloniality*.[21]

Postcoloniality is, hence, a reality materialising not only after the colonial power has physically left the country, but having its beginnings during the actual process of colonisation. A postcolonial situation does not imply the absence of colonial impact. A new period of independence in the history of a nation does not necessarily mean freedom from the previous colonisers. The web of interrelated effects of colonisation binds the country to a situation of dependence extending far beyond the moment of liberation; we need only mention areas like economy, trade, epistemological influences, fashion, culture, and sports.[22]

Postcolonialism, on the other hand, does not refer to the phenomenon studied but to the scholarly discipline studying the phenomenon. There is no consensus about the term *postcolonialism*, just as is the case with almost all terminology within postcolonial studies. Sugirtharajah summarises suggested meanings of postcolonialism as follows,

> Postcolonialism, it has to be stressed, has a multiplicity of meanings, depending on location. It is seen as an oppositional reading practice, and as a way of critiquing the totalizing forms of Eurocentric thinking and of reshaping dominant meanings. It is a mental attitude rather than a method, more a subversive stance towards the dominant knowledge than a school of thought. It is not about periodization. It is a reading posture. It is a critical enterprise aimed at unmasking the link between idea and power, which lies behind Western theories and learning. It is a discursive resistance to imperialism, imperial ideologies, imperial attitudes and their continued incarnations in such wide-ranging fields as politics, economics, history and theological and biblical studies.[23]

---

[21] Cf. Leela Gandhi, *Postcolonial Theory: A Critical Introduction* (New York: Columbia University Press, 1998), 4–8. Segovia, "Mapping the Postcolonial Optic," 48–49.

[22] Cf. Segovia, "Mapping the Postcolonial Optic," 48–49; see also Hall, "When was 'the Post-Colonial'?" 250. Hall emphasises the pervasiveness of colonial history: "With 'colonisation,' and consequently with the 'post-colonial,' we are irrevocably within a power-knowledge field of force. It is precisely the false and disabling distinction between colonisation as a system of rule, of power and exploitation, and colonisation as a system of knowledge and representation, which is being refused. It is because the relations which characterised the 'colonial' are no longer in the same place and relative position, that we are able not simply to oppose them but to critique, to deconstruct and try to 'go beyond' them."

[23] Sugirtharajah, *Postcolonial Reconfigurations*, 15.

According to Sugirtharajah the meaning varies depending on where we locate 'postcolonialism.' In the present study postcolonialism is located within the wider concept of 'postcoloniality' and will be seen as the academic response to postcoloniality—a response, though distinct, very much related to poststructuralism and postmodernism.[24] It had its origins in the field of comparative literature in the 1980's.[25] Postcolonialism thus refers to theories about postcolonial situations (postcoloniality). As Leela Gandhi states, "[t]he theory may be named 'postcolonialism,' and the condition it addresses is best conveyed through the notion of 'postcoloniality.'"[26]

Postcolonialism is, therefore, part of the phenomenon of postcoloniality, since it is a consequence of, and a reaction to colonialism.

Neocolonialism is also part of postcoloniality, since it is a consequence of colonialism. The neo-colonial influences originate from former colonial centres. Consequently, another word for neocolonialism could be 'economic colonialism,' since it is fuelled by the present economic system, which in turn originated and received its structure during and after the modern colonial period.[27]

Even though neocolonialism in many ways is an economic colonialism, it is not by necessity of non-military nature: military concerns are most often connected with economic issues. The United States' involvement in Afghanistan and Iraq, could, for instance, be defined as a neo-colonial enterprise. In the same way, the absence of and reluctance to use military or other means to help free Tibet from its present colonial situation under China's rule is an effect of Western neocolonialism. In the first example the economic aspect of the enterprise is clear, which has also been documented on a popularised level in Michael Moore's controversial movie *Fahrenheit 9/11*.[28] In the second example, it is obvious that military assistance from the West to the

---

[24] Postcoloniality as a non-theorised phenomenon is older than postmodernism. However, on the level of theorising (postcolonialism) the relationship is reversed; postcolonialism is dependent on postmodernism for its conception and growth as well as its inroad into the Western academic world.

[25] Some scholars criticise the fact that postcolonialism has been influenced to such a degree by this philosophical genre. Roland Boer emphasises that the original influences come from Marxism and argues that this is neglected in present discussion within the field. Roland Boer, "Introduction: Vanishing Mediators?" in *A Vanishing Mediator? The Presence/Absence of the Bible in Postcolonialism* (ed. Roland Boer and Gerald West; Atlanta: The Society of Biblical Literature, 2001), 1–12.

[26] Gandhi, *Postcolonial Theory*, 4.

[27] Cf. Loomba's discussion in Loomba, *Colonialism/Postcolonialism*, 1–19.

[28] Michael Moore, "Fahrenheit 9/11," ed. Michael Moore (2004).

opposition in Tibet would harm the West's relations with China—a far too important economic and powerful partner to ignore or oppose.

It should be noted that some scholars prefer to talk about 'neocolonialism' instead of 'postcolonialism' in order to emphasise that today's situation is not a 'post'-situation but an ongoing colonial reality; it just has other ways of expression than people are familiar with. The dependence of a former colony is often so strong that it is in fact misleading to say that the country is independent.

The situation that the term 'neocolonialism' wants to address is when a colonial power has withdrawn from the claim to be the ruler of another country in a political or military sense. Instead, the 'colonisation' is expressed differently using other means of dominance where the 'market' and international trade are often the engine behind the process. When this happens formerly colonised countries become dependent of the former coloniser's trade agreements with them. This is explained by the simple fact that during the colonial period colonised countries were drained economically in a way that prevented them from competing on equal terms with the economical development of the coloniser. It must be emphasised that it was during the colonial period that the foundations of today's international trade were laid, including the power imbalance between colonies and their colonisers.

In addition, formerly colonised countries are often trapped in huge international loans that were taken in order to establish a sustainable economy.[29] In defining the reality in which we live, Spivak is correct, therefore, when she concludes that we live in a "post-colonial neocolonized world."[30]

The problem with using the term neocolonialism, is that it tends to focus more on 'colonialism' than on other related developments that occur as a consequence of and reaction to colonialism. The use of the word 'neocolonialism' implies a focus on centre and periphery in a way that emphasises a 'continuation' rather than a 'transformation.'

---

[29] For a definition of globalisation, see Anna-Karin Hammar, "Globalisering, ekonomi, teologi: ett kristet perspektiv" in *Varför ser ni mot himlen? Utmaningar från den kontextuella teologin* (ed. Thorbjörn Sjöholm and Anders Runesson; Stockholm: Verbum, 2005), 70–89. See especially her discussion of the economic aspects of globalisation, 78–81.

[30] Sarah Harasym, ed., *The Post-Colonial Critic: Interviews, Strategies, Dialogues* (London: Routledge, 1990), 166.

The term 'postcoloniality,' on the other hand, is wider and includes more interrelated phenomena.

Postcoloniality may include references to such diverse aspects as a child's unconscious purchase of a banana produced in a country with a colonial past, an airport's rigorous security check in search for terrorists,[31] or a multinational company's move to Indonesia in order to lower their costs for employees. Even though the word 'post' implies a past, it also indicates both a continuation and a transformation of history in the wake of that past. In this way, 'post' interacts with the 'past,' and the many connections between them form the woven tapestry of the present. As a result, neocolonialism is best seen as one aspect among others, existing *within* a state of postcoloniality.

It is within such situations of postcoloniality that several critical scholarly approaches have developed: e.g., liberation theology,[32] postcolonial feminist studies,[33] subaltern studies,[34] postcolonial and queer studies.[35] These approaches are all consequences of and reactions to colonialism and constitute different 'sub-groups' within the academic field of postcolonialism—the theoretical approaches to postcoloniality.

Modern postcoloniality as a phenomenon has a distinct beginning and can therefore often be dated exactly since its origin is always connected with the beginning of a colonisation (e.g., Vasco DaGama's landing on India's West Coast 1498). It is much more difficult to determine when postcoloniality ends. When does a consequence or a reaction to a phenomenon end?

A common way of defining the postcolonial phenomenon is to talk about it in terms of resistance.[36] If resistance as a reaction is considered

---

[31] Since 'postcoloniality' is about consequences and reactions there exists a connection between the crusades that took place during the 12th and 13th centuries on the one hand, and European colonialism and its out workings in the attack on World Trade Centre in New York on September 11, 2001 on the other.

[32] E.g., Sugirtharajah, *Postcolonial Criticism and Biblical Interpretation*, 103–26.

[33] E.g., Donaldson and Kwok, eds., *Postcolonialism, Feminism, and Religious Discourse*.

[34] E.g., Guha Ranajit, ed., *A Subaltern Studies Reader, 1986-1995* (Minneapolis: University of Minnesota Press, 1997).

[35] E.g., Hawley, ed., *Postcolonial and Queer*.

[36] For example Ian Adam and Helen Tiffin, eds., *Past the Last Post: Theorizing Post-Colonialism and Post-Modernism* (Calgary: University Press of Calgary, 1990), xii; Ashcroft, Griffith, and Tiffin, *The Empire Writes Back*, 2. Aschroft, Griffiths, and Tiffin argue that what makes postcolonial literature postcolonial is that the authors "…asserted themselves by foregrounding the tension with the imperial power, and by emphazising their differences from the assumptions of the imperial centre." Thus, it is in the aspect of resistance that postcolonialism is to be found.

to be the only fundamental part of postcoloniality, then postcoloniality will end as soon as resistance vanishes. The problem with such a definition is that there is no room for other types of consequences and reactions, phenomena that cannot be defined as resistance.

Even if postcoloniality is often associated with resistance, it may also be defined in a broader sense. It includes phenomena such as 'orientalism,'[37] the appearance of Internet cafés in the mountains of Nepal, or even the delivery of a furnace from Steelworks 2 in Torshälla, Sweden, to Bhoruka Steel in Bangalore, India[38]—they are all consequences of a postcolonial situation.

Even if resistance is certainly a reaction within a postcolonial situation and part of postcoloniality, postcoloniality is a much broader phenomenon. The postcoloniality of today is far more global than it has ever been historically and, consequently, it is much more difficult to analyse. Perhaps it is best to maintain a broad criterion when talking about the end of postcoloniality and simply state that when the consequences and the reactions to colonial enterprises cease, the postcoloniality will gradually fade away. When, where, and how is very hard to predict.

As shown above, the definition of postcoloniality should be kept as broad as possible. It is within this reality that postcolonial theoretical systems, including postcolonial New Testament exegesis, are to be located. The essence of postcoloniality is found in the consequences of and the reactions to different aspects of colonisation. This inclusive definition makes it possible to incorporate all aspects of the phenomenon. This in turn, will be helpful when describing and analysing specific postcolonial situations and phenomena.

In order to study postcolonial phenomena we need to work interdisciplinarily. Postcolonialism incorporates a multitude of aspects and theories, and it cuts across different disciplines. Indeed, this fact may be the very reason why it has been difficult to agree on a definition of the issues involved: scholars approach postcoloniality from different academic fields, with different scholarly backgrounds and training.

When we are studying postcoloniality the question is not: who is postcolonial? Or, where do we find postcoloniality? In many respects we are all living in a postcolonial situation—in an almost global postcoloniality—since we live in a world that is permeated by postcolonial-

---

[37] For definition of 'orientalism,' see section 3.1.
[38] Jan af Geijerstam, *Mitt i världen, mitt i tiden* (Stockholm: Ordfront, 1993).

ity. Accordingly, a far more interesting question is: how do we relate to this postcolonial situation? Or, for the purpose of the present study: where is New Testament exegesis located in the postcolonial reality we are living in? How are we to understand the processes of colonisation that formed it, and how do we relate to its embeddedness in the political?

These and related questions are becoming more and more urgent within New Testament exegesis as scholars have come to realise that academia is not isolated from the societies and cultures in which it exists.

In order to understand postcolonialism, it is essential to realise the two fundamental aspects of this field, namely, its close ties to what we may call the 'flesh-and-blood reality' on the one hand, and the 'academic reality' on the other. Some postcolonial scholars refuse to accept any boundaries between academia and social realities. Fernando Segovia and Roland Boer, for example, criticise the fact that the academic postmodern postcolonial discussion has a tendency to ignore the Marxist theories about economy and power.[39] What they mean is that such neglect risks marginalising writers like W. E. B. DuBois,[40] Amilcar Cabral,[41] Kwame Nkrumah,[42] and Frantz Fanon,[43] who lived in or were affected by a colonial situation. These authors represent just a few of several important writers who began to formulate and express the consequences of colonisation. They mirror and transmit to the reader a real flesh-and-blood postcolonial situation. In other words, they function as the flesh-and-blood foundation of postcolonial studies.

---

[39] Boer, "Vanishing Mediators?" 1–12, Fernando F. Segovia, "Postcolonial Biblical Criticism" (paper presented at the SNTS, 59th General Meeting, La Salle Bonanova College in Barcelona, Spain, 5–7 August 2004), 14.

[40] See, e.g., W. E. Burghardt DuBois, *The World and Africa: An Inquiry into the Part which Africa has Played in World History* (New York: Viking Press, 1947); *The Suppression of the African Slave-Trade to the United States of America, 1638–1870* (New York: The Social Science Press, 1954) (his dissertation); and *Dusk of Dawn: an Essay Toward an Autobiography of a Race Concept*, Repr. of the 1940 ed. (New York: Schocken Books, 1968).

[41] See, e.g., Amicar Cabral, *Unity and Struggle: Speeches and Writings* (London: Heinemann, 1980).

[42] See, e.g., Kwame Nkrumah, *Africa Must Unite* (New York: International Publishers, 1970); *Neo-Colonialism: the Last Stage of Imperialism* (New York: International Publishers, 1966).

[43] See, e.g., Fanon, *Black Skin. White Masks; The Wretched of the Earth*, trans. C. Farrington (New York: Grove Press, 1968).

The other 'reality' is the academic reality. Postcolonial studies are deeply rooted in postmodern philosophy and Poststructuralist theories.[44] This fact has appeared to be both beneficial and unfavourable for the discipline. Beneficial because it places postcolonialism, in all its sub-fields, within the most recent, up-to-date research. Unfavourable because postmodern philosophy might seem to employ an unnecessarily complex and complicated terminology, the result being that, instead of including the margin (which is the main focus of the field), the margins are excluded since the language used can only be de-coded by a few trained specialists.[45] Segovia hits the nail on the head:

> The emergence of Postcolonial Studies stands, therefore, as both clear and muddled, understandable and incomprehensible, acceptable and questionable—all at once and inescapably so. This problematic readily extends as well to both the meaning and the scope of these studies.[46]

The development of the discipline has therefore gone in different directions and a consensus concerning definitions and terminology within postcolonial studies has not been, and will perhaps never be, reached.

3.1.1 *Excursus: Who is a Postcolonial Scholar?*

This deceptively simple question turns out to be more difficult to answer than one would first think. It may be answered on several levels. Taking the above discussion into consideration, the following can be said.

---

[44] The Bible and Culture Collective, *The Postmodern Bible* (New Haven: Yale University Press, 1995), 272–308, especially 282–93. See also, Kwame Anthony Appiah, "Is the Post- in Postmodernism the Post- in Postcolonial?" in *Postcolonialism: Critical Consepts in Literary and Cultural Studies*, vol. 1 (ed. Diana Brydon; London: Routledge, 2000), 85–104; repr. from *Critical Inquiry* 17:2 (1991): 336–57.

[45] This was discussed during the conference "*The Politics of Postcoloniality: Contexts and Conflicts,*" at the English Department at McMaster University, Canada 2003. An amusing example of the complexity of postcolonial studies may be found in the winner of the second prize in the *Fourth Bad Writing Contest* (1998), Homi Bhabha. The following sentence is from his book *The Location of Culture*, "If, for a while, the ruse of desire is calculable for the uses of discipline soon the repetition of guilt, justification, pseudo-scientific theories, superstition, spurious authorities, and classifications can be seen as the desperate effort to "normalize" *formally* the disturbance of a discourse of splitting that violates the rational, enlightened claims of its enunciatory modality." Denis Dutton, *Philosophy and Literature* (http://aldaily.com/bwc.htm, 1998 [cited 17 March 2005]).

[46] Segovia, "Postcolonial Biblical Criticism," 14.

First, *terminologically* a postcolonial scholar may be defined as a scholar who describes her/himself as working within the field termed 'postcolonialism.' This is a straightforward and simple definition, but, as we shall se later in this study, it is problematic. Several scholars who do not term themselves postcolonial still use the same or similar approaches to those that are today labelled postcolonial. For example, George Soares-Prabhu, who was active from the 1970s to the middle of the 1990s, never identified his approach explicitly as 'postcolonial.'[47] It is quite clear, however, that his analyses belong within the field today termed postcolonialism. It is therefore, arguably, legitimate to include him among other postcolonial scholars. A second definition would thus be based more on a scholar's *conscious application of methods and perspectives today identified as postcolonial*, than on that author's explicit use of the term 'postcolonial' to describe her/his work.[48]

A third and broader definition takes *postcoloniality* as point of departure. From this perspective, since the West as much as the Two-Thirds World is still very much experiencing the consequences of modern colonialism, all biblical scholars, regardless of whether they are aware of postcolonial issues or not, may be defined as postcolonial. This third definition is most likely to attract criticism because of its broadness. Is it useful at all? An example may clarify the situation.

Let us return to the example of the banana. If an innocent child buys an 'ordinary' banana at a supermarket in Sweden, the child unknowingly participates in an (unequal) postcolonial economic world order. The very fact that a banana can be bought in Sweden at all is a consequence of colonialism. The action of the child is therefore postcolonial, since it is part of postcoloniality.

If the child's teenage cousin consciously chooses to buy an 'alternative' banana, certified as fair trade and organic, we enter another level of postcoloniality: the awareness of oppressive economic systems leads the well-read cousin to act according to ethical standards she deems acceptable. She has identified the web of interconnected actions and consequences in which the society she lives in is entangled, and which

---

[47] See further below for a discussion of his contributions.
[48] Cf. Amy-Jill Levine regarding the definition of who is a feminist, "Anti-Judaism and Postcolonial Biblical Interpretation: The disease of Postcolonial New Testament Studies and the Hermeneutics of Healing—Roundtable Discussion" *JFSR* 20 no. 1 (2004): 91: "Not all the authors considered here define themselves as feminist. I am using the term generally and artificially to name those who write from a liberationist stance and who have a particular concern for women's lives."

she cannot escape, and she acts within that society by making conscious choices. Still, the cousin may not identify herself as a postcolonial activist; terminology is, however, all that distinguishes her from her friends who are involved in starting a movement addressing fair trade issues, identifying what they do as 'postcolonialism.'

While postcoloniality embraces the totality, the most useful definition is perhaps the second. It emphasises the conscious methodological approaches of scholars who are aware of hegemonic and other discrepancies within academia, without limiting such approaches to those explicitly labelled 'postcolonial.'[49] This definition of who is a postcolonial scholar has guided the choice of secondary literature to be discussed in the present study.

In order to understand the phenomenon of postcoloniality, and the postcolonialism within, we will, in the coming section, analyse it within the frames of the theory of episteme. Episteme is a philosophical term used by Foucault in his analysis of power relations and groups considered to belong to the so-called 'margins.'

3.2 Perspectives and Methods

Postcolonial studies are, as mentioned above, closely related to postmodern theories. However, it is important to emphasise that postcolonial studies have their origins and foundation in real life situations.[50] Therefore it is important to keep the balance between theoretical postcolonial exegetical work and 'flesh-and-blood exegesis,' realising that both theories and exegesis as practiced 'on the ground' take place within realities defined by postcoloniality. This fact, that all events, academic or otherwise, take place in perceived realities, rather than absolute realities (even though some discourses present their own perspective as foundational in the sense of 'objective'), makes necessary an analysis of discourses of realities.[51] It is my contention that such

---

[49] Cf. definitions of 'contextual theology.' According to contextual theologians, all theology is contextual, regardless of whether scholars are conscious about/admit it or not. 'Contextual theology' as a term, however, is applied primarily to theologies explicitly acknowledging the contextual nature of theology and taking this fact as point of departure in their scholarship.

[50] Cf. Sugirtharajah, *Postcolonial Criticism and Biblical Interpretation*, 16.

[51] David Scott, "Construction of Postcolonial Studies" in *Postcolonial Studies and Beyond* (ed. Ania Loomba, Suvir Kaul, Matti Bunzl, Antoinette Burton, and Jed Esty; Durham: Duke University Press, 2005), 385–400, 398–99. Scott asks for the "attempts

an analysis is best made taking into account, indeed, taking as point of departure, the analytical category termed episteme by Foucault.[52] Within this analytical frame, we shall then attempt to answer the questions of the location, criticism, and contribution of postcolonial New Testament exegesis in contemporary postcolonial realities.

3.2.1 *Episteme: What is Reality?*

The present study focuses on New Testament exegesis in relation to the concept of knowledge, the historical development of academia, and the larger socio-political context in which people think and act, all aspects of which are defined by the realities of postcoloniality. Therefore, it may be helpful to interconnect the above phenomena and postcoloniality using Foucault's theory of episteme as an explanatory tool for understanding the realities with and within which we work.[53]

Although we are not dealing with epistemic logic specifically, the following definition from *Encyclopædia Britannica* of 'Epistemic logic' may be helpful for understanding the specific contents of episteme intended by Foucault,

> Epistemic logic deals with the logical issues arising within the gamut of such epistemological concepts as knowledge, belief, assertion, doubt, question-and-answer, or the like. Instead of dealing with the essential factual issues of alethic logic (Greek *aletheia*, "truth")—*i.e.*, with what is actually or must necessarily or can possibly be the case—it relates to what people know or believe or maintain or doubt to be the case.[54]

All academic disciplines exist within and on the foundation of a specific episteme. The idea of episteme is concerned with non-factual aspects related to that within which knowledge and beliefs, etc., exist. Further, there is a connection between an episteme and what is produced within

---

to identify the relevant features of the postcolonial problem space in which our investigation takes place."

[52] For an excellent discussion and application of Foucault's approaches to and analyses of perceived realities, although from a different perspective, see Karin Permer and Lars Göran Permer, *Klassrummets moraliska ordning: Iscensättningen av lärare och elever som subjekt för ansvarsdiskursen i klassrummet* (Malmö: Malmö Högskola, 2002), 45ff. As Permer and Permer note (45), Foucault was well aware of the fact that he did not present watertight theoretical systems; rather Foucault invites others to use and transform as they see fit the tools he has suggested. The present study adopts and adapts the theory of episteme to postcolonial discourses.

[53] See, Michel Foucault, *The Archaeology of Knowledge* (London: Travistock Publications, 1972).

[54] "Applied Logic," *Encyclopædia Britannica* 23:281:1b.

it, namely the epistemological concepts. In other words, our modern 'knowledge, beliefs, assertions, doubts, questions-and-answers' have their entire basis in an invisible construct called an episteme. So, what exactly, is an episteme?

An episteme is, as mentioned, not a specific type of knowledge. An episteme functions as a "distinctive structure of thought" that appears during a certain period in history.[55] Barry Smart describes it as

> ...the total set of relations that unite, at a given period, the discursive practices that give rise to epistemological figures, sciences, and possibly formalized systems... it is the totality of relations that can be discovered for a given period, between the sciences when one analyses them at the level of discursive regularities.[56]

An episteme can be characterised as the mortar between the bricks, the bricks symbolising the different discourses mentioned by Smart. Without the episteme the building would have no mortar and would collapse. There is always an episteme present in human societies and collectivities, but it may, and does, change over time.

Foucault explains an episteme as

> ...the lateral relations that may exist between epistemological figures or sciences in so far as they belong to neighbouring, but distinct, discursive practices.[57]

These relations correspond to the 'mortar;' the discourses are dependent on the episteme for their existence. An episteme is not a 'spirit of the age' that comes and goes.[58] An episteme can be portrayed as a web that surrounds and connects different discourses into one system. It cannot hold together without previous and contemporary 'threads.' Changes may occur in the episteme, but historical events and phenomena are always more present in an episteme than they may seem to be at first glance. Consequently, no discourse is to be seen in isolation,

---

[55] Barry Smart, *Michel Foucault* (London and New York: Routledge, 1985), 32.
[56] Smart, *Foucault*, 32, referring to Michel Foucault, *The Archaeology of Knowledge* (London: Routledge, 1989), 191. By 'discursive regularities' Smart understands the similarities that appear between discourses, and that connect discourses that exist conterminously with each other. Inter-discursive similarities' is another way of designating such interconnected similarities. Cf. The Collective, *The Postmodern Bible*, 138ff. See figure 2.
[57] Foucault, *The Archaeology of Knowledge*, 191.
[58] Foucault, *The Archaeology of Knowledge*, 191.

either historically (vertically), or contemporarily (laterally). Foucault writes that the episteme,

> ...opens up an inexhaustible field and can never be closed; its aim is not to reconstitute the system of postulates that governs all the branches of knowledge (*connaissances*) of a given period, but to cover an indefinite field of relations. Moreover, the episteme is not a motionless figure that appeared one day with the mission of effacing all that preceded it: it is a constantly moving set of articulations, shifts, and coincidences that are established, only to give ride to others.[59]

The analysis of an episteme is not just an analysis of a science, or a discourse, and its relation to other sciences/discourses. Rather, the analysis of an episteme relativises the nature of a science altogether, at least in the sense that science has been understood traditionally within the modern paradigm. What kind of relations makes the existence of a science possible? In other words, why does it exist? Foucault writes:

> ...the episteme is not what may be known at a given period, due account taken of inadequate techniques, mental attitudes, or the limitations imposed by tradition; it is what, in the positivity of discursive practices, makes possible the existence of epistemological figures and sciences.[60]

In Foucault's description the episteme is not the actual knowledge—episteme is what constitutes the web in which knowledge is possible. In other words, episteme is composed of the components that determine what knowledge is during a certain historical period. For that reason episteme is not, in the present study, considered to be a method. It is, rather, understood as a description of a reality of interconnected discourses wherein knowledge is formulated.

Consequently, an episteme refers to the relations that create the foundational understanding wherein knowledge and epistemology are constructed. From a broader perspective it is to be considered as the web that constitutes the connections between knowledge discourses within specific cultures.

Orientalism as it expressed itself during Europe's high colonial period (mid 19th until the beginning of the 20th century) is an example of how an episteme functions. 'The other' was constructed from a perspective in which Europe was at the centre and "the people without

---

[59] Foucault, *The Archaeology of Knowledge*, 192.
[60] Foucault, *The Archaeology of Knowledge*, 192.

history" existed in the margin.[61] The Western episteme collided with an episteme in which knowledge was constructed very differently. The solution to this conflict for the colonisers was found in a triumphalistic theory of superiority, in which non-Western cultures became regarded as inferior.

The concept of episteme, applied to the field of postcolonial studies, opens up possibilities for analysing different aspects of constitutive components that finally formed what we today call postcoloniality. In this study episteme will, therefore, be used as a 'theory of reality.'

As mentioned before, an episteme is like a spider's web. In a spider's web the threads are constructed and connected in a way that enables vibrations to go from one part of the web to another. This is a useful metaphor for how postcoloniality is formed. In the moment colonialism had its beginnings, the 'vibrations' in the web began and, over time, transferred to different parts of the web, creating what we today call 'postcoloniality.' The nature of the fact or event itself is not important. What matters are the *effects* colonialism has had. In this sense, postcoloniality is not something that is possible to 'do'—it just 'happens,' which means that the phenomenon may be interpreted with the help of the theory of deconstruction. We shall return to this below.

The understanding of history that is reflected in the theory of episteme ties the scholar to the object that s/he is investigating. Consequently, the theory of episteme turns history into more than just an object to be studied, since the particular discourse with which the scholar is engaging is part of the episteme and interacts with both history and other contemporary discourses through the episteme. Scholarly methods and the perspectives applied should then be seen as resulting from a specific discourse that exists in interaction with the episteme (i.e., the inter-discursive similarities; see figure 2).

In this process, the interconnectedness of methods with a particular episteme within which they were formed may be overlooked. The discourse (within the episteme) within which a certain method is constructed changes over time, and as it changes the discourse-specific origins (which are influenced by the episteme) of the method easily get lost. Using a metaphor, we could say that methods have a 'soul,' which is the *purpose*, or the *meaning*, of the method. This 'soul' is embodied in a discourse, existing in an episteme: the 'body' in which the soul

---

[61] For a survey of the colonial project, see Eric Robert Wolf, *Europe and the People Without History* (Berkeley: University of California Press, 1982).

THE THEORETICAL LOCATION OF POSTCOLONIAL STUDIES 37

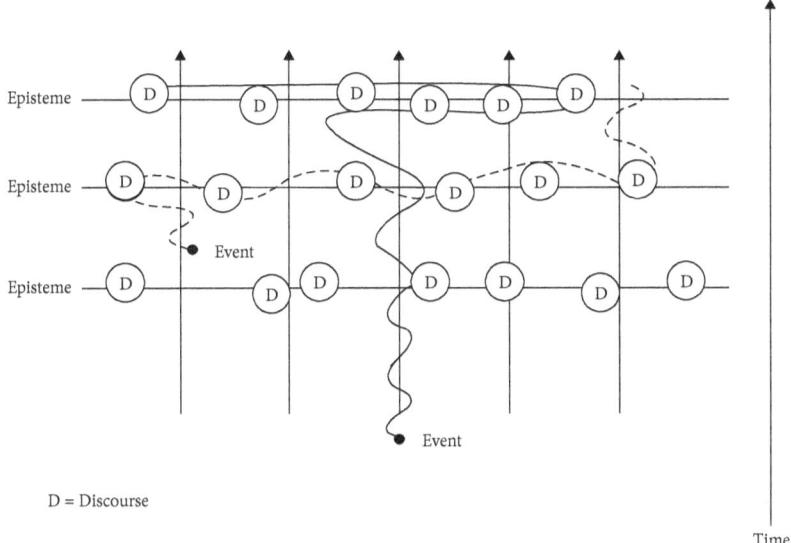

Figure 2. Inter-discursive similarities and inter-epistemic developments.

resides is an episteme-embedded discourse. The 'soul' is never free from the 'body'—a fact that is sometimes ignored by scholars. However, when a method originating within a certain episteme-embedded discourse is transferred into another episteme (i.e., into other cultures with different histories), the discrepancy between the new body and the dislocated soul results in tensions that are not easily resolved. Therefore, in analysing the nature and function of New Testament exegesis in a postcolonial context, it is important to find the 'body' to understand the 'soul.'

In a similar way, Bengt Holmberg discusses the relationship between 'body' and 'soul' in the context of sociology and the New Testament.[62] Holmberg argues, correctly in my view, that we have to avoid "a naive fusing of texts and historical reality," which leads to "the serious methodological mistake of confusing phenomena with the description of them." Applying sociological methods to the study of the New Testament, Holmberg claims, we "take seriously the continuous dialectic between ideas and social structures."[63] In this way a sociological study

---

[62] Bengt Holmberg, *Sociology and the New Testament: An Appraisal* (Minneapolis: Fortress Press, 1990), 2–3.
[63] Holmberg, *Sociology and the New Testament*, 3.

of the New Testament facilitates the study of the 'flesh-and-blood reality' that hides behind the biblical texts. In this sense a sociological method may help us find the 'soul' of the text through searching for the 'body' it lived *as*.[64]

In a transferred sense, then, Holmberg's use of the 'soul-body' metaphor is fruitful for the understanding of the origins of methods within epistemes. Just as it is a mistake to fuse a text with historical reality, it is problematic to fuse historical conclusions resulting from the use of a specific method (e.g., the historical critical method) with unqualified truth claims. The tool has a soul, its purpose, but also a body, the episteme-embedded discourse. Conclusions drawn on the basis of methodologically controlled interpretive exercises using specific methods should be seen as relating to both the soul and the body of the method.

Consequently, a historical critical study of a biblical text has *two* 'bodies' to consider: first, the flesh-and-blood 'body' of textualised ideas, and, second, the epistemic 'body' of the methods used to analyse the socio-historical world of the text. From a postcolonial perspective, this insight is of vital importance since the 'body' of a method has significance for the conclusions resulting from the use of that particular method, conclusions which may be irrelevant—or worse—in an epistemic context foreign to the methods.

If the episteme is shaped by colonialism, the different discourses will most likely be influenced by colonialism. Hence, through an analysis of the episteme it is possible to trace the method's 'soul' back to the 'body' the method lived *as*. Doing so, the methodologically controlled conclusions and their indissoluble interconnectedness with the method's 'body' may be understood from a broader perspective. This may in turn start new motions in the epistemic web that deconstructs former methods and methodological approaches, resulting in a process in which new methodologies are created. One example of such a process of perspectival and methodological deconstruction is the feminist movement and its effects on the Western episteme and its discourses. Postcolonialism, a reaction to and consequence of postcoloniality, is also beginning to cause motions in different contemporary discourses, but it has not yet had the effects on inter-discursive similarities that feminist discourse has had.

---

[64] Holmberg, *Sociology and the New Testament*, 3.

THE THEORETICAL LOCATION OF POSTCOLONIAL STUDIES   39

If we were to depict the above argument in graphic form (see figure 2), we need to take into account the most important parameters mentioned (Discourse, Event, Episteme, Time), and relate them to each other so that their interconnectedness is allowed to emerge in visible form. Note how events may vibrate slowly over a shorter or longer period of time before full epistemic effect is registered. However, the event itself cannot explain all consequences and effects. Rather, a multitude of factors are at work as inter-discursive similarities are created and inter-epistemic developments take place.

3.2.2   Deconstruction—a Theory and a Method

Deconstruction is a widely used concept in postcolonial studies, just as it is in adjacent fields that focus on 'the margins,' e.g., gender studies, queer studies, and liberation theology. In this study, deconstruction will be used in two ways: on the one hand, deconstruction is considered a philosophical term, as developed by Jacques Derrida in the 1960's.[65] On the other hand, deconstruction is understood as a method, developed within comparative literature two decades later by, e.g., Paul DeMan.[66]

According to Derrida, deconstruction is not a method but a course of events that cannot be controlled—something that just 'happens' in a 'passive' sense. Deconstruction is, as John Caputo writes, "what is really going on in things, what is really happening, is always to come." Caputo describes Derrida's deconstruction as something that is not possible to fixate, but which will always "slip away."[67] Deconstruction is what is happening in the process of trying to reach goals that are, ultimately, according to Derrida, unreachable. Segovia captures the core idea of deconstruction in one sentence: "[t]he central tenet is that

---

[65] See John Caputo's interview with Derrida, John D. Caputo, *Deconstruction in a Nutshell: A Conversation with Jacques Derrida* (New York: Fordham University Press, 1997). For further reading see also, John D. Caputo, *The Prayers and Tears of Jacques Derrida: Religion without Religion* (ed. M. Westphal; The Indiana Series in the Philosophy of Religion; Bloomington: Indiana University Press, 1997) and Jacques Derrida, "Letter to a Japanese Friend" in *Derrida and Difference* (eds. Wood and Bernasconi; Warwick: Parousia Press, 1985), 1–5.

[66] Paul DeMan, *The Resistance to Theory* (Manchester: Manchester University Press, 1986). See also, Barbara Johnson, *The Critical Difference: Essays in the Contemporary Rhetoric of Reading* (Baltimore: Johns Hopkins University Press, 1981).

[67] Caputo, *In a Nutshell*, 31.

language is endlessly unstable and indeterminate (*différence*), frustrating all attempts to establish grounds of certainty and truth."[68]

Deconstruction, thus, has things in common with the episteme, in the sense that deconstruction, like the episteme, does not rest on logical developments. Instead, the process continues endlessly as it constantly deconstructs itself. Postcoloniality should be understood within this interpretative frame: it just 'happened/happens.' The seed of postcoloniality was planted when the colonisers entered the respective countries; postcoloniality exists today as a series of phenomena that have undergone constant deconstruction ever since.

Even if Derrida emphasises that deconstruction is *not* a method, the concept has been developed into a method within the field of comparative literature. Deconstruction is today not only a theory about reality; it is also a method, which is applied to texts in order to achieve deeper knowledge and insights about underlying mechanisms of a text. 'The Bible and Culture Collective'[69] describes the method of deconstruction as a tool for locating excluded points in the text. What they mean is that a construction always builds on exclusions: through deconstruction light is shed on such omissions.[70] In a transferred sense, such a procedure may help in the assessment of the place of New Testament studies within postcoloniality as well as in the analysis of specific New Testament passages.

3.3 Postcolonial Studies and New Testament Exegesis

New Testament exegesis has, the last 20 years or so, experienced significant methodological changes and developments.[71] Modern exe-

---

[68] Segovia, "Deconstrucion", 67.

[69] The text is authored by several scholars who do not wish to distinguish between contributions made by individuals within the collective.

[70] The Collective, *Postmodern Bible*, 120.

[71] This is mirrored in recent studies in exegetical methodology. Examples of new methodological approaches that have been more and more accepted during the 1990's and onwards, are structural criticism, narrative criticism, reader–response criticism, poststructuralist criticism, feminist criticism, postcolonial criticism, and socio-economic criticism, e.g., Janice Capel Anderson and Stephen D. Moore, eds., *Mark and Method: New Approaches in Biblical Studies* (2d ed.; Minneapolis: Fortress Press, 2008), The Collective, *The Postmodern Bible*; Steven L. McKenzie and Stephen R. Haynes, eds., *To Each Its Own Meaning: An Introduction to Biblical Criticism and Their Application* (Louisville: Westminster John Knox Press, 1999); and John H. Elliott, *What is Social-Scientific Criticism?* (ed. D. O. Via. New Testament Series; Minneapolis: Fortress Press, 1993). Ten years earlier, introductory books in methodology did not mention

getical approaches have their roots in the epistemology developed during the Enlightenment period, which also marks the beginnings of the modern—and colonial—era. What has happened lately may be described as a change in the epistemological paradigm.[72] The modern era has turned into a postmodern era.[73]

In New Testament studies this development is shown by the introduction of a multitude of new methods and perspectives.[74] Postcolonial approaches within biblical exegesis are located within this development, beginning in the middle of the 1990's, but with roots that are somewhat less recent.[75]

New Testament postcolonial criticism is not to be seen as a discipline coming from the 'outside' and injecting a new approach into New Testament exegesis; rather it originates from and within the field of New Testament studies itself, with scholars aware of their marginalised—post colonial—position. Accordingly, these scholars are now trying to change

---

these approaches, see, e.g., John H. Hayes and Carl R. Holladay, *Biblical Exegesis: A Beginner's Handbook* (London: SCM Press, 1987) and Christopher Tuckett, *Reading the New Testament: Methods of Interpretation* (Philadelphia: Fortress Press, 1987). For excellent discussions in Swedish, see Birger Olsson, "Ett bidrag till metodfrågan," *Svensk exegetisk årsbok* 45 (1980): 110–21, see also by the same author, "Text är arbete att förstå: Om olika textperspektiv i svensk bibelforskning under 1900-talet," *Svensk exegetisk årsbok* 64 (1999): 5–22; and "Förstår du hur du läser?" in *Religio* (ed. René Kieffer and Birger Olsson; Lund: Teologiska institutionen, 1995): 7–22. Methodological changes are fast, but the scholarly community sometimes responds slowly. Resistance to change is one of the most difficult obstacles that postcolonial scholars struggle to overcome. An example from beyond the scholarly community of such reluctance to change with regard to women-oriented methodologies is found in *The Interpretation of the Bible in the Church* (Indian Edition ed. Vatican Document: The Pontificial Biblical Commision; Bangalore: NBCLC, 1995), 69, n. 2. Commenting on the paragraph about "The Feminist Approach" it is stated that, "Out of 19 votes cast, the text of this last paragraph received 11 in favor, 4 against and there were 4 abstentions." Interestingly this is the only footnote (the document has only 3 footnotes) in the document that shows any disagreement among the participants.

[72] Cf. Olsson, "Ett bidrag till metodfrågan." In this article, Olsson maps the development of New Testament methodology from the 'old' historical critical discourse to the beginning of the 'new.' He describes methodology as changing over time, from using one pair of optics to the use of multiple optics that the scholar has to change between when shifting approaches. Olsson's question, "Does all exegetical methods lead to the same goal?" is answered with a 'no.' See also, Birger Olsson, "A Decade of Text-Linguistic Analyses of Biblical Texts at Uppsala," *Studia Theologica* 39 (1985): 107–26.

[73] Cf. The Collective, *The Postmodern Bible*, 8–12.

[74] For a good introduction, see The Collective, *The Postmodern Bible*, 1–15.

[75] For a survey of the history and the place of postcolonial studies within New Testament exegesis, see Segovia, "Mapping the Postcolonial Optic."

both scholarly approaches to a variety of methods, and a politically problematic traditional style of doing exegesis.[76]

It is important, however, to note that, while this research focuses on people and phenomena in the margins, postcolonialism, as an academic discipline within biblical studies in general, is not located in the margins, but in the centre, in the sense that it is currently involved in the renewal of exegetical approaches. Postcolonialism belongs to the most recent approaches in New Testament exegesis, and, as such, it is to be understood as a development taking place in the centre. At the same time, impulses and inspiration come from the margins and the interaction between the margins and the centre.

As noted above, postcolonial studies are very much part of a postmodern critique of European epistemology and its methods for historical research.[77] Kwok Pui-lan,[78] an innovative biblical scholar merging postcolonialism and feminism, uses Foucault's philosophy in her study of how biblical interpretation is formed by the politics of truth.[79] She argues that the context, or, more precisely, the episteme, within which

---

[76] Feminist study, or wo/men study, as Elisabeth Schüssler-Fiorenza prefers to name it, functions in the same way. Schüssler-Fiorenza argues for an inclusive view of wo/men studies. Otherwise, the naming and categorising of sub-fields like gender, race, or class tend to set these fields apart from 'ordinary' exegetical work. That this is still the case is obvious, according to Schüssler-Fiorenza, from the fact that in many libraries and bookstores literature about gender in biblical studies respectively are placed in special, separate bookshelves and not together with the larger field it interacts with. See Elisabeth Schüssler-Fiorenza, *Rhetoric and Ethic: The Politics of Biblical Studies* (Minneapolis: Fortress Press, 1999), 4–5. See also Hanna Stenström's article, "Historical-Critical Approaches and the Emancipations of Women: Unfulfilled Promises and Remaining Possibilities" in *Her Master's Tools? Feminist and Postcolonial Engagements of Historical-Critical Discourse* (ed. Caroline Vander Stichele and Todd Penner; Atlanta: SBL, 2005): 31–46. Stenström describes the struggles of scholar Emilia Fogleklou in Uppsala, Sweden, in the early 20th century. Fogleklou's expectations with regard to the liberating potential of historical critical methodology turned to disappointment as she discovered that, in reality, traditional Christian doctrine still controlled much of exegetical academia (38–39).

[77] Cf. Stephen D. Moore and Fernando F. Segovia, eds., *Postcolonial Biblical Criticism: Interdisciplinary Intersections* (Bible and Postcolonialism; London: T&T Clark, 2005). The interdisciplinary character of biblical criticism is shown by the fact that it interacts with postcolonial theory, poststructuralism, feminism, racial/ethnic studies, and Marxism.

[78] Kwok Pui-lan, *Postcolonial Imagination*; "Mercy Amba Oduyoye and African Women's theology," *JFSR* 20:1 (2004): 7–22; "Jesus/The Native: Biblical Studies from a Postcolonial Perspective" in *Teaching the Bible: The Discourses and Politics of Biblical Pedagogy* (ed. Fernando F. Segovia and Mary Ann Tolbert; Maryknoll, New York: Orbis Books, 1998), 69–85; and *Discovering the Bible in the Non-Biblical World* (The Bible and Liberation; Maryknoll: Orbis Books, 1995).

[79] Kwok, *Discovering the Bible in the Non-Biblical World*, 9.

biblical scholars 'constructed' modern exegesis during the European colonial period often meant the turning of exegetical results into politically correct truths.[80] As an example she brings up the influence orientalism has had on philology.[81]

The modern contemporary context is always present in scholarly conclusions. Segovia,[82] who focuses on postcolonialism and the Gospel of John, argues that "all interpretations, all recreations of meaning from texts, and all reconstruction of history is dependent upon reading strategies and theoretical models."[83] The mainstream reading strategies and theoretical models New Testament scholars apply are often framed by a historical critical perspective, which in turn has its origin in Enlightenment positivism. For this reason, the interpretations and conclusions are less 'factual' historical reconstruction than expressions of epistemological presuppositions originating during the Enlightenment. Segovia holds that it is preferable for postcolonial scholars to approach a biblical text and the historical reconstruction of that text from a postmodern perspective:[84] such an approach will provide the scholar with tools for questioning positivistic truth claims. This will open up the door for other kinds of interpretations—interpretations that acknowledge that which is true for all readings of

---

[80] See her article, Kwok, "Jesus/The Native," especially 75–80.

[81] Kwok, "Jesus/The Native," 77–78. During the early period of philology Kwok states that scholars related "linguistic structures to forms of thought and features of civilization." She gives an example by quoting Renan: "One sees that in all things the Semitic race appears to be an incomplete race, by virtue of its simplicity. This race—if I dare use the analogy—is to the Indo-European family what a pencil sketch is to painting; it lacks that variety, that amplitude, that abundance of life which is the condition of perfectibility." J. Ernest Renan and Henriette Psichari, *Œuvres complètes*, 10 vols., vol. 8 (Paris: 1948), 156.

[82] His most known works are, Fernando F. Segovia, *Decolonizing Biblical Studies: A View from the Margins* (Maryknoll: Orbis Books, 2000); "Introduction: Pedagogical Discourse and Practices in Contemporary Biblical Criticism. Toward a Contextual Biblical Pedagogy" in *Teaching the Bible. The Discourses and Politics of Biblical Pedagogy* (ed. Fernando F. Segovia and Mary Ann Tolbert; Maryknoll, New York: Orbis Books, 1998), 1–27; "Pedagogical Discourse and Practices in Cultural Studies: Toward a Contextual Biblical Pedagogy" in *Teaching the Bible: The Discourses and Politics of Biblical Pedagogy* (ed. Fernando F. Segovia and Mary Ann Tolbert; Maryknoll, New York: Orbis Books, 1998), 137–67; "Reading Readers of the Fourth Gospel and their Readings: An Exercise in Intercultural Criticism" in *"What is John?" Readers and Readings of the Fourth Gospel* (ed. Fernando F. Segovia; Atlanta, Georgia: Scholars Press, 1996), 237–78; *The Farewell of the Word: The Johannine Call to Abide* (Minneapolis: Fortress Press, 1991); and *Reading from this Place: Social Location and Biblical Interpretation in Global Perspective*, 2 vols. (Minneapolis: Fortress Press, 1995).

[83] Segovia, *Decolonizing Biblical Studies*, 119.

[84] Segovia, *Decolonizing Biblical Studies*, 29–33.

texts, namely, the importance of the flesh-and-blood-reader and her or his contemporary situation and perceptions. Segovia's point is, just as Kwok argues, that it is not possible to read the text as if it were only 'plain text;' it is necessary to understand text as part of a larger context, which includes the present reader and her or his perspectives, situations, limitations, and, most significantly, the episteme in which the scholar lives and writes.

One of the most productive scholars in the field, Sugirtharajah, shares the perspectives of Segovia and Kwok. Sugirtharajah criticises the 'Western way' of doing exegesis for being eurocentric.[85] This eurocentrism is applicable not only with regard to Western scholars but postcolonial scholars as well. Sugirtharajah states that they, too, are influenced by a Western scholarly context due to their hybridity.[86] Even if Sugirtharajah himself is a 'hybrid,' born in Sri Lanka, living and working in Birmingham, England, and himself at risk of excluding others, it is noticeable that he is careful to mention and interact with a large number of scholars from all parts of the world. Thus, he is not only aware of his own 'Westernised scholarly hybridity,' but also emphasises how vast and diverse the exegetical and theological world is.

Sugirtharajah also emphasises a broad spectrum of contexts and perspectives when he addresses the issue of (biased) translations of the Bible.[87] Instead of using just one translation of the Bible, he constantly refers to different translations in order to show the variety of translations and their biases—both Western and other. In other words, reading Sugirtharajah rewards the reader with a good sense of the world's 'Four Corners.'

Another important—some would say problematic—contribution to the field is represented by the work of a group of scholars within the Society of Biblical Literature. Two volumes have been published so

---

[85] Sugirtharajah, "From Orientalist to Post-Colonial," 23–24.
[86] Sugirtharajah, *Postcolonial Criticism and Biblical Interpretation*, 23. Sugirtharajah writes, "[P]ostcolonial criticism, like the hybridity it celebrates, is itself a product of hybridity. It is an inevitable growth of an interaction between colonizing countries and the colonized. It owes its origin neither to the First nor the Third World, but is a product of the contentious reciprocation between the two."
[87] Sugirtharajah, *Postcolonial Criticism and Biblical Interpretation*, 6. To avoid the problem of quoting the same translation in his study, and to show the variety instead, Sugirtharajah writes, "The biblical quotations come from different versions of the Bible, indicating that there is no one supreme version, and none which can be definitive, and that each version in its own way elucidates the word."

far in a series named *Reading the Bible in the Global Village*. The first volume appeared in 2000. It derives from the 1999 *SBL International Meeting* in Helsinki, Finland. This volume, together with the second volume, which records presentations and discussions from the conference held in Cape Town 2000, may stand as an example of interaction and dialogue between 'Western' and postcolonial perspectives. These volumes are particularly interesting since the encounter between 'the West/North' and 'the East/South' comes to the fore in a very clear, and for some, upsetting way.

A representative example of this interaction is found in Heikki Räisänen's article and Elisabeth Schüssler-Fiorenza's response, published in volume one. Räisänen states that postcolonial scholars exaggerate their critique of historical critical methodology. Instead, he argues that, "[t]he liberationist enterprise might profit from regarding the historical-critical paradigm, in particular that version which distinguishes between reconstruction and application, as a blessing, rather than as the original sin."[88]

Räisänen refers to Krister Stendahl's definition of 'meant' and 'mean' in his study *Meanings*.[89] He argues that, what postcolonial scholars do fits well into the existing paradigm of the mainstream exegetical community. In other words, the postcolonial enterprise is, to put it bluntly, nothing new. Räisänen claims that the postcolonial critique that he, by and large, thinks is accurate, should not be directed against historical critical methodology but rather against the scholars who have (mis-) used this methodology. As Räisänen states, "[t]hat it was rarely done was not a fault of the method, but of its practitioners."[90]

---

[88] Heikki Räisänen, "Biblical Critics in the Global Village" in *Reading the Bible in the Global Village: Helsinki* (ed. Heikki Räisänen; Atlanta: Society of Biblical Literature, 2000), 9–28, 27.

[89] Räisänen, "Biblical Critics in the Global Village," 11. See also Krister Stendahl, *Meanings: The Bible as Document and as Guide* (Philadelphia: Fortress Press, 1984), 11–44.

[90] Räisänen, "Biblical Critics in the Global Village," 17. Note the similar conclusion Sugirtharajah draws when quoting Amy Ling in her article "'I' am Here." Ling writes, "Tools possess neither memory nor loyalty; they are as effective as the hands wielding them," Amy Ling, "'I' am Here" in *Feminism: Anthology of Literary Theory* (ed. Robyn R. Warhol and Diane Price Hernd; New Brunswick: Rutgers, 1993), 741. Sugirtharajah is however ambivalent about the methodology and, even if he lists all its shortcomings, he sees and acknowledges its advantages for a postcolonial biblical study, just as many other postcolonial biblical scholars do. Sugirtharajah, *Postcolonial Reconfigurations*, 86–87.

Schüssler-Fiorenza, on the contrary, argues that Räisänen misses the point: postcolonialism is not mainly "a battle of methodological 'approaches'... [but]... in reality a battle for power."[91] Asserting that Räisänen misses this aspect of postcolonial studies, Schüssler-Fiorenza believes that he reduces postcolonialism into "a discrete approach within the hegemonic paradigm."[92]

The discussion between Räisänen and Schüssler-Fiorenza may stand as an example of the general discussion of the location of postcolonialism within New Testament studies. Through its many practitioners, postcolonialism embodies a hybridity and a plurality that lead to a variety of approaches to New Testament exegesis, all marked by an awareness of past and present postcoloniality. Postcolonial studies cover, e.g., approaches as disparate as 'traditional' historical critical exegesis,[93] inter-textual studies,[94] general criticism of New Testament exegesis today,[95] historical research into, e.g., Indian philosophical influences on New Testament texts around the 1st and 2nd century,[96] and Western missiological aspects of contemporary educational systems in the Two-Thirds World.[97]

---

[91] Elisabeth Schüssler-Fiorenza, "Defending the Centre, Trivializing the Margins" in *Reading the Bible in the Global Village: Helsinki* (ed. Heikki Räisänen, Elisabeth Schüssler-Fiorenza, Sugirtharajah, Krister Stendahl, and James Barr; Atlanta: Society of Biblical Literature, 2000), 29–48, 35. For further discussion about Schüssler-Fiorenza's view on power relations, see Schüssler-Fiorenza, *Rhetoric and Ethic*.

[92] Schüssler-Fiorenza, "Defending the Centre," 31.

[93] E.g., Soares-Prabhu, who emphasises that historical criticism is pre-requisite for accurate exegesis. George M. Soares-Prabhu, "The Historical Critical Method: Reflections on its Relevance for the Study of the Gospels in India Today," *Theologizing in India* (1981): 314–67.

[94] See Xavier's use of the Upanishads in his reading of the Gospel of John in, A. Xavier, "John's Gospel in the Indian Context" in*dian Theological Studies* 21:2–4 (1984), 347–64. See also George M. Soares-Prabhu, "Two Mission Commands: An Interpretation of Matthew 28:16–20 in the Light of a Buddhist Text," *Biblical Interpretation* (1994): 264–82.

[95] See, e.g., Johnson Teng Kok Lim, "Historical Critical Paradigm: The Beginning of an End," *AJT* 14 (2000): 252–71 and also his study, *A Strategy for Reading Biblical Texts* (New York: Peter Lang Publishing, 2002).

[96] See for example, Zacharias P. Thundy, *Buddha and Christ: Nativity Stories and Indian Traditions* (Leiden: Brill, 1993); J. Duncan M. Derrett, *The Bible and the Buddhists* (Casa Editrice Sardini, 2000); and Augustine Thottakara, "An Indian Poet Contemplates on the Life of Jesus Christ: A Critical Appreciation of the Kristu-bhagavata of Prof. P. C. Devassia" in *Western Encounter with Indian Philosophy: Festschrift in Honour of Prof. Dr. Thomas Kadankavil* (ed. Augustine Thottakara; Bangalore: Dharmaram Publications, 2002), 65–92.

[97] R. S. Sugirtharajah, *Asian Biblical Hermeneutics and Postcolonialism: Contesting the Interpretations* (The Biblical Seminar 64; Sheffield: Sheffield Academic Press, 1999), 135. See also further below, chapter five.

Räisänen's critique does not take this plurality of postcolonialism into account, but rather focuses on historical critical methodology alone. Schüssler-Fiorenza, on the other hand, emphasises the importance of a broad perspective that incorporates not only methods, but also a meta-perspective, which includes rhetorical aspects, ethics of interpretation, and power relations within the academic community.[98]

Räisänen's and Schüssler-Fiorenza's discussion may be understood within the broader question whether a paradigm shift is currently taking place within New Testament studies, a shift that is propelled not only by postcolonialism but also by other expressions of postmodern resistance marked by political overtones.[99]

According to Kuhn, a paradigm consists of 'silent knowledge.' This knowledge is not gained by reading scholarly studies, but mostly through personal interaction with other scholars. Consequently, there is no need to argue for the accuracy of the 'silent knowledge,' since it is taken for granted.[100] When a paradigm shift is about to take place, new ideas, theories, or perspectives, precede it. In this process the 'silent knowledge' is brought up to the surface and discussed: it becomes visible and, at the same time, deconstruction begins.

Quite often the initial response to this process is to ridicule it or diminish its importance. A classic example is Copernicus discovery that the Sun is the centre of the solar system rather than the Earth. Postcolonialism within New Testament studies should be seen as part of a larger movement, in which contemporary 'silent knowledge' is questioned with the aim of bringing change to the traditional exegetical paradigm.

From that perspective, Räisänen's and Schüssler-Fiorenza's discussion mirrors two different understandings of postcolonialism as a phenomenon. Räisänen argues that postcolonial studies are possible *within* the current exegetical paradigm, while Schüssler-Fiorenza believes this to be impossible due to seriously damaged power relations within the scholarly community and globally, which in fact challenge the established exegetical paradigm. It seems to me, however, that both are right.

---

[98] Schüssler-Fiorenza, "Defending the Centre," 30–32, 43–48.
[99] Räisänen states that the shift has already taken place, but he does not agree of its all-pervasiveness in the scholarly world: "There *has* been a shift, and in many ways it is to be welcomed. I think, however, that the radicalness of this shift has been exaggerated." Räisänen, "Biblical Critics in the Global Village," 27.
[100] Torsten Thurén, *Vetenskapsteori för nybörjare* (Malmö: Liber, 1991), 72–73.

Räisänen brings up the aspects of postcolonialism that is already part of the common 'silent knowledge' within the field, while Schüssler-Fiorenza, questioning the ethnocentricity and the hegemonic aspects of New Testament studies in a global context, emphasises parts of postcolonialism that lie beyond and challenge the 'silent knowledge.' The paradigm shift is not mainly about methodological approaches but rather about the ethos prevalent in the scholarly world. *Reading the Bible in the Global Village* should perhaps have a subtitle: *Who is Chief in the Global Village?* Is it the one who has 'Western optics' or the one who has "postcolonial optics?"[101]

3.4 Summary

Chapter three has been an attempt at defining the theoretical location of postcolonial studies in the broader context of biblical exegesis on the one hand and postcolonialism and postmodernism on the other. The first step was to lay a basic terminological foundation on which to build conversation. In order to facilitate discussion of the complex phenomena related to postcoloniality, this and other key concepts were defined. While *postcoloniality* refers to all reactions and consequences of a colonial situation, *postcolonialism*, as the academic pursuit of understanding aspects of such reactions and consequences, is itself one of these reactions. *Postcolonial New Testament exegesis* is a subdivision of postcolonialism. It is aware of the fact that the theoretical background, or matrix of exegesis, is just one way of perceiving reality, a way which emanates from Western dominance in the world and which, in the end, is (consciously or unconsciously) defending this dominance as both right and inescapable. Postcolonial New Testament exegesis is defined by its critical awareness of hegemonic claims within scholarly traditions, and one of the purposes of this approach is to acknowledge and point to a reality that is both ethically responsible and emancipatory.

Fundamental to understanding postcolonialism in context is the adoption and adaptation of the Foucaultian concept of episteme. This concept provides us with an interpretive tool for understanding not only the synchronic context with all its lateral inter-discursive simi-

---

[101] "Postcolonial optic" is Segovia's expression, Segovia, *Decolonizing Biblical Studies*, 119.

larities, but also the diachronic dimensions that may shed light on inter-epistemic developments.

Thinking in terms of perceived realities rather than, as often is the case in the scholarly literature, assuming one's own discourse of truth to be foundational for some sort of objective reality, opens up for epistemic humility and the path towards authentic scholarly progress. Reading perceived realities requires a willingness to read and listen to real life, the 'flesh-and-blood' everyday lives of the contexts in which methodological ideas are born and raised to maturity. Methods are, as much as exegetical results, embedded in epistemic-specific realities; we need to find and define the method's 'body' in order to locate its 'soul.'

Many of the misunderstandings and rather heated debates related to postcolonial biblical studies are based on a neglect to take seriously the diverse epistemic historical and contemporary contexts of divergent methodological approaches, the political implications that follow with them, and the truth-claims they result in. The assumption that, for example, the use of historical critical methods is a neutral endeavour, which will always result in the same answers, regardless of where in the world they are applied, fails to realise the basic epistemic-bound contextuality of all methodological discourses. Further, such an assertion ignores the politics of interpretation.

This does not necessarily mean that historical research would be unsound or impossible in itself; it means however, that the 'McDonaldisation' of this approach, based historically in the Western colonial project, is mistaken, and politically unwelcome.[102] Tensions and conflicts that arise in this regard may be explained by the mechanics set in motion by the injection of epistemic-specific aspects of perceived realities in other epistemic contexts where such aspects and concepts are foreign: the political and the methodological merge, and tension is created in such clashes of epistemes.

With such tensions emerging from lack of fusion or adaptation of epistemes, it is not hard to understand and sympathise with postcolonial critique and its attempt to dismantle and deconstruct Western methodological approaches, specifically the historical critical discourses so connected, as we shall see shortly, with the colonial enterprise. This does not mean that such postcolonial critique is uniform

---

[102] Cf. Anna Runesson, "Historisk-kritisk metod i postcolonial kontext: Stötesten eller nödvändighet?" *Svensk kyrkotidning* 97: 9–10 (2001): 475–79.

or unproblematic; neither does it imply that such critique is without influence from Western academic discourses themselves. We shall now turn to such deconstructive postcolonial endeavours in an attempt to listen carefully to what is being said and how it is said. Then, in chapter five, we shall proceed to take a look at postcolonial constructive exegesis.

CHAPTER FOUR

DECONSTRUCTING WESTERN BIBLICAL STUDIES

4.1 Introduction

The story of biblical criticism shows that even those expounders of the Bible who claim to be indifferent to theories about the history of the sacred texts, from the gnostic preachers of the 2nd century to the structuralists of the 20th have their own hidden historical explanations of how their texts came into existence and of how they are to be read.[1]

These words by William Baird express lucidly what has often been stated in recent debates in New Testament exegesis. The presence of hidden agendas may be either conscious or unconscious. A *conscious* but hidden agenda means that one's research is governed by a specific structure of thought that is not articulated in the text but nevertheless is intended to affect the results.[2] An *unconscious* hidden agenda is present in research done within an epistemological frame that the scholar takes for granted and does not reflect upon methodologically. This agenda will nevertheless affect the scholarly results.[3]

In the strict sense, there are no a-historical or non-methodological readings of text, and any reading that does not explain and make clear its methodological presuppositions must be seen as inherently problematic. In chapter three, we pointed to the necessity of understanding academic activity within broader interpretive frames defined by the theory of episteme. Such an understanding emphasises that there must be an awareness also of where the methods used originated, and that there are political aspects involved.

---

[1] William Baird, "History of Biblical Criticism," *ABD* 1:726–35, 729.
[2] As in colleges and seminars where scholars have to sign a contract in which they agree to stick to the theological doctrines set up by the denomination in charge of the school.
[3] An episteme may serve as the arena wherein the scholar her-/himself is caught and unknowingly formulates results that are in line with the episteme. An example of this is the Enlightenment.

The question of method lies, in many respects, at the heart of postcolonial critique of Western exegesis. The question is, though, how this critique itself is constructed methodologically.

In *Her Master's Tools? Feminist and Postcolonial Engagements of Historical-Critical Discourse*, the editors Caroline Vander Stichele and Todd Penner describe the relationship of feminist and postcolonial studies to historical critical discourse.[4] In the introduction, Vander Stichele and Penner ask whether the aim of feminism and postcolonialism is to 'master the tools' or to 'retool the masters.'[5] The question is important since New Testament scholars in both fields, and of course in other related fields, have to be aware of the role of historical critical discourse when new methodological approaches are formulated.

The reason is simple: methods serve as a guide to the epistemological frame in which research and results should be understood. The construction and use of methods facilitate a *structured understanding* of the material and the sources involved. In addition, from a reversed perspective, methods *mirror the episteme* within which the scholar is socialised, and, to a certain extent, by which s/he is limited. In other words, the research process cannot be understood without the methodological discourse in which it takes place. This discourse serves, if the metaphor is allowed, as the yeast for scholarly cakes: the yeast is the methods, flour and other ingredients are the source material, and fermentation represents the analytical work; in the oven the synthetical work takes place. The cake, of course, represents the final conclusions.

In the present chapter we shall present and discuss postcolonial approaches to methodological questions. An effort has been made to allow the scholars behind the ideas to 'talk' as much as possible in order to accurately represent their critique of historical critical discourse.[6] Focussing on the critique, rather than beginning the analysis by discussing postcolonial contributions to methodological renewal

---

[4] Caroline Vander Stichele and Todd Penner, eds., *Her Master's Tools? Feminist and Postcolonial Engagements of Historical-Critical Discourse* (Global Perspectives on Biblical Scholarship 9; Atlanta: Society of Biblical Literature, 2005), 1–29. 'Historical critical discourse' is a wide concept that includes more than just a specific method. It is more helpful to understand the historical critical discourse as a certain way of thinking, since the postcolonial critique focuses not only on historical critical methodology but also on historical criticism as a hegemonic epistemology.

[5] See Vander Stichele's and Penner's introductory chapter in, *Her Master's Tools?* 1.

[6] Cf. the methodological point of departure by Jussawalla and Dasenbrock described above.

within biblical studies, will prove beneficial to our purposes since it is in the critique that the episteme becomes visible.

Further, putting focus on the critique facilitates the definition and categorisation of the perspectives within which postcolonial scholars are working. This process will, it is hoped, enable us to answer questions like Vander Stichele's and Penner's. As will be shown, the truth seems to lie somewhere in between 'mastering the tools or retooling the masters:' we do not find an 'either-or,' but rather a 'both-and.' And it is not always clear, even within a text by a single author, where the emphasis is to be placed.

A brief overview of the history of New Testament exegesis will introduce the discussion, in order to provide a frame within which the postcolonial critique may be understood. Chapter four will, then, present the critique, categorising the material according to some general patterns that evolve from a close reading of the literature.

4.2 Exegesis in a Nutshell: A Short Presentation of its History

Our purpose here is to give a brief presentation of the history of modern exegesis, guided by the overall concerns of the book. After an exposé of different definitions of exegesis, the epistemological roots of modern biblical studies (especially the importance of the Enlightenment period) as well as the development of methodologies will be dealt with.

4.2.1 *Defining Exegesis*

Exegesis is...

> ...the art of interpretation, the part of theology, that has the interpretation and the explanation of the Biblical texts as its subject. Cf. Hermeneutic. (*Nordisk familjebok*, 1923–1937).[7]
>
> ...methodical interpretation of a text. Especially used of Biblical Studies (Old and New Testament exegesis).(*Nationalencyklopedin*, 1991.)[8]

---

[7] "Exegetik," *Nordisk familjebok: Encyklopedi och konversationslexikon*, 6:1223 (my translation): "...utläggningskonst, den gren av teologien, som har utläggningen och förklaringen av de bibliska skrifterna till sitt föremål. Jfr. Hermeneutik."

[8] "Exegetik," *Nationalencyklopedin*, 6:58 (my translation): "...metodisk uttolkning av text. Termen användes särskilt om bibelvetenskap (Gamla resp. Nya Testamentets exegetik)."

...the critical interpretation of the biblical text to discover its intended meaning. (*Encyclopædia Britannica*, 1991.)[9]

The process of careful, analytical study of biblical passages undertaken in order to produce useful interpretations of those passages. (*ABD*, 1992.)[10]

Exegesis. *See* Reading. (*The Postmodern Bible*, 1995.)[11]

The quotes above reflect different approaches toward exegesis, from 1923 to 1995 (with a focus on the 1990s), and they indicate some of the difficulties in finding a consensus definition.

The first four quotes identify exegesis as interpretation of biblical texts within the field of biblical studies. *Nordisk familjebok* explicitly understands exegesis as part of theology. *Nationalencyklopedin* emphasises the methodological aspect of the subject. *Encyclopædia Britannica* stresses the critical interpretation in order to find the *intended* meaning of the text, as opposed to Douglas Stuart, who authored the entry in *ABD* and who defines the purpose of exegesis to be to find a *useful* interpretation.

Encyclopædia Britannica represents an older, more traditional, view of the nature of exegesis, namely to discover the intended meaning of the text. With that particular perspective the focus is put on the historical context of the text. Stuart's definition, on the other hand, represents an understanding of exegesis that was only formulated as part of scholarly discussions about hermeneutics in the last 15 years. The historical context or meaning is not always the main focus; instead the meaning of the text is said to be located in the interaction between the text and the present context, which the interpreter her/himself is part of. However, the criterion of usefulness is introduced, which limits the range of possible interpretations and at the same time puts emphasis on the contemporary context of the scholars involved in the exegetical enterprise.

The broadest and most inclusive definition is from *The Postmodern Bible* and part of the same postmodern perspective we find in Stuart's definition. The definition in *The Postmodern Bible* abolishes any boundaries between biblical studies and other academic fields: 'exegesis' may refer to interpretation of any texts (religious or not). At the same time, an epistemological claim is made in the reference to the entry 'Readings,' namely that the reader is deeply involved in the interpretive process. (Under 'Reading' we find, consequently, an emphasis on reader response theory.)

---

[9] "Exegesis," *Encyclopædia Britannica*, 4:629.
[10] Douglas Stuart, "Exegesis," *ABD* 2:682–88, 682.
[11] The Collective, *The Postmodern Bible*, 387.

The definitions above show how much definitions are dependent on the historical context of the scholars providing them. The first quote (1923–37) was written during a time when exegesis was commonly known to be part of (Western) theology, which had the Bible as its main focus. The last quote (1995) is written at a time when changes in approaches to and understanding of the processes involved in the interpretation of texts had penetrated the field of biblical studies. However, this should not be taken as evidence of a complete takeover of new (postmodern) perspectives. Rather, today we find a mix of approaches, representing both older and more recent views on what is involved in exegesis.

According to the definition of *The Postmodern Bible*, exegesis is as old as the oldest text and its interaction with its first reader. However, it is not this particular definition of exegesis that postcolonial scholars are addressing in their critique. The main focus of their criticism is the modern exegesis, which has its roots in the Enlightenment period and its connection to the modern colonial era. In other words, the critique found in postcolonial exegetical studies is located in and focuses on the tension between the old exegetical stance, where the search for an intended and historical meaning is the main task, and later developments in which the questions related to finding *a* meaning is formed in the reader's response to the text.

It is worth noting that defining exegesis under the heading 'Reading' leads to an approach in which exegesis is applicable to all historical periods, including the Enlightenment. In other words, regardless of the intentions and epistemology of the scholar, from a postmodern perspective a reading is a reading is a reading…

4.2.2 *The Historical Critical Discourse*

> Historians seek objectivity. They are interested in discovering and reporting what really happened in the past, as opposed to collecting and passing on fanciful stories writing "docudramas," or producing revisionist accounts of the past for propagandistic or ideological purposes.[12]

What Maxwell Miller wants (in somewhat polemical terms) to communicate is a basic distinction between historical work and any other type of storytelling. However, as he continues to argue, it is clear that

---

[12] J. Maxwell Miller, "Reading the Bible Historically: The Historian's Approach" in *To Each its Own Meaning: An Introduction to Biblical Criticisms and their Application* (ed. Steven L. McKenzie and Stephen R. Haynes; Louisville: Westminster John Knox Press, 1999), 17–34, 18.

this distinction is more about the *intention and purpose* of the scholarly endeavour than the actual possibility to produce objective historical reconstructions. Miller writes:

> The historian's own presuppositions, ideology, and attitudes inevitably influence his or her research and reporting. Perhaps it is not an overstatement to say that any history book reveals as much about its author as it does about the period of time treated.[13]

In brief, one could say that this tension between intention and reality in historical exegesis, a tension that is often pointed out in more recent studies such as Miller's, is at the very heart of postcolonial criticism.

The place of historical critical discourse in the history of epistemology has influenced how postcolonial critique of historical criticism has been formulated. The theory of episteme is therefore useful in the search for the origins of historical critical methods in that it can answer the *how and why* questions, not only the *when* and *where*. The advantage of the theory is that it not only locates epistemology in its context, but also addresses problems of what it is that forms our thoughts, actions, lifestyle, theories, relations (including colonial and postcolonial relations) etc. In other words, the episteme is the inevitable network of relations that embraces us and forms us and ties us to previous time periods, the present, and the future.

Historical critical discourse had its beginnings during a period when positivism was deconstructing previous paradigms, and was held high by its proponents. The results and reconstructions of the historians were not only highly valued, but also understood as objective truths. Historical truth became, in the study of religion, *the* truth.

Today epistemological and methodological thinking is going in another direction, and as a result historical research and its results have been re-evaluated by many. A common view is that the interpreter and her/his context are part of the research in such a way that makes it impossible to read the biblical texts from a neutral meta-perspective since, at bottom, a meta-perspective does not exist.

The episteme in which a text was born becomes intertwined with the episteme in which the scholars live and move and have their being. As a result the interpretation becomes dependent on where the scholar is located (e.g., white male in West at a rich university or a woman from India at a college in Bangalore). Consequently, every interpretation is formed in and by the episteme existing coterminously with

---

[13] Miller, "Reading the Bible Historically," 18.

the scholar. However, the text that is the object of interpretation was also formed by the episteme current at the time when the text was authored: to a certain extent, the text is the bearer and transmitter of an episteme that no longer exists. It is arguable that the act of interpretation is by definition a fusion of two epistemes, and inevitably embodies a new phenomenon transcending both epistemes, which in turn affects the current episteme, in which the scholar works.

Historical critical discourse itself is not static: just as interpretations move with and in the epistemes as they slowly and gradually shift, epistemology changes shape as these gradual transformations take place. This is a slow process, and it is within these changes, initially brought about by postmodern thinkers, that postcolonial criticism of Western historical critical methods, as well as attempts at methodological renewal, take place. As a result, historical criticism began as a renewal, and even as a protest movement, claiming to produce new and objectively verifiable truths correcting long held church doctrines and understandings of the New Testament texts. This position of protester is today taken over by postcolonial scholars, criticising what they believe have become oppressing powers preventing them from full participation in the scholarly arena.

4.2.3 *Summary*

The story of exegesis is itself a story of changing epistemes. What some scholars would see as historical interpretations re-constructing first century worldviews, other scholars would claim to be constructions emanating, ultimately, from the powerful episteme dominated by Enlightenment ideas about reality.

Not only do results and conclusions change, so do methodologies and epistemology. Albert Schweitzer's discovery of other scholars' faces in what supposedly should have been portraits of Jesus is just the beginning of the deconstruction of objective certainty.[14] Schweitzer himself was part of the historical discourse within which he criticised his fellow scholars. Postmodern epistemological perspectives open up for new methodological approaches and it is within this larger movement in the history of biblical studies that the postcolonial scholars should be located.

---

[14] Schweitzer, *Leben-Jesu Forschung*. It was George Tyrrell who first used the metaphor of the scholar seeing his or her own face at the bottom of the well of historical Jesus studies.

From this position, postcolonial scholars criticise historical critical discourse, or rather traditional (modern) historical critical discourse. This criticism is related to but not the same as postmodern criticism of historical critical methods. Analysing the postcolonial critique will bring to the fore the methodological and epistemological assumptions and positions of these scholars. Consequently, this strategy will aid our understanding of what is at stake in this growing debate.

4.3 Postcolonial Critique of Traditional Historical Critical Discourse

At the Society of Biblical Literature's annual conference in Denver 2001, one of the participants, Kwok Pui-lan, questioned the relevance of historical Jesus research in a postcolonial context. It does not require much reading of postcolonial literature on biblical interpretation to realise that her statement is representative of much postcolonial exegesis. More specifically, it is the historical critical discourse that constitutes one of the major problems in the field.

In this section, postcolonial critique of historical critical methods will be presented via a discussion of some of the most important scholars in the field: Kwok Pui-lan,[15] Fernando Segovia,[16] Musa Dube,[17] George Soares-Prabhu,[18] R. S. Sugirtharajah,[19] Johnson Teng Kok Lim.[20]

---

[15] See, e.g., Kwok, *Discovering the Bible in the Non-Biblical World*, Kwok, "Jesus/The Native;" and *Postcolonial Imagination*.

[16] See, e.g., Segovia, "Mapping the Postcolonial Optic;" "Postcolonial Biblical Criticism;" Segovia and Mary Ann Tolbert, eds., *Teaching the Bible: The Discourses and Politics of Biblical Pedagogy* (Maryknoll: Orbis Books, 1998); "Contemporary Biblical Criticism," and Segovia and Tolbert, eds., *Reading from this Place*.

[17] See, e.g., Musa W. Dube, "Rahab Says Hello to Judith: A Decolonizing Feminist Reading" in *Postcolonial Biblical Reader* (ed. R. S. Sugirtharajah; Oxford: Blackwell, 2006), 142–58.

[18] See, e.g., Soares-Prabhu, "Historical-Critical Method." See also his other work, "Two Mission Commands." The last study is a collection of some of his better known articles edited by Frances D'Sa after his tragic death in 1995.

[19] See, e.g., Sugirtharajah, who has authored a number of seminal books and articles among which the following are especially noteworthy: *The Bible and Empire: Postcolonial Explorations* (Cambridge: Cambridge University Press, 2005); *Postcolonial Reconfigurations: An Alternative Way of Reading the Bible and Doing Theology* (London: SCM Press, 2003); *Postcolonial Criticism and Biblical Interpretation* (New York: Oxford University Press, 2002); *The Bible and the Third World: Precolonial, Colonial and Postcolonial Encounters* (Cambridge: Cambridge University Press, 2001); and *Asian Biblical Hermeneutics and Postcolonialism: Contesting the Interpretations* (The Biblical Seminar 64; Sheffield: Sheffield Academic Press, 1999).

[20] See, e.g., Johnson Teng Kok Lim, *A Strategy for Reading Biblical Texts* (New York: Peter Lang Publishing, 2002) and "Historical Critical Paradigm: The Beginning of an End," *AJT* 14 (2000): 252–71.

When postcolonial critics analyse the discipline of biblical studies, it is often historical critical methods that are targeted. Sometimes the critique seems to be more routine, lacking detailed arguments; sometimes it is clearly defined and carefully argued.

The nature of the critique makes it convenient to present it under two major headings. First, we find a 'general' critique which postcolonial scholars share with many non-postcolonial scholars, in particular postmodern researchers. Second, we can distinguish a 'specific' critique that is unique to postcolonial scholars. In order to give as full a portrait as possible of the postcolonial critique, it is necessary to include both the general and the unique, since even that which is shared with others acquires specific meanings when it is incorporated into a new context.

4.3.1 *General Critique of Historical Critical Discourse*

The general scholarly debate about historical critical discourse had its beginnings in the 1960s, a decade marked by new epistemological approaches. Until then, historical critical methods had dominated biblical studies as the preferred interpretive perspective. With postmodernism, new methods, like new literary criticism and reader-response criticism, arose and the dominance of historical critical methodology was challenged.

Postcolonialism partly grew from this movement and its criticism of historical critical methods should, consequently, be understood in this context.[21] Soares-Prabhu, for example, illustrates the problems with historical critical methods by explicitly referring to and using insights from postmodernism.[22] In his discussion it becomes clear that traditional historical critical methods belong to an earlier epistemological paradigm—modernism. He states that biblical exegesis has been liberated through the postmodern paradigm and that this liberation has opened up the doors for an Asian biblical exegesis, which does not fit into the positivistic perspective of modernism.[23]

In a similar way, Johnson Teng Kok Lim also criticises the 'old' historical critical paradigm as belonging to the era of modernism. Even

---

[21] However, the origin of postcolonialism is not possible to bind to a specific event. It is comparable with the appearance of feminism in the way that the existence of dissatisfaction gets its acknowledgement during a certain time when the social conditions are favourable. Postcolonialism has other roots but as a scientific endeavour it received its acknowledgement during the 1960s.

[22] Soares-Prabhu, "Two Mission Commands," 264.

[23] Soares-Prabhu, "Two Mission Commands," 264.

if he brings up some advantages with historical critical methods,[24] he argues that these methods are run over by newer methods, which have their basis in a postmodern approach. According to Johnson these newer methods deconstruct the infrastructure of historical criticism; they are "gradually dismantled by the bulldozer of literary and postmodern criticism."[25]

Johnson's point is that there exists an old historical critical methodology that is gradually replaced by a 'new.'[26] He does not seem to entertain much hope for the old historical critical methodology. Johnson belongs among those scholars who do not merely point out the shortcomings of the method, which he argues have caused its failure on the scholarly arena; he also calls into question, on a more fundamental level, its survival,[27] and prophesies that it will become "a footnote in the history of interpretation."[28]

He is not alone in stating this. Segovia, for instance, argues that the historical critical method should be considered obsolete. But this is said from a theoretical point of view only: practically, in the narratives of scholarly discourse, it is still alive, "though at various stages of health."[29] Johnson articulates it even more straightforwardly when he says that "...the old historical criticism is dead and a new historical criticism is reborn singing the same song but in a different tune."[30]

Sugirtharajah argues in a different way than Johnson and Segovia. He does not divide the history of historical critical methodology into an 'old' and a 'new' phase. Instead he states that the historical critical methodology is colonial. Period. This is so because it serves colonial purposes,[31] and, consequently, 'new' methods like social sciences, poststructuralism, narrative theories, and deconstruction should be seen as

---

[24] Johnson, "Beginning of an End," 253. For example he mentions: 1. That it is accurate to apply a historical method to historical religions (Christianity and Judaism) since their scriptures contain elements of God's saving act. 2. That the historical critical method is a good tool for scholars to anchor the biblical text in its historical context and thereby prevent the interpretation from "running wild." 3. That it prevented the text from being exploited, and did not tolerate earlier interpreters' allegorical methods.

[25] Johnson, "Beginning of an End," 258.
[26] Johnson, "Beginning of an End," 258.
[27] Johnson, "Beginning of an End," 252.
[28] Johnson, "Beginning of an End," 259.
[29] Segovia, *Decolonizing Biblical Studies*, 9, n. 8.
[30] Johnson, "Beginning of an End," 257.
[31] Sugirtharajah, *Asian Biblical Hermeneutics*, 125. Cf. Sugirtharajah, *Postcolonial Reconfigurations*, 86–87.

additions to an already existing colonial method. For Sugirtharajah, the postmodern paradigm is, in one sense, just a continuation of the Western epistemological domination.[32]

Postcolonial critique of historical critical discourse is pervasive. For that reason it is important to study the concrete criticism, aiming at inquiring into the central epistemological problems that are at the heart of the debate.

Positivism, objectivism, nature and *intention* are four concepts frequently used within the general critique of the traditional historical critical discourse, and in the following we shall discuss each of them in turn.

4.3.1.1 *Positivism and 'Objectivism'*

Two of the main errors of historical criticism, according to postcolonial scholars, are positivism and 'objectivism.'[33] Soares-Prabhu distinguishes 'objectivism' from 'objectivity,' stating that 'objectivism' is "an illusory 'objective neutrality' emulating the supposed neutrality of the physical sciences."[34] At the very moment objectivism was considered a possible ideology applicable to biblical studies, exegesis became "unidimensional." Soares-Prabhu points out that the aim was to reach the "fixed, objective meaning locked up in" the biblical text.[35] The ideology of 'objectivism' in combination with "philological, grammatical and historical tools" mistakenly led scholars to think it was possible to find the "one true meaning."[36] This enterprise was generally considered not only possible but also universal: "It was always and everywhere the same."[37] From this, Soares-Prabhu concludes that, if that were the case, it should not matter in which culture exegesis is performed—if the methods are properly used, the scholarly results should be the same, globally. Soares-Prabhu writes:

> The *application* of a biblical text (that is, the spelling out its "significance" for the reader) might differ from place to place. But its *exegesis* (the disclosure of its "meaning") would always follow the standard procedures of historical criticism. Attempts at a contextualized interpretation

---

[32] For discussion about domination and hegemony, see 4.3.2.2.
[33] E.g., Soares-Prabhu, "Historical-Critical Method," 319. Segovia, *Decolonizing Biblical Studies*, 12–15, Sugirtharajah, *Asian Biblical Hermeneutics*, 10.
[34] Soares-Prabhu, "Historical-Critical Method," 319.
[35] Soares-Prabhu, "Historical-Critical Method," 319–20.
[36] Soares-Prabhu, "Two Mission Commands," 265.
[37] Soares-Prabhu, "Two Mission Commands," 265.

were dismissed by historical critics as uncritical "readings" (*lectures* in French), which might serve pastoral purposes, but had no place in the serious, "critical" exegesis of the academy.[38]

Inherent in the wish to reach objectivity, Soares-Prabhu argues, is the idea that the real reader necessarily introduces a risk of subjectivity and consequently, the reader must be pushed aside: there was no place for a cultural reading. The reader did not fit into the positivistic pattern of thought, which demanded an objective perspective. For that reason, Soares-Prabhu states that objectivism is the foundation of the failure of historical critical methodology, since it does not include, nor does it permit, a 'real reader' or a culture that is reacting to the intention that is imbedded in a religious text such as the Bible.[39]

According to Segovia, objectivism has its roots in the positivistic ideal within the modern paradigm, and it constitutes a foundation for historical critical methods. He argues that the incentive for this positivistic development was a longing to get rid of tradition and dogmatism.[40] In biblical criticism the guiding star became "to engage in exegesis, not eisegesis"[41]—which meant a ban on interpreting the text from any other angle than the historical.[42]

To use historical criticism on biblical texts was a way to express "the modern light of reason" and to expel "subjectivism and emotionalism."[43] The aim was, according to Segovia, to "decontextualize," i.e., eliminate the presuppositions and preconceptions of the scholar.[44] Or, to put it differently, the purpose was to contextualise the *text* in its own time period. A "reading of the past in the terms of the present" was the "ultimate epistemic taboo."[45] Segovia, just like Soares-Prabhu, considers the idea that it would be possible to sort out the text's context from

---

[38] Soares-Prabhu, "Two Mission Commands," 265.
[39] Soares-Prabhu, "Historical-Critical Method," 319. See also, Mary Ann Tolbert, "A New Teaching with Authority: A Re-evaluation of the Authority of the Bible" in *Teaching the Bible: The Discourses and Politics of Biblical Pedagogy* (ed. Fernando F. Segovia and Mary Ann Tolbert; Maryknoll, NY: Orbis Books, 1998), 168–89, 176–77, where Tolbert contrasts the historical and the transcendent text.
[40] Segovia, *Decolonizing Biblical Studies*, 148–49.
[41] Segovia, *Decolonizing Biblical Studies*, 148–49.
[42] 'Exegesis' means to find meanings out from the text only, and 'eisegesis' means to import a meaning into the text, a meaning that could be coloured by the reader and therefore incorrect and unhistorical.
[43] Segovia, *Decolonizing Biblical Studies*, 149.
[44] Segovia, *Decolonizing Biblical Studies*, 149.
[45] Segovia, *Decolonizing Biblical Studies*, 150.

the real reader's context, or to use his own word "the real flesh-and-blood-reader," to be seriously flawed.⁴⁶

In a similar way, Kwok argues that the historical critical reading strategy, with objectivism as one of its cornerstones, has become "the standard and the norm for judging all other reading strategies."⁴⁷ The reading strategies in other cultures are not valued academically as highly as the Eurocentric historical critical perspective. In addition to Kwok's work, it is worth mentioning John Riches' article "Cultural Bias in European and North American Biblical Scholarship." He argues that biblical interpretation cannot be universal since the biblical reading is a cultural reading just as much as any other reading today.⁴⁸

Since the real reader and contemporary culture are two important parameters in postcolonial exegesis, it follows that the heart of the postcolonial criticism is directed *against the historical critical claim to universality*. Had proponents of historical critical discourse defined their methodological approach as Riches does—i.e., as a cultural reading—much of the New testament postcolonial critique would fall. The universalistic claim is, arguably, closely related to colonial structures; indeed, it originated in the Western episteme within which colonialism was also born.⁴⁹

Joseph Pathrapankal states that the stumbling block in the enterprise of finding the 'situative context' via a historical critical study is objectivism. It "prevents it from appreciating the role the reader and the interpreter have in establishing the total meaning of the text and it remains blind to the authentically new meaning and challenge that a text may have to acquire as it is read in every new situation"⁵⁰ We shall return to this below. At this point, it may be concluded that 'objectivism' and positivism are major targets of postcolonial critical discourse. Such criticism is connected to universalising tendencies and

---

⁴⁶ Segovia, *Decolonizing Biblical Studies*, e.g., 151.

⁴⁷ Kwok, "Jesus/The Native," 73.

⁴⁸ John Riches, "Cultural Bias in European and North American Biblical Scholarship" in *Ethnicity and the Bible* (ed. Mark G. Brett; Boston: Brill Academic Publishers, 2002), 431–48.

⁴⁹ Cf. Musa W. Dube, "'Go Therefore and Make Disciples of All Nations' (Matt 28:19a). A Postcolonial Perspective on Biblical Criticism and Pedagogy" in *Teaching the Bible: The Discourses and Politics of Biblical Pedagogy* (ed. Fernando F. Segovia and Mary Ann Tolbert; Maryknoll, New York: Orbis Books, 1998), 224–46, 237–40.

⁵⁰ Joseph Pathrapankal, "A Re-reading of John 12:20–27 in the Context of Religious Pluralism" (paper presented at the Studiorum Novi Testamenti Societas 56th General Meeting, Montreal, 2001).

a-contextual claims that go hand in hand with colonial attitudes, attitudes that were formed in the epistemic milieu of the enlightenment. As a result, 'objectivism' has political dimensions, which are strongly rejected by postcolonial scholars.

The situation may be compared to the fact, often repeated in New Testament studies, of the non-existence of distinctions between religious and secular spheres of society in antiquity. In the same way, epistemic realities prevent distinctions between the methodological and the political. When postcolonial scholars point to such connections, and bring the political into the discussion, it is not a question of inventing the political in academic contexts. Rather, it is making the already (colonial-)political aspects visible, and then combating them with the intention of replacing them with other (non-colonial) political approaches.[51]

Such criticism, which targets the political and methodological at once, is, however, not the only type of postcolonial critique levelled against traditional Western exegesis. We shall now turn to the problem of the nature and intention of the biblical texts, a major point where postcolonial and postmodern scholars meet in their critique of historical critical discourse.

4.3.1.2 *The Nature and Intention of the Biblical Text*

Soares-Prabhu states that historical criticism is incommensurable with the *nature* and *intention* of the biblical text.[52] The text is not a complete historical work. Instead, he argues that, in its very nature, it is fragmentary because the biblical text constitutes just one component in a long and far-reaching process of interpretation, starting with an ongoing oral tradition that reaches back from before the text was written and into an incalculable future.[53] He understands the biblical text itself as a part of an interpretation of an earlier event, an interpretation that is still proceeding because it was written down and transmitted to us today.

The written text in itself constitutes a limited part of history and the 'truth' of that particular period in history could as well be found outside of the text as within it. Therefore, Soares-Prabhu argues that

---

[51] See further chapter five.
[52] Soares-Prabhu, "Historical-Critical Method," 318. See also, Tolbert, "Teaching with Authority," 176–77.
[53] Soares-Prabhu, "Historical-Critical Method," 319.

the biblical text is "too thin." It does not have the "static entity with a fixed unchanging meaning or series of meanings" that a historical critical study, based on positivistic ideals, tries to find. The biblical text simply does not have that amount of evidence that historical criticism requires.

When Soares-Prabhu states that historical criticism is incompatible with the 'intention' of the biblical text he states that the text, as a religious text, is meant for a receiver—a real reader. For that reason, he emphasises, it is not possible to use a method "fashioned to obtain exact information...to interpret a text which aims at the personal transformation of the reader through his [sic] response in *faith*."[54] It is simply against the intention of the text. Here, Soares-Prabhu introduces another aspect of the real reader, namely, a reader that is responding to the divine message of the text.[55] Johnson holds a similar view. He argues that the text is a complex entity, and as such it is impossible to analyse it without including the entire context. According to Johnson, when engaging in historical criticism there is a risk of atomisation of the text, which might lead to results that will miss the intention of the text as a religious text.[56]

According to Soares-Prabhu the intention of the text, namely the divine message, is impossible to get at through historical critical analyses, since historical criticism is lacking the parameter of 'faith.'[57]

Since the reader of the text is participating in creating the meaning of the text, Soares-Prabhu argues that there cannot possibly exist *one*

---

[54] Soares-Prabhu, "Historical-Critical Method," 318.

[55] This position narrows down the participants in the academic conversation not only to religious persons, but to Christians ready to accept the texts as communicating a message from the divine. It should be remembered, however, that Soares-Prabhu lived in India, in a Christian minority situation in which biblical interpretation was (and still is) a matter of concern almost exclusively to Christians.

[56] Johnson, "Beginning of an End," 256.

[57] On the other hand, Georgi states that the study of the historical Jesus, a study within the historical critical paradigm, often had the parameter of 'faith' as the main incitement for the study—a historical critical study was the gateway to a true faith. He refers here to the overarching view that only "the historical Jesus would prevent theology from sliding into myth, docetism, and mystery religion." Dieter Georgi, "The Interest in the Life of Jesus Theology as a Paradigm for the Social History of Biblical Criticism," *HTR* 85:1 (1992), 51–83, 81. It is interesting to note that in spite of the fact that the parameter of 'faith' is forbidden in a historical critical study, the results and the main goal could very well fit into an apologetic scheme of the scholar. Georgi's purpose with his article is to show how scholarly approaches are influenced by their social history, or, to put it in other words, that it is impossible to be objective.

fixed meaning in the text.⁵⁸ The meaning is dependent on the reader: the text requires a real reader with a religious sensibility, and no one else can find the text's real meaning, which can vary depending on circumstances within the reader's context. But, since the goal of historical criticism is to search out exact information, Soares-Prabhu concludes that it is an impossible enterprise to combine historical critical methods with biblical texts.⁵⁹ The method requires more than the text can provide, partly because of the nature of the text and partly because of its intention. Historical critical study does not take into consideration the importance of a context that reaches beyond the text's historical frames. Consequently, as we noted above, Soares-Prabhu stresses that the project to apply historical criticism to biblical texts is in its very foundation a failure.⁶⁰

The question is, of course, if positivistic ideals really have been "dethroned" and the postmodern climate has opened up for alternatives, such as specific Asian interpretations, as Soares-Prabhu argues.⁶¹ Is the historical critical methodology no longer dominant? Segovia doubts this. He suggests that in a postmodern era the method has lost its importance, but this is only from a theoretical point of view. In reality it is still alive and well.⁶² As a matter of fact, it is more alive in former colonies and the Two-Thirds World than in the postmodern West.⁶³

Even if many postcolonial scholars, embedded in postmodern theory and living in a hybrid situation in the West, agree that the 'old' historical critical methodology should no longer constitute a problem for them, postcolonial scholars living in postcolonial countries in a non-postmodern environment, being theologically trained according

---

⁵⁸ The role of the interpreter in the interpretation has recently been discussed at Vitterhetsakademien's symposium in Uppsala, Sweden, 2006, published in 2007. Birger Olsson comments that the younger generations seem more open to take this into account into their academic work. He also notes that, as a consequence, reception historical perspectives have increased. See Birger Olsson, "Reflektioner vid konferensens slut" in När religiösa texter blir besvärliga (Konferenser 64; ed. Lars Hartman; Stockholm: Kungl. Vitterhets Historie och Antikvitets Akademien, 2007): 147–60, 148. Olsson himself, however, has worked extensively over the last twenty to thirty years with questions of hermeneutics and reception history.
⁵⁹ Soares-Prabhu, "Historical-Critical Method," 319.
⁶⁰ Soares-Prabhu, "Historical-Critical Method," 319.
⁶¹ Soares-Prabhu, "Two Mission Commands," 265.
⁶² Segovia, *Decolonizing Biblical Studies*, 9, n.8.
⁶³ Sugirtharajah, *Asian Biblical Hermeneutics*, 129.

to western traditional historical criticism, often tend to be more traditionally historical critical then those in the West.

In sum, postcolonial and postmodern critique of historical critical discourse overlaps to a significant degree. The main points of contact between these approaches are the epistemologically based rejection of positivistic claims and 'objectivism,' as well as the attention given to the nature of a religious text, and the demand that this nature must be matched by a methodology, which is sensitive to it if an adequate understanding of the text is the purpose of the academic endeavour. Reading postcolonial scholarship, there may come a point when the reader asks, what, then, is new and distinct about postcolonial approaches to New Testament studies?

4.3.2 *Specific Critique of Historical Critical Discourse*

In the previous section we found that postcolonial critique of historical critical methods has much in common with the general critique of the so-called 'old' historical critical discourse. Indeed, the many similarities between postcolonial and postmodern criticism may justify that we talk about postcolonial discourse as being an integral part of postmodern discourse. Postcolonialism finds support and legitimacy in postmodernism. Even so, postcolonial criticism of Western epistemology goes beyond postmodern discourse in that it focuses on the Western colonial enterprise and its impact on biblical studies. Understanding postcolonialism in its own right, it is necessary to narrow down the focus to three interconnected areas, all of which come to the fore in postcolonial scholarship: orientalism, hegemony, and relevance.

One of the main purposes of postcolonial scholars is to criticise and deconstruct epistemological and methodological positions that prevent non-western biblical exegesis from developing in its own right in local contexts. This criticism may take different forms, and it is the purpose of the present section to discuss some of the more important contributions to postcolonial thinking in this regard.

We shall proceed by tracing in the scholarly literature postcolonial perspectives on the role of colonialism, and the episteme in which colonialism was and is formed and maintained, in biblical studies. It is precisely at this point that postcolonial critique of Western exegesis becomes distinct and goes beyond the general (postmodern) critique of historical critical methods. We shall begin with orientalism in biblical studies, and then deal with hegemony and relevance respectively.

4.3.2.1 *Orientalism and the Portrayal of 'the Other'*

One of the most important, indeed fundamental, books in postcolonial discourse is Edward Said's *Orientalism*, published in 1978.[64] The study, which has not escaped criticism, addresses the question of how the West has, and still is approaching the Orient, both theoretically and physically through colonialism. Said insists that the theoretical assumptions and constructions of the Orient made the physical colonial approach towards the East possible; the theoretical construction legitimised colonialism. It is the combination of these two approaches towards the East, the theoretical and the physical, that Said designates 'orientalism.'[65]

The theoretical orientalism imaginatively portrays the Orient in ways suited for Western purposes, creating portrayals which function politically within the episteme as a base for colonial exploitation. Consequently, one of the main points of Said's book is to show that the 'Orient' does not exist in and of itself. As Wong Wai Ching notes, it is

> ...a political, ideological, and imaginative creation of European culture during the post-Enlightenment period. Orientalism was therefore a discourse of the West that controlled the nature and shape of knowledge as well as the ways it was produced and disseminated.[66]

The 'Orient' is, therefore, a construction created within a movement that Said names 'orientalism.' As such it includes everything from academic philological assumptions and representations of the 'oriental' in poems and literatures, to ideas and statements about the intelligence of 'oriental people.' According to Said, academic orientalism is one of the most obvious among the various forms of orientalism. All scholars who are engaged in studies of the 'Orient' are involved in orientalism "...whether the person is an anthropologist, sociologist, historian, or philologist."[67]

---

[64] Edward Said's *Orientalism* was originally published in 1978 by Routledge and Kegan Paul. A second printing with a new Afterword was published in 1994. In the present study I have used the Vintage Books edition from 2003. For a interesting study on Said's educational context and his early formative years, see Maria Småberg, *Ambivalent Friendship: Anglican Conflict Handling and Education for Peace in Jerusalem 1920–1948* (Lund: Lund university, 2005).

[65] Said, *Orientalism*, 73.

[66] Wong Wai Ching, "Postcolonialism," *Dictionary of the Third World Theologies*: 169–70, 169.

[67] Said, *Orientalism*, 1–2. Even if the word 'Orient' is not used today as often as before, 'orientalism' as a phenomenon is alive.

Apart from the academic form of orientalism a more general orientalism exists that has its base in an "ontological and epistemological distinction" made between 'the Orient' and (most of the time) 'the Occident.'[68] In this group we find the poets, the writers, and the philosophers.

A third aspect of orientalism, which is more concrete or physical, emerges during the end of the 18th century. From this time onwards, the West made more explicit statements about the 'Orient' with the purpose of conquering it. This aspect of orientalism became "a Western style for dominating, restructuring, and having authority over the Orient."[69] This development coincides with the peak of the modern colonial period. As such it served the purpose of taking control of the unknown, making way for Western political and military expansion and domination.

The construction of 'the Other' is very much a mirror image of the 'self;' in other words, the two opposed entities are created simultaneously. Therefore, the formation of the 'Orient,' before and during the colonial period, was as much a time for the formation of a Western identity.[70] When the 'Orient' is defined as the *periphery*, it automatically follows that the 'Occident,' or the West, is defined as the *centre*. Said writes, "In addition, the Orient has helped to define Europe (or the West) as its contrasting image, idea, personality, experience."[71]

In this way, neither the 'Orient' nor the 'Occident' exist in reality, since they are only constructions serving Western political and ideological aims.[72] Said's project is to deconstruct the concept of the 'Orient.' However, he does not formulate any alternative theories in

---

[68] Said, *Orientalism*, 2.

[69] Said, *Orientalism*, 3.

[70] Another example of creating an identity in the centre versus an identity in the periphery is to be found in Meyda Yegenoglu's article about the veil. Yegenoglu describes how the West stands out as the norm for 'good' moral living in the discussion of the veiling of eastern women. The Western feminist ideals in the question of veiling do often stand out as the "democratic, advanced, emancipated" norm with a global validity. Meyda Yegenoglu, "Sartorial Fabric-action: Enlightenment and Western Feminism" in *Postcolonialism, Feminism and Religious Discourse* (ed. Laura E. Donaldson and Kwok Pui-lan; New York: Routledge, 2002), 82–99.

[71] Said, *Orientalism*, 2.

[72] Said, *Orientalism*, 5. It should be noted that the same phenomenon occurs in the 'East' in its relation to the 'West,' which is quite clear not least from recent developments in conflicts between people in the Middle East and the West: the east constructs an image of the West serving purposes of identity formation and resistance to what is perceived as Western aggression and dominance.

his study, but leaves that open for other scholars. His purpose is only to unveil the construction of orientalism, not to create a new philosophy.[73] Said's work is seminal, having influenced the debate on the relationship between East and West for almost three decades.[74]

For postcolonial biblical studies, the theory of orientalism has been of critical importance, both in analyses of the modern colonial period, since orientalism was formed in the same episteme as the colonial project, and in modern biblical exegesis, especially the 'old' historical critical discourse. Orientalism is, by default, present in the modern project of biblical exegesis. One of the tasks that postcolonial scholars have taken on themselves is to trace this orientalism as it appears in methods, selections of sources, and results.

Examples of orientalism can be found in a wide range of scholarly productions, dating from the beginning of modern biblical exegesis and continuing to the present day. The series of biblical commentaries known as *The Indian Church Commentaries* completed 1890 presents us with an interesting case.[75] The studies of scholars such as J. B. Lightfoot, B. F. Westcott, and F. J. A. Hort, influenced bishops and missionaries living in India who, in turn, wrote the commentaries. In the commentaries, distinct portrayals of the invader and the invaded evolve. As Sugirtharajah has noted, some parts of the commentaries

---

[73] Said, *Orientalism*, 325.

[74] E.g., Richard King, *Orientalism and Religion: Postcolonial Theory, India and 'The Mystic East'* (London and New York: Routledge, 1999); Qian, *Orientalism and Modernism*; Lisa Lowe, *Critical Terrains: French and British Orientalisms* (Ithaca: Cornell University Press, 1991); and Bryan S. Turner, *Orientalism, Postmodernism and Globalism* (London and New York: Routledge, 1997), 32. These are works that often both acknowledge Said's work and criticise it. Turner, for example, acknowledges Said's work but argues that it is outdated. He argues that the division between the 'Occident' and the 'Orient' has, in Said's work, been too much "organised around the basic dichotomy of sameness and difference; the principal feature of the orientalist discourse has been to emphasize difference in order to account for the 'uniqueness of the West.'" Turner argues for a definition of orientalism as a more dynamic concept that does not always see everything in black and white. It should, for instance, be "permissible to refer to Islam as an occidental religion in Spain Malta and the Balkans and to Christianity as an oriental religion of North Africa, the Fertile Crescent of Asia."(32) According to Turner, orientalism is in fact more diverse than Said allows us to believe. However, as Loomba notes, even if the phenomenon of orientalism was known before Said's study, and even if orientalism has developed further in different directions, his work on orientalism was the beginning of a new kind of study of colonialism. Loomba, *Colonialism/Postcolonialism*, 43.

[75] Sugirtharajah, *Asian Biblical Hermeneutics*, 54–85. I have not been able to locate these commentaries, and have therefore had to rely on Sugirtharajah's presentation and discussion of them. (Sugirtharajah himself notes how difficult it was for him to find and obtain them; p. 84.)

portrayed the Indians as an "orderly, well-mannered, and kindred Christian community with one faith, one Church, and one Lord." This is done in sharp contrast to earlier portraits describing non-Christian Indians as "unruly, vulgar, and diverse."[76]

Sugirtharajah argues that this was a conscious colonial strategy to secure "the consent of the governed through intellectual and moral manipulation rather than through military force."[77] Conversion to the colonisers' religion, Christianity, is the key unlocking the door to the 'civilised world,' making the conquered culturally acceptable to the conquerors. It is easy to see how orientalist ideology is at play in such descriptions of the 'other,' the activity itself best being described as hegemonic.[78]

On the other hand, negative caricatures of Christian Indians are also present throughout the commentaries. Commenting on individual passages, Indians are described as "weeping and wailing openly and uninhibitedly" (Acts). They are, further, depicted as "meek and mild" (2 Corinthians), they are "unreliable and fail to keep promises" (2 Corinthians), and "Indian church workers have a tendency to use church money for private purposes" (Philippians).[79] Such orientalistic constructions of 'the Other' were very common during the 19th century.

Orientalism is, as the above shows, closely related to the phenomenon of hegemony, and the one can hardly be analysed without the other, even if, for purposes of analysis, it is preferable to keep them under separate headings.

4.3.2.2 *Hegemony and Truth Claims*
Orientalism and hegemony go hand in hand. As a result, the deconstruction of hegemony is as crucial as the deconstruction of orientalistic misconceptions about 'the other.' Since postcolonialism implies colonialism, which by definition implies one country's sovereignty over another, the focus on hegemony has become one of the more important characteristics in postcolonial critique.

---

[76] Sugirtharajah, *Asian Biblical Hermeneutics*, 69.
[77] Sugirtharajah, *Asian Biblical Hermeneutics*, 69.
[78] We shall return to hegemony below, 4.3.2.2.
[79] Indian church commentaries, quoted by, Sugirtharajah, *Asian Biblical Hermeneutics*, 71.

Hegemony is a social construction. Loomba, referring to Antonio Gramsci, describes hegemony as "power achieved through a combination of coercion and consent."[80] As such, hegemony is not only created by force, but also by "creating subjects who 'willingly' submit to being ruled."[81] Hegemony may be simply defined as the situation of superiority and subordination. Subordination is a consequence of how, e.g., a person, a gender, an ethnic group or a nation, is defined by a superior power. In the case of the Orient, Said has shown that the Orient's relations to the West are, in many respects, due to a construction mainly created by the West. 'The periphery' is constructed to serve the purposes of the 'centre,' and consequently hegemony is, by definition, intertwined with the activities of the 'centre.' However, even if this is the case and 'the Orient,' 'the West,' and the phenomenon of 'hegemony' itself, are nothing but constructions, they have a concrete impact on the every day life of those living in a postcolonial world. Therefore the effects of these constructions have real 'flesh-and-blood implications.'

Hegemony as the advancement of a colonialist politics also pervades the scholarly world, including biblical studies. Hegemony is at work in the promotion of the view that the epistemology and the methods developed in the West are globally indispensable, indeed fundamental to any scholarly endeavour worldwide. But since scholarly hegemony is a construction it is open to de-construction, just as political hegemony is. These questions are of utmost importance to postcolonial scholars, since Western hegemony prevents non-Western scholars from developing their own interpretive agendas; without worldwide recognition and respect, participation in the global academic dialogue is, in effect, made impossible.

Illustrating the effects that literary and postmodern critique has had on the 'old' historical critical discourse, Johnson Teng Kok Lim emphasises that Western hegemony is now being dismantled.

> For some, it [i.e., new literary criticism] was like a breath of fresh air sweeping across the corridors of biblical studies; while others felt its impact was more like a hermeneutical *El Nino* disrupting the climate of historical criticism and dislodging their hegemony.[82]

---

[80] Loomba, *Colonialism/Postcolonialism*, 29.
[81] Loomba, *Colonialism/Postcolonialism*, 29.
[82] Johnson, "Beginning of an End," 258.

The differences between the two reactions within the biblical scholarly community as Johnson describes them are immense: a breath of fresh air, or an academic climate change that rips apart Western biblical exegetical hegemony. What Johnson describes is how a new theory influences and undermines an already established scholarly hegemony. The question is, however, how much of Johnson's description of a fundamental disruption within biblical studies reflects present day reality, and how much is rather wishful thinking on the part of the author. Are we at the crossroads, where the academic biblical field has to decide the direction of future exegesis? Do we stand before a paradigm shift, or is it just some fresh air slipping through a minor crack in the wall?

According to Thomas Kuhn's theory of paradigm shifts, the purpose of academics is to dislodge hegemonic structures over and over again in order for scholarship to develop. A paradigmatic shift *necessarily involves the dislodging of hegemony*. During the Enlightenment scholars challenged not only other scholars, but also the church's hegemony and its role in academia. One of the better-known examples is, of course, how Copernicus' heliocentric theory about the universe conquered the Ptolemaic worldview. Not only did Copernicus challenge the scholarly community; he also challenged the hegemony of the church, since the church had adopted the Ptolemaic theory as part of its construction of a Christian worldview. However, the more ground Copernicus' theory gained the more the paradigm shift became a fact—both academically and within the church—despite tremendous religio-political resistance.

The role of the church is an important factor to take into account when analysing how hegemony has affected the outcome of scholarly studies. Prior to the Enlightenment and the development of historical critical methods the hegemony of the church was all-pervasive. Church doctrine had a huge influence on academic interpretive work. When historical critical methods developed and gained ground in the beginning of the 18th century, it was not only a new methodological perspective; it was also an immense challenge to the hegemony of the church.

When historical critical methodology became established within biblical studies the authority of the church gradually lost its grip on the discipline. To put it simply, the church began to forfeit its hegemonic power that had previously been controlling the scholarly world to a significant degree. This development represents a clear paradigm shift, opening up a completely new intellectual environment independent of the church.

Today biblical studies are, it seems, changing direction again. Postcolonial scholars are questioning not only the objectivity claim in early historical criticism, but also the *new* hegemony that followed and replaced the old church-based hegemony. The new hegemony is Western university-based. In spite of the fact that both old and new historical criticism was designed for a Western and not for a global context, the epistemological claims of historical criticism have been made global. This process has been part of the modern colonial enterprise, which involved claiming epistemological, as well as political, economical, and military primacy. In other words, postcolonial criticism and methodological renewal represents, just as the Enlightenment paradigm shift, a serious and fundamental attack on an old epistemological paradigm supported by hegemonic institutions.

It may indeed be correct to talk about a paradigm shift. However, it remains to be seen if the thoroughgoing innovations of postcolonial (and postmodern) scholars will penetrate academic society fully. Only then can we determine whether what we now witness is the beginning of a new way of doing exegesis, or whether it will remain a marginal movement that never succeeded in turning the tide.

Johnson defines the methodological development in his own field—literary criticism, which has developed during the last forty years—as part of the same paradigm shift the historical critical discourse is going through.[83] However, Johnson argues that there is a difference between historical and literary approaches to the biblical text. He states that, due to different views of history and different interpretive interests, "...they are incompatible because the diachronist and synchronist ask different questions."[84]

Therefore, Johnson divides historical criticism into an 'old' and a 'new' approach, where literary criticism is part of the 'new' historical criticism. This 'new' historical criticism is more diverse than the old, including a multitude of methods and a re-evaluation of the meaning of 'objectivity.' Johnson deconstructs the hegemony of the 'old' historical criticism and banishes it to an existence as a "footnote in history."[85]

---

[83] Johnson, "Beginning of an End," 258–59.
[84] Johnson, "Beginning of an End," 258.
[85] Johnson, "Beginning of an End," 259.

According to Johnson, the 'old' historical critical methodology has lost its precedence with regard to the interpretation of biblical texts.

Kwok Pui-lan does not describe recent developments in quite the same way. For Kwok, the problem is more complex and diverse. She takes her point of departure in a feminist Two-Thirds World context.

> As an Asian Woman critic, I am painfully aware that contemporary mental and intellectual space is controlled by the cultural hegemony of the West, the white gaze, and the unceasing self-representation of the male. In the field of biblical studies the domination of western epistemology, presuppositions, methods, and solutions is particularly acute.[86]

Kwok argues that even new methods like literary criticism, rhetorical criticism, sociological criticism etc., are "developed from the same cultural matrix and from the Western anxiety about truth, knowledge, and language."[87] In this sense, Johnson's discussion about hegemony may be seen as a debate within the frames of Western biblical epistemology. It is true that the new methods are opening new perspectives in a way that the old 'orthodox' historical criticism could not do, but in the end the new methodological approaches will limp when seen in a postcolonial context; there will always be two or three gear teeth missing in the methodological gear wheel. Or rather, the gear teeth belong in a different machine altogether.

Even though both Johnson and Kwok have a postmodern perspective, they address the problem very differently. Johnson's methodological discussion is located within the 'centre,' i.e., the Western scholarly discourse, while Kwok strives to find solutions where culture and local context are placed at the centre. Kwok's focus is on the problems a Western epistemology creates when it makes global claims.

In Kwok's analysis of the biblical interpretive work of Asian women, she goes beyond the mainstream matrix of Western exegesis. Kwok argues that an Asian woman critic is "...an Other to western biblical scholarship, to white feminist theological discourse, and to male-dominated theological scholarship in Asia."[88] These aspects of marginalisa-

---

[86] Kwok, *Discovering the Bible in the Non-Biblical World*, 26.

[87] Kwok, *Discovering the Bible in the Non-Biblical World*, 26. Kwok emphasises that the discourse of feminist theory is no exception in this. She says that feminism "build[s] on white male scholarships (even if they refute and argue against it) and white feminist theory," and that it is part of the "western women's movement." Therefore, it is also involved in the Western hegemonic structures and insufficient in a global context.

[88] Kwok, *Discovering the Bible in the Non-Biblical World*, 27.

tion show that there exist not only *one* 'Other' but *multiple* 'Others,' which are all bound to their specific context. For that reason, it is not possible for the Western matrix to become a matrix for a global context; the global arena is simply too complex and the marginalisation of people and cultures is too thorough.

When Kwok argues her case, she begins with herself by unmasking her own initial reaction when she was confronted with Asian women's biblical reflections in some anthologies. She reacted negatively, she says, thinking they were "unacademic" and "meant more for a pastoral context than for a theological academy."[89] But after having read Sugirtharajah, among others, she slowly began changing her mind. She finally recognised that she was an Asian woman, trained in a Western academic context implanted in Asia; a scholar formed in a Western biblical interpretive matrix. She realised the tensions between these contexts, which had led to her hesitation when reading Asian theology, and she began re-evaluating the meaning of her Asian heritage for her academic work.

After this discovery, Kwok has emphasised the importance of analysing both the Western and the Asian cultural and religious matrices as foundations for scholarly approaches to theology and biblical studies. She concludes that it will not be possible for the West to understand the hermeneutics of Asian biblical interpretations until the scholarly world takes seriously cultural and religious matrices in different parts of the world.[90]

Johnson and Kwok represent two different approaches toward hegemony. Johnson represents the development within the Western postmodern criticism, while Kwok, from a postmodern/postcolonial perspective, criticises the Western scholarly hegemony and its global claims, both the old and the new. Nevertheless, both Johnson and Kwok agree that the era when it was possible to make clean and tidy exegetical truth claims is over.

Sugirtharajah emphasises, as we have discussed above, the method's colonial aspect. He focuses on the fact that historical criticism is a tool claimed to be universally applicable.[91] This means that the method is not seen just as the foundation of a properly performed exegesis, but also as "universalistically applicable in opening the biblical text" in any

---

[89] Kwok, *Discovering the Bible in the Non-Biblical World*, 27.
[90] Kwok, *Discovering the Bible in the Non-Biblical World*, 27.
[91] Sugirtharajah, *Asian Biblical Hermeneutics*, 126.

given context.[92] Sugirtharajah states that it is this theoretical approach that makes the method part of Western colonialism: Western scholars assume "that their work is universal, comprehensive, and exhaustive."[93] Sugirtharajah argues that this view of historical criticism is alive and well even today. Therefore, it is accurate to speak of historical critical discourse as *modern epistemological colonialism*.

Historical critical discourse was introduced in India during the colonial period for the purpose of serving as a tool to establish biblical faith. Through historical criticism it was possible to proclaim Christianity as an objective and historic religion in contrast to "the mythical and unhistorical" Hinduism;[94] it was used to define the beliefs of the colonisers at the expense of the 'Other,' i.e., the Indians. The biblical text was understood as superior to the Hindu texts, and the colonisers used historical criticism "in the sense that they displaced the norms and practices of...indigenous reading methods."[95]

What Sugirtharajah argues so forcefully is that the historical critical methodology was used in a colonial context with the intention of showing that the scriptures of Christianity were more coherent with historical (and therefore true) events than the scriptures of Hinduism. As a consequence, the indigenous interpretive methods were belittled. Historical critical discourse became hegemonic, and it is not until recently that this hegemony has been challenged.

The more the Western exegetical hegemony loses its grip on the global context, the more the local contexts themselves become a parameter for postcolonial exegetical studies. In this 'localising' process, questions about the relevance of biblical studies and the methods used arise continuously, and they are determined by local-specific, rather than global-general, concerns. Just as orientalism is inextricably intertwined with the problem of hegemony, as we have seen above, the issue of relevance is at the heart of the question of hegemony.

4.3.2.3 *Relevance as a Critical Problem*

In the first half of the 20th century, the quest for the historical Jesus reached a point where many scholars considered a reconstruction of the historical Jesus impossible. This was largely an effect of Schweitzer's

---

[92] Sugirtharajah, *Asian Biblical Hermeneutics*, 126.
[93] Sugirtharajah, *Asian Biblical Hermeneutics*, 127.
[94] Sugirtharajah, *Asian Biblical Hermeneutics*, 10.
[95] Sugirtharajah, *Asian Biblical Hermeneutics*, 126.

conclusion in his seminal study *Geschichte der Leben-Jesu Forschung*, published 1906,[96] that historical study is always at risk to become more a reflection of the scholar's own context than a reconstruction of historical phenomena. The quest for the historical Jesus turned out to be far more methodologically complex and difficult than it had seemed to be 128 years earlier when Reimarus' study was published.

The quest was, however, re-opened in 1953 by Ernst Käsemann, in a famous lecture in Jugenheim on the topic delivered to former students of the quest-doubter Rudolf Bultmann.[97] While most biblical students in the Western world are probably aware of at least a handful of names of well-known historical Jesus scholars, few know that the quest was also being debated by Indian biblical scholars. In 1978 George Soares-Prabhu gave a paper which was later published as "The Historical Critical Method: Reflections on its Relevance for the Study of the Gospels in India Today." The article is a methodological contribution to the discussion of the quest for the historical Jesus. Most importantly, Soares-Prabhu situates the discussion of historical critical discourse in a non-Western context.[98] He agrees with those who reject the possibility of reconstructing the historical Jesus. The real reader's embeddedness in her/his own historical context prevents her/him from finding or reconstructing historical facts.

The perspective of the real reader is always subjective and this fact makes impossible the objectivity claims of the old enlightenment historical critical methodology. However, in addition to the epistemological discussion, Soares-Prabhu puts forward and lays emphasis on another aspect of scholarly work: the question of *relevance*.[99] Historical critical methods are constructed so that scholars are prevented to take into consideration the religious aspect and meaning of the text. A fundamental problem concerns the fact that the texts were written by and for religious people:

> For it is precisely this use of a *historical method* to interpret a *religious text* which explains the failure of critical exegesis to disclose the real

---

[96] Albert Schweitzer, *Von Reimarus zu Wrede: Eine Geschichte der Leben-Jesu Forschung* (Tübingen: Mohr Siebeck, 1906).

[97] Ernst Käsemann, "The Problem of the Historical Jesus" in *The Historical Jesus Quest: A Foundational Antheology* (ed. Gregory W. Dawes; Leiden: Deo Publishing, 1999), 279–313; repr. from *Zeitschrift für Theologie und Kirche* 51 (1954): 125–53.

[98] Soares-Prabhu, "Historical-Critical Method." The article was first presented in 1978 at the seminar on *Theologizing in India* in Pune, India.

[99] Soares-Prabhu, "Historical-Critical Method," 320.

meaning of the Gospel, while supplying masses of information about them; and which explains too why the method fails to come up with generally accepted results.[100]

Soares-Prabhu argues that the difficulty lies in the tension between the approach and intent of the author on the one hand, and of the scholar on the other; the latter searches for exact historical information in a text that "aims at the personal transformation of the reader through his [sic] response in *faith*. The method is, thus, incommensurate with the intention of the text."[101] Soares-Prabhu questions the project of the quest for the historical Jesus as a whole. There is, according to Soares-Prabhu's perspective a correlation between the epistemological issue and the local concern for relevance within Christian faith communities. If the question lacks relevance there would be no reason to search for the historical Jesus, even if there would be accurate methods to do so. Soares-Prabhu goes further than that, however, and states that the historical critical methodology, in its positivistic garments and with its lack of relevance for a non-Western context, results in a methodological failure.[102]

Nevertheless, even if he argues that the method is doomed to fail, he does not consider it a hopeless case completely. Soares-Prabhu considers the method to have a place in an Indian interpretive context on the sole condition that the positivistic objectivism, which *excludes the real reader*, is reduced.[103] He writes as follows about the Indian exegete:

> To a critical consciousness derived from Western modernization, he [sic] must bring a profound and sympathetic understanding of ancient Indian tradition; to a pluriform religious experience he must join a deep and active concern for social issues. His use of exegetical techniques inherited from the West—of a historical criticism freed of its exaggerations and a rhetorical criticism enriched by traditional Indian methods of interpretation, (but not of structuralism, which is, I feel, a passing fashion of no lasting value)—will then be controlled by an Indian pre-understanding, shaped by his own deeply enriching experience of Indian religions, and his passionate involvement in the struggle for justice.[104]

If the exegete meets what we may call the 'criterion of relevance,' the historical critical methodology will consequently appear in a new light.

---

[100] Soares-Prabhu, "Historical-Critical Method," 318.
[101] Soares-Prabhu, "Historical-Critical Method," 318.
[102] Soares-Prabhu, "Historical-Critical Method," 318–21.
[103] Soares-Prabhu, "Historical-Critical Method," 348.
[104] Soares-Prabhu, "Historical-Critical Method," 348.

It is the real reader who is the link between historical critical scholarship and the relevance of its results. We could also say that the search for the historical Jesus is relevant and possible in a postcolonial context only if it is filtrated through the real 'flesh-and-blood reader.'

Johnson seems to be more categorical than Soares-Prabhu. Even if Soares-Prabhu states that the method is a failure, he *does* think it is possible to use it. Johnson, on the other hand, argues that in spite of the advantages of the method it is inadequate, simply because it does not belong in the scholarly discussion of today. There exists a need to interpret the texts from other angles than the strictly historical, and the way forward is literary criticism.[105] Consequently, the old historical critical paradigm is out of order and irrelevant in a postcolonial context. Since the 1960s we can discern the development of a new historical criticism that is more relevant to the present exegetical needs. He does not say what exactly this new method contains, but emphasises the importance of hermeneutics as a decisive element in the methodological approach.[106]

Sugirtharajah agrees with Soares-Prabhu, Johnson, and Kwok, that historical critical methods lack relevance due to their positivistic foundations. We have already presented Sugirtharajah's view on hegemony. Here we need to note that, in relation to the question of relevance, he emphasises hegemony more than epistemological issues, even if the two are intertwined. As a colonial method, Sugirtharajah would not consider historical critical discourse relevant in Indian, postcolonial exegesis. But, seen from another perspective, he argues that the method may nevertheless have some sort of relevance.

Historical critical discourse is used "with great enthusiasm" at the institutions in India today and consequently we can speak of its relevance.[107] He compares historical critical methods with the English language, which originally was colonial but now serves as one of the official languages of India. It takes an "epistemic transformation"[108] for the method to become relevant. This is similar to Soares-Prabhu's view. The method has to be inculturated in order to function as a tool for Indian exegetes.

---

[105] Johnson, "Beginning of an End," 255.
[106] Johnson, "Beginning of an End," 264.
[107] Sugirtharajah, *Asian Biblical Hermeneutics*, 129.
[108] The concept "epistemic transformation" was invented by Spivak and refers to the transformation "of the way in which objects of knowledge...are articulated," Sugirtharajah, *Asian Biblical Hermeneutics*, 129.

Also, the very fact that historical critical discourse is now playing a part in exegetical work aiming at giving a voice to the subaltern (Indian Dalits, Korean minjung, etc.) makes it relevant.[109] It seems as if Sugirtharajah discusses two different kinds or types of historical criticisms that are used in India. On the one hand, there exists an 'old historical critical methodology,' which functions in a traditional way (often more traditional and conservative than in the West). This type of historical discourse is common at the theological institutions in India. On the other hand, a 'new' version of the method that is based on postmodern criticism and used for liberating purposes (not least for the purpose of liberating people from a colonial heritage) has begun to develop. The latter is a clear example of 'epistemic transformation.' This can perhaps be compared to the development of Christianity in Latin America. Having been brought in and used as a colonial tool by the European colonisers, belief in Jesus as liberator among indigenous peoples has turned the (political) role of Christianity around 180 degrees. In the same way, historical critical discourse has been wrested out of the hands of the colonial powers and re-applied in the service of political liberation.

In other words, the episteme of the colonised countries needs to change over time before historical criticism can take on usable forms for others than the former colonial powers. Historical critical discourse must begin to adjust to the changing local episteme. In this process, which is taking place as the present study is being written, (Western) postmodernism has shown itself to be helpful and has been frequently utilised by postcolonial scholars. Historical study of the Bible in an Asian context may be different from European historical study of the same texts.

Kwok identifies different motivations behind European and Asian historical critical study of the Bible. She uses Schüssler-Fiorenza's notion of the Bible as a 'historical prototype.' According to this view the Bible serves as "a formative root-model, rather than a mythical archetype with timeless universal truth."[110] Since the Bible does not have the same function as a historical prototype in an Asian context as

---

[109] Sugirtharajah, *Asian Biblical Hermeneutics*, 129.
[110] Kwok, *Discovering the Bible in the Non-Biblical World*, 40–41. "To read the Bible not as an unchanging archetype but as a structuring prototype is to understand it as an open-ended paradigm that sets experience in motion and makes transformation possible," Schüssler-Fiorenza states in Elisabeth Schüssler-Fiorenza, *But She Said: Feminist Practices of Biblical Interpretation* (Boston: Beacon Press, 1992), 149.

it has in a European context, historical approaches, due to the different epistemes, are not regarded as equally important.¹¹¹ The biblical text in isolation from local cultural and textual heritage is not comprehensive enough a tool for interpretation in an Asian context. This is so despite the fact that colonisation has transformed many Asian nations. Therefore, according to Kwok, it is better to consider the biblical text as a poetic classic.¹¹² Musa Dube argues in a similar way,

> As a predominantly Western discourse, biblical criticism has tended to be text- and logocentric. Other cultures, however, have different ways of articulating their visions of life and perceptions of the divine. Pertinent here is the use of symbols, rituals, drama, poetry, and song—without a focus on text.¹¹³

The question of relevance is dependent on the local context, and cannot be universalised or generalised. In search for meaning in the biblical texts, even historical meaning, postcolonial scholars turn to their own local cultural contexts for interpretive tools. The hegemony of the methodological approaches of the West has been seriously challenged as irrelevant to some degree in non-Western nations, and the basis for this challenge is both hermeneutical and epistemological. As a result, postcolonial scholars have found ways to critique Western exegesis in their quest for locally appropriate methods that unlock the texts and are able to provide interpretations experienced as relevant by their audiences.

4.3.3 *Kwok and the Quest for the Historical Jesus: A Test Case*

As has been shown above, orientalism, hegemony, and relevance are three key concepts in critical exegetical postcolonialism. In order to show how these concepts may interact with each other and more general questions of 'objectivism,' in a given investigation, we shall take a closer look at one scholar's work on an important topic that has been studied for several hundred years—Kwok Pui-lan's critique of historical Jesus research.

Approaching the quest for the historical Jesus, Kwok takes as a point of departure Foucault's theory of episteme, of which one main point is that human beings cannot set themselves free from their own context,

---

[111] Kwok, *Discovering the Bible in the Non-Biblical World*, 41.
[112] Kwok, *Discovering the Bible in the Non-Biblical World*, 41.
[113] Dube, "Postcolonial Perspective on Biblical Criticism and Pedagogy," 237.

culture, or other components of the episteme. Finding inspiration in Foucault, Kwok points out that the quest for the historical Jesus is embedded in its own cultural matrix and, as a result, it is questionable how 'historic' the results from the studies are.[114]

Kwok's analysis of the episteme of which the historical critical discourse is a part leads her to criticise strongly the quest for the historical Jesus. Kwok begins by questioning the assumed objectivity of historical critical methodology. Objectivity is simply not possible; it is an idea belonging to a specific episteme that cannot be realised on any general level. In order to be considered scientific in an 'old' positivistic sense of that word, objectivity must by definition be understood as free from any existing episteme. More specifically, objectivity demands that its "truth" is freed from all kinds of human and worldly influences. Consequently, since the episteme is part of the reality of all humans, just as much as we live in and breathe air, we can never claim to exist or think outside an episteme. Kwok argues that since the quest for the historical Jesus is located within a Western episteme it must be recognised and evaluated within this/these frame/s. Hence, the quest for the historical Jesus is a construction dependent on a Western episteme.

Kwok quite naturally locates the methodological foundations of the quest for the historical Jesus—the historical critical methodology—in the West, originating in the 18th century. During the same period the colonial era experiences rapid development, which eventually will affect at all levels both the Western world and the colonised countries. Since an episteme consists of a series of interconnected discourses, the discursive similarities prompt Kwok to analyse both the discourse of colonialism and the historical critical discourse together. According to Kwok, it is possible and necessary to map connections between the discourse that defines and gives birth to the quest for the historical Jesus on the one hand, and colonial and imperialistic ideals and discourses on the other. She claims, in one sentence, that the historical critical methodology "was influenced by the expansion of Europe."[115]

In her analysis of these intra-epistemic connections Kwok begins by highlighting the confrontation between church authority and

---

[114] Kwok, "Jesus/The Native," 75–80.
[115] Kwok, "Jesus/The Native," 70, 75. Kwok refers to Said in her argument that what the empire building influenced, i.e., "the high cultures of scholarship, novels and arts," thoroughly influenced the episteme in such a way that the study of the Bible could not have been immune.

enlightenment philosophers. Everything that had a "supernatural nimbus" was challenged; the virgin birth, the miracles, and the resurrection. The church "belonged to the old world and did not fit with the emergence of modern science and the ideology of the rising bourgeoisie."[116] The critique delivered by academia became the incentive for biblical scholars to analyse the biblical texts from a 'scientific' angle. In the beginning, the main purpose was precisely to justify Christian belief and to prove that it was trustworthy.[117] It is in this process that scientific historical methods were developed in order to maintain and reinforce that Jesus was a historic person. In this way, the scientific demands of historicity and objectivity became the impetus for the study of the historical Jesus when it began in the larger cities of Europe at the end of the eighteenth century. Thus the Enlightenment 'wave' and its academic effects were contemporary with Europe's colonial expansion and individual nations' struggle for hegemony. Kwok goes on to discuss why this is important.

After pointing out the general influence academia had on biblical studies, Kwok describes the colonial influence that became woven into exegetical studies and most significantly visible in the quest for the historical Jesus. During the 18th and 19th centuries, when the 'quest' was of great interest and researchers like Johann Strauss and Ernest Renan were the leading scholars proposing models for finding the historical Jesus, other mechanisms were at work that Kwok considers must have consciously or unconsciously influenced them. For example, she points out the connection between the interest in Alexander the Great as the "mythological empire-builder" and the tendencies in some studies to classify Jesus as a political leader.[118]

She also brings up the importance of the physical location, where scholars lived, and the political orientation in that specific environment and how that influenced scholarly results. Reimarus, for instance, lived in the important seaport Hamburg, and many of his students were future "merchants, industrial producers, and owners of wharfs."[119] Consequently, he lived, taught, and made his research in an environ-

---

[116] Kwok, "Jesus/The Native," 75.

[117] Subsequently, the aim to justify the Christian belief system transformed into modern scholarly historical study, viewing the Bible as a historical document just as any other historical document.

[118] Kwok, "Jesus/The Native," 76. Here Kwok makes use of Dieter Georgi's article "Social History of Biblical Criticism," 51–83

[119] Kwok, "Jesus/The Native," 75.

ment that was coloured by colonial and expansionist thoughts. Strauss, Kwok continues, was, in addition to his interest in biblical studies, a strong pleader for a united Germany under the Prussian hegemony. He was also influenced by Darwin's theory of natural selection. As to Renan, he was the one who introduced orientalism into the study of biblical philology as a result of his archaeological studies in Phoenicia and Syria.

It is, from a postcolonial perspective, not possible to consider the study of the historical Jesus as an 'objective' and 'neutral' scholarly endeavour unaffected by the European colonial "zenith." The quest for the 'authentic Jesus' should be understood together with ideas about the 'authentic native:' the "two operated on the same episteme and were much related, because the increase of knowledge about the Mediterranean world came at the same time as the expansion of knowledge about the cultures the West had conquered."[120]

The very interest in and ideas about 'origins' were interconnected with the Darwinist idea of an "archimedean point in a primitive and primordial origin."[121] This search for 'origins' was also nourished by the enlightenment assumption that history is linear and progressive. The evolutionary theory created a "myth of origin." Kwok emphasizes the notion of 'opposite' as an important parameter in the modernistic scholarly mind. To be 'primitive' and 'native' were often equivalent with "animistic, superstitious, and profane beliefs" and, consequently, "the origin of Christianity had to be stripped of all mythology, miracle, and the supernatural."[122]

Not surprisingly, Kwok also, benefiting from Said's work, shows that the field of philology was developed contemporarily with the colonial expansion. It was important to master the 'natives' and their texts in order to claim superiority and rule over them. For example, the British wanted to study Sanskrit in order to understand Indian laws, with the aim of, ultimately, acquiring power through knowledge.[123]

There were also tendencies to value Greek as more sophisticated than any other languages. In Renan's mind, which obviously was coloured by orientalism, Semitic languages were just like a "pencil sketch" in comparison to the Indo-European "paintings," of which Greek was the

---

[120] Kwok, "Jesus/The Native," 76.
[121] Kwok, "Jesus/The Native," 77.
[122] Kwok, "Jesus/The Native," 77.
[123] Kwok, "Jesus/The Native," 77.

foremost.[124] For Kwok, Renan's work *La Vie de Jésus* was more of a cultural product than the strict scholarly study that he—and others—claimed it to be.[125]

The belief that the West was "rational, historical, and scientific" and other cultures were "mythical, and unscientific" runs through almost all biblical studies of the time. The concept of the 'native' was prevalent in studies of biblical antiquity as well as in contemporary colonial discourse. Strauss, e.g., explained the mythical element in the Bible as the 'natives'' lack of historical consciousness in biblical times.[126] Biblical peoples were regarded as 'natives,' and, it was argued, as being without historical consciousness, which meant that they were unable to make progress on their own. They could not break loose from their own inability to achieve development.

In the same way, discourse about 'natives' in contemporary conquered nations claimed that these 'natives' lacked historical consciousness: they could only be liberated by European colonisers, who possessed such consciousness and could progress beyond their past. Orientalism was for that reason deeply imbedded in scholarly discourse as well as in contemporary academic and political discourse. Together with hegemony, orientalism represents clear examples of inter-discursive similarities in the (colonial) Western episteme.

Kwok's critique of biblical scholarship, as exemplified by historical Jesus research, is, we may conclude, very much in line with the general criticism directed against mainstream biblical studies. There is a heavy emphasis on the inability of historical critical methods to provide 'neutral' and 'objective' results. The point where postcolonial scholars go beyond the general critique is in their focus on orientalism, hegemony and relevance. For Kwok, the field where her concerns come together and find their analytical solution is the theory of episteme. This basic idea about reality—how interconnected discursive similarities supply the 'material' that forms an episteme—provides the tool used to reveal the contextuality of historical critical discourse, and its inherent fundamental flaws. Historical critical discourse simply cannot be what it claims to be. Kwok concludes that the quest for the historical Jesus is a culture-specific academic endeavour with little or no relevance for Asian exegetes.

---

[124] Kwok, "Jesus/The Native," 78.
[125] Kwok, "Jesus/The Native," 78.
[126] Kwok, "Jesus/The Native," 79.

4.3 Summary

Chapter four has been an attempt to listen to some of the major postcolonial critical approaches to Western historical critical discourse. The critique is diverse and formation of a structured consensus within postcolonial discourse has not yet taken place. It has therefore been necessary to organise and categorise these critical voices.

It has become clear that much of the postcolonial critique of Western historical critical approaches share arguments with (Western) postmodern scholarly discourses. Postmodernism opens up an arena within Western academic study of the New Testament in which postcolonial scholars are increasingly becoming prominent players. Using a metaphor of some repute, from the perspective of traditional Western scholarship, postmodernism functions as the Trojan horse in which postcolonial scholars are brought into the heart of the academic city and can attack it from within. Once there, postcolonial deconstruction of Western epistemological edifices involves more dimensions and perspectives than postmodernism had previously known, at least not in their postcolonial form, but which most of its proponents are willing to embrace. Of these, we have discussed three: orientalism, hegemony, and relevance.

Postcolonial reactions to Western historical critical discourse are best seen against the background of the clashes of epistemes. In brief, when our perspective is globalised to include realities different from our own, differences in epistemes come to the fore. The Western outlook tower constructed and reinforced by colonial means in the self-proclaimed centre of the world is now taken over by new generations of scholars, who are ridding themselves of inherited hegemonic optics and opening their eyes to new landscapes. This opens up dialogue and debate in perceived centres and peripheries, conversations which are bound to change the way New Testament exegesis is defined. This process, it becomes increasingly clear, deconstructs the very tower from which scholars originally spotted new worlds, and constructs platforms for shared academic endeavours.

The constant (re-)making of exegesis through the centuries consists of a continual dialectic between deconstruction and reconstruction of epistemological models. There are no static elements or periods in the history of interpretation of the Bible: everything is constantly changing, although sometimes more radically than otherwise. The postcolonial discourses are, in the same way that historical critical discourses once were, part of major paradigm shifts motivated by what was, and continues to be, seen as oppressing powers. Today, postcoloniality constitutes the epistemic foundation in which traditions are challenged in the same way modernism once formed the matrix in which historical critical discourse was moulded.

Having presented and discussed the deconstructive elements of postcolonial New Testament studies, we must now, consequently, proceed to deal with the constructive aspects of this discourse. Again, these constructive elements are very diverse, and one of the tasks that we need to set before us at this stage is to attempt to categorise the different approaches in order to better understand their contribution to exegesis.

CHAPTER FIVE

CONSTRUCTING POSTCOLONIAL BIBLICAL ANALYSIS

5.1 Redefining Exegesis: Introducing Postcolonial Approaches

> If meaning truly subsists in texts as a quality of the expression itself, why does it remain so elusive even under the conditions most favourable to mutual understanding, and how much more elusive must we admit that meaning to be in the expression of people whom we know hardly at all?[1]

In chapter four we presented and discussed postcolonialism with a focus on its criticism of 'traditional' Western exegetical approaches. Postcolonial exegesis is, however, much more than just an attempt to deconstruct Western exegetical paradigms; it also represents constructive rethinking of what exegesis in a postcolonial situation may be. It is interesting to note that, when postcolonial scholars criticise Western historical critical discourse, this critique is based on a similar approach and the arguments are, with some variety, rehearsed throughout the literature. However, when turning to constructive work, presenting non-Western approaches and methodologies, the same scholars demonstrate a remarkable variety. The present study does not allow a full discussion of all of these approaches. Instead, I have made a selection that is representative of this variety.

Postcolonial exegesis cannot be spoken of in the singular.[2] As mentioned in section 3.1, postcolonialism refers to scholarly theorising, which emanates from the reactions and the consequences occurring within postcoloniality. On one level, postcolonialism represents a basic perspective rather than a method. As a perspective, it can be combined

---

[1] Andrew K. M. Adam, *Faithful Interpretation: Reading the Bible in a Postmodern World* (Minneapolis: Fortress Press, 2006), 5.
[2] Cf. Mary F. Foskett and Jeffrey Kah-Jin Kuan, eds., *Ways of Being, Ways of Reading: Asian American Biblical Interpretation* (St. Louise: Chalice Press, 2006), xiii. "Since its inception, Asian American biblical interpretation has emerged not as a single method or approach but as a discourse that acknowledges both the multicultural and trans-generational infrastructure of Asian American and the social and political dynamics at play in the Asian American experience."

with a variety of exegetical methods, including Western historical critical discourse; a mastering of the tools rather than a re-tooling of the masters.³ On another level, however, it may be justified to speak about postcolonial methods when referring to contextualised methods of interpretation that are used instead of, or in opposition to, Western methodological and interpretive paradigms. Examples of such methods are the dhvani, Dalit, and minjung interpretive techniques. We shall return to discuss these in some detail below in section 5.3. Such methodologies would constitute attempts to retool the masters.

Postcolonialism is best referred to as an umbrella term that covers both perspectives and methods, which provides scholars with a range of opportunities to read the biblical texts anew.[4]

In this chapter we shall take a closer look at some important areas of research where we find postcolonial perspectives and methods employed. Even if scholars seldom reflected on the matter 50 years, or so, ago, it is today a truism that the approaches and methods chosen by the researcher control and determine much of the results of her or his studies. In the same way, perhaps, 50 years from now, the importance of the socio-political and cultural context in which scholars live for the methods they choose and the conclusions they reach might be universally acknowledged in the scholarly community, even if there is no consensus on this today.[5]

We shall approach the diversity evident within postcolonialism by attempting to sort the contributions into two major categories. The first of these is *postcolonial analysis within the historical critical paradigm*. The second brings together *postcolonial methodological approaches beyond Western historical critical discourses*.

It goes without saying that any categorisation is to a certain degree arbitrary, and that there will always be difficulties involved when listing scholars and approaches under a specific category. As the titles of the categories indicate, I have taken as a basic point of departure the degree to which a certain approach can be seen as working within a specific paradigm. Important here are the methodological choices

---

[3] Cf. the title "Mastering the Tools or Retooling the Masters?" in Vander Stichele and Penner, eds., *Her Master's Tools?* 1.

[4] Cf. Dube, "Post-Colonial Biblical Interpretations," *Dictionary of Biblical Interpretation* 2: 299.

[5] See for example recent studies such as Foskett and Kah-Jin Kuan, eds., *Ways of Being, Ways of Reading*; Vander Stichele and Penner, eds., *Her Master's Tools?* and Adam, *Faithful Interpretation*.

made by scholars, the perspectives, but also the contexts in which scholars live. Also important to keep in mind is that, as with all categories, there is always a certain amount of overlap between them. Some scholars would fit into both categories. However, it is still useful to draw the line at some point in order to clarify the broader picture.

Some approaches within the two categories are broad and fundamental for all postcolonial studies, e.g., tracing colonial elements and abuses in New Testament texts, or mapping the spread of Western biblical criticism in the footsteps of colonisation. Other approaches are narrower and aim at understanding specific texts from the horizon of certain socio-cultural contexts with which the scholar has a strong familiarity (e.g., inter-textual comparisons, or 'culture based' studies such as Dalit and minjung biblical exegesis).

Within the categories it is possible to find the use of historical approaches as well as contemporary and contextualising interpretations from a confessional (Christian) perspective. Still, there are common elements in all of these approaches that justify that we define and discuss these as postcolonial studies; these common elements will be outlined in the summary below (5.4).

If we return to the individual categories, we find in the first group approaches operating within and using historical critical arguments in order to shed light on and analyse matters colonial. To this category belongs, e.g., analyses of colonial elements in New Testament texts and inter-textual comparisons between biblical texts and other religious texts (e.g., the Baghavad Gita). A special case here concerns Bible translations in an Indian context. In the second category we find methodologies and perspectives originating within and addressing questions existing in local-specific contexts.

The aim in the following is to present the diversity of postcolonial studies in a structured way in order to show how different epistemes are merging, and in what ways this affects the making of present and future exegesis.

5.2 Category One: Postcolonial Analysis within the Historical Critical Paradigm

> As Asians we cannot ignore the history of the research and trap ourselves into an exclusivistic methodological practice suited to hold and affirm our own values and biases. We must be open to exegetical insights and hermeneutical options that are made available by scholars of different

nationalities and faith-communities. In this respect, though we should avoid the hazards of the historical-critical method we cannot turn a blind eye to the necessity of historical evidence and its importance to the historical research. We need to seek ways to modify historical-critical method in order to make it an effective tool for the understanding of the New Testament.[6]

[The]...use of exegetical techniques inherited from the West—of a historical criticism freed of its exaggerations and a rhetorical criticism enriched by traditional Indian methods of interpretation...will then be controlled by an Indian pre-understanding, shaped by...[the]...deeply enriching experience of Indian religions, and...[the]...passionate involvement in the struggle for justice.[7]

As has been shown in chapter four the effectiveness and value of historical critical discourse has been thoroughly debated and examined by both postcolonial scholars and others. However, even if the critique is massive, this, strangely enough, does not mean that scholars have abandoned historical critical methodology. Some would go so far as to consider invalid an exegetical study that left out the historical critical paradigm.

A case in point is Soares-Prabhu. Even if he argues that the historical critical methodology is a failure in itself, and especially in a context like the Indian, he, nevertheless, states that historical critical discourse has to be applied when analysing text in order to achieve exegetically viable results.[8] He even argues that historical critical methodology may bring liberation to India (cf., above on relevance, section 4.3.2.3), in the sense that it shows a way around fundamentalism and "pre-critical dogmatism," just as it did in Europe during the Enlightenment period.[9] This does not mean, however, that the methodology's epistemic location during the Enlightenment should be repeated in an Indian context. Soares-Prabhu warns that scholars have to be careful not to let historical criticism become the dominant method. It must only retain an "ancillary role."

Pathrapankal also places his work in a historical critical frame when he argues for a *situative context*. By this he argues that the text must be "further interpreted by successive generations of readers in their own respective social, cultural and religious situations without losing sight

---

[6] Joseph G. Muthuraj, "New Testament and Methodology: An Overview," *AJT* 10 (1996): 253–77, 260.
[7] Soares-Prabhu, "Historical-Critical Method," 348.
[8] Soares-Prabhu, "Historical-Critical Method," 348.
[9] Soares-Prabhu, "Two Mission Commands," 273.

of the original context and its original meaning."[10] With this claim, Pathrapankal strives to combine historical attempts to find original meanings in biblical texts with the present reader's need to contextualise the New Testament corpus to make it understandable. We find a similar argument in Stendahl's famous study *Meanings*, where he distinguishes between what a biblical text *meant* and what it *means*.[11] 'Meant' refers to the historical, original meaning, and 'means' to the present meaning of a biblical text, a meaning that may vary depending on the context in which the biblical text is interpreted, and for what purpose.

This tension between meant and means is also present in Sugirtharajah's work. Sugirtharajah's critical approach to historical critical discourse is not to be understood in an absolute sense. Rather, as we noted above, the criticism has its roots in questions related to hegemony and the resistance hegemony evokes. For Sugirtharajah, historical critical methodology is inherently colonial.[12] How could it, then, be used?

For Soares-Prabhu, one could say, relevance counters hegemony and finds a place for historical critical discourse in a modified form, even within a postcolonial thought-pattern. Sugirtharajah would express it somewhat differently but still puts emphasis on relevance.[13] Indeed, several of his works are historical studies from a postcolonial perspective. This is true both when he engages biblical texts and when he analyses Western colonialism and how it changed the Indian educational system.[14]

Sugirtharajah, like several other postcolonial scholars, does not construct a methodology of his own. He applies existing interpretive techniques, Western and otherwise, and argues that it is not possible to construct an altogether Indian model of interpretation. Western epistemology has become too intertwined in Indian exegesis in a way that is not possible to untie. In other words, aspects of the Western episteme have merged with the Indian episteme, and the result is a *postcolonial methodological hybridity*.

---

[10] Pathrapankal, "Re-reading of John," 2. See also, by the same author, chapter one in *Text and Context in Biblical Interpretation* (Bangalore: Dharmaram Publications, 1993), 1–16.
[11] Stendahl, *Meanings: The Bible as Document and as Guide*, 1–8.
[12] Sugirtharajah, *Postcolonial Reconfigurations*, 87ff.
[13] Sugirtharajah, *Postcolonial Criticism and Biblical Interpretation*, 114–15.
[14] Sugirtharajah, *Postcolonial Criticism and Biblical Interpretation*, 91–94.

In the following, we shall present and discuss some examples where this type of hybridity comes to the fore, when postcolonial scholars use the tools of colonisers in order to create liberating conclusions based on historical investigations.

5.2.1 Tracing Colonial Elements and Abuses in New Testament Texts

The books of the New Testament were all written in a postcolonial situation, which comes to the fore in different degrees in the individual texts. Obvious examples of passages include the Gerasa miracle when demons are sent into a swine herd which drowns in the Sea of Galilee (Mark 5:1–20), the Herodians' question to Jesus about paying taxes to the Roman Emperor (Matt 22:15–22), the tax collector Levi (Luke 5:27–32), the Samaritan woman (John 4:7–42), the Canaanite woman (Matt 15:21–28), the execution of Jesus and the events leading up to it (the colonial threat of national destruction: John 11:47–50; the political power to execute: John 18:28–38).

The examples could easily be multiplied. On a general level, postcolonial interest in colonial aspects of the texts may be compared to the now common knowledge that people bring their own background and interest with them to the texts. This is, of course, true of all interpretive activities, including traditional Western historical critical studies. On a more specific level, postcolonial historical analyses aim explicitly at *relevant* interpretations, and acknowledge this interest as they proceed in their work.

An intriguing dimension of 'interested' postcolonial historical analyses in comparison with so-called 'dis-interested' traditional historical critical approaches to the New Testament is that the former scholars live in, or relate closely to, a postcolonial reality in which oppression and different forms of violence are either directly or indirectly present. Such lived realities have alerted postcolonial scholars to signs in the texts of similar realities in the first century. With Segovia, we may talk about a postcolonial 'optic.'[15] Put another way, there are certain epistemic similarities between current and ancient postcolonial situations that connect postcolonial scholars with ancient realities that have traditionally been missed behind comfortable and unthreatened middle-class Western desks. Because of such epistemic similarities,

---

[15] Segovia, *Decolonizing Biblical Studies*, chapter five and six, 119–42.

postcolonial scholars, despite the fact that they search for *relevant* interpretations, may arrive at historically more valid conclusions than their traditional Western counterparts—even when judged from a Western epistemological point of view!

A text that has received attention among postcolonial scholars as well as scholars who would not label themselves postcolonial, is Mark 5:1-20. Empire-perspectives are becoming increasingly popular in New Testament exegesis, and here we find a bridge being built between postcolonial historical critical studies and scholars who come to this topic from a Western background and perspective.[16]

From a reception-historical perspective, Sugirtharajah notes that Mark 5:1-20 has been (mis-)used to legitimise missionary activities among indigenous peoples. Historically, however, the text's focus is rather on a situation of colonial oppression; the story is meant to be and describe an act of resistance against Roman presence in the land. According to Sugirtharajah, the Roman military presence in the Decapolis area is described by an identification between the soldiers and demons called 'Legion,' which possess a man living among (ritually unclean) graves. Jesus commands the demons to leave the man and enter into a herd of swine, related to the animal represented on the standard of the tenth Roman legion (Legio X Fretensis); the swine rush down the hill into the Sea of Galilee and drown.[17]

According to Sugirtharajah, this is a metaphorical way of describing the annihilation of the Roman armies and their return to the waters of chaos.[18] When confronted with the powers of the legitimate Son of God (as opposed to the Emperor), who brings the Kingdom of God, Roman colonial occupation must cease. Such an interpretation is, obviously, the very opposite of Western traditional missiological

---

[16] See, e.g. John Dominic Crossan, *Jesus: A Revolutionary Biography* (San Francisco: Harper, 1994), 88-91; Warren Carter, *Matthew and Empire: Initial Explorations* (Harrisburg: Trinity Press, 2001); see also, Richard A. Horsley, ed., *Paul and Empire: Religion and Power in Roman Imperial Society* (Harrisburg: Trinity Press, 1997).

[17] The animal depicted on the standards of the tenth legion was the boar, rather than swine kept for domestic purposes. In addition, it is worth noting that Roman military presence in this area was a post-70 phenomenon; no Roman legion was located here during Jesus' lifetime. Historically, we would be dealing with Mark's historical context rather than Jesus.'

[18] Sugirtharajah, *Postcolonial Criticism and Biblical Interpretation*, 91-94; see also references to Sugirtharajah's studies in, Anna Runesson, "'Legion heter jag för vi är många:' En postkolonial läsning av Mark 5:1-20" in *Jesus och de första kristna: Inledning till Nya testamentet* (ed. Dieter Mitternacht and Anders Runesson; Stockholm: Verbum, 2006), 475-81.

interpretations validating European missionary claims. One could say that postcolonial scholars have wrested the weapon out of the colonisers' hands and now turn it against their (former) oppressors with the explicit aim of breaking free and gaining academic status and credibility in the West. Postcolonial historical critical studies are instrumental in a special way for clearing a path into the Western academic arena: a similar language is used and researchers are made to listen.

Another field that has occasioned much debate, and needs to be mentioned, is the relationship between feminism, postcolonialism, and anti-Jewishness. As has been the case within (Christian) feminist exegesis, postcolonial exegesis has sometimes used metaphorical language, or drawn conclusions, that may be interpreted as anti-Jewish.[19] This problem has been noted and, on the basis of experiences from previous discussions regarding feminism, such awareness has to a large degree prevented developments in this direction. A text that has been the centre of some debate in this regard is the story about the Canaanite woman in Matt 15:21–28.[20]

Closely related to postcolonial historical analyses of New Testament texts is, of course, the very fact that historical critical discourse was

---

[19] Thanks to the dialogue between Jewish and Christian feminists, the anti-Jewishness in feminism has largely vanished in favour of other modes of expression. However, in the field of postcolonial biblical studies this is, unfortunately, not yet the case. One of the reasons that might explain, but not justify, why anti-Jewish interpretations are to be found in some postcolonial scholarly works today could be that such perspectives were included in 'the export' of the old exegetical historical paradigm that spread with the modern colonial era. The old historical paradigm, as we know today, was fermented with anti-Jewish theology. However, anti-Jewish theology has just recently been (and still is in the process of being) dismantled in the West. The same development is, unfortunately, not as strong in other parts of the world where the old historical-critical paradigm is still strong—this is symptomatic of the embeddedness of anti-Jewish theology in the old historical paradigm. Amy-Jill Levine is surely correct, therefore, when she points out that there is gap between the West and the Two-Thirds World regarding the question of anti-Jewish interpretations. She notes, "Today, the majority of (Western) feminist academic reading of biblical materials are explicitly cognizant of this problem" (Amy-Jill Levine, "Lilies of the Field and Wandering Jews: Biblical Scholarship, Women's Roles, and Social Location" in *Transformative Encounters: Jesus and Women Re-Viewed* [ed. Ingrid Rosa Kitzberger; Leiden: Brill, 2000], 331). See also by same author, "Anti-Judaism and Postcolonial Biblical Interpretation: The disease of Postcolonial New Testament Studies and the Hermeneutics of Healing—Roundtable Discussion" *JFSR* 20:1 (2004): 91–99, and Kwok, *Discovering the Bible in the Non-Biblical World*, 76–79.

[20] See, e.g., Amy-Jill Levine, "Matthew's Advice to a Divided Readership" in *The Gospel of Matthew in Current Study* (ed. David E. Aune; Grand Rapids: Eerdmanns, 2001), 22–41, especially 24 and 39.

spread to colonised nations by the colonisers. We shall thus need to say a few words on how this fact is handled by postcolonial scholars.

5.2.2 Mapping Colonial Spread of Western Biblical Criticism

Postcolonial scholars, and not only those who use (modified) forms of historical critical discourse, have a need to analyse how and in what ways Western academic discourse was spread in colonised countries. Mapping such historical developments helps shed light on current situations and gives important background for postcolonial analytical work itself. Most postcolonial scholars have met, in one form or another, the Western educational system and been influenced by it. Reflecting on this helps situate their own contributions theoretically. Here, questions of hegemony come to the fore in quite obvious ways.[21]

The history of Christian mission in India is crucial for understanding postcolonial approaches today. Christianity arrived in India long before the modern colonial enterprise.[22] When the European colonisers arrived, after papal rejection of the Syrian Christians in the country, they strove to convert both Christians and non-Christians in the areas where they settled. An important part of the colonial project was to establish (Christian) schools, and here we find the first inroads of Western academic principles.[23]

Through educational reforms in India, biblical studies came to be based on Western epistemology, which was understood to be superior to indigenous interpretive techniques. Historical critical discourse was

---

[21] E.g., "Having gone through a lengthy period of colonial education, I am interested in exploring the steps necessary for a postcolonial intellectual to dislodge herself from habitual ways of thinking, established forms of inquiry, and the reward system vigilantly guarded by the neoliberal academy." Kwok, *Postcolonial Imagination*, 3.

[22] Cf. Harold W. Attridge, "Christianity from the Destruction of Jerusalem to Constantine's Adoption of the New Religion: 70-312 C.E." in *Christianity and Rabbinic Judaism: A Parallel History of Their Origins and Early Development* (ed. Hershel Shanks; Washington, DC: Biblical Archaeology Society, 1992), 151-94, 340-50, here 155, n. 9. Note especially the mention in Eusebius *Eccles. Hist. 5.10.1-4* of a certain Pantainos, a learned Stoic from Alexandria who became a Christian. He was appointed to proclaim the Gospel for the peoples of the East, and it is said that he reached as far as India in the second century. Eusebius notes that in India he encountered Christians who read the Gospel of Matthew—in Hebrew—which they had received from Bartholomew.

[23] For a brief discussion, see Anna Runesson, "Kontextuell exegetik i en postkolonial värld: Bibeltolkning i en postkolonial värld" in *Varför ser ni mot himlen? Utmaningar från den kontextuella teologin* (ed. Anders Runesson and Torbjörn Sjöholm; Stockholm: Verbum, 2005), 122-49, 131-34.

played out against 'mythical and a-historical Hinduism.'[24] Hinduism, the (Western) logic proclaimed, is false, because it lacks historical proof supporting its mythology.

Indian Christian priests and pastors were educated within an epistemology originating in the Western episteme. Christianity, in this way, was estranged from its Indian cultural context. Postcolonial scholars analysing the exegetical situation in India are now highlighting this clash, or merge, of epistemes, lamenting the fact that many Western influenced Indian colleges and seminaries still work within traditional Western paradigms. Indeed, many educational institutions remain within 'older' Western paradigms, untouched by postmodern critique and preserving, as if frozen in time, what would best be described in the West as an educational anachronism.

Many factors have contributed to this situation, one of them directly related to socio-economic situations created as a direct consequence of the colonial enterprise. In brief, due to the lack of financial resources, educational institutions cannot afford to build modern libraries (and books donated by Western scholars are almost without exception outdated, with publication dates in the first half of the 20th century. Sometimes donated books are not even in English. See Figure 3). In the same way, financial restraints prevent many scholars from travelling to conferences in the West and other places.[25]

By focussing on and mapping how and why Western epistemology made its way to non-Western cultures, postcolonial scholars contribute to the process in which current situations begin to change.[26] The criterion of relevance is, indeed, at work here.[27]

---

[24] Cf. Sugirtharajah, *Asian Biblical Hermeneutics*, 10–11.

[25] This fact is now on the agenda of the Society of Biblical Literature and other organisations, which, increasingly, try to find ways to support conference participants from non-Western countries.

[26] Joseph Pathrapankal, at Dharmaram Vidya Kshetram, the Roman Catholic college in Bangalore, has been involved for many years in trying to get permission from Western publishers to re-publish scholarly studies in India for a fraction of the cost of importing them. Note also the indisputable importance of the 2nd Vatican Council for radical change in Roman Catholic approaches to theological education in the Two-Thirds World.

[27] Limtula Longkumar points to the problem of achieving a holistic education, which takes into account the specific contexts in which people live today in Nagaland; see Limtula Longkumar, "In Search of a Holistic Educational Ministry in the Churches of Nagaland," *Journal of Tribal Studies* 7 (2003): 177–91, especially 182.

Figure 3. An interesting example, involving a significant lack of linguistic match, is found in the library of the United Theological College in Bangalore: a full collection from the mid 20th century of *Svensk teologisk kvartalskrift*—in Swedish. This library is one of the largest and most important Christian libraries in southern India.

5.2.3 *Translating the Bible in an Indian Context*

Bible translations are always a very complex and difficult matter, so also in a postcolonial situation. Here, however, further dimensions are added: the merging of epistemes comes to the fore when translation work is analysed, as is evident in studies made by Sugirtharajah.[28]

As in all translations of biblical texts, the hermeneutics of meaning demands consideration of the nature and function of the different languages—the primary languages, in our case Greek and Hebrew, and the secondary language, the language into which the translation is intended to transfer meaning. Translations may follow different hermeneutical principles. Some aim at a more literal translation, others focus more on conveying the main ideas of a text.

For postcolonial scholars, an important parameter is to what degree a translation has to take into account different cultures, and how differences in cultures will affect the meaning of the text. For example, Sugirtharajah notes that the translation of 'lamb' is problematic

---

[28] Sugirtharajah, *Postcolonial Criticism and Biblical Interpretation*, 155–71.

in India since it does not evoke the same connotations as it would have in a Middle Eastern context. He points out that 'cow' would be a closer match. This might seems a bit strange in a Western context where 'cow' has connotations very different from 'lamb.' In an Indian context, however, 'cow' makes sense because of the holiness attributed to cows in this cultural context—a status not applicable to lambs.[29] The example points effectively to the immense difficulties of 'making sense' in different epistemic contexts, especially with regard to metaphors and symbols.

Devadasan Premnath argues that it was the Protestant missionaries in the 18th century who first translated the Bible into native languages. The reason for this was the Protestant focus on the biblical text for its missionary enterprise. The Lutheran missionary Ziegenbalg, who arrived in Tranquebar in 1706, was the first missionary to translate the Bible into Tamil.[30] Later, more systematic work with translations took place at the Serampore Mission in Calcutta, one of the more important missionary stations in India. The Serampore Mission produced translations of the Bible in thirty local languages. Like Sugirtharajah, Premnath notes the difficulties inherent in many of these translations and their reception. As an example he brings up the word for 'heaven'—*svarga*—which was avoided by the translators because it had such strong connections with the god Indra. Instead, the word *devaloka* was chosen due to its more neutral association to the 'world of the god,' which the translator thought catches the 'original' meaning better.[31]

Despite the difficult questions arising from such translations, one problem is more dire than the rest, from a postcolonial perspective. As Johnsson Chakkuvarackal points out, most of translations are made using other languages than the original Greek and Hebrew.[32]

---

[29] Sugirtharajah, *Postcolonial Criticism and Biblical Interpretation*, 163. Note also his remark on the problems in India with biblical texts mentioning sacrifices of cows, the father's offering of the calf to the prodigal son's party etc. These and other biblical texts resulted in the upper class seeing Christianity as a low class pariah religion. In order to change these preconceptions the Roman Catholic Church made translations more suited to address this audience, (162–63).

[30] Devadasan N. Premnath, "Biblical Interpretation in India: History and Issues" in *Ways of Being, Ways of Reading: Asian American Biblical Interpretation* (ed. Mary F. Foskett and Jeffrey Kah-Jin Kuan; St. Louis: Chalice Press, 2006), 1–16, 3–4.

[31] Premnath, "Interpretation in India," 4.

[32] See his article in full, Johnson T. Chakkuvarackal, "Translating Bible in the Indian Context," *BiBh* 28:4 (2002): 656–71.

The English of the King James Version turns out to have been used as the primary source language. The reason for this development goes back to the colonial period, when "colonial infiltration of English culture and language [...] created the tendency for Indians to rely on English versions as the primary sources."[33] From a modern scholarly perspective, an absurd connection between the coloniser and the religion missionised was established, and encouragement to learn Greek and Hebrew in order to translate the Bible was non-existent. In other words, English values and perspectives were not only imported via the English language culture imposed on the colonised country; it was effectively transferred via a multitude of local languages into which King James Version was translated.[34]

It should also be noted that the idea of 'holy text' never was as strong in India as it was in the West.[35] Sugirtharajah argues, in addition, that the tradition of translation in India has never been the same as in the West. Indian translators "were more interested in the aesthetic flavour than literal accuracy."[36]

Chakkuvarackal points out the difficulties involved in translation work in today's India, a task that involves the merging of aspects from two epistemic contexts in the midst of a postcolonial awareness. He goes as far as to claim that, because of the country's complex multi-cultural and multi-linguistic heritage, Indian translators have one of the most complex assignments in the world of translations. While Sugirtharajah, on the one hand, argues for a "wider intertextuality which will link biblical texts with Asian scriptural texts" when translations are made,[37] Chakkuvarackal, on the other, argues for a more historical critical and text linguistic approach because "[t]he mere dependence upon the vernacular versions may lead us to distant conclusions, different from the original sources."[38]

---

[33] Chakkuvarackal, "Translating Bible in the Indian Context," 656. Cf. Sugirtharajah, *Asian Biblical Hermeneutics*, 91.

[34] The *KJV* is not the only English version critiqued by postcolonial scholars. *NRSV* has also received its share of criticism; see, e.g., Sugirtharajah, *Postcolonial Criticism and Biblical Interpretation*, 168.

[35] Sugirtharajah, *Asian Biblical Hermeneutics*, 90. He states that it was only after the arrival of the missionaries that the Indian texts, e.g., Bhagavad Gita, were considered a 'holy book.' Before the missionaries there was no such need since the religions worked well without a focus on a certain holy scriptural source.

[36] Sugirtharajah, *Asian Biblical Hermeneutics*, 91. See also 5.3.1 Dhvani Exegesis.

[37] Sugirtharajah, *Asian Biblical Hermeneutics*, 92–94.

[38] Chakkuvarackal, "Translating Bible in the Indian Context," 671.

Translating the Bible in a postcolonial Indian context is a matter that is far from solved today, and the debate is likely to continue as changes occur.

5.2.4 Inter-Textual Comparisons

> Truly I tell you, just as you did not do it to one of the least of these, you did not do it to me.
>
> (Matthew 25.45)
>
> If you do not tend one another, then who is there to tend you? Whoever would tend me, he should tend the sick.
>
> (Vinya Mahavagga 8.26.3)[39]

The comparative study of New Testament texts in relation to non-canonical literary works is not a new field within New Testament study. Comparisons are made with other Jewish and Christian texts as well as texts from the Graeco-Roman world. Individual examples are innumerable: Josephus, Philo, Qumran literature, the Talmud, the Nag Hammadi library, the Apostolic Fathers, Stoic texts, etc. The common denominator is, not surprisingly, that the comparative material comes from roughly the same time period and it originated in the same Middle Eastern or Southern European cultural sphere. The purpose of comparisons has been to shed light on and provide a context, which facilitates the understanding of the first Christians and their texts, more specifically the historical and theological meanings of these texts.[40]

Traditionally, all such textual comparisons have excluded texts from beyond the Mediterranean world, which has caused some scholars to point to the fact that close parallels actually exist between Asian

---

[39] Marcus Borg, ed., *Jesus and Buddha: The Parallel Sayings* (London: Duncan Baird Publishers, 2002), 23. For other important studies on comparisons between Christianity and Buddhism, see Albert Joseph Edmunds, *Buddhist and Christian Gospels*, ed. Masaharu Anesaki, 4 ed., 2 vols. (Philadelphia: Innes & Sons, 1914); J. Edgar Bruns, *The Christian Buddhism of St. John: New Insights into the Fourth Gospel* (New York: Paulist Press, 1971); Thundy, *Buddha and Christ*; Derrett, *The Bible and the Buddhists*; Sarvepalli Radhakrishnan, *Eastern Religions and Western Thought* (New York: Oxford University Press, 1959); Roy Amore, *Two Masters, One Message* (Nashville: Abingdon, 1978).

[40] Sometimes scholars have gone too far in their search for parallels; the term 'parallelomania' has been put forward by Samuel Sandmel to describe overzealous attempts at drawing conclusions about Christians texts from sometimes far-fetched comparative material. See Samuel Sandmel, "Parallelomania," *JBL* 81 (1962): 1–13.

and Middle Eastern texts. The question is *why* Western scholars have ignored this.

Zacharias Thundy's study of Buddhist texts in relation to the New Testament addresses precisely this problem. Thundy's focus is on nativity stories in Buddhist, Hindu, and New Testament texts, and his purpose is to illuminate the many parallels between these texts and what they mean for the study of Christianity, Buddhism, and Hinduism. In addition, he also wants to emphasise the historical parallels between India and the Middle East. Unlike historical critical study of parallels between Christian and other texts, however, Thundy's aim is not only to illuminate the biblical texts and their meaning in history. His purpose has an added dimension which, according to him, is very relevant: he wants to achieve religious dialogue across the (traditional) boundaries between East and West, to go beyond the "religious narcissism" that ends with "Christians associating with Christians and Buddhists with Buddhists in splendid isolation."[41]

Here again we see an example in which historical discourse is important, but the choice of topic and the broader aims lie very much in line with postcolonialism. The new and somewhat surprising element is, of course, the claim that Indian texts may have a bearing on the understanding of the New Testament. Thundy, and others engaged in the same approach, go beyond the biblical Mediterranean world and search for trans-cultural and trans-religious connections that might have something to contribute to the understanding of biblical texts, both historically and in contemporary settings.

The immediate problem from anyone socialised in a Western academic context is usually that, if connections are to be established between these diverse texts, it needs to be proven that, historically, there was a cultural exchange between India and the Mediterranean world. Where is the evidence? We shall return to this question under the next heading (5.2.5). At this point, in order to clarify the discussion of this approach, we shall take a brief look at a study by Soares-Prabhu, which is representative of much of this type of work.

---

[41] Thundy, *Buddha and Christ*, 13; see also 14–17. Cf. Premnath, "Interpretation in India," 15: "The presence of scriptures in other religions presents challenges as well as exciting prospects. The challenge is to refrain from making absolutist claims from one's perspective. In a context with many religions and scriptures, the claims of one group cannot become normative for everybody else... [i]t is not a matter of giving up one's beliefs but rather redefining them."

In the article "Two Mission Commands: An Interpretation of Matthew 28:16–20 in the Light of a Buddhist Text," Soares-Prabhu produces an inter-textual study comparing two texts from two different traditions: the Christian-Jewish text of Matthew 28:16–20 and the Buddhist text Mahavagga I.10–11.1 from Vinaya Pitaka in the Pali canon. In this study, Soares-Prabhu uses a historical critical approach in order to make a comparison between the two texts and reach an Asian understanding of the mission command in Matthew. Rather than the traditional Western interpretation of the mission command in Matthew, Soares-Prabhu's aim is to show that the mission command receives a very different meaning with an Asian inspired reading. This reading, he claims, might even be a more historically valid interpretation than interpretations used in colonial settings supporting aggressive missionary activities. In his reading, mission according to Matthew is spreading the teachings of Jesus, which implies love, compassion, and serving others. This is important, since Western interpretations have failed to produce these qualities and have served triumphalism, hegemony, arrogance, and violence. To counter such effects, Mahavagga is allowed to inform and inspire the interpretation of Matthew; the below indicates in which ways:

Go therefore and make disciples of all nations, baptizing them in the name of the Father and of the Son and of the Holy Spirit	Go now, O Bhikkus, and wander for the profit of many, for the happiness of many and out of compassion for the world, for the good, profit, and happiness of gods and human beings.

Soares-Prabhu is not claiming a direct relationship between the texts. Rather, Matthew's text is infused with a culturally appropriate and relevant meaning when interpreted from the perspective of the mission command in the Mahavagga. In addition, such meaning is no less historically probable than a Western imperialist interpretation.[42]

Soares-Prabhu emphasises the necessity of not getting trapped in Western patterns of interpretation, exported to India during the European colonial period, or for that matter, as spread today in Western paradigms of exegesis. This example shows how, from a postcolonial perspective, a very problematic New Testament text, used in the

---

[42] For a more comprehensive discussion of Soares-Prabhu's interpretation of Matthew's mission command, see Runesson, "Kontextuell exegetik i en postkolonial värld."

colonial process, may be reinterpreted and given a culturally adequate meaning.[43]

5.2.5 Mapping Historical Contacts: The Ancient World Beyond the Euphrates

As seen in the previous section, there are several, sometimes striking parallels between New Testament and Buddhist texts. So many are the similarities that it has made scholars wonder about what exactly the relationship between Christian and Buddhist tradition is. Were there close contacts in antiquity between Asia and the Middle East? Scholars have long known about trade routes from India, and, of course, Alexander's imperial ambitions took him all the way to the Indus valley.

But just how much mutual influence was there? What about religious and philosophical interchange? Did merchants on the Silk Road, which passed through legendary Petra in modern day Jordan, bring with them religious beliefs that influenced the peoples around the Mediterranean? And what about the well established fact of the sea trade between India and Southern Arabia already in the 6th century B.C.E.?[44]

It seems clear that Christians very early, already in the late first century, journeyed to India to spread their belief in a Jewish Messiah. If this is correct, it is highly likely that there were Jewish communities established along the way, tracing their origins further back in time than the first century.[45] Perhaps the contacts between these vast areas were much more common and intense than Western scholars have traditionally been willing to admit. Thundy writes,

> [A]t least the educated people of the period knew India well and could even identify Indian doctrine as Indian. Therefore, there existed really no insurmountable barrier preventing Christianity and Indian religions

---

[43] By way of comparison, biblical texts that are perceived as very problematic from a feminist perspective have been given new interpretations using a variety of methods. In both cases, it is the real-life circumstances of the interpreters, circumstances that have not been part of real-life for previous traditional scholarship, that have initiated the new interpretive strategies and conclusions.

[44] See, e.g., Hananya Goodmann, "Introduction. Judaism and Hinduism: Cultural Resonances" in *Between Jerusalem and Benares: Comparative Studies Between Judaism and Hinduism* (ed. Hananya Goodmann; Delhi: Sri Satguru Publications, 1997), 1–14, 10.

[45] That Christianity spread rapidly throughout the Mediterranean world has been attributed to the use of synagogues as places where social networks could be established and the message could find the socio-religious context needed for it to spread.

from influencing each other during the formative years of Christianity. However, there exists in the West a mental barrier or the prejudicial "Orientalism" that would protest against the view that it is quite possible and even probable that Indian thought could have influenced the Christian gospel.[46]

While some of Thundy's conclusions will not convince all historians, it is quite clear that he has managed to establish as a fact that contacts between the Mediterranean world and India and other Asian lands existed and were important enough to leave traces in the historical records, both regarding trade and religious and/or philosophical thought. The reason that this has not been considered in older Western research most likely has a lot to do with the phenomenon designated by the term orientalism, and very little to do with historical critical approaches.

This said, however, the question of the exact nature and extent of mutual influence remains to be established. This is work that still, to a large degree, needs to be done.[47] In any case, though details are missing, the fact that mutual influence between Christians and peoples of India was possible opens up for historical critical discourse a basis for textual comparisons between diverse religious scriptures.

This marks a distinct difference between postcolonial scholars working with an Indian context and those working from other cultural spheres, such as, e.g., Latin America, or Korea. While all would emphasise the desirability of interpreting the New Testament in indigenous contexts using local textual traditions as comparative material, the latter would have to work from outside historical critical discourse.[48]

This brings us to the second of the two categories we have proposed in order to organise the diverse postcolonial approaches to the New Testament. In the following we shall present and discuss postcolonial scholarly discourses that go beyond Western historical critical methodologies, but which may still be defined as exegetical approaches.

---

[46] Thundy, *Buddha and Christ*, 266ff.
[47] Cf. Borg, ed., *Jesus and Buddha: The Parallel Sayings*, who explains similarities as not genetic in nature but rather based on common experiences: "similarity of underlying structure is not cultural borrowing, but commonality of religious experiences. Both Jesus and Buddha had life-transforming experiences of 'the sacred.'" (10).
[48] Note that Indian Christians may, in this context, point both to contacts between ancient Christianity and Indian religions, and Christian missionaries on the continent already in the late first century. See, e.g., Muthuraj, "New Testament and Methodology," 264–68.

5.3 Category Two: Postcolonial Methodological Approaches Beyond Western Historical Critical Discourses

With the development of biblical studies within the field of comparative literature, psychology, and social theory, etc., exegesis opens up towards the field of theology. It is important, however, to keep separate theology and exegesis since the theoretical foundations, the history of scholarship, and current discourses and aims are different. The distinction between exegesis and theology does not run along the attempted demarcation line between confession-neutral and confessional approaches, even if that is sometimes assumed; both exegesis and theology may be found on either side of the fence.

For postcolonial scholars working constructively to interpret exegetically New Testament texts in local-specific cultural contexts, the criterion of relevance connects them both with their colleagues' work within a modified historical critical paradigm (c.f., above, section 5.2) on the one hand, and constructive contextual theologising on the other. Still, the aim of these scholars, which is the understanding of text, belongs within and should be designated as exegesis, even though they work beyond traditional Western epistemic discourses of scholarly logic.[49] The search for meaning in New Testament texts involves, by necessity, analyses of the religio-cultural foundations both of the primary (the historical) culture, which is to be 'translated,' and the secondary (the present) culture into which the meaning of the message is to be transferred and made available.[50]

As examples of postcolonial exegetical approaches beyond the Western historical critical discourses, I will discuss *dhvani*, *Dalit*, *minjung*, and the approach that Kwok calls *postcolonial imagination*. It goes without saying that these approaches are but a few among many examples. The discussion below is not intended to be exhaustive, but rather to present some of the more important approaches within the field.[51]

---

[49] Cf. Samuel Byrskog's note on the church fathers' categorisation of Biblical studies as exegetical, Samuel Byrskog, "Nya testamentets forskningshistoria" in *Jesus och de första kristna: inledning till Nya testamentet* (ed. Dieter Mitternacht and Anders Runesson; Stockholm: Verbum, 2006), 33–41, especially 33–34, 40–41.

[50] This should, arguably, also determine the 'how' of historical critical studies of any ancient material.

[51] For other examples from a Hindu Indian context, see, e.g., Richard De Smet, "Hindu and Neo-Hindu Exegesis;" Richard De Smet, "Some Characteristics of Buddhist Exegesis;" and Thomas Manickam, "Cross Cultural Hermeneutics: The Patterns

According to many postcolonial scholars, Western historical critical discourse does not provide enough proper tools for exegesis in the context in which they live. This is especially apparent when focusing on a multi-religious context such as Asia. The aims of the scholarly studies are connected to the addressees of said studies, the real readers, and this in turn determines the choice of methods. Methods chosen must be moulded so that they respond to the sense of relevance desired by the audience.

It is important to recognise that the new methodologies are context-bound, but not more so than the historical critical methods, even if it may seem that way. This is because the Western episteme in which historical critical discourse emerged has imbedded in itself a discourse of global truth claims; this is not the case with the Asian approaches here mentioned. The Western claims to objective and universal truth, however, are no more universal than these approaches, despite the rhetoric (although, admittedly, the Western claims are more ethnocentric). In other words, Western discourses are interwoven with a specific episteme just as much as any other set of discourses, and therefore are as locally limited as any other discourses.

The approaches discussed below put focus on the human being as an interpreting being, and proceed from there to reading texts in contemporary and relevant socio-cultural contexts in order to discover and understand their meanings.

5.3.1 *Dhvani Exegesis*

As a theory of interpretation of Sanskrit poetry, applied to texts like the Baghavad Gita and the Mahabharata, dhvani exegesis is not as well known in the Western world as the Dalit and Minjung approaches. Dhvani is an ancient exegetical method, developed before the modern colonial era. Its origins are traced back to Anandavardhana of Kashmir, who presented the approach in his study *Dhvanyaloka*, dated to the 9th century C.E. His theory was a contribution to the linguistic discussion at the time within the science of Alamkarasastra, a 'Science of Beauty,' focusing on the interpretation of poetic texts.[52] Dhvani as

---

of Jaimini, Bharthari and Sankaracharya," all in *Indian Theological Studies* 21:3–4 (1984): 250–67.

[52] Anand Amaladass, "'Dhvani' Theory in Sanscrit Poetics," *BiBh* 5:1 (1979): 261–75, 261. See also Amaladass' full-length work *Philosophical Implications of Dhvani: Experience of Symbol Language in Indian Aesthetics*, vol. 11. (Publications of the De Nobili

a method has been applied to biblical texts by, e.g., Francis D'Sa, Sr Vandana, and Soares-Prabhu.[53]

Dhvani exegesis is neither concerned with the grammatical construction of the text (the primary meaning of a word, in Sanskrit *adhidha*), nor with the metaphorical meaning (the secondary meaning, in Sanskrit *laksana*). Both the primary and the secondary meanings of texts are, according to Anandavardhana, 'concrete' and 'direct' meanings, available for structural analysis. Dhvani both lies within and goes beyond these two levels of meaning. Dhvani is the suggested meaning that goes beyond what is to be found in the text as written artefact. As such, dhvani is a notion of meaning sensed and incorporated in the text by its author through *adhidha* and *laksana*, but not directly visible in the grammatical and metaphorical structure of the sentences.[54]

Dhvani exegesis illuminates the importance of the context and culture of both the milieu in which the text was authored and the setting in which the text is being received (read or heard). Since dhvani is only 'indirectly' visible in the text itself, it is dependent on the reader's response and sensibility to what is written. In order to identify dhvani, Anandavardhana argues for three types of dhvani, which in turn can be sorted into two categories. The first category is *dhvani of attribution* (the extrinsic, or the open, dhvani), which is constituted by two underlying dhvanis: *vastu-dhvani* and *alamkara-dhvani*. The second category is *rasa-dhvani*.[55] The dhvani Anandavardhana focuses on is the *rasa-dhvani* (also called the proper dhvani). In graphic form, the relationship between these forms of dhvani may be portrayed as follows:

Research Library; Vienna: Gerold, 1984) and his study *Indian Exegesis: Hindu-Buddhist Hermeneutics* (Satya Nilayam Publications: Chennai, 2003), see spec. 102-26.

[53] Francis X. D'Sa, "'Dhvani' as a Method of Interpretation," *BiBh* 5:1 (1979): 276-94, Sr Vandana, "Water—God's Extravaganza: John 2.1-11" in *Voices from the Margin: Interpreting the Bible in the Third World* (ed. R. S. Sugirtharajah; Maryknoll: Orbis Books, 1995): 156-67; and George M. Soares-Prabhu, "And There Was a Great Calm: A 'Dhavani' Reading of the Stilling of the Storm" in *BiBh* 5:1 (1979): 295-308.

[54] Amaladass, "'Dhvani' Theory," 263-66.

[55] Amaladass, "'Dhvani' Theory," 270.

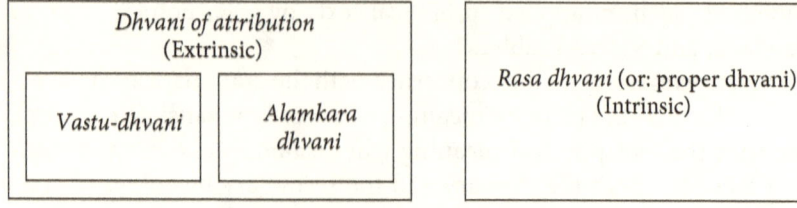

Figure 4. The relationship between dhvani of attribution, vastu-dhvani, alamkara dhvani, and rasa-dhvani.[56]

In order to understand rasa-dhvani, we have to explain the dhvanis of attribution, vastu-dhvani and alamkara-dhvani. Vastu-dhvani is the suggested meaning in an expressed sentence. For example, the sentence 'it is cold outside,' understood as a factual statement told to a child on her/his way out into the snow, has the vastu-dhvani (the suggested meaning) of 'put on warm clothing.' If the child puts on a jacket, a hat, and mittens suitable for the weather, the child has grasped the vastu-dhvani of the sentence.[57] Often, even the tone of voice may evoke specific feelings or actions. In the example, however, there is nothing in the sentence that grammatically suggests the action of the child. In that sense vastu-dhvani goes beyond the grammatical meaning and points beyond the text; nevertheless vastu-dhvani is extremely important, even from the point of view of authorial intention. The function of vastu-dhvani is simply to mediate a fact or initiate an action or evoke feelings through means other than the grammatical structure of a sentence.

Alamkara-dhvani is different. Alamkara-dhvani suggests how to interpret one phenomenon using another, including the underlying or metaphorical meanings of either phenomenon. The author may use suggested (metaphorical) similarities for comparisons. For example, if a woman tells her beloved, 'your eyes are like blue lakes,' the alamkara-dhvani's suggested meaning is that there is a similarity between 'eyes' and 'blue lakes,' not in a literal, but in an allegorical sense. The language in alamkara-dhvani is more charming and poetic than in vastu-

---

[56] Cf. Amaladass, "'Dhvani' Theory," 266.

[57] As an example of vastu-dhvani on worldviews and meanings, see Stephen Westerholm, *Understanding Matthew: The Early Christian Worldview of the First Gospel* (Grand Rapids: Baker Academic, 2006), 11–14.

dhvani, but both points in the direction of underlying meanings not grammatically expressed in the text.[58]

Anandavardhana's contribution to the science of Alamkarasastra (the Science of Beauty) is, however, not the two dhvanis in category one, but instead the dhvani in category two, the *rasa-dhvani*. Rasa-dhvani can never be expressed (contrary to vastu- and alamkara-dhvani), but only hinted at by the author, who wants to evoke a certain response from the audience. As Anand Amaladass states, "[t]he poet keen on evoking rasa-dhvani has to create the atmosphere by providing the conditions."[59]

Rasa-dhvani refers to emotional moods, appearing when a person reads or hears a text, pointing towards a reality that goes beyond the written text itself. The author of the text guides the reader to this experience of dhvani through the language of the text itself. The author's task is to express her/himself in a way so that the reader grasps the rasa-dhvani.

Amaladass states that the rasa-dhvani "comes into play between the evocative language of the poet and the aesthetic sensibility of the reader."[60] This means that when the text merges with a reader who is sensitive to rasa-dhvani, the grasping of the rasa-dhvani should happen simultaneously to the text being read.[61] The nature of rasa-dhvani is expressed well by D'Sa,

> Dhvani in the strictest sense of the word is that use of language which through either the primary or the secondary meaning or through both of them takes the reader to a depth meaning which is experienceable but not expressible.[62]

D'Sa adds, however, that *rasa-dhvani* emanates only from the existing sentences in the text. D'Sa explains the function of dhvani by comparing it with a radio broadcast:

> Both the relaying quality of the text as well as the receiving antenna of the reader together make the dhvani-broadcast possible. The attuned antenna of the reader alone would not succeed in catching the dhvani-message if the text does not transmit.[63]

---

[58] Amaladass, "'Dhvani' Theory," 270.
[59] Amaladass, "'Dhvani' Theory," 266.
[60] Amaladass, "'Dhvani' Theory," 272.
[61] Amaladass, "'Dhvani' Theory," 267.
[62] D'Sa, "'Dhvani' as a Method of Interpretation," 279.
[63] D'Sa, "'Dhvani' as a Method of Interpretation," 279.

Even if this school is dealing mostly with poetic texts from Baghavad Gita and Mahabaratha, the theory has proven to be fruitful in the study of New Testament texts.

Soares-Prabhu discusses the contributions of *rasa-dhvani* in his article "And There Was a Great Calm: A 'Dhvani' Reading of the Stilling of the Storm (Mark 4:35–41)." Soares-Prabhu compares a historical critical reading of Mark 4:35–41 with a dhvani reading of the same text. His conclusion is that the historical critical study "detects various strata in it, and reconstructs with some plausibility the history of the transmission." Soares-Prabhu agrees that this study is good and useful, but that it misses the "heart of the story" since it does not take into consideration that the analysed text is a religious text. Historical critical study does not take the reader to the full experience and understanding that is the dhvani of the text. Soares-Prabhu illustrates his suggested dhvani of Mark 4:35–41 as follows:

> It is only when we have experienced (as our world is beginning) the terrible frailty of human life, lived out in a tiny planet spinning like a fretful midge in the vast emptiness of space and pulsing with titanic forces that threaten any moment to blow it apart; or when we have looked with terror into the cauldron of savage violence and destructiveness that seethes in each human heart—it is only then that we can reach the great calm which recognizes behind the fragile patterns of human existence the unshakeable stability of the ground of our being. It [is] this experience of ultimate stability behind the turmoil of our agitated and threatened existence that the story of the Stilling of the Storm evokes.[64]

If it is possible at all to talk about related areas of analyses in the Western academic world, some similarities do exist between different aspects of dhvani and biblical studies inspired by the field of comparative literature and the use of methods like narrative analysis, reader-response criticism and rhetorical analysis. Perhaps these methodologies, or developments of them, may help to provide bridges in the future between Western and Indian scholarly discourses, and resolve some of the epistemic tensions of today that result in misunderstanding and an inability to listen to the 'other.'

The contribution of dhvani exegesis to postcolonial studies is its potential as an Indian indigenous exegetical methodology to allow the

---

[64] George M. Soares-Prabhu, "And There Was a Great Calm: A 'Dhvani' Reading of the Stilling of the Storm," *BiBh* 5:1 (1979): 307–8. For another interesting example of a dhvani analysis of a New Testament text, see Vandana, "God's Extravaganza," 156–67.

scholar to pick up and use the culture and context of India in her/his interpretation of the New Testament texts. In addition, a dialogue between dhvani exegesis and the Western methodologies just mentioned may prove valuable in constructively building understanding between exegetical cultures.

5.3.2 Dalit Exegesis

Dalit refers to the 16% of the Indian population that do not belong to any of the four castes (priests, rulers, traders, and labourers). These people are not only outsiders in the society, they are also considered ritually unclean and not worthy even to look at.[65] Despite the fact that India's civil law no longer acknowledges the caste system and the discrimination that follows from it, the social-political realities for the Dalits in their everyday life have not changed. The Dalits live in religiously legitimised misery.

In such a social context it is not hard to understand that a Christian proclamation of a God that loves and acknowledges those who have no standing in society and live in distress has been well received within the Dalit community. Today, about two-thirds of the Dalits are Christians.[66] From the community of Christian Dalits has emanated what is termed Dalit theology. Interestingly, despite the fact that the majority of the Christians in India are Dalits, this has not meant that they have been allowed to access leading positions in the churches and take active part in the theological discussions in India and globally. The explanation is, tragically, that the caste system has been and to some degree still is, reflected not only in Indian Hindu society, but also within the Christian community itself. Traditionally, the Brahmin Christian perspective has been the dominant perspective.[67] It was not until the last 10 years or so that Dalit theology has emerged and achieved status and importance both in the Indian Christian community and globally.

---

[65] Sathianathan Clarke, "Dalit Theology," *Dictionary of Third World Theologies*: 64–65, 64. Cf. another of Clark's studies, *Dalits and Christianity: Subaltern Religion and Liberation Theology in India* (New Delhi: Oxford University Press, 1998) and John C. B. Webster, *The Dalit Christians: A History* (Delhi: ISPCK, 1992).

[66] Clarke, "Dalit Theology," 64.

[67] Arvind P. Nirmal, "Towards a Christian Dalit Theology," *Asian Journal of Theology* 6:2 (1992): 297–310, 299.

Arvind Nirmal, who has been called the father of Dalit theology,[68] describes Dalit theology as being *about* the Dalits, *for* the Dalits, and *by* the Dalits.[69] As such, Dalit theology is a liberation theology, aimed at addressing specific religious, social, economical, and political aspects of life as lived by members of this community.[70] As in many liberation theologies, the Exodus story has a central place in Dalit theology; Deut 26:5–11, specifically, is frequently used and referenced.[71] As Premnath states, "[i]t is in the dalitness of Jesus that the dalits ought to recognize the mystery of their 'exodus.'"[72] One of the express goals of Dalit theology is to strive to become the image of God, to achieve full humanity (Gen 1:26).

An informative example of how biblical exegesis from a Dalit perspective plays out in relation to a specific, and for Dalit Christians extremely relevant, topic, is Soares-Prabhu's study on Jesus and table fellowship.[73] Here, first century concerns about purity and pollution are brought directly to bear on the Indian context. After what is by and large a historical critical study of Jesus' and the early church's attitudes towards purity and holiness,[74] Soares-Prabhu proceeds in a later section to read his own Christian-Indian context, contrasting Jesus' position and the current situation in which separation still occurs between Dalit Christians and other Christians.[75]

Dalit biblical exegesis is set within a context where the overarching hermeneutical key is a socio-economically liberating message. From this socially informed theological perspective the texts are interpreted

---

[68] See Clarke, "Dalit Theology," 65.
[69] Nirmal, "Christian Dalit Theology," 301.
[70] Cf. James Elisha, "Liberative Motifs in the Dalit Religion," *Bangalore Theological Forum*, 34:2 (2002): 78–88.
[71] Premnath, "Interpretation in India," 7. Cf. Arvind P. Nirmal, "A Dialogue with Dalit Literature" in *A Reader in Dalit Theology* (ed. Arvind P. Nirmal; Madras: Gurukul, 1991), 64–82.
[72] Premnath, "Interpretation in India," 7.
[73] George M. Soares-Prabhu, "The Table Fellowship of Jesus: Its Significance for Dalit Christians in India Today" in *Jeevadhara* 22:128 (1992): 140–59.
[74] Note, however, that Soares-Prabhu allows his own experience of Indian society to inform his historical analysis; he explicitly critiques E. P. Sanders for inadequate conclusions based on his lack of experience of Indian society (which is epistemically closer to first century Judea): "Had Sanders experienced the working of cast in India, he might not so easily have dismissed the significance of purity/pollution in the table fellowship of Jesus." ("Table Fellowship of Jesus," 140, n. 2).
[75] George Soares-Prabhu, "Table Fellowship of Jesus," 154–59.

in ways meant to convey a liberating message.⁷⁶ Through this fundamental hermeneutical key, Dalit exegetical analyses are connected to other emancipating biblical readings in other parts of the world. The common concerns that run through such analyses, are concerns that are less related to specific cultural contexts and more to issues of class and socio-economic conditions. Still, Dalit biblical analysis is deeply embedded in Indian socio-cultural and religious realities and can only be understood and explained from such a perspective.

If the contribution of dhvani exegesis to global exegetical communities and Western academic discourses lies primarily in building bridges between textual methodologies, Dalit exegesis connects the reader with disadvantaged groups working with liberating theologies in different parts of the world. From a postcolonial perspective, it is interesting to note that the effects of colonisation, for the Dalits, have not been entirely negative, but rather meant increased possibilities for liberation from an oppressive indigenous religio-political structure. The religion of the colonisers, despite hegemonic aspects involved in colonisation, has provided them with a tool that they have adapted for liberation. Indeed, this conclusion extends to include the intrusion into the Indian episteme of historical critical discourse, as Soares-Prabhu's analysis, mentioned above, suggests.

5.3.3 *Minjung Exegesis*

'Minjung' is a Korean word, written with two Chinese characters, meaning 'people.' It refers to those in the Korean population who are silenced, powerless, economically exploited, and marginalised in different ways. This marginalisation is taking place in both the socio-political structures in Korea and, from a global perspective, in the socio-political structures of neo-colonialism in a postcolonial world.⁷⁷ Minjung, in a strict sense, does not refer exclusively to the Korean Minjung but might apply as well to other suppressed groups in a global and historical context.

Minjung approaches had their origin during the 1970s when minjung became a major force in Korean liberation theology. During the

---

⁷⁶ Cf. the definition of exegesis in *Nordisk familjebok*, above, section 4.2.1; see also the definition provided by *ABD*, especially the focus on "*useful* interpretations." The same definitions of exegesis apply to minjung exegesis; see further below.

⁷⁷ Cf. David Kwang-sun Suh, "Minjung Theology," *Dictionary of Third World Theologies*: 143, and Kwok, *Discovering the Bible in the Non-Biblical World*, 15.

1980s the minjung movement went through two different phases: the minjung church movement and the feminist minjung theologies. The latter has been an important group, and particularly Chung Hyun Kyung, who has pointed out the fact that women often are the "minjung within the minjung," and as such require a separate field of inquiry.[78] It is within Minjung feminist theology that we find the initiative to inaugurate comparative study between biblical texts and non-Christian Korean religious perspectives, e.g., the shaman tradition.[79]

Han and *han-puri* are two key concepts within minjung theory. *Han* refers to feelings of

> ...resentment, anger, sadness, and resignation experienced by the people that arises from injustices suffered, from the sinful interconnection of classicism, racism, sexism, colonialism, neocolonialism, and cultural imperialism that are part of the people's daily lives.[80]

Han is, in other words, the concise pain in reaction to oppression taking place in history and in everyday life, a pain that is both physical and psychological.[81] *Han-puri*, a word that originates from the Korean shaman tradition, is the release from *han* in the sense that it untangles the oppression, sexism, racism, etc., in both history and in the present. The solution to the reality of *han* lies in the process of *han-puri*.[82] One of the main tasks of minjung theology is to reclaim the history from which the minjung has been excluded and made invisible and speechless, both historically and in the present. Such a recovery of a place lost in history and society is part of the process of *han-puri*. It is in this context that minjung exegesis, as part of minjung theology, takes place and plays a part in Korean society.

Minjung exegesis may be described as a perspective in which different methods may be applied depending on the task chosen. The minjung postcolonial reality is one of suffering and humiliation (*han*). Minjung (liberation) theology represents Christian resistance in the face of this violence, and as such is part of the process of *han-puri*. One of the tools of resistance within minjung theology is minjung

---

[78] Chung Hyun Kyung, "Han/Han-puri," *Dictionary of Third World Theologies*: 96–97. See also Chung Hyun Kyung, *Struggle to be the Sun Again: Introducing Asian Women's Theology* (Maryknoll: Orbis Books, 1990), 23, where Chung Hyun Kyung describes the Korean women's struggle to reclaim their 'womanity.'

[79] Kwang-sun Suh, "Minjung Theology," 143.

[80] Chung Hyun Kyung, "Han/Han-puri," 96.

[81] Chung Hyun Kyung, *Struggle to be the Sun Again*, 42.

[82] Chung Hyun Kyung, "Han/Han-puri," 96.

biblical exegesis. Minjung exegesis makes use of the full range of methodological approaches (grammatical, historical, reception history etc.), all refracted in the prism of minjung suffering realities.

One of the pioneers of minjung exegesis is Ahn Byung-Mu.[83] Ahn is known, among other things, for his study of the Gospel of Mark through minjung optics.[84] In his study he analyses the author's use of ὄχλος instead of the more commonly used term for people, λαός. Ahn argues that, even if 'the people' in Mark is an important group, the analysis of this character-group has been less than satisfying. Ahn uses experiences from minjung studies and applies them to the Markan ὄχλος in order to understand the text in a way that might be closer to the original meaning. In other words, we have here a variant of historical critical methodology.

The reason for him to assume that ὄχλος is socially equivalent to the minjung is Mark's way of applying the term in his narrative. The author is alone in the New Testament using the word repeatedly and in combination with a complete avoidance of λαός. The reason for this is that λαός for Mark represents the upper strata in society, i.e., the opposite of the minjung. Those who followed Jesus were, in other words, the minjung of the time: the 'sinners,' the tax collectors, the sick, and the outcasts of the society.[85] The ὄχλος is not a strong and violent group like the zealots, but rather a quiet group which both welcomes Jesus, and betrays him. What Mark is saying about Jesus is, according to Ahn, that he "stands with the minjung, and promises them the future of God."[86] With Ahn's interpretation a connection is established between the oppressed in contemporary societies, Korean and others, and the New Testament texts.

Comparing minjung exegetical approaches with Dalit exegesis, we find several similarities. Both focus on unjust structures and oppression

---

[83] For an example of minjung exegesis on Hebrew Bible texts, see Cyris H. S. Moon, "A Korean Minjung Perspective: The Hebrews and the Exodus" in *Voices from the Margin: Interpreting the Bible in the Third World* (ed. R. S. Sugirtharajah; Maryknoll: Orbis Books, 1995), 228–43.

[84] Ahn Byung-Mu, "Jesus and the Minjung in the Gospel of Mark" in *Voices from the Margin: Interpreting the Bible in the Third World* (ed. R. S. Sugirtharajah; Maryknoll: Orbis Books, 1995), 85–104. See also the full study Ahn, *Minjung Theology: People as the Subject of History* (Maryknoll: Orbis Books, 1981).

[85] Ahn, "Minjung in the Gospel of Mark," 88–96. Note the risk of an anti-Jewish interpretation when Ahn draws such a sharp line between the ὄχλος (as the suppressed people) and the λαός (a word used for the people of God). Ahn does comment on this risk.

[86] Ahn, "Minjung in the Gospel of Mark," 102.

in society; both are used as interpretive tools within a larger theological response to those injustices; both make use of a variety of existing methodologies. As feminist exegesis, both are best described as perspectives. The hermeneutical key for the exegetical investigations is derived from real life suffering and struggle for liberation. A difference between the two, however, lies in the fact that Dalit exegesis is very much focused on this specific group and its unique position in Indian society. Minjung, on the other hand, is explicitly meant to encompass other minorities and oppressed groups, both in history and in other nations and societies. It is, for example, possible to talk about the minjung of Sweden, but not of the Dalits of Sweden.

5.3.4 *Postcolonial Imagination*

We began section 5.3 by discussing a text-centred method for interpreting non-textual aspects present in the text (dhvani); then we continued to look at two perspectives characterised by social activism and applied within larger theological frameworks with the aim of achieving liberation (Dalit and minjung). In the present section we shall turn to a different kind of postcolonial approach, namely what Kwok Pui-lan has termed *postcolonial imagination*. This approach focuses primarily on the researcher, and suggests strategies for opening up the scholar's mind for new solutions. As will be shown, postcolonial imagination represents the broadest and most general approach so far.[87]

Postcolonial imagination refers to,

> ...a desire, a determination, and a process of disengagement from the whole colonial syndrome, which takes many forms and guises.[88]

Originally, in 1995,[89] Kwok introduced the concept of 'dialogical imagination.' In her study from 2005, however, she has expanded the

---

[87] Cf. Hjamil A. Martínez-Vázquez, "Breaking the Established Scaffold: Imagination as a Resource in the Development of Biblical Interpretation" in *Her Master's Tools? Feminist and Postcolonial Engagements of Historical-Critical Discourse* (eds. Todd Penner and Caroline Vander Stichele; Society of Biblical Literature: Atlanta, 2005), 71–91. See also Soares-Prabhu, "Stilling of the Storm," 300, who uses the example of a parable: "A parable, therefore, is to be understood not through intellectual abstraction but through imaginative participation. It is through the imagination that one enters into a parable, experiences that shock of the "dislocation of the familiar" that its story conveys, and is brought into a fleeting, vertiginous confrontation with the limits of one's world."

[88] Kwok, *Postcolonial Imagination*, 2.

[89] Kwok, *Discovering the Bible in the Non-Biblical World*.

definition of the concept into three subsections (*historical imagination, dialogical imagination* and *diasporic imagination*) and sorted them under the umbrella term of 'postcolonial imagination.'[90]

The idea behind 'imagining' is to find non-Western ways to reach knowledge. A quote may clarify:

> How do we come to know what we know? How do postcolonial intellectuals begin the process of decolonization of the mind and the soul? What are the steps we need to take and what kind of mind-set will steer us away from Eurocentrism, on the one hand, and a nostalgic romanticizing of one's heritage or tradition, on the other?[91]

What Kwok does is look into how the imagination of human beings functions, and how it can be used in scholarship involved in analyses of past, present, and future realities. She argues that, in the postcolonial search for new images and meanings, the ability to imagine is essential for the effort to find what 'does not fit,' because it is within these 'errors' or 'gaps' that new knowledge may be acquired. Imagining does not take place in the mainstream, but in the periphery where we find gaps which

> ...refuse to be shaped into any framework... These disparate elements that staunchly refuse to follow the set pattern, the established episteme, the overall design that the mind so powerfully wants to shape... they have the potential to point to another path, to signal radically new possibilities.[92]

Making this argument, Kwok touches upon one of the most important qualities for a successful scholar: the courage to go beyond already familiar knowledge. This is an ability that is often connected to the capacity to discover what is 'on the other side of the fence.' For example, the importance for unhindered imagination is especially noticeable in processes where paradigm shifts are initiated. Earlier we mentioned Copernicus as one such example of scholarly courage.[93]

Kwok brings up three types of imagination: historical, dialogical, and diasporic imagination, through which she herself has been formed as an Asian scholar. *Historical imagination* refers to the imagination that allows the scholar to discover gaps in history that, if brought to light and incorporated into the analytical discussion, may significantly

---

[90] Kwok, *Postcolonial Imagination*, chapter one.
[91] Kwok, *Postcolonial Imagination*, 30.
[92] Kwok, *Postcolonial Imagination*, 30.
[93] See section 3.3. We also find examples of imagination in history that did not bring the scholarly world to a paradigm shift—alchemy is one of them.

change our perception of the past. As an example, Kwok brings up the 'semicolonisation' of China and variant historiographies written about the Christian mission in this country. Here, Kwok points to the neglect of official historiography to mention the poor peasant women, living in rural areas, who converted to Christianity.[94] To study women's history does not mean only to 'add' them; historical accounts of women need to ask questions not usually asked in order to look from perspectives usually ignored.

In Kwok's case, it means to ask why these women converted, what appealed to them, how it felt to worship together with males in a society that required separation between sexes, or what role they played in founding and developing the churches of China. Historical imagination represents a way to search and find the women in history whose contributions became permanent and changed the course of history. Historical imagination is, Kwok argues, crucial also for scholars working within biblical studies.

Turning now to *dialogical imagination* and biblical texts, Kwok searches for new connections not only between different cultures but also between "the bible and our lives."[95] In this search, she states, we have to use our imagination.

> ...we have to imagine how the biblical tradition—formulated in another time and in another culture—can address our burning questions of today. On the other hand, based on our present circumstances, we have to reimagine what the biblical world was like, thus opening up new horizons hitherto hidden from us.[96]

Kwok argues that dialogical imagination bridges "time and space" and brings meaning to the biblical text when read in contemporary contexts. The strategies for employing dialogical imagination may be summarised in two main fields:[97]

1. The use of indigenous myths, legends, and stories in biblical reflection.
2. Finding the hermeneutical key that is the social biography of the people in order to understand both the reality in which we live and the Bible itself in relation to us.

---

[94] Kwok Pui-lan, *Chinese Women and Christianity, 1860–1927* (Atlanta: Scholars Press, 1992).
[95] Kwok, *Discovering the Bible in the Non-Biblical World*, 13.
[96] Kwok, *Discovering the Bible in the Non-Biblical World*, 13.
[97] Kwok, *Discovering the Bible in the Non-Biblical World*, 13.

Focusing on the minjung experiences, both in Korea and in other places, provides a starting point for this hermeneutical reflection, which is intended to lead to contextualised understandings of biblical texts. Approaching the biblical texts only from a historical perspective is too limited and cannot achieve a full understanding. Scholars have to consider the Bible a "talking book" and not a "dead book."[98]

Dialogical imagination is a way to merge biblical and Asian sacred scriptures and traditions.[99] In such a fusion of traditions, it is important to take into account the Asian multi-cultural and multi-religious context and, as Kwok points out, pay attention to the fact that "an Asian reads the Bible from a situation of great alienation."[100] She takes her methodological point of departure in the Chinese characters that translate into English as 'dialogue.' Dialogue in China refers to giving and receiving, equally, by both parties.[101] Kwok points out that this dialogue should take place between different traditions as well, like the Christian and the Asian religions. The dialogue has to take place in the midst of these traditions in order to create authentic Asian theology. Likewise, she suggests that, "biblical interpretation in Asia must create a two-way traffic between our own tradition and that of the Bible."[102] Therefore, in dialogical imagination it is important not to see people of non-Christian faiths as potential objects for mission, but to treat each other with respect, searching together for a common perception of truth—and a better society in Asia.[103]

---

[98] Kwok, *Discovering the Bible in the Non-Biblical World*, 32.
[99] Cf. Soares-Prabhu, "Two Mission Commands," 324.
[100] Kwok, *Postcolonial Imagination*, 39.
[101] Kwok notes, however, in her study *Postcolonial Imagination and Feminist Theology*, that this enterprise is difficult due to former colonisation and recent neo-colonisation. It is not possible to find a 'pure' West and a 'pure' East and compare them since cultures and traditions are never static. Kwok, *Postcolonial Imagination*, 43. It is difficult to take and receive equally in a global situation where cultures are without boundaries.
[102] Kwok, *Discovering the Bible in the Non-Biblical World*, 12.
[103] Kwok, *Discovering the Bible in the Non-Biblical World*, 12-13. See also Lucien Legrand, "Inculturation and Biblical Studies in India" in *Indian Theological Studies* 20:1 (1984): 61-70. Legrand does not talk about dialogical imagination, but he states in his study that, "...as in the case of any dialogue, exegesis must be able to understand the language of its partner," (70). Kwok also adds a feminist perspective to dialogical imagination: "With multiple subjectivity an Asian woman critic sees not only the fusion of horizons but also the rupture of the order of things, not only the cogency of argument but also the arbitrariness of the construction of meanings, not only unity and coherence but also asymmetry and fragmentation. The possibilities of creative dialogues because of the multiple consciousness of the female investigating

The third type of imagination, *Diasporic imagination*, takes as point of departure the global phenomenon of migration, either voluntary or involuntary. Diaspora as a term has been used within biblical studies and in Jewish tradition for the Jewish experience of displacement from the land of Israel.[104] Today it is also a concept used to refer to the vast migration of peoples in the wake of de-colonisation and globalisation. As such it is generally applicable to people in a situation of "forced or voluntary migration," including the experiences, and interpretations of experiences, that follow from this situation.[105] Kwok writes,

> A diasporic consciousness, which is located here and there, reads back metropolitan history and regimes of knowledge from multiple vantage points because people in diaspora are "outsiders" from within.[106]

She continues,

> Diasporic imagination recognizes the diversity of diasporas and honors the different histories and memories. The diasporic experiences of being a Chinese in the United States are different from those of a Chinese in Indonesia or in Peru. The Jewish, Armenian, Chinese, Japanese, Asian Indian diasporic communities in the United States are different not only because of history and religious traditions, but also because of class, race, and ethnicity.[107]

Putting emphasis on imagination, Kwok challenges scholars to use knowledge from different contemporary situations relevant for biblical studies in order to open up new ways of thinking about things biblical and contemporary, finding the gaps and the errors in current historiography and exegesis. The goal is to reach culturally relevant

---

subject enable multiple readings and open new arrays of interpretation." Kwok, *Discovering the Bible in the Non-Biblical World*, 27.

[104] Within biblical studies, 'diaspora' usually refers to Jews living outside Israel. In a postcolonial context, however, the phenomenon of diaspora is wider and is used for the physical movement of people beyond their original homelands due to colonisation, past or present. Kwok, *Postcolonial Imagination*, 44–45. Cf. Sugirtharajah, *Postcolonial Criticism and Biblical Interpretation*, 180–85. See also Cooppan, "The Ruins of Empire," 87.

[105] Kwok, *Postcolonial Imagination*, 44.
[106] Kwok, *Postcolonial Imagination*, 49.
[107] Kwok, *Postcolonial Imagination*, 49.

interpretations of biblical texts through non-Western ways of creating knowledge.[108]

Postcolonial imagination has, like Dalit and minjung exegesis, a focus on matters of oppression, and, implicitly or explicitly, takes the position of the oppressed with the goal of achieving liberation in both society and academia. We find in postcolonial exegetical approaches a close connection between real-life settings and the academic world. Both the academic world, which is increasingly globalised (in the sense of increased interaction between scholars from different cultures), and societies affected by postcoloniality, display hegemonic aspects that postcolonial scholars attempt, from within the academic arena, to address and correct. There is no place, from a postcolonial point of view, where to stand, which can be declared non-political. Dhvani is a special case. In and of itself, the exegetical method may be insensitive to such aspects of hegemony and oppression. However, set within a postcolonial context and used by scholars working explicitly within the field of postcolonial biblical exegesis, dhvani is used in a similar way to oppose hegemonic Western methodological claims and point towards indigenous resources for exegetical analyses.

5.4 Summary

The aim of chapter five has been to present and discuss constructive postcolonial contributions to New Testament exegesis, categorising them under two main headings: postcolonial analysis within the historical critical paradigm and postcolonial methodological approaches beyond Western historical critical discourse. The field of postcolonial exegesis is extremely diverse, as we are yet in the beginning of its development as an independent academic approach. In order to enable a fair evaluation of the contributions, it has been necessary first to establish a structured account of its achievements. It must be emphasised though, that the presentation has not aimed at a comprehensive discussion of all the diverse fields of study. Rather, the goal has been to introduce a representative cross section of some important contributions.

---

[108] Kwok points to fields of dialogue, history, and diaspora. One might add other aspects of current immediate relevance, such as environment and economy.

It will be of some help in the discussion to distinguish between perspectives and methods. Postcolonialism as an umbrella term represents what we may call a primary perspective. Within this overall perspective, we find both secondary perspectives and methods. Category one represents, to a large degree, (modified) historical critical methodologies set within the primary perspective of postcolonialism. As such, these approaches represent a kind of (embryonic and still developing) fusion between aspects of Western and Eastern epistemes. In the second category, we find both secondary perspectives and methods. For example, Dalit exegesis is set within a Dalit theological context, which does not necessarily provide a method, but rather a secondary perspective or hermeneutical key with which the texts are approached. Within this secondary perspective, a variety of methods may be used, including historical critical discourses, in the search for Dalit-inspired meaning. Both the secondary perspective and the methods used within it are embedded in the larger primary perspective of postcolonialism, which is a phenomenon within postcoloniality. A graphic representation of the relationship between these aspects may be drawn as follows.

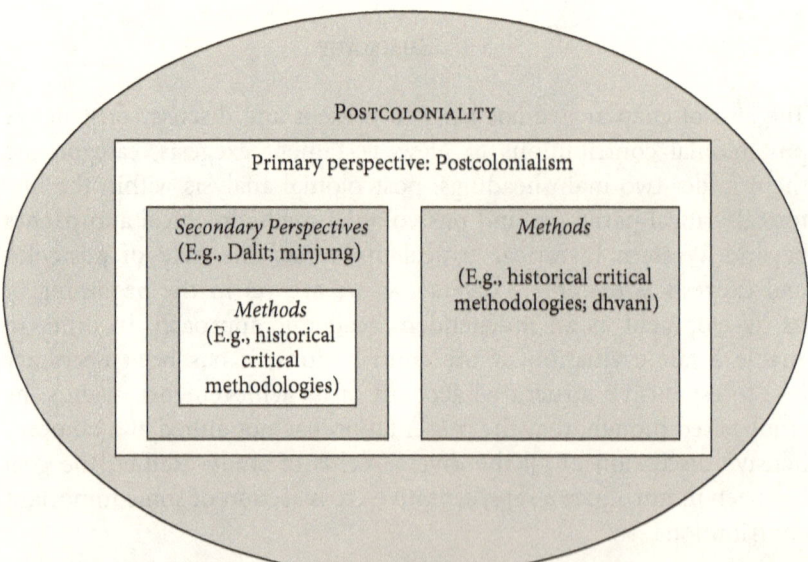

Figure 5. The relationship between perspectives and methods in postcolonial exegesis.

While 'perspective' may be defined as a *general* approach to a specific question or task using a basic hermeneutical key guiding the interpretation, 'method' is, in this study, a structured search for meaning—based on theories or unspoken assumptions of how 'things work,' embedded in the episteme and taken for granted—using *specific* questions as tools to solve a perceived problem.

Combining primary or secondary perspectives and methods lends to all postcolonial approaches a specific, basic (political) point of departure for exegetical endeavours. Issues relating to hegemony, displacement, oppression, and other consequences of postcoloniality, come to the fore.[109]

It goes without saying that there are many ways of categorising the material at hand. For example, one might consider placing Dalit and minjung exegesis in category one, since historical critical discourse may be used as part of these approaches. The choice of the present study to locate them in category two is the embeddedness of the exegetical methods used, historical or otherwise, in indigenous theological secondary perspectives.

In conclusion, what makes it possible to speak about postcolonial biblical exegesis in the midst of this diversity of approaches is the centripetal force of the primary perspective to highlight the common underlying concerns of each approach. Even an exegetical method like dhvani, which was not originally developed as a response to modern postcoloniality, may be listed among postcolonial exegetical approaches once it has been incorporated under the umbrella of the primary perspective of postcolonialism.

---

[109] Of course, non-postcolonial approaches also have primary perspectives (regardless of whether they are explicitly expressed or unconsciously at work), which are intrinsically political, including Western traditional historical critical discourse. Both that which is focused on and that which is left unsaid constitute political acts.

CHAPTER SIX

SUMMARY AND CONCLUSION: POSTCOLONIALISM AND
THE SEARCH FOR "AUTHENTIC EXEGESIS"

> Academics have never been just professionals in their field of expertise. They are also men and women of a particular generation, ethnicity, race, sexual orientation, and culture. These realities also shape—to varying degrees—the university world.[1]

We live in postcoloniality. It affects us as human beings in our everyday lives—and when we practice our profession as academics. New Testament exegesis cannot escape this reality any more than anything else in modern life. The clash and merge of epistemes, Western and Eastern, registers to different degrees on the Epistemic Richter scale, but wherever it erupts violently, as in Mizoram (in the introductory story of this work), it is not only an isolated incident but reveals a global state of affairs, a symptom of a growing concern that will, eventually, have to be dealt with by scholars in all parts of the world. We are now, it seems, at a point in history when political fantasies of universal power and global truth claims embedded in the Western episteme are falling apart as ghosts disintegrate at the crack of dawn. Postcolonialism has realised this, and by actively taking a stance in this process, exegetes prepare the ground for this to happen.

We are not, however, talking about a Hegelian development with Marxian cataclysmic revolutions, which by necessity will come and replace whatever existed before them. Rather, with a postcolonial optic, what we see is a situation where epistemes meet and results are mixed in a struggle against a variety of forms of oppression, within and beyond academia. For New Testament exegesis, and biblical studies generally, what is especially at stake is the colonially conceived, reared, and nurtured historical criticism, which currently dominates exegetical studies in the West and its former colonies, and prevents other forms of (indigenous) methodological approaches, often with an

---

[1] "Striving for Equity: Voices from Academe: How Far Have We Come? Where are We Going?" *Academic Matters* (February 2007): 3.

emancipatory agenda, from taking a place in the academic discourses and claim legitimacy.

The present study has attempted to do three things, namely, a) to locate theoretically postcolonial New Testament exegesis, b) to present, categorise, and discuss the postcolonial critique of traditional Western historical critical discourse, and c) to present, categorise, and discuss constructive postcolonial perspectives and methodological contributions.

The first task was achieved through adopting and adapting Foucault's theory of episteme in the analysis of different perceptions of reality and the relationship between different methodological discourses. Understanding exegetical approaches as part of distinct epistemes achieves a connection between 'flesh-and-blood realities' and methodologies. The purpose and meaning of a method, its 'soul,' is embodied in a discourse, which resides in an episteme. The methodological soul is never free from its epistemic body. This allows for the consideration of a variety of perceived realities and truth claims as just that: perceived truths from a certain epistemic-theoretical location. This is so despite the universalising or totalising rhetoric that may occur within a specific methodology, such as traditional Western historical critical discourse. Such rhetoric is local but thinks itself global and consequently does not fit into inter-epistemic reality. This is revealed by the postcolonial critique of Western methodologies.

Western historical critical discourse came into being during the same period that saw the birth and development of modern colonialism; colonial ideology and historical criticism have the same epistemic mother. The universalising claims of both went hand in hand as Western powers established their colonies. Through the colonial process, the Western episteme was injected into the epistemes of the colonised nations, and cemented through educational reforms in those countries. Historical critical discourse served the function of establishing the Western culture of knowledge, including biblical exegesis, as superior to indigenous interpretations, as well as non-Christian religions generally. The latter were regarded as false, and one of the strategies used to undermine local indigenous religions was to claim that their 'mythological doctrines' could not be analysed historically. Western New Testament exegesis became a tool for colonial mission.

Crucial for understanding the contemporary situation is the fact that epistemes are not static, but are constantly—slowly—changing.

SUMMARY AND CONCLUSION 129

Postcoloniality, which is defined as all reactions and consequences of colonialism, means that a movement of epistemes towards each other is taking place. This has developed over several centuries, but it is only during the last two decades that discursive similarities have multiplied to such a degree that we may speak about a merging of epistemes and the beginnings of a major paradigm shift. The emergence of postcolonialism, which is defined as an academic reaction to postcoloniality in which theories about this postcoloniality are developed, is a sign of the beginnings of such a paradigm shift.

The second task of this work, the presentation, categorisation, and discussion of postcolonial deconstruction of Western exegesis, began with an attempt to define exegesis in its historical context. The major postcolonial critique of Western exegesis may be divided into two fields, of which the first uses existing postmodern criticism of objectivism and positivism in biblical studies. Postcolonial scholars unanimously agree that objectivity is elusive and cannot be reached. However, this does not mean that all of them give up historical critical discourses. Several of the scholars discussed in the present study still argue that modified forms of historical criticism are acceptable and indeed may serve emancipatory purposes.

The second kind of postcolonial critique, which includes parameters such as orientalism, hegemony, and relevance, is more its own creation, with emphases unique to its own discourse. The combination of general postmodern critique of traditional historical criticism and specific postcolonial contributions creates an interesting situation with regard to its reception in a Western context. Postmodern critique functions as a kind of Trojan horse, with the help of which specific postcolonial perspectives are brought into the centre of Western academic discourse. Once inside the 'city,' deconstruction may take place, as well as construction of new epistemologies and methodologies. In this way, a re-making of exegesis may take place, and does take place, in which voices from the margin enter into the Western academic mainstream.

In one sense this is nothing new. The liberating element, which is fundamental to postcolonial exegesis in its opposition to the hegemony of (Western) historical criticism, was present in the very process in which historical criticism emerged on the historical scene; historical criticism was itself a liberating movement, protesting against the hegemony of the church and its exegetical primacy. The contextual parameters are to a certain degree similar. This is also one of the arguments in favour of understanding what is now happening as the beginning of a new paradigm shift.

The third task of categorising, presenting and discussing constructive postcolonial contributions to New Testament exegesis led to a need to think again about what 'exegesis' means, as well as to define 'perspective' (primary and secondary), and 'method,' and the relation between these concepts. 'Perspective' refers to a *general* approach to a specific question or text, using a basic hermeneutical key to guide the interpretation of said question or text. 'Method,' on the other hand, refers in the present study to a consciously structured search for meaning in a text, using a *specific* set of questions as tools to solve a perceived problem. Both methods and perspectives are episteme-specific; therefore methods need to be sensitive to, and adapted, to local cultures.

In present day postcolonial realities, there are seldom neat distinctions between indigenous and global Western methodologies; most often, we find a mix of methods and perspectives on the one hand and indigenous and Western-global approaches on the other. In Dalit exegesis, e.g., we find a very distinct Indian theological perspective as the general point of departure for exegetical work with the biblical texts. However, the specific methods used within the perspective may include historical critical discourse. In other words, this is one of the cases where merging epistemes become visible in the exegetical work. The overall purpose of the exegesis is, ultimately, to understand the liberating meaning of the texts. This purpose lies embedded in both the primary perspective (postcolonialism) and the secondary (Dalit theology) perspective (cf. above, figure 5).

Contrary to Dalit exegesis, dhvani exegesis had, originally, no general primary or secondary perspective in which the method was embedded. However, once scholars consciously working in postcoloniality took up dhvani, a primary perspective of postcolonialism with its overall purpose of emancipation was added to the use of the method. The context in which a method is used is crucial to how it is played out in actual interpretation. Whatever the original purpose of dhvani was, today it is used by some scholars as a postcolonial method.

In sum, it is an incontestable fact that, today, epistemic developments have taken a new turn and we see developments of discursive similarities across epistemes, and a rather rapid merging of epistemes as a

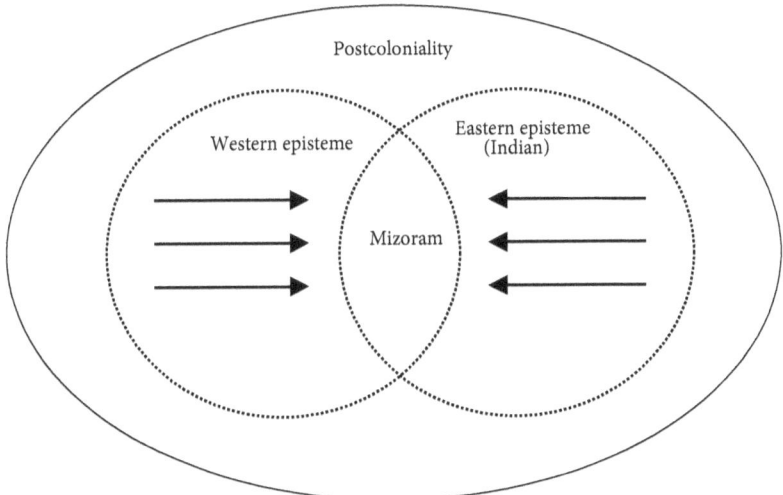

Figure 6. Understanding and illustrating the Mizoram incident.

consequence. Sometimes this process is smooth, almost indiscernible; at other times we find conscious efforts to negotiate various aspects of different epistemes to achieve the goal of understanding meaning. On yet other occasions, there are violent clashes of epistemes. All this may seem abstract and more about academic fine points than lived reality. It should not be forgotten, however, that what we have discussed in the present study, in fact, plays out in real life settings. Academia and 'flesh-and-blood realities' are, in postcolonial studies, inextricably interwoven.

Returning to the introductory story about the book-burning event in the village in Mizoram, we are now in a position to suggest answers to the questions that arose from that incident. In brief, what we see in the story may be described as a clashing/merging of epistemes, with a turbulent outcome.

When the two epistemes meet, friction appears that ignites a violent event. Other phenomena connected to the merging of the epistemes are not violent, but rather perceived as acceptable cultural changes. That the young man was sent to England to do biblical studies is an indication of a culture in which Western hegemony is pervasive, due to the colonial, missionary, and educational history in the area. Still, the result of the educative journey was intensely unexpected by the people, including the Presbyterian pastor. The merging of two epistemes was materialised in this event, a burning glass through which the epistemic beams were momentarily focused, creating a violent reaction.

Authentic exegesis, in whichever way it is constructed, is indeed a political act.

PART TWO

POSTCOLONIAL READINGS

CHAPTER SEVEN

INTRODUCTION

In PART ONE we traced the theoretical location of postcolonial studies and its critique of, and contributions to, the theoretical and methodological area of biblical studies today. In order to illustrate and exemplify the discussion of PART ONE, we shall now turn to a selection of Postcolonial interpretations of comparative interest, representing applications of postcolonial analyses on specific New Testament passages. The five articles, although not covering all of the fields that we have discussed above, are representative within their own perspective and approach. In addition to exemplifying and illustrating the above analysis, it is hoped that the reader will find these contributions to postcolonial studies critical and stimulating in ways that not only summarises what has been done, but also point forward in new and important directions.

A word on selection criteria is in order. There are many different parameters to take into account when choosing articles for a volume such as the present. One of them is to make the selection as broad as possible, which is a task hard to fulfil within a limited number of pages. My ambition has been to choose articles that will illustrate as much as possible of the methods and perspectives described in PART ONE. Further, postcolonial studies are sensitive to ethnic, cultural and other socio-religious and political parameters. The present selection has taken the following parameters into account as much as possible, although complete satisfaction in this regard has been beyond reach. a) Land of origin: the articles represent three continents (Africa, Asia and North America) and four/five countries (Botswana, USA/China, Canada and India). b) Regarding New Testament passages interpreted, there is an emphasis on the synoptic gospels: six passages from the gospels and one from the Pauline corpus (Matt 8:28–34; 15:22; 10:8, Mark 5:1–20, 4:35–41, Luke 15:30, and 1 Cor 8:1–13). While this may seem overly focused on the gospels, consideration of other parameters made such a choice preferable. The same is true for c) the aspect of gender: among the authors are one woman and four men. d) Finally, I have aimed at diversity regarding the publishers of the journals in which these articles have previously been published. SAGE Publications (USA) for Musa W. Dube, Brill (the Netherlands) for Khiok-Khng Yeo, St. Thomas Apostolic Seminary for George M. Soares-Prabhu (India), and Asian Women's Resource Centre for Culture and Theology (Sri Lanka) for George Zachariah. The fifth article by Gregory D. Wiebe is authored for the present volume.

While the present selection of studies represents key contributions to the field, there are, of course, many others of great importance. The reader is strongly encouraged to explore further publications in this rapidly expanding field; I have listed a few excellent places to continue this quest in the footnote that follows.[1]

A few words on the content of articles. In the first study, "Consuming a Colonial Cultural Bomb: Translating *Badimo* Into 'Demons' in the Setswana Bible (Matthew 8:28–34; 15:22; 10:8)," by Musa W. Dube,[2] we are introduced to the difficult question of the politics of Bible translation in the context of colonisation. Dube exegetically approaches the 'colonial bomb' produced by the use of the Setswana word *Badimo* when translating the Greek δαιμόνιον ('demon'). In Setswana, *Badimo* is a positive word referring to 'The High Ones' or

---

[1] For selections of articles on postcolonial studies and biblical interpretation see e.g., *Voices from the Margin: Interpreting the Bible in the Third World* (ed. R. S. Sugirtharajah; Maryknoll: Orbis Books, 1991, 1995 [2 d ed.] and 2006 [3d revised and expanded edition]); *Postcolonial Biblical Reader* (ed. R. S. Sugirtharajah; Oxford: Blackwell, 2006); *Reading from this Place: Social Location and Biblical Interpretation in Global Perspective* (eds. Fernando F. Segovia and Mary Ann Tolbert; 2 vols.; Minneapolis: Fortress Press, 1995); *Her Master's Tools? Feminist and Postcolonial Engagements of Historical-Critical Discourse* (eds. Caroline Vander Stichele and Todd Penner; Atlanta: SBL, 2005); *A Postcolonial Commentary on the New Testament Writings* (eds. Fernando F. Segovia and R. S. Sugirtharajah; London: T&T Clark, 2007). See also journals from the Two-Thirds World e.g., *The Bible Bhashyam, Jeevadhaara, Journal of Hispanic/Latino Theology, Journal of Asian and Asian American Theology, Journal of Theology in Southern Africa*. For a good collection focusing the second and third generation postcolonial 'hybrid' biblical scholars in North America, see *Ways of Being, Ways of Reading: Asian American Biblical Interpretation* (eds. Mary F. Foskett and Jeffrey Kah-Jin Kuan; St. Louise: Chalice Press, 2006).

[2] Other works by Dube include, e.g., *Postcolonial Feminist Interpretation of the Bible* (St. Louis: Chalice Press, 2000); "Divining Ruth for International Relations" in *Postmodern Interpretations of the Bible: A Reader* (ed. Andrew K. M. Adam; St. Louis: Chalice Press, 2001), 67–79; "'Go Therefore and Make Disciples of All Nations' (Matt 28:19a). A Postcolonial Perspective on Biblical Criticism and Pedagogy" in *Teaching the Bible: The Discourses and Politics of Biblical Pedagogy* (ed. Fernando F. Segovia and Mary Ann Tolbert; Maryknoll, New York: Orbis Books, 1998), 224–46; "Rahab Says Hello to Judith: A Decolonizing Feminist Reading" in *Postcolonial Biblical Reader* (ed. R. S. Sugirtharajah; Oxford: Blackwell, 2006), 142–58; "Readings of Semoya: Batswana Women's Interpretations of Matt. 15.21–28," *Semeia* 73 (1996): 111–29.

'Ancestral Spirits.' Dube argues that through colonial hegemony and cultural differences between colonisers and the colonised, scholars have twisted the meaning of the word in the indigenous language in ways that not only changes the sense of the word but also attacks a central aspect of the culture. This, she argues, has been part of the colonial program to transform the colonised people and the way they perceive life in order for them to conform to the new culture that is being imposed on them. In this way, the colonised themselves are made to take over and perpetuate the colonisation of their country or culture.

The reception of the translation by the people of Botswana, however, has taken another turn. Reading the Setswana Bible, people often use the written text together with their own unwritten 'canons' (indigenous tradition and culture). This creates a hermeneutic in which tradition filters the biblical text in ways creating channels through which the positive connotations of *Badimo* may reappear.

In Khiok-Khng Yeo's article, "The Rhetorical Hermeneutic of 1 Corinthians 8 and Chinese Ancestor Worship,"[3] we are introduced to Confucian philosophy as an 'inter-text' to 1 Cor 8:1–13. Yeo criticises the use of Paul for the (missionary) purpose of undermining ancestor worship in China. Applying rhetorical criticism, Yeo analyses Paul's interaction with the Corinthians regarding the question of idol meat. The traditional (metaphorical) Christian reading of this Pauline passage in China has implied a rejection of the legitimacy of ancestor worship. Nuancing the perception of ancestor worship and rereading 1 Corinthians from that perspective, Yeo explores aspects of openness in Paul's rhetoric. He draws "the hermeneutical implications of Paul's rhetoric for a new audience—the Chinese pietists who are steeped in the belief in and practice of ancestor worship." Yeo's rhetorical-hermeneutical approach is in itself part of a Western methodological context, although he takes it in new directions as he combines it with indigenous traditions.

---

[3] Other works by Yeo include, e.g., *Musing with Confucius and Paul: Toward a Chinese Christian* (Eugene, Ore: Cascade Books, 2008); "On Confucian Xin and Pauline Pistis," *Sino-Christian Studies* 2D (2006): 25–51. "Li and Law in the Analects and Galations; A Chinese Christian Understanding of Ritual and Property," *AJT*, 19:2 (2005): 309–32; What Has Jerusalem to Do with Beijing? *Biblical Interpretation from a Chinese Perspective* (Harrisburg: Trinity Press International, 1998); Chairman Mao Meets the Apostle Paul: *Christianity, Communism, and the hope of China* (Grand Rapids: Brazos Press. 2002).

In the third article, "The Demonic Phenomena of Mark's 'Legion:' Evaluating Postcolonial Understandings of Demon Possession," Gregory David Wiebe takes on the question of how scholars have interpreted the concept of 'demon' in Mark 5:1–20. He deals with traditional Western approaches as well as postcolonial scholarship, critiquing them for interpreting the text on the basis of preconceived and anachronistic conceptions of the phenomenon of demon belief. Wiebe notes that scholars tend to diagnose the Gerasene demoniac (e.g. with dissociative-identity disorder) and bundle him off as mentally ill. However, doing so is not only an implicit rejection of ancient worldviews as uninformed and superstitious, it is also a marginalisation of the vast proportion of the world's population today that acknowledges the existence of demons and therefore have access to other, and for the text more relevant, interpretive options. When such options are explored, the text makes sense in new ways, beyond Enlightenment rationalism.

The last two articles bring non-Western methodologies to the fore: the Sanskrit exegetical method of dhvani, and the real-life perspective that emerges when the Dalit experience is made into an interpretive key to unlock the biblical texts. Both approaches are related to what Kwok Pui-lan calls postcolonial imagination. As mentioned above in PART ONE, postcolonial imagination does not refer to some kind of vivid imagination leaning towards escapism. On the contrary, the postcolonial reality demands creative imagination that reaches beyond traditional Western exegetical approaches.

In Soares-Prabhu's article, "And There Was a Great Calm: A 'Dhvani' Reading of the Stilling of the Storm (Mk 4:35–41)," we are introduced to the advantages of rhetorical criticism as this method easily merges with dhvani analysis.[4] With dhvani exegesis the mind "...jolts...into a new insight into the reality compared, so that one moves through the metaphor to a new level of meaning."[5] The interpreter enters into a method based on and interacting with experience rather than expres-

---

[4] Other works by Soares-Prabhu include, e.g., Frances X. D'Sa, ed., *The Dharma of Jesus. An Interpretation of the Sermon on the Mount* (Maryknoll, New York: Orbis Books, 2003; a collection of Soares-Prabhu's works published post mortem); "Two Mission Commands: An Interpretation of Matthew 28:16-20 in the Light of a Buddhist Text," *Biblical Interpretation* (1994): 264-82; "The Historical Critical Method: Reflections on its Relevance for the Study of the Gospels in India Today," *Theologizing in India* (1981): 314-67; "The Table Fellowship of Jesus: Its Significance for Dalit Christians in India Today," *Jeevadhara* 22:128 (1992): 140-59.

[5] Soares-Prabhu, "Stilling of the Storm," 301.

sion. The article, notably, combines dhvani interpretation with historical critical analysis of the same text, with the aim of showing how dhvani may add to historical understandings of the passage. While historical criticism may reveal, technically, various levels of the narrative, dhvani analysis takes the reader to the heart of the story, from which the traditional historical critical reader is excluded.

Finally, "The Parable of the not so Prodigal Daughters: A Postcolonial Dalit Womanist Reading," by George Zachariah, offers a new understanding of Luke 15:30.[6] He brings our attention to those who are completely silenced in the text: the prostitutes whom the prodigal son visited as he travelled the world beyond his father's farm. Reading from a Dalit perspective, Zachariah highlights the conditions under which prostitutes live in contemporary society, and allows this to elucidate the cultural mechanisms underlying the biblical text.

Zachariah notes that the situation for the prostitutes in the story not only remains after the re-union between the father and the son, but is also a necessary narrative component, functioning as one of the contrasts carrying the Lukan parable. Indeed, this reading of the story puts focus on a problematic aspect that interconnects narrative and reality: the 'need' of the subjugated in society, in the biblical text, and in interpretations of the text. In this way, relevance[7] becomes intertwined with the interpretive technique itself.

The selected studies represent only a few examples of approaches in the rapidly growing field of postcolonial New Testament studies. In this field, resistance and renewal take on multiple forms, and radical dismissal of Western interpretive approaches mix and merge with interpretive techniques finding authentic value in both old and new. Still, a key unifying element is the aim of giving voice to those who are marginalised and oppressed due to colonisation past and present, within and beyond academia. It is of some importance to note, as this field grows, that when light has been shed on one aspect of the

---

[6] Other works by Zachariah include, e.g., *Alternatives Unincorporated: Earth Ethics from the Grassroots* (London: Equinox Press, 2010); "Musings on Climate Justice: A Subaltern Perspective," *JLE* 9:4 (April 2009), n.p. On line: http://www.elca.org/What-We-Believe/Social-Issues/Journal-of-Lutheran-Ethics/Issues/April-2009/Musings-on-Climate-Justice.aspx. See also Monica Jyotsna Melanchthon and George Zachariah eds., *Witnessing in Context: Essays in Honor of Eardley Mendis* (Tiruvalla: Christava Sahitya Samithi, 2007).

[7] Cf. above, section 4.3.2.3.

margins, another is still waiting in the shadows to be discovered. What we experience now is just the beginning of a long journey. As postcolonial scholarship moves towards the centre, and the centre is transformed, the field of New Testament studies will be enriched and more deeply connected to the real (global) world of which it is a part.

CHAPTER EIGHT

POSTCOLONIAL ANALYSIS, HISTORY, AND HERMENEUTICS

8.1 Musa W. Dube (University of Botswana). Consuming a Colonial Cultural Bomb: Translating *Badimo* Into 'Demons' in the Setswana[1] Bible (Matthew 8.28–34; 15.22; 10.8)[2]

Matthew 8:28–34	
²⁸When he came to the other side, to the country of the Gadarenes, two demoniacs coming out of the tombs met him. They were so fierce that no one could pass that way. ²⁹Suddenly they shouted, 'What have you to do with us, Son of God? Have you come here to torment us before the time?' ³⁰Now a large herd of swine was feeding at some distance from them. ³¹The demons begged him, 'If you cast us out, send us into the herd of swine.' ³²And he said to them, 'Go!' So they came out and entered the swine; and suddenly, the whole herd rushed down the steep bank into the lake and perished in the water. ³³The swineherds ran off, and on going into the town, they told the whole story about what had happened to the demoniacs. ³⁴Then the whole town came out to meet Jesus; and when they saw him, they begged him to leave their neighbourhood.	[28] Καὶ ἐλθόντος αὐτοῦ εἰς τὸ πέραν εἰς τὴν χώραν τῶν Γαδαρηνῶν ὑπήντησαν αὐτῷ δύο δαιμονιζόμενοι ἐκ τῶν μνημείων ἐξερχόμενοι, χαλεποὶ λίαν, ὥστε μὴ ἰσχύειν τινὰ παρελθεῖν διὰ τῆς ὁδοῦ ἐκείνης. [29] καὶ ἰδοὺ ἔκραξαν λέγοντες· τί ἡμῖν καὶ σοί, υἱὲ τοῦ θεοῦ; ἦλθες ὧδε πρὸ καιροῦ βασανίσαι ἡμᾶς; [30] ἦν δὲ μακρὰν ἀπ' αὐτῶν ἀγέλη χοίρων πολλῶν βοσκομένη. [31] οἱ δὲ δαίμονες παρεκάλουν αὐτὸν λέγοντες· εἰ ἐκβάλλεις ἡμᾶς, ἀπόστειλον ἡμᾶς εἰς τὴν ἀγέλην τῶν χοίρων. [32] καὶ εἶπεν αὐτοῖς· ὑπάγετε. οἱ δὲ ἐξελθόντες ἀπῆλθον εἰς τοὺς χοίρους· καὶ ἰδοὺ ὥρμησεν πᾶσα ἡ ἀγέλη κατὰ τοῦ κρημνοῦ εἰς τὴν θάλασσαν καὶ ἀπέθανον ἐν τοῖς ὕδασιν. [33] οἱ δὲ βόσκοντες ἔφυγον, καὶ ἀπελθόντες εἰς τὴν πόλιν ἀπήγγειλαν πάντα καὶ τὰ τῶν δαιμονιζομένων.

---

[1] The word Setswana denotes the language and culture of Botswana. The inhabitants, on the other hand, are Batswana (plural) and Motswana (singular).
[2] First published in *Journal for the Study of the New Testament* 1999; 21; 33–59.

	[34] καὶ ἰδοὺ πᾶσα ἡ πόλις ἐξῆλθεν εἰς ὑπάντησιν τῷ Ἰησοῦ καὶ ἰδόντες αὐτὸν παρεκάλεσαν ὅπως μεταβῇ ἀπὸ τῶν ὁρίων αὐτῶν.

Matthew 15:22	
²²Just then a Canaanite woman from that region came out and started shouting, 'Have mercy on me, Lord, Son of David; my daughter is tormented by a demon.'	[22] καὶ ἰδοὺ γυνὴ Χαναναία ἀπὸ τῶν ὁρίων ἐκείνων ἐξελθοῦσα ἔκραζεν λέγουσα: ἐλέησόν με, κύριε υἱὸς Δαυίδ· ἡ θυγάτηρ μου κακῶς δαιμονίζεται.

Matthew 10:8	
⁸Cure the sick, raise the dead, cleanse the lepers, cast out demons. You received without payment; give without payment.	[8] ἀσθενοῦντας θεραπεύετε, νεκροὺς ἐγείρετε, λεπροὺς καθαρίζετε, δαιμόνια ἐκβάλλετε· δωρεὰν ἐλάβετε, δωρεὰν δότε.

...the domain in which the encounter with the mission made its deepest inroads into Setswana consciousness was that of literacy and learning. Those who chose to peruse the Setswana Bible learned more than the sacred story, more even than how to read. They were subjected to a form of cultural translation in which vernacular poetics were re-presented to them as a thin *sekgoa* narrative—and their language itself reduced to an instrument of imperial knowledge.[3]

Introduction:
Language and the Art of Colonizing Minds and Spaces

Because colonizers tend to install their languages among the colonized, thus displacing the local ones, the subject of language is central to post-colonial debates.[4] Questions such as why do the colonizers give their languages to their subjects? What happens to the languages of the colonized? What exactly is lost when the colonized begin to speak, read and write in the colonizer's language and neglect their own

---

[3] Jean Comaroff and John Comaroff, *Of Revelation and Revolution: Christianity, Colonialism and Consciousness in South Africa, I* (Chicago: The University of Chicago Press, 1991), 311.
[4] See Bill Ashcroft, Gareth Griffiths and Helen Tiffin (eds.), *The Post-colonial Studies Reader* (London: Routledge, 1995), 285–314.

languages?⁵ The question, What strategies are adopted by the colonized to resist the imposition of the colonizer's language?⁶ remains central to postcolonial debates. Frantz Fanon, a postcolonial critic of the sixties, addressed the issue of language back then. Fanon opened his book, *Black Skin White Masks*, with a chapter on 'The Negro and Language,' where he stated that he 'ascribe[s] a basic importance to the phenomenon of language,'⁷ for to speak a language is not only to use its syntax or to grasp its morphology, but it is 'above all to assume a culture, to support a civilization.'⁸ Thirty years later, Ngugi wa Thiongo, one of the present-day postcolonial critics, echoes Fanon when he maintains that 'language carries culture, and culture carries...the entire body of values by which we come to perceive our place in the world.'⁹ Their statements speak for themselves insofar as the imposition of the colonizer's language on the colonized and the loss of their own languages is concerned. The colonized, who speak, read and write in the colonizer's language adopt the culture of their subjugators. They begin to perceive the world from the perspective of their subjugators. In this way, the colonizer takes possession of the geographical spaces and the minds of the colonized. The imposition of the language of the colonizer is thus an effective instrument for colonizing the minds of the subjugated, for it alienates them from their own cultures. On these grounds, Ngugi holds that

> the biggest weapon wielded and actually daily unleashed by imperialism against that collective defiance [of the colonized] is the cultural bomb. The effect of a bomb is to annihilate a people's belief in their names, in their languages, in their environment, in their heritage of struggle, in their unity, in their capacities and ultimately in themselves.¹⁰

Ngugi describes colonization as a violent undertaking that proceeds by demolishing the cultural world views of the colonized. The suppression of their cultures 'makes them want to see their past as one wasteland of non-achievement and it makes them want to distance themselves from

---

⁵ See Frantz Fanon, *Black Skin White Masks* (New York: Grove Weidenfeld, 1967), 17–40, and Ngugi wa Thiongo, *Decolonising the Mind: The Politics of Language in African Literature* (London: James Curry, 1986), 4–33.
⁶ Bill Ashcroft, Gareth Griffiths and Helen Tiffin, *The Empire Writes Back: Theory and Practice in Post-Colonial Literatures* (New York: Routledge, 1989), 38–59.
⁷ Fanon, *Black Skin*, 17.
⁸ Fanon, *Black Skin*, 17–18.
⁹ Thiongo, *Decolonising*, 16.
¹⁰ Thiongo, *Decolonising*, 3.

that wasteland.'¹¹ Describing the violence of colonialism on native cultures, Fanon holds that 'Every colonized people—in other words, every people in whose soul an inferiority complex has been created by death and burial of its local cultural originality—finds itself face to face with the language of the civilizing nations.'¹² Fanon equates colonization with the 'death and burial' of one's culture. Fanon also regards the suppression of colonized cultures as a means to an end: it leaves the colonized confronted by the culture or the language of their subjugator. It serves, therefore, to clear the way for the implantation of the colonizers' language or culture.

Evidently, the explosion of the colonial cultural bomb shatters and alienates the colonial subjects from themselves, their lands and their cultures. But, more importantly, cultural colonization has ensured that the colonizers remain in power regardless of whether geographical and political independence has been won by the colonized, or not. It ensures that the institutions of the colonized are generally permeated by the colonizer's world view, for the colonized subjects themselves embody the values of their subjugator and become the instruments of their own colonization. Language, which is the crucible of culture, is the effective instrument that constructs the colonized subject, as imitators, devotees and ambassadors of their oppressors, but, of course, not as equal subjects. This structural construction of the colonized subjects has indeed ensured that long after the colonizer's departure and absence from the former colonies, their domination is freely furthered by the colonized on themselves.¹³ It is also this aspect of colonialism that makes postcolonial reading of texts a necessary exercise in what seems to be a largely post-independence era.

In this paper, I will examine the use of language to colonize from a slightly different angle. Most postcolonial debates focus on the imposition of the colonizer's language on the colonized, its impact on the colonized and the strategies of resistance, but I will examine the use of

---

[11] Thiongo, *Decolonising*, 3.
[12] Fanon, *Black Skin*, 18.
[13] The use of language in postcolonial contexts is not only limited to the imposition of the colonizer's language on the colonized. Many postcolonial writers have shown that colonizers are highly dependent upon language to claim, describe and mark foreign lands and people as their own. The representation of foreign lands and people that legitimates their subjugation in the colonizer's literature is accomplished through language. See Elleke Boehmer, *Colonial and Postcolonial Literature* (Oxford: Oxford University Press, 1995).

the languages of the colonized to subjugate them. I will be examining 'the colonization of local language[s]'[14] such that they no longer serve the interest of their original cultures, but indeed, become weapons that victimize the original speakers. This examination will look at the translations and definitions of words in the Setswana Bible and dictionaries, which were first carried out by London Missionary Society (henceforth LMS) agents between 1829 and 1925.[15] The first Setswana Bible and dictionary were subsequently revised by many other LMS agents and church missionaries of other societies. This paper will limit itself to the LMS work, for it was the most influential among Batswana who reside in the present-day Botswana. Although this paper will be specific to Botswana, I believe that such an investigation will be of interest to many other former colonized subjects who read colonial biblical translations and interpretations.

In assessing the colonization of the Setswana language, I will focus on the biblical and dictionary translations and definitions of 'Ancestors' (*Badimo*), 'doctor' (*Ngaka*), 'diviner' (*Ngaka ya ditaola*), 'demons and devils' (*mewa e e maswe*), terms that are all somewhat related to the divine arena. I will pay attention to the time and ideology that informed their renderings as well the readers themselves. The Bible and dictionaries are treated together for they are closely interconnected: the dictionaries drew their vocabulary from the Setswana Bible. They were also produced by the same institution and personalities. Second, I will highlight the response of the colonized, for a planted colonial cultural bomb may explode, but the scattering fragments of the colonized subjects continue to proclaim their existence even in their fragmentation. Indeed, to consume a colonial cultural bomb, or anything, is also an attempt to take power over something: it is a dangerous gesture of resistance. My exposition begins with my own story as a colonized subject and how I came to discover colonizing translations of the Setswana Bible only four years ago—after at least twenty years of personal and academic biblical reading.

---

[14] See Comaroff and Comaroff, *Of Revelation*, 218–20.
[15] See Alexander Sandilands, *The History of The Setswana Bible* (Cape Town: Bible Society of South Africa, 1989). Robert Moffat first translated the Gospel of Luke in 1829, completed the New Testament in 1840 and the whole Bible in 1857.

How I Discovered *Badimo* Dressed in the Skins of Demons

I was lucky to do my graduate studies during the reader age, when the theories of a neutral and expert reader had been sufficiently disputed in biblical studies. Taking advantage of this spirit, I returned home from my First World graduate school to read the Bible 'with' Batswana women readers for my dissertation. I wanted to collect interpretations of Mt. 15.21–28 and Jn 4.1–42 by women of African Independent Churches (henceforth AICS).[16] These are readers with very low or no literacy skills, hence I decided to find a Setswana and Kalanga Bible for my field work.[17] I chose the local languages since most people with low levels of literacy can at least read or listen to their own languages.

Thus I first went to the Botswana Bible Society to buy Bibles. I found Alfred J. Wookey's Bible of 1908. Wookey's Bible was an upgraded version of Robert Moffat's Bible of 1857.[18] Wookey's Bible has remained the most popular version among Batswana ever since its first printing. The recent 1992 Morolong Bible, which was produced by a group of Batswana, has yet to establish itself against Wookey's Bible of 1908. The second one was Sandilands' Setswana New Testament, which was launched in 1957 and was completed in 1970. The latter was sanctioned for the centenary celebration of Robert Moffat's first Setswana Bible of 1857. The Sandilands version was accomplished through a number of Setswana scholars such as Moabi Kitchen. It is readable, for it is written in the orthography of the Setswana language of the present-day Botswana. Wookey's Bible, on the other hand, uses an old orthography and its Setswana language is a mixture of Sesotho and Sepedi, which are languages spoken in South Africa and Lesotho. The latter languages are different from the Setswana language spoken and written in present-day Botswana. It therefore made sense that I should use Sandiland's s Centennial New Testament version. I also bought *Ndebo Mabuya*, a Kalanga Gospel of Matthew.

---

[16] See Musa W. Dube, "Readings of *Semoya*: Batswana Women's Interpretations of Matt. 15.21–28," *Semeia* 73 (1996): 111–29, for some of the published account of their readings.

[17] Kalanga is one of the many Bantu languages spoken in Botswana. It is different from Setswana and much closer to Shona, a language spoken in Zimbabwe.

[18] I had no access to Robert Moffat's original Bible in Botswana national archives and LMS related institutions. It is currently displayed in Kuruman, South Africa.

Armed with biblical texts written in the languages of my respondents, I began my fieldwork. But as soon as my Setswana speaking respondents heard me read from Sandiland's version, they said, '*O ko o mphe Baebele yame hoo. Eo ga ke utlwe sentle,*' that is, 'Let me get my own Bible. I do not properly understand the Bible you are reading.' And yet this was the Bible written in our present day Setswana language! What they brought out was Wookey's Bible. Here one must imagine a present day English reader who maintains that they understand the King James Version better than contemporary versions. Similarly, when I read out *Ndebo Mbuya* to my Kalanga respondents, my listeners/readers said, '*Anto iwa. Ma ditole Baele yangu,*' that is. 'I cannot understand that Bible. Let me get my own.' Once again, they brought Wookey's Bible with its foreign and difficult Setswana language. This was particularly amazing, for most elderly Kalanga people are not good Setswana speakers. Moreover, most Kalanga speakers take great pride in their language, and they do not like to speak Setswana, which is our national language. In the case of these Kalanga readers, one must imagine a present-day non-English speaker who insists that s/he can understand the King James Version much better than modern English versions. While I had thought my respondents would welcome their own languages and understand them better, I had grossly miscalculated. My respondents had a close intimacy with Wookey's Bible, and reasonably so, for it had been the main Bible among Batswana for the past eighty years.

I must say I had always known that in many AICs in Botswana the South African languages, which were first used to translate the Bible, had become languages of worship. Many non-Sotho and non-Ndebele speakers of Botswana preach and pray in these languages once they enter church. Nonetheless, I did not expect readers/hearers to insist on these languages even when their own languages are now available in written forms. This, however, is a graphic example of what depending on a language other than your own at an institutional level can do to a reader. These AICs readers can rightfully be said to be regionally colonized.

I went back to the Botswana Bible Society and bought Wookey's Bible for my fieldwork research. But here a minefield awaited me. I had trodden on dangerous and deadly ground. I found out that where the Canaanite woman said, 'My daughter is severely possessed by demons,' in Mt. 15.22, it was translated '*morwakiake o chwenwa thata ke Badimo.*' That is, 'my daughter is severely possessed by the High

Ones or Ancestors.' I was stunned. The word *Badimo* literally means the 'High Ones' or 'Ancestral Spirits' in Setswana cultures. *Badimo* are sacred personalities who are mediators between God and the living in Setswana cultures. They consist of dead members of the society and very old members of the family who are attributed divine status and sacred roles. *Badimo* hold the welfare of their survivors at heart, both at individual and community level. They bless the living and make sure that they are well provided for and successful in their plans. They also punish those who neglect their social responsibilities and taboos, by removing their protective eye and leaving the concerned individual or society open to the attack of evil forces. In addition, the institution of *Badimo* serves as the centre of social memories or history of the society. For an oral people, the role of *Badimo* as an institution of social memories cannot be overemphasized. *Badimo* are the thread which connects the present society and families with their past and directs them to the future, for here the people of the past are kept alive and actively involved in the events of contemporary society.[19] *Badimo* therefore are sacred beings who regulate the norms of the society and ensures its stability or health. Yet here, in Wookey's Setswana Bible of 1908, the *Badimo* had been translated into 'demons' and 'devils.'[20]

But this late discovery on my part begs an explanation. If Wookey's Bible had been in circulation for more than 80 years and had remained the main Bible until four years ago, why had I not known that *Badimo* were devils and demons in the Setswana Bible despite my long years of reading the Bible? The answer to these questions points to my own colonization, which involved both church and academic structures. To begin with my educational story: although I went to the so-called Setswana medium schools, all the subjects were taught in English except for the Setswana language itself. Like most students who undergo this

---

[19] Paul Stoller, *Embodying Colonial Memories: Spirit Possession, Power and the Hauka in West Africa* (London: Routledge, 1995), illustrates these roles quite well.

[20] Although I had no access to Robert Moffat's original Setswana Bible, secondary sources trace the translation of *Badimo* into 'demons' to him. See, for example, Comaroff and Comaroff, *Of Revelation*, 218. Further, Alfred J. Wookey, does not use the word *Badimo* for demons in the translated text of Matthew in his commentary, *Phuthololo Ea Efangeleo e e Kwadilweng ke Mathaiao* (Tiger Kloof: LMS Book Room, 2nd edn, 1902). He uses 'modemona/Bademona' the hybrid word derived from 'demon/s.' But he uses the word *Badimo* to refer to demons when he comments on the verses (see p. 54). This suggests that the use of *Badimo* for demons, which Wookey maintained in his 1908 Bible, can be traced to Moffat himself, as attested by other secondary sources.

national system of education, by the time I finished high school I found it easier to read and write in English than in Setswana. The problem of being a slow Setswana reader was further compounded by the fact that the circulating local Bible was written in a foreign Setswana and an old orthography. Further, my mother language is Ndebele and not Setswana. I could not be bothered to read Wookey's Bible, which was the only complete Setswana Bible then. It follows that I used English Bibles.

When it came to church, my fellowship was primarily among the middle-class, educated young people, who felt more at home preaching and praying in English than in Setswana. In contrast to the AICs, who are largely of low class and low level of education, who use Sesotho and Ndebele/Zulu as their holy languages, English was the language of worship in my church. So when I returned from the USA, aware of my colonized biblical methods and schools of interpreting the Bible, I was determined to read the Bible 'with Batswana women' of the AICs. Thus I bought my first Setswana Bible. I rightly imagined AICs readers to be slightly insulated from colonial institutions and strategies of reading, since they are the resisting readers who historically walked out of the colonial missionary-founded churches to start their own.[21] They walked out of these churches to read the Bible and worship God from their African cultural perspectives. AICs' Christian practitioners are also renowned for holding on to African cultural world views and infusing them with Christian perspectives. And yet, I discovered *Badimo* sadly dressed in the skins of demons and devils in their favourite biblical text.

THE SETSWANA BIBLE AND THE COLONIZATION OF THE SETSWANA LANGUAGE

In my shock, I turned to other passages in Matthew to confirm my disbelief. I found the story of Jesus and the demoniac of Gadarene (Mt. 8.28-34). There I found our sacred *Badimo* scared in front of another divine being: they trembled and begged Jesus to leave them alone, to spare them or at least to cast them out to the pigs (vv. 29-31). And

---

[21] See John B. Ngubane, "Theological Roots of the AICs and their Challenge to Black Theology," in *The Unquestionable Right to Be Free: Black Theology from South Africa* (ed. Itumeleng Mosala and Buti Tlhagale; New York: Orbis Books, 1992), 71-100.

150   CHAPTER EIGHT

Jesus cast the *Badimo* out, sending them into pigs that ran away and drowned in the sea (v. 32). Here was a textual burial of *Badimo*! I turned to the commissioning of the disciples in Mt. 10.1–15. There I found Jesus instructing the disciples to go out, preach, heal and 'cast out *Badimo*,' (v. 8). This reading experience was chilling to say the least. My reading moment itself was a violent experience which accelerated my heartbeat. The text exploded, shattering the very centre of my cultural world view. It invited me to see myself and my society as people who had believed in and depended on the demons and devils before the coming of Christianity. Could there be any more evidence for the dark and lost continent of Africa than the one I was reading in this Setswana Bible?[22] It is important to name this translation, its aims, and how it achieves its purposes.

In this translation, the roles of Badinio are reinvented: *Badimo* are equated with demons and devils, when any Motswana reader expects them to be friends with Jesus, or with divine powers. The translation is a minefield planted in the Setswana cultural spaces, warning every Motswana Christian believer and reader of the Bible to stay away from the dangerous and deadly beliefs of Setswana. It marks boundaries and designates the Setswana cultures as a 'dangerous, devil and death zone,' to be avoided at all costs. The translation invites us, the Batswana biblical readers, to distance ourselves from *Badimo*, the demons, and to identify ourselves with Jesus, a Christian divine power. It achieves its aims through literary techniques of writing and characterization. The characterization maintains Jesus' holy role, but *Badimo* are given a new role, that of demons. The Comaroffs are correct to note that 'Moffat's use of *Badimo* ("ancestors") to denote "demons"...did violence to both biblical and conventional Tswana usage.'[23] Be that as it may, the Christian tradition hardly lost anything central to its faith in this translation, while the Setswana tradition lost its very centre. The

---

[22] This colonial strategy of characterizing the colonized in a particular way and then creating evidence to support the claims has been called the 'retrospective consent,' that is, 'subject people be subjugated first and then be assumed to have consented to their enslavement' (see Edward Said, *Culture and Imperialism* [New York: Alfred A. Knopf, 1993], 107). See also Michael Taussig, *Shamanism, Colonialism and the Wild Man: A Study in Terror and Healing* (Chicago: University of Chicago Press, 1987), who documents how colonizers first characterized natives of South America as cannibals and then forced them to eat human flesh. In this way, the savagery of the colonized can be concretely documented in the diaries and letters of the colonizer. The same ideology underlines the translation of *Badimo* as 'demons' in the Setswana Bible.

[23] Comaroff and Comaroff, *Of Revelation*, 218.

translation is, therefore, a structural device of alienating natives from their cultures, or what Ngugi describes as the colonizing art of making the colonized 'see their past as one wasteland of non-achievement and... want to distance themselves from that wasteland.'[24] Who, indeed, would not want to distance her/himself from demons and devils?

At this stage of my reading, I was an adequately educated biblical scholar, who could consult the Greek New Testament texts and lexicons for the 'original' meanings of words. I was also sufficiently conscious of the politics of interpretation or translation. Yet I could not help but wonder about the masses, the oral readers who read or hear only the Setswana Bible. It was hard to avoid thinking about the Setswana readers/hearers who first read the Setswana Bible in 1857 and those who continued to read it for the next 150 years that followed: Did these Setswana readers/hearers discover their own *Badimo* as devils and demons? Did the written Setswana Bible prove to them that they were lost and knew no God, so much so that they venerated demons and devils as sacred beings? The implications and impact of these translations cannot be overemphasized for readers who were originally non-literate. As Tiffin and Lawson note, 'it is when the children (in both senses) of colonies read such texts and internalize their own subjection that the true work of colonial textuality is done.'[25] The construction therefore portrayed Setswana perspectives as evil powers, in order to promote the Christian and English world view as the necessary light. But who were these translators and what kind of era informed their thinking?

Reading the Translated Time and the Time Translator

In 1840 Robert Moffat completed his Setswana New Testament translation and in 1857 he finished translating the Hebrew Bible. In 1908 Wookey produced the enduring revised version of Moffat's Bible. In 1870 John Brown compiled a Setswana dictionary, which drew most of its words from Moffat's Setswana Bible. He produced its revised version in 1895. His son Tom J. Brown brought forth an upgraded

---

[24] Thiongo, *Decolonising*, 3.
[25] Chris Tiffin and Alan Lawson, eds., *De-scribing Empire: Post-colonialism and Textuality* (London: Routledge, 1994), 4.

version in 1925. The latter remained the main dictionary until 1993, when Z. I. Matumo's version was published. What is significant in these dates is that the translations were carried out between the last half of the nineteenth century and the First World War. The latter half of the nineteenth century was the height of the British empire, a time when the certainty of the empire seemed unquestionable. The First World War, however, heralded the revolt of the colonized voices, a period that has stretched to the nineties. How is this colonizer–colonized power struggle reflected in the Setswana Bible translations and dictionaries?

As the first writer of Setswana, Moffat's achievement was undoubtedly outstanding. Yet as the Comaroffs tell us,

> those who chose to peruse the Setswana Bible learned more than the sacred story, more even than how to read. They were subjected to a form of *cultural translation* [emphasis mine] in which vernacular poetics were re-presented to them as a thin *sekgoa* narrative—and their language itself reduced to an instrument of imperial knowledge.[26]

The Comaroffs use the word *sekgon* with a small 's' to describe the way European colonizing agents constructed themselves in the colonial frontiers against native cultures.[27] Moffat, the Browns and Wookey were missionaries who built schools, hospitals and churches for the natives. Yet their work was actively involved in the construction of '*sekgoa* narrative.' In short, they were men of their time and place: a time of European imperialism and a time of the glory of the British empire. They were also well placed at the colonial frontier of Southern Africa. Accordingly, colonizing ideology found its way into their written accounts of Setswana language. As their translations of *Badimo* attest, they indeed 'reduced Setswana to an instrument of imperial knowledge.' Their translations seized the symbols that are central institutions of Setswana cultures and equated them to the evil powers.

I know that many have defended, and still vigorously defend, missionaries of colonial times, separating them from other colonizing agents and showing how they built schools, churches and hospitals for the natives; how they were often spokespersons for the natives against other colonizing agents of their time. Missionaries were certainly different from other colonial agents such as traders and politicians.

---

[26] Comaroff and Comaroff, *Of Revelation*, 311.
[27] Usually Sekgoa defines white Europeans (particularly the British) and their cultures.

This difference, however, does not exempt most, if any, missionaries of colonial times from the game of colonizing. What such arguments tend to overlook is that there are 'diverse forms of the colonizing cultures.'[28] In fact, missionaries of colonial times did not have to regard themselves openly or consciously as advancing the rule of their countries to be part of the colonizing squad, although many did. Missionaries of colonial times were inevitably colonizing agents. That is, if we agree that missionaries were people who 'set out to save Africa [and other continents]: to make people the subjects of a world wide Christian commonwealth,' we should also agree that 'in so doing they were self-consciously acting out a new vision of global history, setting up new frontiers of European consciousness, and naming new forms of humanity to be entered onto its map of the civilized mankind.'[29] To establish any form of world wide 'commonwealth'—be it Christian, economic, political, social, ideological, environmental, military—always involves the suppression of cultural differences and the imposition of a few universal standards. It involves the promotion of certain powerful centres and the creation of some satellites cultures. Its establishment is accomplished through such institutions as schools, hospitals and trade centres, which become the crucibicle that proclaims and disseminates the colonizer's consciousness and finally establishes the institutions of the colonizer over against the native ones. These very institutions, which many missionary defenders are quick to remind us 'civilized' or helped us, are the most important part of colonizing minds and spaces. Moffat, Wookey and the Browns' work, for example, looks like an immense service to Batswana. Yet when put in its context, when its intentions are interrogated, and when its contents are examined, one realizes that their tasks were carried out to serve the establishment of a 'world wide Christian commonwealth,' and that such a task entailed the 'death and burial' of Setswana cultures in order to '[set] up new frontiers of European consciousness.'

The Colonization and Decolonization of Setswana in the Dictionaries

As I have said, the compilation of the Setswana dictionary was interconnected with the Setswana Bible. The first dictionary was compiled

---

[28] Comaroff and Comaroff, *Of Revelation*, 313.
[29] Comaroff and Comaroff, *Of Revelation*, 309.

in 1870 by John Brown and it was followed by revised versions in 1895, 1925 and 1993. The 1995 Morulanganyi Kgasa and Joseph Tsonope[30] dictionary was the first to be produced outside LMS religious institutions. How, then, was the Setswana language colonized in these dictionaries'? Can we also detect the forces of resistance and decolonization in these dictionaries? To answer these questions, I will comment on the structures, contents and definitions of words in the dictionaries.

To begin with the first question, both the first Setswana Bible and the first dictionary marked the beginning of the reconstitution of the Setswana language for services other than those of Batswana. Setswana was being transformed from an oral to a written language. Its written form, however, was designed to serve institutions other than those of Batswana. It served primarily in the mission schools, hospitals, church and colonial trade centres. These institutions set themselves against the local ones and competed with or replaced the established institutions of Batswana, such as *Bogwera* (boys school), *Bojale* (girls school) and *Bongnka* (healing institutions).[31] The written Setswana form was an instrument of disseminating a worldwide Christian commonwealth, European trade systems, European medical and educational practices; by extension, it was employed to suppress its own cultural institutions.

Second, the structural organization of Brown's dictionary itself is instructive. The dictionary is divided into two parts. In the first part, its entries follow an English-Setswana language format: it lists English words first and explains them in Setswana, then in English again. In the second part, the dictionary entries follow a Setswana-English format, listing Setswana words and explaining them in English. This structural organization presupposes readers who have an English vocabulary and who are looking for the meaning of their words in the Setswana language. These will be foreign English readers who have some interest in Batswana. Even though we can posit native Batswana readers, the dictionary portrays them as anglicized Batswana who will only read their language with and through the English language. On

---

[30] See Morulanganyi Kgasa and Joseph Tsonope, *Tlhanodi ya Setswana* (Gaborone: Longman, 1995).
[31] See Comaroff and Comaroff, *Of Revelation*, 206–38. The competition of local and missionary institutions of health and education were intense and are well documented among various writers.

POSTCOLONIAL ANALYSIS, HISTORY, AND HERMENEUTICS 155

the issue of the intended readers, Tom J. Brown's introduction to his 1925 edition is explicit:

> The Revs. John Brown and Alfred Wookey gave to their share of the work many years of willing service, in the hope that it would prove useful to all Europeans, who were desirous of acquiring a knowledge of the Secwana language, and also to such Becwana[32] as were seeking to gain an acquaintance with English.[33]

Further, the structural arrangement of the dictionary itself symbolically captures the colonization of the Setswana language. The very placement of Setswana side by side with English structurally indicates that, as a language, Setswana no longer stands by itself. It is now a language that is enveloped by English. Moreover, English takes priority over it, since it is the language that is listed first and covers more space. Such a structural organization largely remained with us from 1870 to 1995, when A. Kgasa and J. Tsonope's *Tlhanodi ya Setswana* appeared.

Third, the colonization of the Setswana language is evident in the definitions ascribed to the listed words and the content of words in the different parts of the dictionary. To illustrate the former point I will look at the definition of *Badimo* and *Ngaka*, and some related words. Here we will see how the language itself was reduced 'to an instrument of imperial knowledge' and agendas. The definition of the word *Badimo* and its centrality to Setswana cultures has already been explained above. *Ngaka* in Setswana cultures is a diviner-herbalist. *Ngaka* is not only a physician, rather, his/her role is priestly for s/he mediates between the living and the divine powers, *Badimo*. *Ngaka* is in touch with *Badimo* on behalf of the society on issues of their welfare. Both *Badimo* and *Ngaka* are, therefore, central to Setswana religious thinking. Let us now look at how the dictionaries define these words. I will chronicle the words according to the order of publications available to me.

---

[32] Please note that it took a while before the spellings became standardized. Thus Botswana was often spelt Becwana, Bechwana or Bechuana(land). Setswana was also spelt Secwana, Sechwana and Sechuana.

[33] Tom J. Brown, *Secwana Dictionary: Secwana-English and English-Secwana* (Tiger Kloof: LMS Book Room, 1925), iii.

Contents and Definitions in John Brown's Dictionary of 1895

In the first part of Brown's dictionary, 'Ancestors' is defined as *Bagolo*,[34] which means 'elders.' 'Ancestral Spirits' is not listed. Under the word 'Spirit' Brown has a sub-entry of the phrase 'evil spirits.' According to Brown, the definition of 'evil spirits' in Setswana is *badimo*.[35] Coming to the word 'diviner-herbalist,' Brown lists the word 'diviner' and defines it as *moloi*, which means 'wizard' or 'sorcerer.' He then lists the word 'divination' and explaines it as *too*, which means the practice of *boloi* or witchcraft.[36] He also lists the word 'doctor' and correctly defines it as '*naka (ngaka)*;[37] *moalahi*. To doctor, *alaha*; to protect a person from danger, *upelela*'.[38] It is significant that in the English part of the dictionary, Brown does not list the words 'demon,' 'devil' and 'Satan,' a point which I will return to below.

Turning to the second part of Brown's dictionary (the Setswana part), the word *Badimo* is listed and flatly defined as 'evil spirits.'[39] Although he lists the word *moea*, 'spirit,' he does not list the phrase *moea oo maswe*, or 'evil spirits.' He also lists the word *modemona*, a hybrid word, drawn from 'demon.'[40] The words *diabolo* and *satane*, hybrid words from devil and Satan, are not listed. The word *Ngaka* or *naka*, meaning 'doctor,' is not listed. The word *naka* is defined simply as 'a pipe of dagga.'[41] But the reader realizes that Brown knows that *naka* also means 'doctor,' for he defines 'doctor,' in the English part of his dictionary, using this word. What, then, is the significance of resisting to identify *naka* as a doctor in the Setswana part of the dictionary? This question will be clearer below.

With these definitions, Brown has subverted the Setswana language for imperial ends. If he wished to be fair to the Setswana language and culture, he could have defined the word 'Ancestors' as both *bagolo*

---

[34] John Brown, *Secwana Dictionary: English-Secwana and Secwana-English* (Tiger Kloof: LMS Book Room, 1895), 25.
[35] John Brown, *Secwana Dictionary*, 203.
[36] See John Brown, *Secwana Dictionary*, 78, for the definitions of both 'diviner' and 'divination.'
[37] Please, note that *naka/ngaka*, meaning 'doctor,' is another reflection of the fluidity of spelling before its current stabilization.
[38] John Brown, *Secwana Dictionary*, 79.
[39] John Brown, *Secwana Dictionary*, 253.
[40] John Brown, *Secwana Dictionary*, 374.
[41] John Brown, *Secwana Dictionary*, 391.

and *Badimo*. But in both parts of the dictionary, Brown categorically states that *Badimo* are evil spirits. A diviner is also a *moloi* or wizard. A *ngaka* who is also a diviner in Setswana cultures is thus identified as an agent of the evil powers for English readers and Christianized Batswana. The omission of *Ngaka* in the Setswana part of the dictionary thus becomes clear: it is a categorical dismissal of his/her status. It is a denial that a doctor exists in Setswana cultures. Brown's refusal to recognize a diviner-herbalist as a doctor can be explained since we know that he defines a diviner as *moloi*, or wizard. Since a *Ngaka* is not only a physician but also a diviner with spiritual roles in Setswana cultures, Brown identifies him/her as a *moloi*; a real doctor is only the European type.

Turning to the contents, it is significant that Brown omits the words 'Satan,' 'devil' and 'demon' in the English part of the dictionary. This is particularly notable for a dictionary produced in a religious institution and whose main purpose was to evangelize the natives. The omission implies that the role of negative spiritual powers is played only by *Badimo* and found only in Setswana cultural thinking. The presentation purges English language or culture of any knowledge of evil and pushes evil powers onto Setswana cultures. Here we glean a '*sekgoa* narrative' that is, the imperial construction and marketing of English (language) as a civilized, humane and Christian culture, over against colonized cultures that only appear as devilish, childish and savage. This construction is glaringly attested to by the fact that Brown lists the hybrid word *modemona* in the Setswana part of the dictionary, while he does not list its proper form, 'demon,' in the English part of the dictionary. The omission that infomed this '*sekgoa* narrative' reflects the thinking of the time and is well captured by Josiah Young's words of 1885. Young, a missionary of colonial times and at the height of British empire, confidently said,

> Is there room for reasonable doubt that this race...is destined to dispossess many races, assimilate others, mold the remainder, until in a very true and important sense it has Anglo-Saxoned mankind. Already English language, saturated with Christian ideas, gathering up into itself the thought of all ages is the great agent of Christian civilization throughout the world, at this moment molding character of half the human race.[42]

---

[42] Josiah Strong, "Josiah Strong on the Anglo-Saxon Destiny, 1885," in Louis Synder (ed.), *The Imperialism Reader: Documents and Readings in Modern Expansionism* (New York: D. Van Nostrad Company, 1962), 123.

Young's eulogy of Anglo-Saxons displays no conflict between his Christian faith and the values or impact of imperialism on other races. The Anglo-Saxons' project of dispossessing, assimilating and moulding foreign nations into Anglo-Saxons does not bother him as a missionary. The mentality that freely dispossesed Batswana of their cultural agency can be fairly understood within this framework of thinking. But what is even more instructive here is Young's perception of English as a language and a culture. Young describes English as a language 'saturated with Christian ideas' and 'the great agent of Christian civilization.' The English language is almost identical to Christianity in Young's description, which is why he finds the conversion of the world into Anglo-Saxon unproblematic. His words reflect the *'sekgoa* narrative' behind the dictionary entries that purged the English language of demons, devils and Satan, while it constructed a Setswana counter culture, which is characterized as a realm of negative spiritual powers.

Turning to the local informants, it is inconceivable that any Motswana of Moffat, Brown and Wookey's day could have defined *Badimo* as evil spirits and a *Ngaka* as a *moloi*, for the welfare of individuals and the society as a whole hinged and revolved on the loving care of *Badimo* and *Ngaka*. Another point which makes it very unlikely that Setswana informants could have likened demons to a diviner-herbalist and *Badimo* pertains to the fact that a *Ngaka* does not get spirit possessed or lose control at any point of her/his professional duties. In short, 'Setswana did not include a tradition of possession or ecstasy.[43] Although Ancestral Spirit possession is found in some Southern African cultures (Nguni, Shona), among Batswana speakers *Badimo* do not make their houses in people such that they lose control.[44] A *Ngaka*, performs all her/his duties fully composed, even when s/he consults the divine powers in Setswana cultures. It is also difficult to imagine that Moffat and Brown, who, together with other LMS agents, had been working among Batswana for at least fifty years, would have grossly misunderstood this particular aspect of Setswana cultures: the central aspect. What we are reading here is, therefore, a planted colonial cultural bomb, a cultural landmine. It is a deliberate design, aimed

---

[43] See Comaroff and Comaroff, *Of Revelation*, 239.
[44] Yet even among some Nguni groups, where Ancestral Spirits come and temporarily take possession of living human beings and speak their desires and give advice through them, they cannot be equated to demons, for evil spirits are institutionally debarred from possessing people.

at exploding away the cultural validity of Setswana cultural spaces for the purposes of furthering a world wide Christian commonwealth. It was a cultural landmine that marked Setswana cultural spaces as dangerous death zones to be totally avoided by Batswana Christian readers of the Bible. The establishment of a Christian commonwealth together with the accompanying European hospitals, schools and trade necessitated this strategy for, unless the colonial missionaries defined other worlds as realms of evil, danger and death, it would be hard to justify their agenda. Brown's dismissal of Setswana cultures as a realm of evil spirits and wizards indeed reflects his time: he compiled his work at the height of the British empire, when the imperial success seemed indisputable. This was a time when the so-called 'savages' and 'children' of colonies seemed destined to remain under the tutelage of the colonizer, but World War I would usher in a different era.[45]

Structure, Content and Definitions in Tom J. Brown's Version

Tom J. Brown's revised version of the Setswana dictionary was published in 1925, just after World War I. This was a time when the confidence of the empire was beginning to be shaken, both from inside and outside. The devastating war was a rude awakening that forced the colonizers to question their own civilization, for it graphically revealed that they were not at all purged of demonic, satanic and demonic spirits. The war had torn the thin veil of '*sekgoa* narrative' apart and showed that there were evil spirits in the civilized continent of Europe. In addition, many colonized subjects began to insist on their autonomy. It would take several decades for most colonized countries to attain their political and geographical independence, but the ball had begun to roll. As we shall see, Tom J. Brown's dictionary reflects both the colonization of language and the tremors of decolonization in its structure, content and definitions of words.

To begin with the structure of the dictionary, there is a notable change. Whereas John Brown's dictionary begins with entries for English words, Tom Brown begins with Setswana words! While John Brown's dictionary is entitled *Secwana Dictionary: English-Secwana*

---

[45] These images are very common in the colonial literature. A good example here is Rudyard Kipling's poem, 'The White Man's Burden.'

and Secwana-English, the latter is entitled *Secwana Dictionary: Secwana-English and English-Secwana*. Nonetheless, the Setswana words are still defined in English. The Setswana language is still intertwined with English and is without an independent life of its own. When we look at the definitions of *Badimo* and *Ngaka* similar changes are discernable.

To start with the word *Badimo*, Tom Brown defines it as follows: 'Spirits. Used generally of both good and bad spirits, but principally the latter.'[46] He also lists the word *Naka [Ngaka]* and explains it as follows: 'a doctor; a witch doctor; a heathen doctor of any description.'[47] In the second part of the dictionary (the English-Setswana part) Tom Brown lists the word 'Ancestors,' and, like the former Brown, translates it as *Bagolo; bagolwane*, meaning elders.[48] Here the word is stripped of its Setswana religious tones. He also lists the word 'Spirit' and explains it as 'departed spirits, *badimo*.'[49] It is notable that in the latter entry he has striven to be neutral by leaving out the qualifiers bad or good. Tom Brown also lists the words 'doctor,' 'diviner' and 'divination.' The word 'doctor' is defined as follows: 'A healer, *moalahi*; a native doctor, *mophekodi, naka; naka ea sedupi; naka ea moupo*; a rain doctor, *moroka*; a witch doctor, *naka; moloi*.'[50] Divination is to practice '*go laola ka bola; go diha boitsaanape*. (*Nape* is one of the Secwana demi-gods).[51] In short, divination is the art of getting in touch with *Nape*. Tom Brown goes on to define a diviner, as a *Moitseanape* which is a compound word made of *moitse* (one who knows) and *Nape*, the Setswana divine power.[52] It means one who knows or who is in touch with *Nape*. When one looks back to his first section of Setswana, one finds that he defines the word *Motseanape* as follows: 'A diviner; a soothsayer; one familiar with Spirits; one who works divination; a magician.'[53]

In Tom Brown's definitions we very much sense a colonial mentality that dismisses the local cultures and equates them with evil: *Badimo* are primarily 'evil spirits'; *Ngaka* is still a 'witch-doctor and heathen doctor of any description' and a diviner is a magician. But

---

[46] Tom J. Brown, *Secwana Dictionary*, 13.
[47] Tom J. Brown, *Secwana Dictionary*, 234.
[48] Tom J. Brown, *Secwana Dictionary*, 345.
[49] Tom J. Brown, *Secwana Dictionary*, 547.
[50] Tom J. Brown, *Secwana Dictionary*, 401.
[51] Tom J. Brown, *Secwana Dictionary*, 401.
[52] Tom J. Brown, *Secwana Dictionary*, 400.
[53] Tom J. Brown, *Secwana Dictionary*, 205.

something has begun to happen. Tom Brown, unlike his father, lacks that categorical dismissal of Setswana cultures 'as perfect specimens of absolute error, masterpieces of hell's invention, which Christianity was simply called upon to oppose, uproot and destroy.'[54] Here Tom Brown acknowledges *Badimo* as Spirits who have goodness. He acknowledges that there is a Setswana doctor, although he proceeds to qualify it from his colonizing perspective. A gleam of light is also discernable in his definitions of doctor, diviner and divination. The Setswana religious world view no longer appears as an absolute realm of evil spirits, demons and wizards.

The contents of Tom Brown's dictionary also reflects a different era. Like the former Brown, he lists the hybrid word *modemone* and explains it as 'a demon.'[55] He also omits *diabolo* and *satane*, hybrid words from 'devil' and 'Satan.' But unlike the former Brown, Tom J. Brown includes the words 'demon' and 'devil' in the English Bible. He defines them as '*moea o o mashwe*' (evil spirit) and '*moea o o mashwe; oa ga Dinwe*': (evil spirit; the spirit of an ogre)[56] respectively. This inclusion reflects the tremors of decolonization that were beginning to shake the confidence of the empire in the post-World War I era.

Structure, Content and Definition in Z. I. Matumo's Version

Although Z. I. Matumo's *Setswana English Setswana Dictionary* of 1993 was still produced within LMS institutions, it was the first full-fledged revision of Tom J. Brown's edition by a Motswana. The preface states that 'the whole of the earlier dictionary has been reviewed' and that 'there has been a careful study of definitions and a revision of grammatical apparatus in terms of the current understanding of the language.'[57] As its title indicates, there is a change: the title privileges the local language, suggesting that English is now enveloped by Setswana. The title, however, is not matched by structure and contents for they still follow Tom J. Brown's arrangements of Setswana-English

---

[54] William H. Gairdner, *An Account and Interpretation of the World Missionary Conference* (London: Oliphant & Ferrier, 1910), 137.
[55] Tom J. Brown, *Secwana Dictionary*, 198.
[56] Tom J. Brown, *Secwana Dictionary*, 395, 392.
[57] Derek Jones, 'Preface,' in Z. I. Matumo, *Setswana English Setswana Dictionary* (Gaborone: Macmillan, 1993), viii.

and English-Setswana categories (maybe in terms of the number of Setswana words and definitions). The Setswana language still does not have an independent life. As his definitions of words will show, Matumo is at once a decolonizing and colonized subject, like most postcolonial subjects.

How then did Matumo define the words *Badimo* and *Ngaka*? To begin with the former, Matumo defined *Badimo* as follows: 'spirits; ancestors, ranging from one's parents who are alive to the dead and long forgotten ones; believed to influence or control events.'[58] *Ngaka* is defined as 'a doctor; a witch doctor; a physician; one who holds the highest university degree in any faculty.'[59] *Moloi*, on the other hand, is a 'wizard; a witch; a poisoner; one who acts treacherously.'[60] The hybrid words of *Modimona, Diabolo, Satane* are not listed. Turning to the English part of his dictionary, Matumo lists the word 'Ancestors' and defines it as *'bagologolo; badimo*: the ancestors have responded, i.e. have heard people's prayers.'[61] A diviner is defined as '*Ngaka ya sedupe; moitseanape*,' which means 'a diviner-herbalist, a clever person.'[62] A doctor is defined as 'a healer, *moalafi, mophekodi; Ngaka ya moupo*; rain doctor, *moroka*; a witch doctor; *ngaka ya Moloi*.'[63] Following his predecessor, he lists the words 'devil' and 'demon,' but not 'Satan.' The devil is defined as '*mowa o o maswe*,' that is, evil spirits.[64] The word 'demon' is defined in the same way.[65]

What is significant in Matumo's definitions? To begin with *Badimo*, his definition is a world apart from the Browns' definitions, who first defined *Badimo* as evil spirits and then as primarily evil spirits. In Matumo's definitions *Badimo* are part and parcel of Setswana family and society, ranging from the living to the dead. *Badimo* includes one's parents. In his English definition, Matumo does not suppress the religious meaning of *Badimo*, by simply defining the word as elders or ancient people. Rather, Matumo brings out its religious meaning by pointing out that these are sacred figures who answer prayers in Setswana cultures.

---

[58] Matumo, *Setswana*, 10.
[59] Matumo, *Setswana*, 281.
[60] Matumo, *Setswana*, 259.
[61] Matumo, *Setswana*, 463.
[62] Matumo, *Setswana*, 505.
[63] Matumo, *Setswana*, 506.
[64] Matumo, *Setswana*, 501.
[65] Matumo, *Setswana*, 499.

A significant aspect is also discernable in his definition of *Ngaka*. Matumo outlines a number of types of doctors, defining them according to their speciality or qualifications as healers, rainmakers, diagnosers of problems and PhD holders. Matumo acknowledges that a doctor who tends to forget that his/her task is to save or enhance life and uses his/her knowledge to bring harm is also to be included. Such a doctor would be called a 'witch doctor.' But in Matumo's dictionary, a *Ngaka* is by no means identical to a *moloi* or a 'witch doctor' as in the previous dictionaries. A wizard or *moloi* is one whose role is absolutely evil and his/her role is a world apart from the Setswana *Ngaka*, the diviner-herbalist.

Further, in Matumo's definition evil powers are distinct from powers of good. The evil powers consist of demons and the devil found in the English vocabulary and *moloi* found in the Setswana language. These are not identical to *Badimo* and *Ngaka*, or the diviner as we have seen in the previous dictionaries. With these definitions, Matumo has made significant strides towards decolonizing Setswana.

Matumo's efforts to decolonize the Setswana language have been continued by M. Kgasa and J. Tsonope's Setswana dictionary of 1995. The latter not only redefined the words according to Setswana understanding, but also restructured the dictionary. Unlike all other dictionaries that came before, the Kgasa and Tsonope dictionary does not treat the Setswana language side by side with English. For the first time, the Setswana language earned the right to stand by itself, after over a century (125 years) since the first dictionary appeared. This structural change is the most significant contribution of the Kgasa and Tsonope dictionary in the decolonization of the Setswana language.

Consuming the Colonial Cultural Bomb: Strategies of Resistance

As a colonized subject whose daily bread was that of consuming a different form of colonial cultural bomb (reading the English Bible and the Greek Bible), the cultural death of AICs Setswana Bible readers seemed certain to me. I could not see how they could ignore the fact that *Badimo* are negative spiritual powers in the Setswana Bible. Further, most AICs readers are hardly literate and have little or no way of researching the 'original' Greek meanings, or reading for themselves about the historical background that gave us the New Testament.

What was given to them is what they received: It is the Word of God. AICs certainly marched out of missionary-founded churches, protesting against the white-only church leadership and preaching roles in colonial times. They started their own churches in search of autonomy, yet they still depended on the missionary Bible, for they had no financial power or academic skills to initiate their own Bible versions. Yet as I soon found out during my fieldwork research, they were not helpless consumers of the colonial cultural bomb. They managed to harness and redirect the energy of a destructive bomb for their own wellbeing. They did not observe the colonial boundaries that marked Setswana cultural spaces as a 'no-go dangerous death zone.' Instead, the readers rolled on minefields, detonating them with their methods of reading; namely, by divining through the Bible, reading the Spirit and through the Spirit, telling and retelling the text but hardly interpreting.[66] While these methods are closely interconnected, I will focus on the method of divining through the Bible as a decolonizing strategy that reasserts the Setswana cultural agency.[67]

In Setswana cultures, divining is the skill of a trained diviner-herbalist (*Ngaka*) who throws down a divining set to diagnose individual and community problems, their causes and solutions. The set can contain a minimum of four pieces, which represent key social relationships on their own, with the designs drawn on them and with the patterns they form in their fall, that is, their relationship to one another once they have been thrown down and with the directions they face. What a diviner-herbalist reads in the process of diagnosis is a combination of these aspects of the set.[68] The point here is that a Setswana diviner-herbalist uses the divining set to get in touch with *Badimo*. They are asked to reveal the problem, the causes and the solutions through

---

[66] See Dube, 'Readings,' 111–29, for a detailed account of reading a Spirit canon and through the Spirit, and of the telling and re-telling of the biblical texts among AICs readers. The former method was captured by Virginia Lucas, one of my respondents, who said, 'when God spoke to me through the Spirit, God never opened the Bible' (114).

[67] Some Africans who first heard biblical reading and preaching immediately regarded it as divination. See Comaroff and Comaroff, *Of Revelation*, 229.

[68] See Musa W. Dube, "Divining the Texts for International Relations (Mt. 15.21–28)," in Ingrid Kirtzberger (ed.), *Transformative Encounters: Jesus and Women Reviewed* (Leiden: E. J. Brill, 2000), for more details on divination among Botswana and as a method of reading the Bible. See also, Phillip M. Peek (ed.), *African Divination Systems: Ways of Knowing* (Indianapolis: Indiana University Press, 1991).

the divining set. Among the AICs, church leaders are also faith healers, who are consulted for various health issues. Instead of divining through the traditional set, they use the Bible. The structural similarities of the church and traditional institutions are evident in the healing practices and roles of spiritual leaders.[69] In a study where G. C. Oosthuizen focused on AICs' faith-healers, he found that 'there are a few who do not have this double-barrel approach, but none reject diviners, or oppose them.'[70] Oosthuizen's respondents, who were themselves faith-healers, had this to say about their work: '[I] work under the power of the Holy Spirit but the Ancestors may be consulted'; another one said, 'I...always start working as the prophet and if nothing happens then I would apply everything which a diviner would use because I am using both,' and another one held that 'I use *impepho* to dream and then the ancestors visit me; the cords on me fight illness and keep demons away. Then the Holy Spirit comes...'[71] These quotes from one study attest to a phenomenon that has been widely documented by AICs scholars; namely, that AICs freely draw from the Christian and African traditions in their business of maintaining life.

Accordingly, my arrival in AICs church compounds for field work research, on days and times when the worship service was not on, was often regarded as my wish to consult a faith-healer for her/his healing services. Thus when I was brought before them they treated me like any other consulting client: they handed me a closed Bible, asked me to hold it with my two hands, to open it and to hand whatever passage I opened to them. The business of healing was on! Had I complied, they would have diagnosed my life through reading whatever passage I happened to open. In Setswana cultural thinking good health is almost equivalent to healthy relationships and success, while ill health is also closely associated with unhealthy relationships and misfortune. To divine one's life, therefore, they would examine one's relationships: the unhealthy and healthy ones. Depending on what the

---

[69] That AICs' theological practices draw from both Christian and African traditions is widely documented by scholars of these churches. AICs recognize Jesus and pay allegiance to African Ancestors at the same time. There are a few exceptions, but generally scholars agree that they are 'syncretistic.' See Gerhardus C. Oosthuizen. *The Healer-Prophet in Afro-Christian Churches* (Leiden: E. J. Brill, 1992), 165–93.
[70] Oosthuizen, *The Healer-Prophet*, 167.
[71] Oosthuizen, *The Healer-Prophet*, 166–67.

passage reveals, through the help of divine powers, who are indispensable partners in these reading sessions, a problem is identified and solutions are advanced.

This usage of the Bible and method of reading is stunningly subversive to colonizing narrative designs. The AICs' readers resist the translation that turned *Badimo* into demons and devils in the Setswana Bible, the '*sekgoa* narrative' that constructed Christian and Setswana traditions as opposites. Instead, they perceive the Bible from their own cultural perspectives as a book that diagnoses relationships and promotes the healing of relationships between people and the divine powers. Insofar as it is a book that detects bad relationships and recommends solutions that build for good relationships between people and divine powers, Batswana AICs readers see no difference between the biblical aims and their religious thinking. They see the Bible as a divining set. Hence once they were in control of biblical interpretation in their own churches, the Bible took its rightful place as one among many other divining sets. *Badimo* and Jesus/Holy Spirit also took their rightful place as divine powers that promoted good relationships and health in communities where the Bible is read. This AICs strategy of resistance entailed a method of reading the written Setswana language through and with the unwritten text of Setswana cultures. In short, while colonial missionaries took control of the written 'Setswana,' they could not take control of the unwritten Setswana from the memories of Batswana readers and hearers. In this way, the Batswana AICs readers resurrected *Badimo* from the colonial grave site where they were buried; they detonated the minefields planted in their world views and reclaimed their cultural worlds as life-affirming spaces.

Conclusion

In this article, I have examined the Setswana biblical and dictionary texts, the age that informed its authors-readers (missionaries), how they reflect the colonization of the Setswana language and the methods of resistance adopted by Batswana readers and writers. I have treated translation and definitions of words as an interpretation, which allows us to see how the Setswana language was reconstructed for imperial ends. Missionary literary works of translation have been shown to be heavily engaged in the colonization of the minds of natives and for advancing European imperial spaces. The death and burial of Setswana culture here was primarily championed through the colonization of their language such that it no longer served the interests of the original speakers. Instead the written form of language had equated their cultural beliefs with evil spirits, demons and wizardry. This colonization of Setswana was in itself the planting of a colonial cultural bomb, meant to clear the ground for the implantation of a worldwide Christian commonwealth and European consciousness. It was a minefield that marked Setswana cultural spaces as dangerous death zones, to be avoided by every intelligent Motswana reader or hearer of the translated text. Here, as elsewhere, we realize that

> imperial relations may have been established initially by guns, guile and disease, but they were maintained in their interpellative phase largely by textuality, both institutionally and informally. Colonialism (like its counterpart, racism) then, is an operation of discourse, and as an operation of discourse it interpellates colonial subjects by incorporating them in a system of representation. They are always already written by that system of representation.[72]

But as much as Batswana readers swallowed a colonial bomb for over a century and walked over cultural minefields, they also developed methods of resistance. The Setswana Bible that was once used to champion the degradation of *Badimo*, became now one of the divining sets, used to get in touch with *Badimo* and Jesus among the AICs' Bible readers. This method of reading among the AICs resists the suppression of diversity and cultivates liberating interdependency between the Christian and Setswana world views. It reads two canons simultaneously: the written and unwritten Setswana canons. The approach tears away the colonizing strategy that translated *Badimo* into evil spirits and demons in the Setswana Bible. But above all, divining through the Bible is a method that reconciles the divine with the divine: *Badimo* and Jesus are friends at last as they should be.[73]

---

[72] Tiffin and Lawson (eds.), *De-scribing Empire*, 3.
[73] I am grateful to Tiro Sebina, Seratwa Ntloedibe, Peter Mikwisa and Andrew Chebanne at the University of Botswana, my colleagues who read this article and gave me constructive feedback. *Leka muso bagaetsho!*

8.2 Khiok-Khng Yeo (Garrett-Evangelical Seminary, USA/ Beijing University, China). The Rhetorical Hermeneutic of 1 Corinthians 8 and Chinese Ancestor Worship[74]

1 Corinthians 8:1–13

¹Now concerning food sacrificed to idols: we know that 'all of us possess knowledge.' Knowledge puffs up, but love builds up. ²Anyone who claims to know something does not yet have the necessary knowledge; ³but anyone who loves God is known by him. ⁴Hence, as to the eating of food offered to idols, we know that 'no idol in the world really exists', and that 'there is no God but one.' ⁵Indeed, even though there may be so-called gods in heaven or on earth—as in fact there are many gods and many lords—⁶yet for us there is one God, the Father, from whom are all things and for whom we exist, and one Lord, Jesus Christ, through whom are all things and through whom we exist. ⁷It is not everyone, however, who has this knowledge. Since some have become so accustomed to idols until now, they still think of the food they eat as food offered to an idol; and their conscience, being weak, is defiled. ⁸'Food will not bring us close to God.' We are no worse off if we do not eat, and no better off if we do. ⁹But take care that this liberty of yours does not somehow become a stumbling-block to the weak. ¹⁰For if others see you, who possess knowledge, eating in the temple of an idol, might they not, since their conscience is weak, be encouraged to the point of eating food sacrificed to idols? ¹¹So by your knowledge those

[1] Περὶ δὲ τῶν εἰδωλοθύτων, οἴδαμεν ὅτι πάντες γνῶσιν ἔχομεν. ἡ γνῶσις φυσιοῖ, ἡ δὲ ἀγάπη οἰκοδομεῖ·
[2] εἴ τις δοκεῖ ἐγνωκέναι τι, οὔπω ἔγνω καθὼς δεῖ γνῶναι·
[3] εἰ δέ τις ἀγαπᾷ τὸν θεόν, οὗτος ἔγνωσται ὑπ' αὐτοῦ.
[4] Περὶ τῆς βρώσεως οὖν τῶν εἰδωλοθύτων, οἴδαμεν ὅτι οὐδὲν εἴδωλον ἐν κόσμῳ καὶ ὅτι οὐδεὶς θεὸς εἰ μὴ εἷς.
[5] καὶ γὰρ εἴπερ εἰσὶν λεγόμενοι θεοὶ εἴτε ἐν οὐρανῷ εἴτε ἐπὶ γῆς, ὥσπερ εἰσὶν θεοὶ πολλοὶ καὶ κύριοι πολλοί,
[6] ἀλλ' ἡμῖν εἷς θεὸς ὁ πατὴρ ἐξ οὗ τὰ πάντα καὶ ἡμεῖς εἰς αὐτόν, καὶ εἷς κύριος Ἰησοῦς Χριστὸς δι' οὗ τὰ πάντα καὶ ἡμεῖς δι' αὐτοῦ.
[7] Ἀλλ' οὐκ ἐν πᾶσιν ἡ γνῶσις· τινὲς δὲ τῇ συνηθείᾳ ἕως ἄρτι τοῦ εἰδώλου ὡς εἰδωλόθυτον ἐσθίουσιν, καὶ ἡ συνείδησις αὐτῶν ἀσθενὴς οὖσα μολύνεται.
[8] βρῶμα δὲ ἡμᾶς οὐ παραστήσει τῷ θεῷ· οὔτε ἐὰν μὴ φάγωμεν ὑστερούμεθα, οὔτε ἐὰν φάγωμεν περισσεύομεν.
[9] βλέπετε δὲ μή πως ἡ ἐξουσία ὑμῶν αὕτη πρόσκομμα γένηται τοῖς ἀσθενέσιν.
[10] ἐὰν γάρ τις ἴδῃ σὲ τὸν ἔχοντα γνῶσιν ἐν εἰδωλείῳ κατακείμενον, οὐχὶ ἡ συνείδησις αὐτοῦ ἀσθενοῦς ὄντος οἰκοδομηθήσεται εἰς τὸ τὰ εἰδωλόθυτα ἐσθίειν;

---

[74] First published in *Biblical Interpretation* 2:3 (1994): 294–311.

weak believers for whom Christ died are destroyed. ¹²But when you thus sin against members of your family, and wound their conscience when it is weak, you sin against Christ. ¹³Therefore, if food is a cause of their falling, I will never eat meat, so that I may not cause one of them to fall.	[11] ἀπόλλυται γὰρ ὁ ἀσθενῶν ἐν τῇ σῇ γνώσει, ὁ ἀδελφὸς δι' ὃν Χριστὸς ἀπέθανεν. [12] οὕτως δὲ ἁμαρτάνοντες εἰς τοὺς ἀδελφοὺς καὶ τύπτοντες αὐτῶν τὴν συνείδησιν ἀσθενοῦσαν εἰς Χριστὸν ἁμαρτάνετε. [13] διόπερ εἰ βρῶμα σκανδαλίζει τὸν ἀδελφόν μου, οὐ μὴ φάγω κρέα εἰς τὸν αἰῶνα, ἵνα μὴ τὸν ἀδελφόν μου σκανδαλίσω.

Christian missionaries have used 1 Corinthians 8 to deal with the issue of ancestor worship in Chinese church history. Missionaries such as William Martin, Young Allen, and Timothy Richard took a compromising and tolerant position—a minority position. Most missionaries, both Protestants and Roman Catholics,[75] prohibited the ritualistic practice of ancestor worship on the grounds that ancestor worship is rooted in filial pietism, a religious exercise in which the Chinese are unintentionally offering food to idol-demons instead of to their ancestors. Since worship is to be rendered to God alone, for "God is One" (1 Cor. 8:6), can one say that ancestral worship is idolatry? How are we going to suggest alternative responses from Paul's rhetoric and theology in 1 Corinthians 8? How are we going to imitate Paul rhetorically?

---

[75] Protestant missionaries were represented, for example, by those of the "China Inland Mission" between 1807 and 1860. Other protestant missionaries holding the same position prior to 1860 include Walter Henry Medurst and John L. Nevius, and even present day mainline protestant churches in Asia take this line. Cf. Ro Bong-rin ed., *Consultation on Christian Response to Ancestor Practices, Christian Alternative to Ancestor Practices* (Taichung, Taiwan: Asia Theological Association, 1985), 45-80; W. A. P. Martin, "The Worship of Ancestor—A Plea for Tolerance," in *Records of the General Conference of the Protestant Missionaries of China Held at Shanghai* (1890), 619-31; idem, "How Shall We Deal with the Worship of Ancestors?" in *Chinese Recorder* 33 (1902), 117-19; and idem, "The Worship of Confucius: is it Idolatry?" in *Chinese Recorder* 34 (1904), 92-93.

The Jesuits, represented by Matteo Ricci, held a compromising position towards ancestor worship at the end of the 16th century. But the 17th century Dominicans and Franciscans held the opposing view which (coupled with the issue of the translation of "God") eventually led to the proscription of Jesuit missionary work. For more on the various responses to ancestor worship, see Henry N. Smith, "A Typology of Christian Responses to Chinese Ancestor Worship," in *JES* 26 (1989), 628-47.

Because of the significance of ancestor worship in Chinese culture and the lack of Christian response to this issue,[76] this paper seeks to respond from a rhetorical-hermeneutical perspective. Thus, the purpose of this paper is twofold: first, it seeks to observe how Paul interacts with the Corinthians rhetorically over the issue of idol meat;[77] second, the paper attempts to transmit the hermeneutical implications of Paul's rhetoric for a new audience—the Chinese pietists who are steeped in the belief in and practice of ancestor worship.

Paul's Rhetorical Interaction with the Corinthians

A rhetorical study of 1 Corinthians 8 would begin with the reconstruction of the rhetorical situation.[78] The three interlinking issues that are relevant to the rhetorical analysis of this pericope are: (1) the social environment which gives rise to the dissensions and their theologies; (2) the occasion for eating idol-meat (temples, market-place, homes or social clubs); (3) the audience hypotheses and their identities: the knowledgeable "Gnostics" and the "weak-conscience" ones. Here I will focus on the identities of the "strong" and the "weak." The "strong" are the proto-gnostics who are influenced by the Hellenistic Jewish thought prominent in the Wisdom tradition and the writings of Philo.[79] These proto-gnostics hold that knowledge is divinely given by God or by his consort sophia to make one wise, righteous or perfect.[80] These gnostics believe they are undefileable by the idols because of the knowledge they have (8:1) and their belief that "an idol is nothing in the world" (8:4b). The weak, however, abstain themselves from eating the idol meat because: (a) they believe that idols are real; (b) their past association with idols convinces them that idols are real and that to eat idol food now is to relapse into the previous guilty experience. The gnostics want to demonstrate their divine knowledge, their power and spirituality. The weak refuse to eat the idol food because their experience informs them that eating idol food will defile their bodies and

---

[76] Most of the Christian scholarly material is mentioned in the previous footnote.
[77] The first part of the discussion below is a summary of a larger section in my Ph.D. dissertation, "Rhetorical Interaction in 1 Corinthians 8 and 10: Potential Implications for a Chinese, Cross-Cultural Hermeneutic" (Ph.D. diss., Evanston: Northwestern University, 1992), 282–332.
[78] See my "Rhetorical Interaction in 1 Corinthians 8 and 10," 117–241.
[79] "Rhetorical Interaction in 1 Corinthians 8 and 10," 189–241.
[80] 6 Cf. Wisd. 7:17; 10:10; Quod Deus 92; Op. 70–71.

thus betray Christ. For Paul, the questions arising out of this conflict of stasis concern knowledge (theology) and love (ethics). As we will see, the best approach for Paul is not to judge, or to praise or blame one party, but to "talk it over" with them.

Rhetorical Disposition of 1 Corinthians 8

The genre of 1 Corinthians 8 is deliberative and has the following rhetorical structure: (a) the *exordium* of 8:1 a in which Paul secures the attention of his audience and hints at the desired goal of his rhetoric. (b) Paul states clearly the desired goal of the discourse by which he desires to persuade/dissuade in the *propositio* (or thesis) of 8:1b: "Knowledge puffs up, but love builds up." (c) In the *proof* (or *confirmatio*) of 8:2–10, Paul advances his argumentation regarding what is honorable, edifying, and right as he, the rhetor, speaks for the many voices of the congregation. (d) In the *epilogue* (or *peroration* or *conclusio*) of 8:11–13, Paul restates with all possible force factors that are alluded to in the *exordium* and factors that are adduced or developed in the proof for the purpose of urging the audience into the right course of understanding and action. The response of Paul in vv. 10–13 reveals his view that knowledge without love is destructive to the weaker brothers and disastrous to the salvific work of Christ. Verse 13 is an exhortation by personal example to the gnostics (i.e., the knowers in the congregation), who have no other choice but to practice their knowledge with love for their brothers/sisters.

Rhetorical Techniques Used in Argumentation

Vv. 1–6 1 Cor 8:1–3 reminds the audience of chaps. 1–4 of the contrast between the knowers and Christ. In the light of the distinction between "spiritual" (πνευματικός) and "unspiritual" (ψυχικός) in 1 Corinthians 2, the former claim to have a gnosis that the latter do not possess. That is, πάντες γνῶσιν ἔχομεν ("we all have knowledge") is used by the gnostics to claim knowledge for themselves exclusively. In v. 7 Paul clarifies that οὐκ ἐν πᾶσιν ("not all") have the knowledge the gnostic congregation claims to have. The Corinthian gnostics claim that "we know that we all have knowledge." But Paul quotes them and considers himself as one of the "we" in οἴδαμεν ("we know") used by the Corinthians. The "we" Paul uses is inclusive of himself and the weak in the community.

By partially quoting the Corinthians' slogan in the first five verses, Paul has gained strong footage in his persuasion. It is a way of gaining attention from the audience also, letting them know their argument has some validity. But Paul does not just quote, he also clarifies. In 8:1 b for example, he states his position: ἡ γνῶσις φυσιοῖ ἡ, δὲ ἀγάπη οἰκοδομει ("knowledge puffs up, but love builds up"). Note that γνῶσις and ἀγάπη are not exclusive of each other, but this antithetical parallelism indicates a contrast in the fundamental understanding between Paul and the Corinthian gnostics. The contrast between φυσιόω ("puff up") and οἰκοδομέω ("build up") is significant. Φυσιοῖ ("it puffs up") is a kind of inflating, boasting with the purpose of putting down or hurting, "against one another" (as indicated in 1 Cor 4:6, κατὰ τοῦ ἑτέρου). This thesis (8:1b) pinpoints the heart of the matter: puffing up in knowledge or building up with love.

"Love" is the positive quality which describes one's inclusive and mutual relationship with God and with other people through the death of Christ. Love therefore is a willed relationship which demands that one be considerate for another's benefit without any boasting, inflating, or destructive motive.[81] Paul persuades by attempting to alter (in 8:2–3) the static cognitive argument of the gnostics into a dynamic affectional relationship, from knowledge of God to being known by God. Paul gives the gnostics' view a correction: knowing in the sense of self-edification means that one does not really know; but if one is known by God as God elects and redeems, one really knows.

In *v. 5a*, Paul paraphrases (he does not quote) the argument of the Corinthian gnostics and smoothly extends it with a hymn in v. 6. The Oneness-Lord-Creator God is affirmed by both the audience and the rhetor. But the cosmological and redemptive motifs of the person Jesus Christ appear in the hymn in a subtle way. An initial look at the creed in v. 6 suggests the idea that it merely reinforces the gnostics' argument. It is in fact purposely used to set up the Pauline argument of creation *and redemption*; Paul's argument is "God created all, he is one; but note Christ redeems all. Therefore do not be a stumbling block!"

V. 7 In verse 1 the gnostics assert that they have γνῶσις. Here Paul says οὐκ ἐν πᾶσιν ἡ γνῶσις ("not all have the knowledge"). Verses 1 and 7 sound contradictory. But rhetorically they are not: in v. 1 Paul

---

[81] Cf. Rom. 13:10, 14:15, 1 Cor. 14:1, Gal. 5:13, Phil. 2:1–3.

accepts the gnostics' claim of knowledge, whereas in v. 7 he explains to them that not all have the knowledge they claim.

Vv. 8-9 In the light of the reconstruction of the gnostics' theology of knowledge and monotheism, I surmise that the gnostics' edification campaign for the weak is probably a strategy to persuade the weak to eat idol food so that they might overcome their weak conscience. In that sense, βρῶμα ἡμᾶς παραστήσει τῷ Θεῷ ("food will bring us to God"). However, Paul reverses their argument by adding οὐ before the παραστήσει. Paul has shown already the negative effect of idol food on the weak in 7b. Now in 8b he elucidates his reasoning on the effect of βρῶμα to the gnostics: οὔτε ἐὰν μὴ φάγωμεν ὑστερούμεθα, οὔτε ἐὰν φάγωμεν περισσεύομεν ("we are no worse off if we do not eat, and no better off if we do").

The final self-justification by the gnostics for their course of action is seen in the word ἐξουσία they use in v. 9. For the gnostics, knowledge means the right to act in freedom, because freedom is self-realization in the realm of the divine (monotheism). For Paul, however, love is the giving up freely of one's right for the sake of the other because of the creative and redemptive works of God and Christ (monotheism).

Vv. 10-13 The key word of the gnostic argument is ἐξουσία ("authority/right"), but Paul formulates the result of their ἐξουσία: ἐξουσία ("right") without ἀγαπή ("love") equals πρόσκομμα ("a stumbling block"). To convince them fully of his logos (argument), Paul is going to use the following rhetorical devices:

(a) a rhetorical question,[82] which includes a pedagogical dialogue in v. 10, with the change from a plural to a singular "you," σε.[83] Paul also seems to be turning to an imaginary interlocutor.[84] The rhetorical technique is probably not a diatribe. In any case, the function of the rhetorical question is twofold: it recapitulates the issue discussed above; and it acts as *proserotonta*, i.e., it puts questions as to the rhetorician's strongest point and the opponent's weakest point.[85] According

---

[82] Cf. Heinrich Lausberg, *Handbuch der literarischen Rhetorik: Eine Grundlegung der Literaturwissenschaft* (2 vols.; Munich: Max Heuber, 2nd edn 1973), 1:379-84.

[83] Papyrus 46 B F G and latt lack σέ. But it is more likely for the copyist to omit rather than insert it. See Bruce M. Metzger, *A Textual Commentary on the Greek New Testament* (London/New York: United Bible Societies, 1971), 557.

[84] For interlocutor in rhetoric, see Chaïm Perelman, *The New Rhetoric and the Humanities: Essays on Rhetoric and its Applications* (Dordrecht: D. Reidel, 1979), 30-40; idem, *The Realm of Rhetoric* (Notre Dame: University of Notre Dame Press, 1982), 15-16.

[85] As discussed by Aristotle, *Rhetoric* 3.18.

to hellenistic rhetorical tradition, the use of an interlocutor in a rhetorical question depicts and exposes the "moral contradiction"[86] of the opponents, in this case, the gnostics. This persuasion is reinforced by the fictional interlocutor, who lends a degree of detachment from theoretical prejudices, thus adding an objective judgment to the rhetor's argument. The pedagogical use of the question in vv. 10–11 evokes irony and forces the audience to accept the rhetor's persuasion; thus indicating the pastoral sensitivity of Paul as a missionary.

(b) A serious didactic tone follows the rhetorical question. The answer to the rhetorical question is clear: a brother with a weak conscience will not be built up. So Paul draws the conclusion from their action in v. 11. The conclusion entails, however, a reluctant respect for their behaviour: the knowledge of the gnostic is destructive!

(c) The *conduplicatio* of their action, its purpose being to amplify or appeal to actions,[87] is given in verse 12, which shows beyond a shadow of doubt that their knowledge alone is not enough; it can end up as sin against Christ, and that is not love. If Christ died for the brethren out of love, how can they sin against their brethren? That is the biggest mistake one can make in having knowledge.

(d) While the audience ponders the right course of action (though by now they are convinced by Paul's argument), the rhetorician exemplifies personally what he would surely do (in verse 13). The personal example Paul gives in verse 13 is more than a guide to the Corinthians; it is a forceful way of saying "μιμηταί μου γίνεσθε καθὼς κἀγὼ Χριστοῦ" (11:1 "Imitate me as I am imitating Christ"). Implied in v. 13 is the right to eat; but the primary concern is that one's action will result in the "eternal trapping"[88] (σκανδαλίζει) of others, the direct opposite of one's intention. The radical nature of the Gospel—love—is manifested in Paul's response. Love cannot be merely stated; it must be demonstrated, demonstrated in the rhetoric of Paul and in his exemplary conduct (in the last verse).

In short, Paul seems to agree with the factual knowledge of the gnostics about monotheism (cf. 10:26); but he cares for the conscience, the instinctual knowledge of the weak. He counters arrogance with love,

---

[86] Cf. Stanley K. Stower, *The Diatribe and Paul's Letter to the Romans* (SBLDS 57; Chico: Scholars Press, 1981), 110.

[87] Cf. *Rhetorica Ad Herennium* 4.28.38.

[88] See Gustav Stählin, "Σκάνδαλον" *TDNT* 7: 339–43; Liddell and Scott, *Greek-English Lexicon*, s.v. "σκάνδαλον."

clarifies partial knowledge with conviction, and turns abstract theory into a real-life issue of caring for the weaker members of the community. And that is a rhetoric of knowledge practiced in love.

Pauline Rhetoric in 1 Corinthians 8 as a Whole

Paul's rhetorical style is dialogical. It functions well in a polemical situation such as that in Corinth. Meeks rightly draws upon the insight of Bakhtin to argue that Paul's rhetoric is not dialectical but "polyphonic."[89]

First, Paul identifies with the most dominant and articulate voice of the Corinthian community, which is the "we" voice in 8:1 and 4. After asserting and granting the validity of their claim to possess knowledge in 8:1–4, Paul then relativizes their assumed superiority in 8:7, 8 and 9. Also, by using "we" in the first four verses, Paul is certainly including the "weak" who are left out; this "we" is used therefore to create a community discourse among the Corinthians; the weak in conscience are probably weak in rhetoric. This community discourse is one of the Paul's intentions as we hear the voice of the weak in vv. 7–9, and 11 with the help of Paul, their spokesperson. Pauline rhetoric therefore fosters a more inclusive community.

This community discourse is intentional in the Pauline rhetoric in 1 Corinthians 8. Paul's rhetoric of knowledge and love, in short, creates a rhetorical process whereby all parties can talk and listen to one another for the sake of edification. The result of such community discourse is that the weak are taught by Paul to be eloquent and the gnostics are taught to edify others. The way they can all grow up is to listen to each other's voices.

Implications of Paul's Rhetoric for the Chinese Context

A Cross-Cultural Hermeneutic: An Interpathic Understanding

Has Pauline rhetorical interaction with the Corinthians concerning idol food in 1 Corinthians 8 any affinity with the practice of ancestor worship in Chinese culture? If there is any relevance and relation, it is in the *hermeneutical implications* of the rhetorical analysis of

---

[89] Wayne A. Meeks, "The Polyphonic Ethics of the Apostle Paul," *Annual of the Society of Christian Ethics* (1988): 18.

1 Corinthians 8 for ancestor worship. The task of hermeneutics is to prevent cultural isolation and to help resurrect the power of Paul's s rhetoric and theology. Thus, 1 Corinthians 8 can provide us insights and paradigms for how to interact with the Chinese Christians who are sincere filial pietists.

Before addressing ancestor worship hermeneutically at both the contextual and indigenous levels, there is a prior task which serves as a bracket between exegesis and hermeneutics. This task concerns the interpathic nature of cross-cultural understanding of a particular issue. The approach of "interpathy,"

> is an intentional cognitive envisioning and affective experiencing of another's thoughts and feelings, even though the thoughts rise from another process of knowing, the values grow from another frame of moral reasoning, and the feelings spring from another basis of assumptions. In interpathic caring, the process of 'feeling with' and 'thinking with' another requires that one enter the other's world of assumptions, beliefs, and values and temporarily take them as one's own.[90]

Our interpathic exercise will focus on the values the filial pietists ascribe to ancestor worship.

Ancestor Worship and Hsiao: Cosmic and Spiritual Value

Ancestor worship is rooted in the ethics and spirituality of "*hsiao*" ("filial piety"). The word "*hsiao*" is made up of two radicals: an old person and a child, perhaps denoting the responsibility of a child in bearing or supporting the old person. Why is this responsibility of the child conceived by the Chinese to be both spiritual and ethical?

Hsiao Ching ("The Classics of Filial Piety") says that "Filial Piety is the first principle of heaven, the ultimate standard of earth, the norm of conduct for the people. The people ought to follow the pattern of heaven and earth, which leads them by the rightness of the heavens and the benefits of the earth to harmonize all under heaven" (chap. 7). Here the dialectic between cosmology and anthropology, between metaphysics and ethics, between universe and family are conceived and symbolized in Chinese thinking. In other words, this dialectical thinking is a typical Chinese or Confucian worldview, which I will name the value of *Tao Te* ("the Way and the Moral"). *Tao* is the relation-

---

[90] David W. Augsburger, *Pastoral Counseling Across Cultures* (Philadelphia: Westminster Press, 1986), 29.

ship with the cosmos, *Te* is the relationship with humanity.[91] The *Tao* denotes the actualization of the self in harmony with the cosmic and spiritual realm; the *Te* denotes the actualization of the self in wholeness with the social and ethical realm. Filial piety encompasses these two notions together. In other words, filial pietists seek selfhood and cosmic harmony, and hence the value of *Tao Te*. Since the virtue of filial piety is central and well-developed in Confucius' thought, I will locate his metaphysical and ethical values of filial piety as concretely as possible, most notably in his understanding of the "Transcendence/Immanence"—*T'ien* ("Heaven").

The book Confucius (551-479 BCE) loved, *The Book of Odes*, says: "*T'ien* gave birth to the multitude of people; where there is a thing, there is a principle; that is why people hold to rightness and like this natural, beautiful virtue." (*Ta-ya*, III: 3, 6; 505 and 541) This religio-philosophical understanding of human life assumes that all humans come from *T'ien* the Creator; and that morality is derived from *T'ien*. A similar concept of this "transcendence/immanence" *T'ien* is expressed in the *Analects*. This concept is best summed up by a Confucian scholar, Donald L. Alexander, who argues that Confucius' religious-metaphysical understanding of ultimate reality is couched in the bi-polar conception of *T'ien*; and out of that conception comes Confucian metaphysics and ethics.[92] The *Tao* of *T'ien* ("the heavenly principle/way") is the way of the Heaven which not only gives birth to people but continues to regenerate and sustain them. The transcendence is best known in the immanence. Furthermore, Confucius seeks to popularize and democratize that way of Heaven to all people so that all can cultivate selfhood and attain the wholeness of life.[93]

Confucianism emphasizes filial piety as one of the central teachings in the more immanent realm while seemingly neglecting those aspects in the transcendent realm. In philosophical understanding, the immanent aspect is seen as the expression of the transcendent aspect. Therefore, filial piety is regarded not merely as human responsibility, but also as a spiritual or heavenly-ordained way of life.

---

[91] Cf. Chae-Woon Ng, "Filial Piety in Confucian Thought," *North-East Asia Journal of Theology* 28 (1982): 40.
[92] Donald L. Alexander, "The Concept of *T'ien* in Early Confucian Thought," *His Dominion* 3 (1985), 11-14.
[93] Sung-Hae Kim, "Silent Heaven Giving Birth to the Multitude of People," *Ching Feng* 31:4D (1988), 195-96.

When Confucius is asked what is the greatest virtue, he replies: "Filial Piety is the first principle of heaven, the ultimate standard of earth, the norm of conduct for the people. The people ought to follow the pattern of heaven and earth, which leads them by the rightness of the heavens and the benefits of the earth to harmonize all under heaven" (*Hsiao Ching*, 7). This virtue is promoted by Confucius as a means to restore harmony in the midst of the political disintegration, social unrest, intellectual anarchy, and moral disorder of his age. Confucius' ingenuity here is to portray to the people the whole vision of life; that is, familial values, social values, and other immanence values are actually transcendental values. This vision is summed up in *Hsiao Ching* chapter 9 in a hierarchical mode: "Human beings excel all other beings in heaven and earth, and of all human actions, none is greater than filial piety. In the practice of filial piety, no aspect is greater than paying due respect to one's parent, and in paying respect to one's parent, none is greater than venerating him as a mediator of God *T'ien*." The *Hsiao Ching* says that "The relation and duties between parent and child thus belong to the Heaven-conferred nature" (*Hsiao Ching*, 9). The virtue of filial piety, which underlies the practice of ancestor worship, is therefore rooted in the cosmic and spiritual value systems of Confucius.

Social Values: Personhood and Selfhood

Not only is filial piety a virtue that is endowed by Heaven, *Hsiao Ching* continues "The son derives his life from his parents, and no greater gift could possibly be transmitted...Hence, the one who does not love her parents, but loves other people, is called a rebel against virtue; and he who does not revere his parents, but reveres other people, is called a rebel against propriety" (*Hsiao Ching*, 9). This proverbial saying expounds the social values of ancestor worship which are delineated in the following intricately interrelated tenets: (a) Personhood in individuation as practiced in *Jen* and *Li*[94] and (b) Selfhood actualization as practiced in the dynamic dyadic social relations.

---

[94] On the differences between *Jen* and *Li*, see Ng, "Filial Piety in Confucian Thought," 37–38.

Personhood in, Jen and Li

The importance of ancestor worship for the filial pietists is demonstrated in the Confucian notion of selfhood and personhood cultivation. The whole of Confucius' philosophy can be summed up succinctly in his words, "to demonstrate illustrious virtue, renovate the people, and rest in the highest excellence."[95] Confucius regards filial piety as the root of all virtues. When Tseng Tsu asked Confucius "Is filial piety the highest of all the virtues possessed by a great sage?" Confucius replies: "There is nothing so great in the world as a human being, and there is nothing so great in a man as filial piety" (*Hsiao Ching*, 1). But Confucius also regards *jen* as the fountain head of all virtues. Thus, he advocates that all should actualize the mandate of *T'ien* by committing ourselves to *jen*[96] because what makes human beings human is *jen*.[97] In other words, the will of God for any community is to practice a life-style of love.

Filial piety then is the first concrete step in actualizing *jen* in a person. In this respect, Hsiao Ching notes that "The effect of education upon the minds of the people was well known to the good emperors of old. They made all people love others by loving their parents first." (7) Mencius extends the practice of *jen* even further: "The superior man should love his parents and be lovingly disposed to people in general; and he should also be kind to all living creatures" (Mencius 7.45).

Filial piety is the root of all virtue together with *jen*, and filial piety is related to *li* ("propriety") also. Confucius observes that "Parents, when alive, should be served according to *li* (propriety); when dead, they should be buried according to *li* (propriety); and they should be sacrificed according to *li* (propriety)" (*Analects* 2:5).

---

[95] The Great Learning 1.1. The naming of that way of life as philosophy, ethics, or spirituality is itself an intellectual controversy. T'ang Chün-I for example explains that "love and respect for one's parents, is not biological but is moral, being based on a sense of obligation or a debt of gratitude, and is therefore spiritual." Charles A. Moore, ed., *The Chinese Mind; Essentials of Chinese Philosophy and Culture* (Honolulu: University of Hawaii, 1971), 186.

[96] Milton M. Chiu, *The Tao of Chinese Religion* (Lanham: University Press of America, 1984), 191–92.

[97] Translated variously as human-heartedness (E. R. Hughes), benevolence, love (Derk Bodde), benevolent Love (H. H. Dubs), humane, human-at-its-best, goodness (A. Waley), humanity, virtue (H. G. Creel), human-relatedness, charity, humanity (W. T. Chan), morality, etc. Cf. Fung Yu-lan, *A History of Chinese Philosophy* (trans. Derk Bodde; Princeton: Princeton University Press, 1952), 69–73.

How is the cultivation of personhood related to *jen* and *li*? It is possible that one loves another merely for the sake of ritual; and this is what Confucius warns against: "Merely to feed one's parents well...even dogs and horses are fed" (Analects 2:7). That means that merely to fulfil the obligations of *li* is superficial, what is essential is a higher principle, and that is *jen*. So *li* without *jen* can degenerate into formalism or insensitivity (cf. *Analects* 3:3). Therefore, *li* must be grounded in *jen*.[98]

Selfhood in Dyadic Social Relations

Confucius includes in his idea of liberal education or wide culture not only book learning but also ritual and cultural practice which reinforce the interaction of the self with the larger community (from self to home to society to nation to the world). That constant reinforcement serves as a process of self-cultivation if it is practiced in a spirit of loyalty, filiality, brotherhood, discipleship and so forth (*Analects* 1). The parent-child relationship is the basic one in self-cultivation. Hsieh Yu-Wei rightly observes that "With genuine and comprehensive love toward one's own parents, in its developing process, one may naturally learn to be benevolent to all living creatures, affectionate toward humankind as a whole, loyal to one's country and to the duties of a free citizen, faithful in keeping obligations, righteous in action, peaceful in behavior, and just in all dealings."[99] *Hsiao Ching* declares that "It is filial piety which forms the root of all virtues, and with it all enlightening studies come into existence." (1)

Family Values: Preservation and Support

Ancestor worship also seeks to promote the continuity of lineage and family in terms of identity. Thus the responsibility of the children and grandchildren, particularly the eldest son and the grandson, is to perform ritual services to the ancestor. Ancestor worship is "a cult that contributed substantially to the integration and perpetuation of the family as a basic unit of Chinese society."[100]

---

[98] This is what Tu Wei-ming means by "the primacy of jen over li and the inseparability of li from jen." See his "Li as Process of Humanization," *Philosophy East and West* 22 (1972): 188.

[99] Moore, *The Chinese Mind*, 174.

[100] Ching Kun Yang, *Religion in Chinese Society* (Berkeley: University of California Press, 1967), 29.

The social functions of ancestor worship are many. Among them are the following: (1) It provides an occasion for the reunion of the family; thus, the ancestral shrine ("she") is the meeting place of the family. (2) It provides economical, social and psychological support to bereaved families.[101] Ahern, for example, emphasizes the economic motivation for ancestor worship from her studies in Taiwan.[102] The ancestor's property provides the economic stability for the descendant but also shows the prosperity of the ancestor. (3) Socially the cult of ancestor worship is therapeutic in coping with "the emotionally shattering and socially disintegrating event of the death..."[103] The meal with the dead is conceived as a common meal both with the dead and the living. Meyer Fortes says that "Food dependence is from the moment of birth the vital bond that unites child to parent. To share a meal is, as is well known, an expression of amity and trust..."[104] The form, time, and place of meals are fixed, as for example in ancestor festivals;[105] therefore a meal ritual shows not only mutual dependence but also the trust and affection of living and dead.

Conflictual Values of Ancestor Worship

So far, the approach through interpathic research has made use mostly of the philosophical and some of the religious traditions. The mythological sources for ancestor worship, coupled with the religious practice of the little tradition, often portray different values that contradict (thus are in conflict with) the idealized values of the great tradition.[106] The fear and myth of ancestor worship are real and substantial in the value systems of the filial pietists. To categorize more concretely what

---

[101] Cf. Yang, *Religion in Chinese Society*, 31–38, on the social functions of ancestor worship: for the benefit and salvation of the soul, for the protection of the living from the dead, for the expression of grief, for the reassembling the family group and reasserting family status.

[102] Emily M. Ahern, *The Cult of the Dead in a Chinese Village* (Stanford: Stanford University Press, 1973), 121: "an adult man who is a direct descendant of the lineage ancestors and who has married, sired male children and handed down property to his sons is a paradigm of the person with a right to have his tablet placed in the hall. "

[103] Yang, *Religion in Chinese Society*, 29.

[104] Meyer Fortes, "An Introductory Commentary," in *Ancestors* (ed. William H. Newell; Haugue/Paris: Mouton Publishers, 1976), 11.

[105] Cf. Francis L. K. Hsu, *Under the Ancestor's Shadow: Kinship, Personality, and Social Mobility in China* (Stanford: Stanford University Press, 1971), 182ff.

[106] The conflictual value is similar to the discrepancy or inconsistency between the operative, conceived and desirable values proposed by Charles W. Morris; see his *Varieties of Human Value* (Chicago: University of Chicago Press, 1956), 9–12.

the fear and myth are, one needs to understand (a) the Chinese belief in spirit/god, ghost, and ancestor; and (b) the practice of geomancy (*fung shui*).

Many filial pietists do look for supernatural power in the deceased parents or ancestors for blessing, guidance, protection from evil, or forgiveness from wrongs. So in popular culture or the little tradition there is another philosophical understanding of ancestor worship which is over-clouded with superstitious baggage.

The superstition concerning the ancestor becoming a haunting ghost originated from a very ancient Chinese belief that there are three categories of spiritual being: ghosts (*kui*, or evil spirits), gods (*ciengsin*), and ancestors (*kong-ma* or *co-kong*). One has a different attitude towards each of them: "One propitiates (*ce*) *kui*, but honors (*hok-sai, kieng-hong,* or *pai*) god"[107] and ancestors. Gods, ancestors, and *kui* are all thought of by the masses as former human beings. Living humans inhabit the *yang* world, the others the *yin* world or *im-kan* ("prisons of the earth"). The Chinese believe that a human being becomes a person when the spirit (*hun* that comes from heaven) and the soul (*p'o* that comes from the earth) enter the body. The spirit and the soul will return to heaven and the earth respectively while the body decays upon a person's death. But the spirits and the souls have powers beyond those of humans, and they are mediators between human beings and supernatural beings.

Many Chinese worship their ancestors for their supernatural power, often for selfish reasons. Moreover, they worship out of fear because they believe that when the souls and the spirits return to their descendants' homes, they need to be well taken care of through sacrifice and divinations. Otherwise they become ghosts or *kui* (literally "returning") who will haunt people.[108] Good ghosts called spirits will bring blessing and wisdom to their descendants; evil ghosts called *kui* will bring bad luck, disaster and torments. An infant that dies prematurely is believed to be a reincarnation of, or possessed by, the evil spirit.[109] Thus, dying infants are never sacrificed to and seldom remembered.

---

[107] Stephan Feuchtwang, "Domestic and Communal Worship in Taiwan," in *Religion and Ritual in Chinese Society* (ed. Arthur P. Wolf; Stanford: Stanford University Press, 1974), 107; similarly Hsu, *Under the Ancestor's Shadow*, 144–45.

[108] Chiu Milton M., *The Tao of Chinese Religion* (Lanham: University Press of America, 1984), 343.

[109] Therefore, dead infants are often not remembered ritually, nor burried with a coffin.

One of the ways to deal with the fear of the curse of barrenness from past ancestors is through geomancy. The technique is to relocate the grave to a better site involving mediation by shamans between the living and the dead, or employing shamans and intermediaries to manipulate fate or circumstances as much as possible. De Groot seems to overemphasize that in a patriarchal society of authority and respect, absolute obedience and worship of the dead "signifies that family ties are by no means broken by death, and that the dead continue to exercise their authority and to afford their protection."[110]

A Pauline Response

How one ought to respond to such practices in the light of Christian faith continues to create an impasse in missiological practice to this day. To advise the Chinese not to offer food and not to eat the food in ancestor worship may be implicitly advising them not to love their parents, not to practice love, and ultimately not to be Chinese. Yet the fear and myth of this practice carries with it a conflictual side. In this section I will attempt to construct a Pauline response by using the rhetorical insights of Paul in 1 Corinthians 8.

First, in 1 Corinthians 8 Paul never resorts to absolute prohibitions concerning idol-meat eating. To begin from the prohibition would contradict the "in-Christ" gospel he so preached. The gospel of Christ is not a right/wrong ethical system. Therefore, for the missionary to preach the Gospel with prohibitions—however wrong the audience's practice is—contradicts Paul's rhetoric and the very nature of the Gospel he proclaimed. Paul rarely corrects sub-Christian or non-Christian behavior by prohibition.[111] To do so would "turn ethical response into legal obligation."[112] In short, Paul's strategy is to deal with the more basic issue of the nature of the Gospel, since our existence is qualified always by the fact that Christ the Sophia is the Creator and Redeemer of us all (8:6). None is superior or better or more righteous than the other even if we are "in-Christ."

---

[110] Jan Jacob Maria de Groot, *Religion in China* (American Lectures on the History of Religions; New York, London: The Knickerbocker Press, 1912), 178.
[111] Gordon D. Fee, "Εἰδωλόθυτα Once Again: An Interpretation of 1 Corinthians 8–10," *Biblica* 61:2 (1980): 197.
[112] Fee, "Εἰδωλόθυτα Once Again," 197.

Second, Paul would affirm that prohibition alone, unless being informed by knowledge and practiced in love, is unwise.[113] I will deal with the "practiced in love" clause later. Here I want to focus on the "informed by knowledge" clause. Though Paul does not totally accept the viewpoint of the Corinthians, he does (a) begin his argument from their slogans or points of view, and (b) affirm some of their beliefs. The strategy of point (a) draws the audience onto common ground with the responder, as we have discussed above. The strategy of point (b) allows them to feel accepted. Both strategies keep them open for dynamic community discourse. But both strategies required him to be knowledgeable of the audience's belief and arguments.

In order to formulate a responsible attitude to the Chinese ancestor worship issue, one needs an interpathic understanding of the issue and the values of the practice. This is a necessary step towards being "informed by knowledge" as one suggests a viable response. In other words, to advise the Chinese not to practice ancestor worship, or not to offer food to ancestors, is implicitly advising them not to be Chinese, not to love their parents, not to practice love, etc.

Third, Paul is sensitive to the needs of the audience as he interacts with them, for example, the need of the strong to be less overbearing, and the need of the weak to be more eloquent. The needs of the Chinese pietists are likewise real and varied. This is where the gospel of Christ can grant them hope, freedom, and salvation. We observe that most filial pietists do look for supernatural power in deceased parents or ancestors, for blessing, guidance, protection from evil, or forgiveness of wrongs. Much is done out of fear and bondage. Many Chinese filial pietists are living in fear of the supernatural power of the ancestors, who might punish them if they either do not worship or worship inappropriately. Others worship with manipulative motives. Here, the Gospel of the Lord summarized in 8:6 can be indeed Good News to the fearful filial pietists: "there is one God, the Father, from whom are all things and for whom we exist, and one Lord, Jesus Christ, through whom are all things and through whom we exist."

Fourth, however one interacts with the pietists concerning ancestor worship, one needs to learn from Paul, whose rhetoric is not only informed by knowledge but also "practiced with love." Paul's rhetorical techniques and strategies are shaped and influenced by the classical

---

[113] See Fee, "Εἰδωλόθυτα Once Again," 196.

rhetoric of his day; even more, his rhetoric is guided and controlled by the gospel of love. Paul's rhetoric in 1 Corinthians 8 could have been strictly judicial and could have provided absolute imperatives about what the Corinthian Christians are supposed to do regarding the eating of idol-meat. Instead, we see a rhetor with pastoral sensitivity to both the strong and the weak for mutual and social edification. Paul's rhetorical strategy is wisdom practiced with *jen*, demonstrating the Gospel he believes in.

I believe that the Gospel of Christ is the gospel of love which cares for one's relationship with God in Christ as expressed in one's relationship with one's neighbours. In other words, seeking to draw the Chinese closer in relationship to the Christian God by issuing imperatives is to begin at the wrong point. Such presentation of imperatives as divinely ordained, without respect for an individual's needs and context, is not an act of love. Also, ancestor worship is a Chinese "gospel of love" for the ancestors by showing respect and love for them. One has no right to criticize this practice just because it is shaped by a different culture. In fact, understanding ancestor worship from the perspectives of its cosmic, spiritual, social, and family values, one cannot but affirm and encourage its practice. Whatever view one holds concerning ancestor worship, I am convinced that the next point speaks to the heart of Paul's response.

Fifth, the Pauline response establishes a deliberative, community discourse and does not attempt to give an easy answer of "yes or no." Such a response will create an on-going process of interaction as all parties commit themselves to that rhetorical event. The Pauline response is more concerned with the process than with the answer. This is not to say that Paul's theology has no content. It only means that to absolutize Paul's theology in 1 Corinthians 8 (especially without observing the rhetorical context) is inadequate. It also means that without a rhetorical understanding of his argument, one will misappropriate his theology. My attempt to create a discoursed community in this paper is seen in the dialogical rhetoric I analyze in 1 Corinthians 8 (part one) and in the way I need to listen to the Chinese pietists (hence interpathic understanding in part two) before I give a response. The use of rhetorical criticism of 1 Corinthians 8 reveals that both the gnostics and the "weak" are being nurtured in love as they participate in the community discourse.

A rhetorical analysis of 1 Corinthians 8 is necessary and helpful because it helps to overcome the traditional focus on the content of

Paul's theology alone. This rhetorical analysis has focused on and appreciates the way Paul approaches the issue within the Corinthian historical context, and has viewed Paul's theology or ethics in light of and in relation to his rhetoric. My hope is that this provides the means to construct an indigenous theology that speaks beyond the original historical context. What Paul explicitly says in 1 Corinthians 8 is not *necessarily* universal, absolute, and applicable to all in all situations. But with a broader understanding of rhetorical-hermeneutical study, which takes the twentieth-century audience and situation seriously, I believe the Bible can be appropriated and addressed to new audiences and situations. Perhaps it is in this type of combined exegesis-hermeneutic that we can say that the Bible is eternal and life-changing.

The analysis of 1 Corinthians 8 reveals that Paul's theology is expressed in the rhetoric of knowledge and love. Paul's theology and rhetoric suggest to the global community that all traditions can participate in the interpretive process whereby the uniqueness of each is differentiated, affirmed, and esteemed, while the commonalities of all are shared, identified, and celebrated. The purpose of Pauline rhetoric is to encourage the confluence of traditions to the edification of humanity and to the glory of God.

8.3 Gregory David Wiebe (McMaster University, Canada). The Demonic Phenomena of Mark's "Legion": Evaluating Postcolonial Understandings of Demon Possession

Mark 5:1–20	
¹They came to the other side of the lake, to the country of the Gerasenes. ²And when he had stepped out of the boat, immediately a man out of the tombs with an unclean spirit met him. ³He lived among the tombs; and no one could restrain him any more, even with a chain; ⁴for he had often been restrained with shackles and chains, but the chains he wrenched apart, and the shackles he broke in pieces; and no one had the strength to subdue him. ⁵Night and day	[1] Καὶ ἦλθον εἰς τὸ πέραν τῆς θαλάσσης εἰς τὴν χώραν τῶν Γερασηνῶν. [2] καὶ ἐξελθόντος αὐτοῦ ἐκ τοῦ πλοίου εὐθὺς ὑπήντησεν αὐτῷ ἐκ τῶν μνημείων ἄνθρωπος ἐν πνεύματι ἀκαθάρτῳ, [3] ὃς τὴν κατοίκησιν εἶχεν ἐν τοῖς μνήμασιν, καὶ οὐδὲ ἁλύσει οὐκέτι οὐδεὶς ἐδύνατο αὐτὸν δῆσαι [4] διὰ τὸ αὐτὸν πολλάκις πέδαις καὶ ἁλύσεσιν δεδέσθαι καὶ διεσπάσθαι ὑπ' αὐτοῦ τὰς ἁλύσεις

among the tombs and on the mountains he was always howling and bruising himself with stones. [6]When he saw Jesus from a distance, he ran and bowed down before him; [7]and he shouted at the top of his voice, 'What have you to do with me, Jesus, Son of the Most High God? I adjure you by God, do not torment me.' [8]For he had said to him, 'Come out of the man, you unclean spirit!' [9]Then Jesus asked him, 'What is your name?' He replied, 'My name is Legion; for we are many.' [10]He begged him earnestly not to send them out of the country. [11]Now there on the hillside a great herd of swine was feeding; [12]and the unclean spirits begged him, 'Send us into the swine; let us enter them.' [13]So he gave them permission. And the unclean spirits came out and entered the swine; and the herd, numbering about two thousand, rushed down the steep bank into the sea, and were drowned in the sea. [14]The swineherds ran off and told it in the city and in the country. Then people came to see what it was that had happened. [15]They came to Jesus and saw the demoniac sitting there, clothed and in his right mind, the very man who had had the legion; and they were afraid. [16]Those who had seen what had happened to the demoniac and to the swine reported it. [17]Then they began to beg Jesus to leave their neighbourhood. [18]As he was getting into the boat, the man who had been possessed by demons begged him that he might be with him. [19]But Jesus refused, and said to him, 'Go home to your friends, and tell them how much the Lord has done for you, and what mercy he has shown you.' [20]And he went away and began to proclaim in the Decapolis how much Jesus had done for him; and everyone was amazed.

καὶ τὰς πέδας συντετρῖφθαι, καὶ οὐδεὶς ἴσχυεν αὐτὸν δαμάσαι·
[5] καὶ διὰ παντὸς νυκτὸς καὶ ἡμέρας ἐν τοῖς μνήμασιν καὶ ἐν τοῖς ὄρεσιν ἦν κράζων καὶ κατακόπτων ἑαυτὸν λίθοις.
[6] καὶ ἰδὼν τὸν Ἰησοῦν ἀπὸ μακρόθεν ἔδραμεν καὶ προσεκύνησεν αὐτῷ
[7] καὶ κράξας φωνῇ μεγάλῃ λέγει· Τί ἐμοὶ καὶ σοί, Ἰησοῦ υἱὲ τοῦ θεοῦ τοῦ ὑψίστου; ὁρκίζω σε τὸν θεόν, μή με βασανίσῃς.
[8] ἔλεγεν γὰρ αὐτῷ· Ἔξελθε τὸ πνεῦμα τὸ ἀκάθαρτον ἐκ τοῦ ἀνθρώπου.
[9] καὶ ἐπηρώτα αὐτόν· Τί ὄνομά σοι; καὶ λέγει αὐτῷ· Λεγιὼν ὄνομά μοι, ὅτι πολλοί ἐσμεν.
[10] καὶ παρεκάλει αὐτὸν πολλὰ ἵνα μὴ αὐτὰ ἀποστείλῃ ἔξω τῆς χώρας.
[11] Ἦν δὲ ἐκεῖ πρὸς τῷ ὄρει ἀγέλη χοίρων μεγάλη βοσκομένη·
[12] καὶ παρεκάλεσαν αὐτὸν λέγοντες· Πέμψον ἡμᾶς εἰς τοὺς χοίρους, ἵνα εἰς αὐτοὺς εἰσέλθωμεν.
[13] καὶ ἐπέτρεψεν αὐτοῖς. καὶ ἐξελθόντα τὰ πνεύματα τὰ ἀκάθαρτα εἰσῆλθον εἰς τοὺς χοίρους, καὶ ὥρμησεν ἡ ἀγέλη κατὰ τοῦ κρημνοῦ εἰς τὴν θάλασσαν, ὡς δισχίλιοι, καὶ ἐπνίγοντο ἐν τῇ θαλάσσῃ.
[14] Καὶ οἱ βόσκοντες αὐτοὺς ἔφυγον καὶ ἀπήγγειλαν εἰς τὴν πόλιν καὶ εἰς τοὺς ἀγρούς· καὶ ἦλθον ἰδεῖν τί ἐστιν τὸ γεγονὸς
[15] καὶ ἔρχονται πρὸς τὸν Ἰησοῦν καὶ θεωροῦσιν τὸν δαιμονιζόμενον καθήμενον ἱματισμένον καὶ σωφρονοῦντα, τὸν ἐσχηκότα τὸν λεγιῶνα, καὶ ἐφοβήθησαν.
[16] καὶ διηγήσαντο αὐτοῖς οἱ ἰδόντες πῶς ἐγένετο τῷ δαιμονιζομένῳ καὶ περὶ τῶν χοίρων.
[17] καὶ ἤρξαντο παρακαλεῖν αὐτὸν ἀπελθεῖν ἀπὸ τῶν ὁρίων αὐτῶν.

[18] Καὶ ἐμβαίνοντος αὐτοῦ εἰς τὸ πλοῖον παρεκάλει αὐτὸν ὁ δαιμονισθεὶς ἵνα μετ' αὐτοῦ ᾖ.
[19] καὶ οὐκ ἀφῆκεν αὐτόν, ἀλλὰ λέγει αὐτῷ· Ὕπαγε εἰς τὸν οἶκόν σου πρὸς τοὺς σοὺς καὶ ἀπάγγειλον αὐτοῖς ὅσα ὁ κύριός σοι πεποίηκεν καὶ ἠλέησέν σε.
[20] καὶ ἀπῆλθεν καὶ ἤρξατο κηρύσσειν ἐν τῇ Δεκαπόλει ὅσα ἐποίησεν αὐτῷ ὁ Ἰησοῦς, καὶ πάντες ἐθαύμαζον.

Introduction: Phenomenal Remainders

It is, perhaps, a defining characteristic of postcolonial scholarship to *demythologize* empire; that is, to denude the myths of exceptionalism and historical ascendancy that constitute it. The quintessential form this demythologization takes is the unveiling of voices and resistances suppressed by the vectors of imperial power that make empire and its organising mythologies possible. As postcolonial sensibilities get taken up within biblical scholarship in the late twentieth and early twenty-first century, scholars who yearn for justice for those "voices at the margins" see analogous voices in biblical texts and other ancient literature that deserve to be heard, and that might teach us to listen better to those silenced voices of our own day. Of course, as the language of *empire* has fallen out of favour, and as the techniques of its subtle exercise advance, the cannons of criticism are aimed not just against imperialism, but against neo-imperialism, the logic of imperialism wherever it appears, that attitude of hegemony that sacrifices the other on the altar of its own pride of place.

Yet it does not come by this task without its own desires. On the contrary, postcolonial biblical scholarship is marked by a desire that is so zealous to overturn the injustices of colonialism that it is as suspicious of the traces of imperialism in the resistance to empire as it is of empire itself. This is its conspicuous *ambivalence*, as Stephen D. Moore has identified it, following Homi K. Bhabha.[114] And New

---

[114] See Stephen D. Moore, *Empire and Apocalypse: Postcolonialism and the New*

Testament literature—particularly the gospels in their imperial *Sitz im Leben*—has proven a fecund subject for ambivalent postcolonial biblical criticism: was Jesus' alternative vision ambitious enough in its challenge to the colonial apparatus? Did it forego any substantive alteration of the relationship between oppressor and oppressed, ultimately upholding the status quo?[115] To the extent that there is a vision of resistance, does it overturn empire simply by reversing the vectors of its operation? Is the messianic victory merely the re-inscription of empire writ large?[116] True to form, postcolonial criticism is often critical of itself: are the postcolonial criticisms of the insufficiency of New Testament resistance themselves incomplete? Have the voices of those *more* marginalized (like those of indigenous women) been silenced in the attempt to hear other marginalized voices?[117]

In few texts do the problems of marginalized voices and the zealous expectations of imperial overthrow come together in a passage in which the Roman Empire itself bubbles so titillatingly close to the surface as Mark's Gerasene demoniac. The pericope is pregnant with suggestion for understanding the encounter with empire in ancient Palestine, and potentially even today. However, though it can be seen to have recorded an ancient marginalized voice that speaks of resistance to the imperial order, we will find it only does so whetted, keenly cutting to the heart of the sensibilities of postcolonial biblical critics and biblical scholars in general. For the marginalized voice it contains, contrary to the naturalistic assumptions of many, is that of a man possessed by scores of demons, a *legion* of them. Yet it is difficult to find a current scholar willing to allow the "meaning" of this passage to pass through any positive affirmation of the narrative's postulation of the existence of active demons;[118] it would seem that many are not yet ready to listen to the voices issuing from this afflicted man's mouth.

Testament (The Bible in the Modern World 12; Sheffield: Sheffield Phoenix, 2006), 90. Moore is engaging Bhabha's *The Location of Culture*.

[115] R. S. Sugirtharajah, "Coding and Decoding: Postcolonial Criticism and Biblical Interpretation," in *Postcolonial Criticism and Biblical Interpretation* (Oxford: Oxford University Press, 2002), 74–102, 88–90.

[116] Moore, *Empire and Apocalypse*, 97–121; the language of "empire writ large" is from p. 121.

[117] Laura E. Donaldson, "Gospel Hauntings: The Postcolonial Demons of New Testament Criticism" in *Postcolonial Biblical Criticism: Interdisciplinary Intersections* (ed. Stephen D. Moore and Fernando F. Segovia; London: T&T Clark, 2005), 97–113.

[118] There are a few notable exceptions. Among the better of these are Father Cyrille Argenti, "A Meditation on Mark 5:1–20," *Ecumenical Review* 23 (1971): 398–408; J. Duncan M. Derrett, "Contributions to the Study of the Gerasene Demoniac," *JSNT* 3

John Dominic Crossan is typical in his terseness: "I myself, for example, do not believe that there are personal supernatural spirits who invade our bodies from outside and, for good or evil, replace or jostle for place with our own personality."[119] Biblical scholars in the West have for a long time now be content to challenge the accuracy of the biblical text; it is no longer uncommon to postulate that Mark "got it wrong," or that not all of the events he recounts "actually happened." But, as Crossan concedes, "seventy-five percent" of the world's people still claim to hold belief in spiritual beings, a fact that mitigates one's ability to be so dismissive. His solution, ever the true scholar, is to make a distinction: "So while I may not accept their *explanation*, I tread very carefully in discussing the *phenomenon* that leads them to that diagnosis."[120]

Consider, however, what "explanation" and "phenomenon" denote. Although he does not himself make the difference explicit, we can safely presume that the "explanation" Crossan does not "accept" refers narrowly to the specific naming of "possession." He might have in mind Mark's use of the language of being "in an unclean spirit" (ἐν πνεύματι ἀκαθάρτῳ) to describe the man that immediately meets Jesus when he steps ashore. On the other hand, the "phenomena" are presumably those things that would have been observable to anyone present at such an event, but which were subsequently misinterpreted by Mark and his sources as being the effect of unclean spirits: the excessive strength of the man, his self-destructive behaviour, the bizarre conversation he has with Jesus about where he is to go and the swine herding nearby. In short, the "phenomena"—that is, the historical materials Crossan still feels compelled to "very carefully discuss"—are those matters that can be assimilated into contemporary scientific or social-scientific discourse (e.g. naturalism, realism, psychopathology, etc.).[121]

(1979): 2–17; *idem*, "Spirit Possession and the Gerasene Demoniac," *Man* New Series 14 (1979): 286–93. Less demanding on scholars' cosmologies is Solomon K. Avotri, "The Vernacularization of Scripture and African Beliefs: The Story of the Gerasene Demoniac Among the Ewe of West Africa," in *The Bible in Africa: Transaction, Trajectories, and Trends* (ed. G. O. West and M. Dube; Leiden: Brill, 2000), 311–25. For such accounts pertaining to texts related to Mark 5, see R. E. K. Mchami, "Demon Possession and Exorcism in Mark 1:21–28," *Africa Theological Journal* 24 (2001): 17–37; W. D. Davies and Dale C. Allison, *A Critical and Exegetical Commentary on the Gospel According to Saint Matthew II, 8–18* (ICC; Edinburgh: T&T Clark, 1991), 77–78.

[119] John Dominic Crossan, *Jesus: A Revolutionary Biography* (San Francisco: Harper, 1994), 85.

[120] Crossan, *Jesus*, emphasis original.

[121] Crossan maintains, however, "in linking colonial domination with demonic possession, we are not simply retrojecting modern sensibilities back into first-century

Possession phenomena are always "possession" phenomena, which means, for example, the alien voices of Mark's Gerasene demoniac are probably symptoms of dissociative identity disorder.[122] Making such a distinction within a possession narrative, as Crossan does between the phenomena of Mark 5 and the spiritual explanation of them, can sometimes leave a phenomenal remainder, however, wherever the given phenomena cannot be intelligibly recounted without postulating the spiritual to account for its logical coherence. (The question that remains for Crossan is which came first: the decision that this event could not have happened historically,[123] or the decision that "personal supernatural spirits" do not exist?).

What is interesting about the Gerasene demoniac is that it presents us with just such phenomena. For in the absence of the explanatory postulation of spirits, it is difficult to know how to link—scientifically or otherwise—the herd of pigs rushing to their deaths and the other components of the pericope. In the face of this difficulty, some, like Crossan, simply deny the historicity of the account.[124] Most commentators sidestep the issue by treating the pericope as *mere* pericope. This avoids the problem because the demons, despite their significance, are treated as real only within the logic of narrative; the narrative as a whole retains its "meaning" without confronting the historicity of its content.[125]

---

minds" (*Jesus*, 90). I am inclined to reserve a space in which to agree with Crossan, but the primary task of this essay is to qualify this agreement.

[122] Commonly known as multiple personality disorder.

[123] Crossan, *Jesus*.

[124] E.g. Roger David Aus, *My Name is "Legion": Palestinian Judaic Traditions in Mark 5:1-20 and Other Gospel Texts* (Studies in Judaism; Lanham: University Press of America, 2003). Although they do not come right out and say it, this is also the sentiment of John R. Donahue and Daniel J. Harrington, *The Gospel of Mark* (SP 2; Collegeville: Liturgical, 2002), 168.

[125] This is typical of commentaries in general, explicitly so in Donahue and Harrington, *Mark*, 169. See also, Eduard Schweizer, *The Good News According to Mark* (trans. D. H. Madvig; Richmond: John Knox, 1970), although his comment about the pericope being a combination of stories suggests scepticism regarding its historicity (111); Henry Barclay Swete, *Commentary on Mark* (Grand Rapids: Kregel, 1977). Also, Morna D. Hooker, *The Gospel According to Saint Mark* (BNTC 2; Peabody: Hendrickson, 1991). She pleads agnostic: "it is useless for us to try to reconstruct what might have happened" (144). This claim presupposes that the account given *cannot* have happened as it is told; yet this does not preclude her from expositing the significance of the passage in the crumbling of Satan's kingdom (144). It is interesting to note that the greatest problem the pericope presents is the fact that Jesus allows an entire herd to perish. See also Kelly Iverson, "First Journey into Gentile Territory" in *Gentiles and the Gospel of Mark: "Even the Dogs Under the Table Eat the Children's Crumbs"* (London: T&T Clark, 2007), 20-39; and C. E. B. Cranfield, *The Gospel According to Saint Mark* (Cambridge: Cambridge University Press, 1959). Cranfield actually names the point I am trying explore, namely that "we must...take seriously

Some, however, shrewdly attempt to show that it is the historical phenomena themselves that suggest the obsolescence of demonic language. Richard A. Horsley's account,[126] for example, ignores the debates and proceeds to give serious treatment to the phenomena as if they are historical. When he does, he rather compellingly finds that the phenomena recounted in the story of the demoniac are indicative of a causal link with the colonial context of first-century Palestine,[127] suggesting strongly that the exorcisms of Jesus are encounters not with spiritual entities but political oppressors. Because his account is so suggestive, and because the story is so fecund at the level of its phenomena, the present analysis will felicitously follow Horsley's approach and treat the pericope as if it is historical, though it is well beyond the scope of this project to argue this.

This essay will evaluate Horsley's account of the phenomena of the Gerasene demoniac—an analysis he inherits in part from Crossan—and follow his uncovering of their political origins via their demythologization. Then, by way of Phillip H. Wiebe's work on possession,[128] I will discuss spiritual language as a theory postulated in order to render intelligible seemingly related phenomena. This discussion will put us in a position where we must discern the phenomena presented to us in Mark's story, asking whether Horsley's account of demythologization is a sufficient enough explanation of the phenomena to supplant the language of spirits present in the pericope, or if, in inheriting Crossan's analysis, he also inherits Crossan's phenomenal remainder. As we will see, the only reason I am at odds with Horsley is because the only way he can get from exorcism to political confrontation is through the demystification of the demonic, which is not only unnecessary, but

---

the possibility that Jesus permitted real demons to enter the herd of swine" (180). However, this merely leads him to Hooker's question, as if economic loss exhausted the significance of the demonic.

[126] Richard A. Horsley, "The Struggle Against Roman Rule" in *Hearing the Whole Story: The Politics of Plot in Mark's Gospel* (London: Westminster John Knox, 2001), 121–48.

[127] Here he explicitly follows Crossan's analysis from *Jesus*, 88–91, as well as the work of Paul W. Hollenbach, "Jesus, Demoniacs, and Public Authorities: A Socio-Historical Study," *JAAR* 49 (1981): 567–88. See also Moore, *Empire and Apocalypse*, 24–44; and Laura E. Donaldson, "Gospel Hauntings." Interestingly, Donaldson traces neo-colonialisms in the works of Crossan and Horsley mentioned here.

[128] Phillip H. Wiebe, *God and Other Spirits: Intimations of Transcendence in Christian Experience* (Oxford: Oxford University Press, 2004); "Finite Spirits as Theoretical Entities," *RelS* 40 (2004): 341–50.

actually undermines the conclusion itself. The essay will conclude with an interrogation of how Horsley's political insights might survive the refutation of his demythologization.

This study is intended to contribute internally to postcolonial scholarship by reproducing its objective of unveiling hidden voices. The materials I engage make a concerted effort to uncover the voice of a man sacrificed to the fragile idol of stability in the face of colonial oppression. And although I share this sympathy, in their effort to do so, these scholars have unearthed one voice only to deposit their detritus upon another. Thus, as is customary within postcolonial scholarship, I will be reading against readings, attempting to find miniature neo-colonialisms in the postcolonial interpretation of the Gerasene demoniac. Yet the specific content of the voice I attempt to hear will also afford us an opportunity to evaluate some of the common political expectations of postcolonial study that may have obfuscated it in the first place.

Ademonic Politics

By now, it has become quite acceptable to infer political references in Mark's Gerasene Demoniac, whether one follows the critical path[129] or eschews it.[130] The name of the demon(s), *Legion* (λεγιών), carries almost unbearable symbolic weight all its own when the division of Roman troops bearing that name is taken to be its referent; it seems to name the source of the demoniac's affliction.[131] Mark has already set a precedent for the language of exorcism connoting political subjection or conquest in 1:25, 27.[132] J. Duncan M. Derrett's excellent

---

[129] To the list in n. 127 above, we might add Ched Myers, *Binding the Strong Man: A Political Reading of Mark's Story of Jesus* (Maryknoll: Orbis, 1988), 190–94; Swete, *Commentary*, 95; Christopher Burdon, "'To the Other Side': Construction of Evil and Fear of Liberation in Mark 5:1–20," *JSNT* 27 (2004): 149–67, who also mentions Gerd Theissen, Werner Kelber, as well as Joel Marcus and Joachim Gnilka, both of whom are more cautious. See the discussion of 157–63; see 158 n. 20 for a bibliography of those that have rejected or ignored this line of interpretation.

[130] E.g. Moore, *Empire and Apocalypse*, who sidesteps the question of whether "Legion" is a military or numeric reference by interpreting the passage allegorically (27–29).

[131] Horsley, "The Struggle," 140. Cf. Moore, *Empire and Apocalypse*, 24–27; and Sugirtharajah, "Coding and Decoding," 92–93, who identifies Mary Baird as the first to uncover the term's "colonial associations," in her "The Gadarene Demoniac."

[132] Horsley, "The Struggle," 137–38. In this he refers to Howard Clark Kee's "The Terminology of Mark's Exorcism Stories."

collection of insights into the Gerasene Demoniac helps us to see those undertones extended into Mark 5.[133] The term ἀγέλη, though rightly translated *herd*, was also a local term for a group of military recruits. The demon begs not to be *dispatched* (ἀποστείλῃ) out of the country, as though they were a troop appealing to their commanding officer. When Jesus permits the Legion to move into the swine, the word ἐπέτρεψεν is used, which, though rightly translated as *permission*, carries a well established association with the issuing of a military command, an *order*. When ὥρμησεν ἡ ἀγέλη down the steep cliff into the sea, it did what pigs have no business doing; on the contrary, ὥρμησεν is much more naturally used to describe the movement of troops *rushing* or *charging* into battle. Moreover, as has been well pointed out, the Galilean body of water is hardly a θάλασσα, a *sea*. Such language calls to mind rather the Reed Sea, suggesting in our own pericope the representation of the Egyptian armies drowning at the hands of God in their pursuit of the Israelites.[134] It also reminds of the Mediterranean, whence the Roman legions have come in conquest.[135]

According to Richard Horsley, the political orientation of the story reveals the symbolic turning of the tables on the occupying Roman legions in the genuflection of the demoniac before Jesus. The readers of Mark are "treated to the picture of (the Roman) Legion 'bowing down before' Jesus and 'desperately begging him not to send him/them out of the country' that they had taken possession of!"[136] With the ultimate destruction of the Legion with the pigs in the sea, "the episode thus tells of the people's liberation from the Roman legions and the destruction of those legions, as it evokes memories of God's original deliverance of Israel from Egyptian bondage in the exodus."[137]

But for Horsley and others who see Mark's demoniac as politically suggestive, the pericope remains resistant to what otherwise seems a rather sensible reading; for despite the military vocabulary, Jesus' encounter is not with a Roman army or anyone therefrom, but with a (legion of) demon(s). How do we traverse the gap between the given narrative account of phenomena about which modern sensibilities

---

[133] The following references all come from Derrett, "Contributions," 5. Cf. Horsley, "The Struggle," 141, and Myers, *Binding*, 191.
[134] Cf. Derrett, "Contributions," 8; Horsley, "The Struggle," 141; Myers, *Binding*, 191.
[135] Horsley, "The Struggle," 141.
[136] Horsley, "The Struggle," 140.
[137] Horsley, "The Struggle," 141.

remain incredulous, and that narrative's political "meaning" which modern sensibilities are convinced is of the utmost relevance? To put it otherwise, how does Mark's unbelievable story about demon possession teach Mark's modern readers about what *seems* to be its point, namely the political rescue of God's people by the Messiah?

Paul W. Hollenbach, writing in the early eighties, takes it upon himself to correct what he identifies as the dearth of biblical scholarship dealing with the sociological details of Jesus' exorcisms. Scholars have given undue attention to answering what beliefs Mark's early readers would have held regarding demon possession, neglecting the actual lives of demoniacs, and hence overlooking the task of situating exorcisms within Jesus' broader career. He is unequivocally certain, however, that the task of uncovering the socio-political significance of exorcisms can only be performed through the development of a kind of "social science of demoniacs, exorcists, and exorcism."[138] In fact, the phenomena once explained with reference to the miraculous are now exhaustively explained with reference to the social sciences. The language of possession and exorcism for Hollenbach is utterly obsolete: "In modern terms [exorcism] means that Jesus healed people who had various kinds of mental or psychosomatic illnesses."[139]

Though he is less explicitly enthusiastic about the explanatory capabilities of the social sciences, Horsley takes up Hollenbach's project to ascertain what role Jesus' exorcisms play within Mark's story of the renewal of Israel vis-à-vis its rulers,[140] in an attempt expand upon his socio-psychological account with a consideration of the politico-historical (i.e. colonial) dimensions.[141] Their differences are minimal and will be discussed below. For the moment, however, they are unimportant, for both Horsley and Hollenbach enlist Frantz Fanon's *The Wretched of the Earth*[142] to establish a causal relationship between colonial oppression and "demon possession," and identify the integral role of the "possessed" in colonial stability. Fanon's account of Algerian experiences under French colonialism helps the two exegetes situate the phenomena of possession within the extensive pressures

---

[138] Hollenbach, "Jesus, Demoniacs," 568.
[139] Hollenbach, "Jesus, Demoniacs," 567.
[140] Horsley, "The Struggle," 136.
[141] Horsley, "The Struggle," 274 n.33. Myers also notes this weakness in Hollenbach's account in *Binding*, 192–93.
[142] Frantz Fanon, *The Wretched of the Earth* (trans. C. Farrington; New York: Grove, 1968).

exerted by colonialist presence and oppression.[143] Horsley recognizes in Fanon an opportunity to see that the struggle between spiritual forces is "also a this-worldly *political* struggle."[144] What follows is a brief account of Horsley's adaptation of Fanon's work to the story of the Gerasene demoniac.

Colonization operates by setting up a basic dualism between the colonizer and the colonized that is, in its essence, Manichaean. The colonizer, beyond being a vector of physical force, inhabits and demonstrates prescriptively the life of strength, high-moral value, and satiety. The force of this demonstration homogenizes the native and his[145] way of life, which is correspondingly subjected, the enemy of values, destitute. The native becomes "absolute evil."[146] Concomitant with this is the development within the native social-psyche of a reversed Manichaeism that idealises the native way of life and mocks the colonizer's. Here, the settler is the absolute evil, though the native lacks the sheer force of the colonizer to reverse the social order.[147] This engenders a state of "permanent tension"[148] that, for some, is actually unbearable. It divides the mind of the native, for he desires the overthrow of the oppressor, desires to be the oppressor; through his hatred of this absolute evil, he is simultaneously absolutely opposed and irresistibly drawn to his enemy.[149] There is additional pressure in the ancient Palestinian setting because Israel's God is supposed to be in charge of history, the

---

[143] Horsley is clear that the colonisations of Palestine by the Romans and Algeria by the French are not exact parallels. He still contends that there are enough similarities for Fanon's account of the Manichaeism of colonization to be suggestive for this pericope ("The Struggle," 142). This rests partly on his claim that Roman troops would have, in recent Galilean experience, "more than once…attacked their villages unmercifully, burning their houses, slaughtering or enslaving the people, plundering their goods, either in their own or nearby areas" (140). Horsley expands upon this setting on 51–52 of "'My Name is Legion': Spirit Possession and Exorcism in Roman Palestine," in *Experientia, Volume 1: Inquiry into Religious Experience in Early Judaism and Christianity* (ed. F. Flannery, C. Shantz, and R. A. Werline; SBL Symposium 40; Leiden: Brill, 2008), 41–57. Though this claim is contested, it need not be strictly true in order to soundly develop his account of possession. Possession will be linked below to states of tension and their effect on the psyche of the colonised that, as Hollenbach notes, does no not *require* localized events, and are "attributable to the state of general social disruption" ("Jesus, Demoniacs," 575).
[144] Horsley, "The Struggle," 141, author's emphasis.
[145] Pronouns are here consistent with my sources.
[146] See Horsley, "The Struggle," 142.
[147] See Horsley, "The Struggle," 143.
[148] Horsley, "The Struggle," 144; also, Fanon, *The Wretched*, 52.
[149] Cf. Hollenbach, "Jesus, Demoniacs," 573.

one capable of their salvation from this abject subjection.[150] Its invasion by Rome constitutes in the community's psyche an invasion of the people of God by rival, evil spiritual forces (Belial, Satan).[151]

The native of divided mind is "hemmed in,"[152] delimited by colonial power on all sides, touching even his innermost reaches.[153] The demonstrations of power by the oppressor serve not only to remind the native of the futility of his resistance, it keeps his anger virile as well while depriving it of any outlet. It is here that the mythology of possession has its intelligibility. On the one hand, the development of demonic mythology within the constitutive narrative of the social body allows the Israelites, in our case, to persist in a particular way of life.[154] It does this in two ways. First, it avoids the blasphemy of blaming God for their plight. Second, it avoids the suicide of directly confronting their human oppressors. This is the choice of the "lesser evil," the diversion of the body's attention for the sake of its own physical and cultural survival. Possession mythology becomes a way to cope with oppression without threatening the social position of the colonizer.[155] In Fanon's words, "Believe me, the zombies are more terrifying than the settlers.... We no longer really need to fight against [the settlers] since what counts is the frightening enemy created by myths."[156] This is concomitant to the apocalyptic imagination that is convinced that in the face of massive injustice and power imbalance, all will be decided at once and for all.[157]

---

[150] This assumes that the demoniac is Jewish, which is not a given. See e.g., Iverson, "First Journey"; also Hooker, *Mark*, 143, and Cranfield, *St Mark*, 177. On the other hand, Derrett argues that the unqualified use of ἄνθρωπος in the Synoptics means *Jew*, and estimates the mission on the far side of the Sea of Galilee was to nominal Jews as much as to Gentiles, who together have failed to call upon the name of the Lord ("Contributions," 16 n. 26, 6, 9). Either way, however, the pressures of imperial domination can easily be said to affect all in the region, regardless of whether one is Jew or Gentile.

[151] Horsley, "The Struggle," 143.

[152] Horsley, "The Struggle," 144, quoting Fanon, *The Wretched*, 52.

[153] Cf. Moore's comment regarding the ἐν from ἐν πνεύματι ἀκαθάρτῳ of Mk 5:2: "The peculiar *en* should be allowed its full, engulfing force here. It signifies that the possessed subject's identity has been utterly submerged in that which possesses him—as is indeed evident from that fact that, in the dialogue that ensues, *it* speaks in him, through him, and for him. One would be hard-pressed to find a more apt image—or allegory—of the colonial subject's self-alienation when compelled to internalize the discourse of the colonizer" (*Empire and Apocalypse*, 28).

[154] See Horsley, "The Struggle," 144.

[155] Cf. Hollenbach, "Jesus, Demoniacs," 575–76.

[156] *The Wretched*, 56, quoted in Horsley, "The Struggle," 144.

[157] See Horsley, "The Struggle," 143.

On the other hand, being so hemmed in can have a profound effect on the psychology of individuals specifically, beyond mere diversion. Hollenbach and Horsley see this in two slightly different ways. Hollenbach follows Fanon's lead more closely. In his account, when the permanent state of oppressive tension becomes too much for the mind to bear, the mind loses its ability to cope with the conditions presented to it and mental illness sets in.[158] For Horsley, the Gerasene demoniac is seen as a man whose sanity is sacrificed to protect himself from his own suicidal rebellion, and to turn him into a diversion away from political confrontation in the manner discussed above.[159] What is common to both is the perception of a general causal relationship between military possession and "demon possession." The exposure of this link makes it possible for Hollenbach to see how Jesus' exorcisms seem to play such a large role in fomenting the opposition of local and Galilean authorities (scribes, Pharisees, Herod Antipas). Because of the integral role that the mental illness of "demon possession" played in social control and public order, Jesus' prolific practice of exorcisms, not to mention his interpretation of them as signs of the coming kingdom, made Jesus' disruption of the social order, and challenge to the prevailing system, inevitable.[160] In placing Hollenbach's analysis within the context of the Roman occupation, however, Horsley understands the political threat of exorcisms not to be a natural consequence, but the deliberate operation of the exorcisms themselves. Because of the causal relationship between military occupation and "demon possession," Jesus' exorcisms must be seen as modes of political confrontation, intentionally disrupting the social order for the sake of the kingdom.[161]

---

[158] Hollenbach, "Jesus, Demoniacs," 573–75.

[159] Horsley is reticent to speak of individual psychological conditions and so focuses on the manner in which the demoniac becomes, by virtue of his condition, the repository for the community's resentment over Roman domination ("The Struggle," 145).

[160] See esp. Hollenbach, "Jesus, Demoniacs," 582–84.

[161] For another, though altogether more brief, account of the Gerasene demoniac that uses Fanon, see R. S. Sugirtharajah, "Coding and Decoding," 91–94. Like both Hollenbach and Horsley, Sugirtharajah sets the demoniac within the context of colonialism and refers to Fanon to identify the "possession" as an effect of Roman occupation. Unlike those two, however, he is more equivocal about whether this exorcism is a good thing: in upsetting the delicate balance, does Jesus' exorcism manifest his hostility to the Roman powers, or does it rob the Gerasenes of their one articulation of resistance, their coping mechanism, treating the symptom without confronting its source?

Thus, though Horsley lacks the explicit confidence in the ability of the social sciences to exhaustively explain (i.e. demystify) possession, his account entails no less a suppression of the ancient explanation of these phenomena than Hollenbach's does. They both find the political significance of Jesus' exorcism in its ability to disrupt the stable relation of colonizer-colonized. The strength of these accounts is in rightly seeing exorcism as a political activity; their weakness is that they can only reach this point by bracketing possession itself. As we initially saw with Crossan, the problem is this: colonialism never causes demon possession, it only causes "demon possession." Hence, the political meaning of exorcism for Horsley is redirected away from the possession that bears it:

> Once Jesus has forced out the identification of the demonic forces as (the surrogates of) the Roman political and military forces in the exorcism of the Gerasene demoniac, the veil of mystification has been pulled back. The casting out and naming of "Legion" is a demystification of (the belief in) demons and demon possession. It is now evident to Jesus' followers and to the hearers of Mark's story that the struggle is *really* against the rulers, ultimately the Romans.[162]

It is not without irony that these postcolonial biblical scholars join with Fanon in out-narrating the "seventy-five percent of the world" that still believe in spiritual beings by showing us what demon possession *really* is; such an interpretation bears a colonialist relationship not only over these people of today's world, but also over those of the past and the text of Mark itself, despite their sensibilities to the contrary.[163] In order to reach a compelling political account of the

---

[162] Horsley, "The Struggle," 147, emphasis mine.

[163] Since the publication of *Hearing the Whole Story*, Horsley has published another essay on Mark's Gerasene demoniac, which was unfortunately brought to my attention too late for me to give substantive treatment here. See "My Name is Legion." Having said that, he simply discusses examples strengthening the connection between the demonic and the colonial, without fundamentally changing his position on the matter. In fact, if anything, he is more audacious in "My Name is Legion," as he castigates other scholars for "explaining away" spirit possessions with modern western psychological explanations that do not "take indigenous cultural beliefs and representations seriously" (41-42), unaware that he is doing precisely the same thing. For despite his desire to "investigate the portrayal of spirit possession and exorcism in its own cultural context" (44), in claiming that spirit possession is the mystification of "concrete power relations," implying again that it was a mistake for the Galileans to believe their misfortunes were caused by demons and not the Romans or their own sins, taking seriously the *specific content* of indigenous beliefs and representations is precisely what Horsley does not do (see p. 56).

Gerasene demoniac they have had to efface the demons themselves with the oppressive sobriety of the social sciences, effectively silencing all those for whom Jesus' power to exorcise is meaningful, all of those who depend upon this power. It seems as though the demonic cannot survive the political, but this has only been accomplished by setting certain phenomena within the pericope aside. The remaining questions before us are thus twofold. Do these phenomena provide us with a scratch from which to reassert the plausibility of the demonic, beyond the pejorative "blind faith"?[164] And, if they do, can the political survive the demonic?

Demons as Postulated Entities

At this point in the development of the modern sciences, any theory in the West that tries to make sense of demons has the heavy burden of a long history of demythologization to bear.[165] Phillip Wiebe thus restricts himself to the relatively modest task of inquiring whether there is any room within a rational account of the world for demons and other spirits. An account of spirits that resists naïveté requires

---

[164] My work should be delimited on the other side by accounts that do posit the demonic, although I do not have the space here to give it proper treatment. However, the majority of such accounts remain popular in nature, and lack the subtle scholarship that would make them suitable dialogue partners. In any case, often appearing under the rubric of "Spiritual Warfare Theology," these accounts tend to make the inverse mistake of the demythologizing scholars by allowing the demonic to elide the political. Beyond being unable to account for what I think are helpful insights from political readings of exorcism, such accounts often unwittingly bolster extremely conservative, moralistic, and often patriotic concerns, problematically reproducing the kind of imperialist politics I take Jesus' exorcisms to be opposing. There is a small contingent of scholars at present willing to admit the reality of superhuman agents. Foremost among these are Clinton E. Arnold and Graham H. Twelftree. Unfortunately, the former, though responding to some of the extremes of Spiritual Warfare, is still too simplistic morally and politically. The latter argues in his latest work that Mark's exorcism stories are precisely not socio-political in nature, although this rests upon a narrow understanding of the socio-political. See *In the Name of Jesus: Exorcism among Early Christians* (Grand Rapids: Baker, 2007), 105–11. Nevertheless, he does have some helpful comments in the conclusion that temper the excesses of Spiritual Warfare Theology (279–95).

[165] Wiebe highlights the role of Rudolf Bultmann in the demythologization process of theology and biblical study (*God and Other Spirits*, 3). But Max Weber rightly identified "disenchantment" as the very character of the rationalization and intellectualization of modernity. See "Science as a Vocation," in *From Max Weber: Essays in Sociology* (ed. and trans. H. H. Gerth and C. W. Mills; New York: Oxford University Press, 1946), 129–56.

specificity regarding their modern critique and dismissal. It is a prerogative of modern science to continually evaluate explanatory theories of phenomena. As a matter of course, many theories are eliminated whose basic concepts are either unnecessary or defective in such a way as to warrant the abandonment of the theory altogether, and its replacement by something completely different.[166] It is commonly held that the postulation of demons is just such a theory, and that modern science is able to give a better, more coherent and consistent accounts of the phenomena that spirits (now inadequately) explain. Wiebe concedes that any defender of such a theory in our time must demonstrate the existence of phenomena for which the postulation of the theory of spirits still provides the most plausible explanation.[167] Our present task is more modest still, and that is to show that the particular phenomena presented to us by Mark's Gerasene pericope is still most plausibly explained in accordance with the explanation given within the narrative, which is with reference to the demonic.

It is noteworthy that Horsley and Hollenbach did not take the easy way out of the challenge of the demonic by calling into question the historicity of the story. Instead of finding political elements merely by invoking reader-response or authorial intent, in recalling Fanon they have boldly taken up an historical claim. They have postulated an alternative theory to Mark's that attempts to explain the historical phenomena themselves—presumably limited to the behaviour of the "demoniac," his countrymen, and Jesus. Horsley is more reticent than Hollenbach to diagnose the Gerasene demoniac, and even Hollenbach does not get any more specific than "mental illness." But no mental illness—including dissociative-identity disorder, which is often invoked to explain phenomena like the voices from the demoniac that the narrative attributes to unclean spirits—is able to account for the pig's behaviour.[168] It is thus significant that in their account, the movement

---

[166] Wiebe calls this the "eliminative approach" in *God and Other Spirits*, 18–20. So, e.g., biology has seen this with genes, evolutionary theory with natural selection, geology with tectonic plates, and psychology with the unconscious ("Finite Spirits," 344). Note also the obsolescence of theories of substances such as ether and phlogiston in *God and Other Spirits*, 134–36.

[167] Wiebe, *God and Other Spirits*, 127.

[168] Cf. Wiebe, "Finite Spirits," 342. It is possible that the pericope in Mark is a combination of exorcism tales attributed to Jesus, and that a basic exorcism could be historical and the transfer not. See, e.g., Hooker, *Mark*, 141–42, and Rudolph Pesch, "The Markan Version of the Healing of the Gerasene Demoniac," *Ecumenical Review* 23 (1971): 349–76, esp. 367–68. I submit, however, that it is no coincidence that such

of the spirits from the demoniac to the swine drops completely out of view. As such, we have the dismissal of a theory without a full examination of the phenomena it is enlisted to explain; Horsley even pushes the elimination of Mark's theory by his own to constitute the very meaning and significance of the passage. But if we take Wiebe's project seriously, this reading is not adequate to eliminate the demonic; it is not a thorough enough examination to persuasively demythologize Legion. For such a dismissal can only be "won by careful argument and *more complete attention* to the phenomena that have been alleged as best explained by hypotheses postulating transcendent beings."[169]

As I suggested above, the behaviour of the demoniac himself does not occlude a purely psychopathological interpretation. What *does* occlude one is the confluence of a variety of observable phenomena that are seemingly linked in a causal manner.[170] Upon exiting the boat, Jesus is met by a self-destructive man in an unclean spirit, whom no man is strong enough to subdue, even by binding him with chains. It seems at first that Jesus engages in conversation with the *man*, who proceeds rather unusually to bestow upon Jesus the title of "Son of the Most High God," and attempt to make Jesus swear to God that he will not torture him. Verse 8, however, retroactively makes it clear that Jesus is not conversing with the man, but is addressing the spirits possessing him; it is they who are aware of Jesus' identity. The conversation continues and the demon—who appears to be speaking on behalf of a multitude of demons[171]—begs Jesus not to send them out of the country but into the pigs visibly feeding on the nearby hillside. Jesus grants them this permission, whereupon more or less at once the pigs rush down the bank into the lake and drown, and the man ceases his destructive behaviour.

---

arguments come from those who cannot abide belief in superhuman agents. Pesch is particularly pretentious and derisive: Jesus' behaviour is embarrassing to the sceptic, feeding the credulity of the unsophisticated and naïve (349). With such demeaning rhetoric, it is difficult to see this as other than a (colonialist) strategy to find the "meaning" of the passage on one's own rationalist terms without giving any ground to inferior cosmological beliefs. Pesch's self-righteousness notwithstanding, the decision to lop off the swine is still conjecture rather than necessary, and in any event, Horsley and Hollenbach have opened up the door to historicity without making this distinction.

[169] Wiebe, *God and Other Spirits*, 20, my emphasis.
[170] Cf. Wiebe, *God and Other Spirits*, 32.
[171] See Wiebe, *God and Other Spirits*, 14, on the use of "we" and the possession of someone by a group of spirits.

The "unclean spirits" of Mk 5 play the causal role Wiebe refers to as a postulated entity. In terms of its relation to an historical account, this means that we can understand these spirits, which are *unobservable*, as a theory postulated to explain the seemingly causal relationship between *observable* events.[172] The sequence of events, their timing, their proximity, and the intelligibility of the conversations conducted, which themselves include an interpretation of the events, all suggest the causal connection of the exorcism event and the erratic behaviour of the pigs.[173] To deny this we might suggest that the events are so anomalous that coincidence could be postulated just as easily as spirits. It should be noted, however, that there have been other reports, even contemporary ones, which bear sometimes strikingly similar marks of demonic transfer or "contagion."[174] Moreover, to claim these events as a coincidence is to "deny them the intelligibility we find in human life, where speech and actions appropriate to a particular context and past events occur."[175] The behaviour of the man and the suicide of the pigs seem to be observable effects of an independent unobservable power; they exist in a particular order of succession, joined in narrative by a conversation that includes a command by Jesus to that unobserved causal power to leave the man and enter the pigs. To arrive at Horsley's theory—that the mythology of possession is a diversion from the "real" problem, and that Jesus' exorcism constitutes a demythologization of possession—one has to ignore everything that makes the pericope what it is: the content of the conversation between Jesus and the

---

[172] Cf. Wiebe, "Finite Spirits," 347: "Spirits are postulated entities that can be understood primarily by the causal relationships that they have with phenomena whose existence is not in doubt." Part of the strength of Wiebe's project comes from his observation (adapted from the work of philosopher David Lewis) the regularity with which all manners of discourse—both scientifically credible and not—make use of postulated entities as a matter of course in recognizing the intelligibility of everyday phenomena. He cites an example from physics (the baryon II particle) and folk-psychology (anger); Wiebe, "Finite Spirits," 343-44.

[173] Cf. Wiebe, *God and Other Spirits*, 12.

[174] It is part of Wiebe's project to collect and analyse such reports. He relays a powerful account of an exorcism in Adelaide, Australia, that involved the transfer of a demonic contagion (*God and Other Spirits*, 11-15). I draw here from Wiebe's analysis of this case as much as I do from his analysis of the Gadarene demoniac (he uses Matthew's text as opposed to Mark's), as the contours of the stories bear striking resemblances.

[175] Wiebe, *God and Other Spirits*, 13. Note also his comment from the same page: For this study, "the relevant background appears to be the human sciences, where claims about causal connections are often tentative and incompletely supported by observation."

demon, the actions of the swine, and the apparent connection between the two.[176] Horsley is unable to eliminate demons from the pericope; in the absence of other hypotheses, they remain the best explanation of the phenomena of the Gerasene demoniac.

Political Demons, Demonic Politics

I have suggested with Wiebe that we might understand Mark's "unclean spirits" as a theory postulated to account for the connection between evental phenomena. It seems, however, unsatisfactory to call Mark's use of the term "unclean spirits" a "theory," if for no other reason than the unlikelihood of either him or much of his early communities of readers thinking of spirits as "theoretical entities." On the contrary, the pericope is what Wiebe calls a theory-laden description;[177] that is, we cannot neatly distinguish between the observable phenomena and the unobservable spirits postulated to give the account intelligibility. The existence of unclean spirits is assumed in the very telling of the story.

Consider what we would be left with were we to attempt to give an account of the historical event without the postulation of spiri-

---

[176] Wiebe, *God and Other Spirits*, 12. Hooker notes that some have attempted to explain the movement of the swine by suggesting that at his healing the demoniac was paroxysmal, but this seems to be grasping at straws. As I noted in n. 168, she thinks that it is useless to try to reconstruct the historical event. Significantly for our study, she gives the following concluding comment: "The interpretation given to the incident by Mark was the natural deduction from the available facts, granted the basic belief of those concerned that the man had been possessed by a large number of unclean spirits, and that these had been driven out" (*Mark*, 144). She seems here to admit reluctantly that even if a scientifically-minded contemporary were to witness the historical exorcism, no more observable phenomena (such as a paroxysm of some sort) would come to light that would satisfactorily suggest an alternative theory to Mark's. Ironically, she here agrees with Derrett, who is much less reluctant to grant that the phenomena suggest demons, particularly given a little knowledge of animal behaviour: "[Pigs] are very liable to panic, and then they scatter: they do not stampede in the manner familiar in horses, cattle, etc. The miracle in the story lay in the pigs' forming themselves up up to two thousand strong, and rushing over the cliff. If such a thing happened any onlooker would say they were bewitched" ("Contributions," 5).

[177] See Wiebe, "Finite Spirits, 345: "All description is sometimes said to be theory-laden, but this might only be a way of saying that assumptions about existent things and their properties and relations are involved in all description. A more important sense of the theory-laden character of descriptions is illustrated by the case of the Gadarene demoniacs, where the description itself requires presupposing the entities whose existence the theory postulates."

tual entities.[178] Upon exiting the boat, Jesus is met by a self-destructive man, whom no man is strong enough to subdue, even by binding him with chains. Jesus engages in conversation with the man as he proceeds rather unusually—and, except for the voice from heaven at his baptism and another demon, without precedent—to bestow upon Jesus the title of "Son of the Most High God," and attempt to make Jesus swear to God that he will not torture him. There is a conversation with unknown content. Jesus utters something resembling a command, whereupon more or less at once the pigs rather inexplicably rush down the bank into the lake and drown, the man ceasing his destructive behaviour.

What intelligibility is left in this story? In fact, it is no longer a story at all, but a loose collection of discrete events that coincidentally occur around the same time.[179] But this is not Mark's story: Horsley's demythologization thesis has rendered a number of important elements in his pericope inadmissible. The very name *Legion* becomes suspect, for who are the *we* whose number justifies the name, and who is the *them* begging not to be sent out of the country? The pronouns betray an intelligence not belonging to the Gerasene man yet speaking "through" him. Although this *could* be explained by Hollenbach's reference to mental illness (e.g. dissociative identity disorder) and remain applicable to the political reading, other elements are not so retainable. Jesus' command to *come out* of the man (ἔξελθε) which is a performative utterance,[180] becomes unintelligible if spoken to the man (what would it mean to be told to come out of oneself?) and histrionic if spoken to a mental illness. Of course, without this performative utterance we lose any semblance of Jesus' hand in the healing of the mentally ill Gerasene; when Jesus says "Go home to your friends, and tell them how much the Lord has done for you," we cannot be certain of what he is speaking. Without demons there is nothing for Jesus to order (ἐπέτρεψεν) into the swine, nothing to be dispatched (ἀποστείλῃ). And as every connection to the swine is severed—for what is Horsley's point but to say that there is precisely *nothing* in the man to enter the swine—we lose the swine themselves and any descriptions associated with them: the herd (ἀγέλη), the charging (ὥρμησεν), and the plunge

---

[178] See Wiebe, *God and Other Spirits*, 124.
[179] Cf. Wiebe's example of a description that is more "topic-neutral" (*God and Other Spirits*, 125).
[180] Cf. Wiebe, *God and Other Spirits*, 124–25.

into the sea (ἐν τῇ θαλάσσῃ). But is not all of this precisely the narratological material that suggested the political reading of the pericope to Horsley et al. in the first place?

The loss of these elements through the elision of the demonic utterly destroys the integrity of the pericope. In order to arrive at his political reading, Horsley has to elide the very material that makes it possible. It is the *demons* that have military associations, not a collection of abstract phenomena.[181] This mistake is most obvious in the blunder of attributing to the man what the narrative attributes to the demons. Hollenbach, for example, claims that the *man* gives the name *Legion* to the "demon."[182] But, as we have already noted, v. 8 makes it clear that it is to the demon and not the man that Jesus is speaking; the two are not substitutable without consequence. This is simply a matter of wanting to have it both ways. Horsley tries to argue against the existence of demons by using an event that is still, even today, best explained by postulating a theory of the demonic. His positing of what possession "really is," which he takes to be the significance of the passage, has radically compromised the integrity of his interpretation; it is not logically tenable.

If we keep the demons in, however, we may retrieve the phenomena that suggest a political reading. It seems as though it is all or nothing: either the pericope is about both demons and political oppression, or it is about neither. Horsley's reading is still compelling in certain ways. First and foremost I think that Horsley and Hollenbach are right to suspect a sort of causal connection between military occupation and the kind of affliction we see in the demoniac. But moreover, this account lends intelligibility to the reaction of the people of the area, showing the manner in which exorcism turns Jesus into a political threat. And I think it correct to understand exorcism as freeing one to do a kind of political work. That his analysis is not tenable when taken as a whole suggests not that we should throw it out, but that we ask how to think about the story such that the Fanonian colonialist

---

[181] Cf. Derrett, "Contributions," 5: "It is of interest that specialists in spirit-possession have come across many instances where the 'spirits' speak of their military associations and prowess."

[182] Hollenbach, "Jesus, Demoniacs," 581. This section is replete with sloppy analysis such as this, attributing "demonic possession" to the man's agency. This should be seen as problematic even if we were to concede that many possession accounts were attributable to mental illness, as if people "choose" to be mentally ill. Cf. Horsley, "The Struggle," 145: "In becoming possessed and violently crazy, the man sacrificed his sanity, but at least he was still alive."

accounts and the uniquely tenable hypothesis of demon possession can coexist. At one point, Horsley worries that, compared to the Manichaean structure of colonialism, his theory with regards to the politics of demon possession may be considerably more difficult to grasp.[183] In actual fact, it may be far simpler than he suspects.

I submit that if Mark's Gerasene demoniac contains political references to the Roman occupation of Palestine, it is because there is, in fact, a connection between the military possession and demon possession. To be clear, this is distinct from Ched Myers' postulation that "the meaning of [exorcism] must be found by viewing it in terms of symbolic reproduction of social conflict."[184] Myers wants to take seriously the language of demon possession,[185] but he fares no better than Horsley in his treatment of the phenomena: exorcism *qua* exorcism is political, but only metaphorically. For both however, it seems that the distance to be traversed for a more accurate reading spans no more than a single word. When Horsley says the struggle of exorcism is "*really* against Roman imperial rule,"[186] he is admitting the phenomenal connection but suggesting that the mythology is a distraction; when Myers says that exorcism is a "public *symbolic* action,"[187] he recognizes the connection between the mythology and the political, but the connection remains metaphorical and not phenomenological. In fact the *really* and the *symbolic* may be dropped; demons are not beside the point, and there is no literary distance between exorcisms and the political. For in Mark, exorcism is *actually* public action against Roman imperial rule. The "hemmed in" native is the one susceptible to unclean spirits; the exorcism of his spirits is Jesus' chosen response to the colonial pressures that possess him. There is thus no gap that must be traversed to see exorcism in the political career of Christ. It is an act of confrontation not in a war of myths, as Myers suggests,[188] but in a very political battle.

---

[183] Horsley, "The Struggle," 144.
[184] Myers, *Binding*, 142.
[185] See Myers, *Binding*, where he describes demythologization as "historicism at its crudest."
[186] Horsley, "The Struggle," 147, emphasis mine.
[187] Myers, *Binding*, 193, I have removed Myers' emphasis on "public," which is no longer controversial as it may have been in 1988, and placed it upon symbolic.
[188] Myers, *Binding*, 143.

CHAPTER EIGHT

The Phenomenological Consequences of Ritual Impurity and Imperial Pride

So, demons and imperial politics seem to exist together in some broadly causal relationship; the exorcisms of Jesus may be seen to constitute a direct response to the Roman occupation of first-century Palestine. Unfortunately, we are a long way from unravelling the exegetical consequences of this postulation. Nevertheless, we can already suggest a couple of ways to conceive of this strange relation, which has implications not only for the relation between discursive spheres we are normally inclined to keep separate, but also for our understanding of theological concepts.

Consider that *cleanliness* is commonly understood as pertaining to bodily rituals that function *socially* and *symbolically*. Rarely, it seems, would anybody claim that there are phenomenal consequences to being ritually unclean.[189] Roger David Aus, however, notes that the Latinism *legion* developed negative connotations particularly with the stationing of *Legio X Fretensis* in Syria, near our demoniac.[190] The connection between the Gerasene demons and the swine they ultimately enter is well linked via the name *Legion* due to the fact that the Tenth Legion used the image of a wild boar on its military standards. That the boar is considered unclean in terms of Jewish ritual purity is obviously suggestive for the literary connection between the name *Legion*, the demoniac's unclean spirits, and their transference to the swine. But Aus notes a reference from the Tosefta that should suggest to us that the link between the Roman legion and the legion of demons is more than symbolic. According to *m. Hul.* 9:2, the skin of a human being is unclean. And so the Tosefta at 8:16 says, "A legion which is passing from place to place—he who overshadows it is unclean. You have no legion in which there are no (human) scalps." Aus also notes the commentary on this passage in *b. Hul.* 123a: "Our Rabbis taught: If a [Roman] legion which passes from place to place enters a house, the house is unclean, for there is not a legion that does not carry with

---

[189] In fact, many Christians understand Jesus in Mark 7:1–23 to be marking precisely the obsolescence of ritual purity, Christianity being understood to supersede such concerns. And so we snicker in church at the puerile fastidiousness of the Pharisees and their hand washing, all the while not realizing that Jesus is not abolishing cleanliness laws, but relocating the loci of defilement.

[190] Aus, *Legion*, 17.

it several scalps."¹⁹¹ More than simply suggesting the symbolic fecundity of the "demonic" correlation between the Romans and swine,¹⁹² this suggests including considerations of purity in the causal nexus of oppression and possession. It was, after all, an "unclean spirit" that possessed this man whose innermost psyche has been laid bare through colonialist pressure.

However, their ritual impurity is not the only, or even the primary, way by which the Roman occupying forces have been associated with demons. Though we can point to instances where ritual cleanliness is understood as a practice of keeping the community pure from demonic pollution,¹⁹³ a much more straightforward connection can be made by way of the Judeo-Christian tradition that the gods of the nations are demons,¹⁹⁴ and how this assertion gets picked up in apocalyptic sensibilities. In the imagery of the dragon and the two beasts in Rev 13, the very structure of Empire is revealed to the seer of Patmos. The beast of the sea, which is the seat of the imperial authority and dominion of Babylon, has the power, throne, and great authority of the dragon (Rev 13:2b), "who is called the Devil and Satan, the deceiver of the whole world" (12:9). The beast metonymically denotes the empire itself in the monstrous body of the emperor, whose worship is enforced by the beast of the earth (13:12). If we think the problem of idolatry this demonic fellowship manifests is simply a matter of the pantheistic worship of the people, we are only revealing the extent of our own demythologization of the political. On the contrary, the authority Satan gives empire is manifest in idolatry that takes the form of imperial war and conquest (13:7), economic oppression and exclusion (13:16–17), and most importantly the pride of its blasphemy and glorification of its own imperial power (13:4–8). In other words,

---

[191] See Aus, *Legion*, 18.

[192] Cf. Aus, *Legion*, 18.

[193] We might think of the fastidiousness of the Qumran community, for example, in terms of the correlation between ritual cleanliness and spiritual cleanliness. Cf. 1QS 2:25–4:26 and CD fragment 4Q266 fr. 6 i 1:5–7, and see Philip S. Alexander, "The Demonology of the Dead Sea Scrolls," in *The Dead Sea Scrolls After Fifty Years: A Comprehensive Assessment, Vol. 2* (ed. P. W. Flint and J. C. VanderKam; Leiden: Brill, 1998–1999), 348–50. But, a little closer to our own text, the eating of meat sacrificed to idols in 1 Cor 8 can also be read as a debate about precisely these matters. See Dale B. Martin, *The Corinthian Body* (New Haven: Yale University Press, 1995), 179–89.

[194] See Deut 32:17; Ps. 95:1–5 (LXX); 106:37; *1 En.* 19:1; *Jub* 1:11; and 1 Cor 10:20.

all the oppressive imperial conditions that made possible the possession of our Gerasene[195] were themselves the natural outcome of the demonic fellowship of the deceived nations; empire grows great under the lordship of demons,[196] and so it is to be expected that a corollary of the spread of empire would be an outbreak of the demonic contagion that animates it.

Conclusion: Postcolonial Expectations and the Mystery of the Political

It is a paradigmatic task of postcolonial scholarship to uncover those voices that are veiled by the media of colonialist culture, whether it is scholarly analyses, literature, or what have you. My primary task in this essay has been to apply this sensibility to postcolonial scholarship itself: I have attempted to reveal how the uncovering of the political voice of the Gerasene demoniac by setting it within the dynamics of empire has, in this case, obfuscated the presence of the demonic elements of the story. By implication, Horsley, as well as Hollenbach and Fanon, have effaced those voices that tenaciously cling to belief in the activity of invisible superhuman agents. I have also argued that the two voices can coexist, and, in Mark, already do. Of course, to turn the methodological cannons of postcolonialism against itself is nothing novel. But my hope has been that the particular content of my argument might play a secondary role in providing some groundwork to call into question some of the assumptions of much postcolonial biblical scholarship itself.

Contra Horsley, Jesus' struggle with the demons does not exactly promise to liberate the people from Rome's legions.[197] It is hard to believe Mark's early readers would hear the pericope telling them of their liberation from Roman legions, as Horsley suggests; regardless of

---

[195] Cf. Horsley, "My Name is Legion," 52.

[196] The early Christian judgement that the problem with the nations is their fellowship with demons finds perhaps its greatest expression in Augustine's political critique of Rome in *The City of God Against the Pagans*. Here Augustine links empire in all ages—the Athenians, Assyrians, Egyptians, Romans—within the notion of the earthly city, which is defined by its proud rejection of God in a fellowship with demons that fuels its lust for mastery. For Augustine, all such empires have risen (and continue to rise?) to power under the lordship of fallen angels. See Augustine, *The City of God against the Pagans* (ed. and trans. R. W. Dyson; Cambridge Texts in the History of Political Thought; Cambridge: Cambridge University Press, 1998) 16.17 and 19.24.

[197] Horsley, "The Struggle," 147.

whether Mark was written before or after the war, in its context, for an "exorcism" to "tell" of liberation in the absence of the Messiah's substantive encounter with Rome's occupying forces would have been nothing more than milquetoast soteriology. It is significant to note, however, that where Horsley argues that the struggle is really against the oppressive empire, presuming that spiritual agents do not exist, ancient Christ-believers argued the inverse. Most believed in active angels and demons, and conceived the *real* battle to be spiritual. For them, one could be *free* under an oppressive power that has yet to be unambiguously and catastrophically overturned; one could be emancipated while still being employed and abused as a slave, and deliverance was conceived spiritually, often as release from the power of unclean spirits. My suspicion is that, ever attuned to the injustices of empire—and perhaps rightly so, in many ways—Horsley is too preoccupied with the Romans to realise that, for early Christ-believers, the Romans were simply the latest in the line of imperial demon-worshippers; just as the occupying forces that bear the unclean contagion in Mark's pericope are contained to literary references within a story more evidently about spirit possession, so too imperial domination is but the manifestation of a more significant and immemorial spiritual struggle. Not only do Jesus' exorcisms deal directly with the subject of colonial oppression; they address the problem more to the point than would a straightforward confrontation between the Messiah and the Roman generals.[198] Far from treating the symptom without addressing the disease,[199] Jesus' exorcisms cut directly to the heart of the matter, even if a single exorcism leaves much more work to be done.

After Mark's Jesus demystifies the belief in demons and demon possession, as Horsley interprets the episode, the story focuses in upon Jesus' confrontation with the Romans themselves in the trial and crucifixion. This is why, he notes, "the dramatic battles against demons leave off just as the explicit political conflict comes to a head."[200] Of

---

[198] Fanon suggests that, just like demon mythology, pacifism serves to stabilize the colonial order; they both occlude the real change that comes only from insurrection (*The Wretched*, 59). It may be interesting to view Jesus' exorcisms in light of his renunciation of violent political force. His call to his followers to love their enemies has left him vulnerable to the charge of political quietism. Though this charge is misguided for several reasons, this account of exorcism suggests one more important way in which Jesus and his followers are to remain politically active in a manner fully consistent with their commitment to enemy-love.

[199] Sugirtharajah, "Coding and Decoding," 94.

[200] Horsley, "The Struggle," 147.

course, a demystified cross does not make for much of a confrontation, particularly from the viewpoint of the zealous messianic expectation of unambiguous liberation that postcolonial scholarship often entertains. But the cross has traditionally been understood as mystifying the expectation, not being demystified by it. To the extent that Jesus does liberate the faithful from Roman oppression, he does so *staurologically*,[201] but the content of this liberation at present is discipleship—and if we insist on speaking of "politics," we must assert that discipleship is staurology's proper political medium. Of course, this means nothing other than to continue the work he did and commissioned them to do in the appointing and sending of the twelve (Mk 3:13–19; 6:6b–13). In the appointing, casting out demons is one of only two authorities Jesus bestows upon his disciples; in the sending, their authority over unclean spirits is renewed. Thus, if we are looking for Jesus' confrontation to the Roman occupation in the hope that we might see his response to the powers throughout the ages, we ought to reinterpret the discipleship he is purported to have commissioned and made possible in light of the tradition that follows him in taking the *mystery* of the political a great deal more seriously. We close with just such a tradition, from Paul's Epistle to the Ephesians, which—being the precise inverse of Horsley's conclusion—begins to sound a lot less symbolic, resonating with renewed political fervour: "For our struggle is not against enemies of blood and flesh, but against the rulers, against the authorities, against the cosmic powers of this present darkness, against the spiritual forces of evil in the heavenly places" (6:12).

---

[201] As in, ὁ σταυρός (cross). Cf. Stanislas Breton, *The Word and the Cross* (trans. J. Porter; Perspectives in Continental Philosophy 22; New York: Fordham, 2002), 48.

CHAPTER NINE

POSTCOLONIAL APPROACHES BEYOND WESTERN HISTORICAL CRITICAL DISCOURSES

9.1 George M. Soares-Prabhu (De Nobili College in Pune, India [†1995]). And There Was a Great Calm: A 'Dhvani' Reading of the Stilling of the Storm (Mk 4:35-41)[1]

Mark 4:35-41

³⁵On that day, when evening had come, he said to them, 'Let us go across to the other side.' ³⁶And leaving the crowd behind, they took him with them in the boat, just as he was. Other boats were with him. ³⁷A great windstorm arose, and the waves beat into the boat, so that the boat was already being swamped. ³⁸But he was in the stern, asleep on the cushion; and they woke him up and said to him, 'Teacher, do you not care that we are perishing?' ³⁹He woke up and rebuked the wind, and said to the sea, 'Peace! Be still!' Then the wind ceased, and there was a dead calm. ⁴⁰He said to them, 'Why are you afraid? Have you still no faith?' ⁴¹And they were filled with great awe and said to one another, 'Who then is this, that even the wind and the sea obey him?'

[35] Καὶ λέγει αὐτοῖς ἐν ἐκείνῃ τῇ ἡμέρᾳ ὀψίας γενομένης· διέλθωμεν εἰς τὸ πέραν.
[36] καὶ ἀφέντες τὸν ὄχλον παραλαμβάνουσιν αὐτὸν ὡς ἦν ἐν τῷ πλοίῳ, καὶ ἄλλα πλοῖα ἦν μετ' αὐτοῦ.
[37] καὶ γίνεται λαῖλαψ μεγάλη ἀνέμου καὶ τὰ κύματα ἐπέβαλλεν εἰς τὸ πλοῖον, ὥστε ἤδη γεμίζεσθαι τὸ πλοῖον.
[38] καὶ αὐτὸς ἦν ἐν τῇ πρύμνῃ ἐπὶ τὸ προσκεφάλαιον καθεύδων. καὶ ἐγείρουσιν αὐτὸν καὶ λέγουσιν αὐτῷ· διδάσκαλε, οὐ μέλει σοι ὅτι ἀπολλύμεθα;
[39] καὶ διεγερθεὶς ἐπετίμησεν τῷ ἀνέμῳ καὶ εἶπεν τῇ θαλάσσῃ· σιώπα, πεφίμωσο. καὶ ἐκόπασεν ὁ ἄνεμος καὶ ἐγένετο γαλήνη μεγάλη.
[40] καὶ εἶπεν αὐτοῖς· τί δειλοί ἐστε; οὔπω ἔχετε πίστιν;
[41] καὶ ἐφοβήθησαν φόβον μέγαν καὶ ἔλεγον πρὸς ἀλλήλους· τίς ἄρα οὗτός ἐστιν ὅτι καὶ ὁ ἄνεμος καὶ ἡ θάλασσα ὑπακούει αὐτῷ;

---

[1] First published in *The Bible Bhashyam* 5:1 (1979): 295-308.

A. 'Dhvani' in New Testament Exegesis Today

1. *Historical Criticism*

Anyone acquainted with recent parable exegesis will be aware of how closely the interpretation of a text through *dhvani* resembles recent attempts at understanding the parables of Jesus as metaphor.[2] These attempts are quite new. Ever since the scientific revolution of the 16th and 17th centuries which ushered in the modern world, it is historical criticism that has been the dominant method of biblical exegesis. The scientific revolution which gave rise to empirical science brought it also new 'scientific' methods for the study of literature and history. Historical criticism applies these methods to the Bible. Through the use of a series of rigorous techniques, the so called 'criticisms' (text, literary, form, redaction and historical criticism) it attempts to recover the original form of a biblical text and lay bare its original meaning.[3]

What is the 'Meaning' of Text?

But just what is the 'meaning' of a text? Is it what the author intended to say (*speaker* or *author meaning*); or what the text does in fact say whether the author intended it or not (*discourse* or *text meaning*)—for intent and expression need not always coincide, and an author may not fully express what he intended or even say more than he wished to; or is it what his readers or listeners understood (or misunderstood) him to have said (*listener* or *reader meaning*)?[4] The problem becomes even more acute when we are dealing with texts like the Gospels, which are not the products of a writer's workshop—creative compositions of individual authors—but are the end products of a long and complex process of community tradition. Stories about and sayings of Jesus were handed down orally in the post-Easter Church for some thirty or more years before they were first incorporated into a continuous narrative, a Gospel. And in course of their transmission these traditions were continually reinterpreted as they were handed down,

---

[2] See Robert Funk, *Language, Hermeneutic and the Word of God* (New York: Harper, 1969), 133–62.

[3] See Edgar Krentz, *The Historical Critical Method* (Philadelphia: Fortress Press 1975).

[4] See Vern Poythress, "Analysing a Biblical Text: Some Important Linguistic Distinctions," *SJT* 32 (1979): 113–37.

acquiring new meanings as they were applied to new situations, until they received a fixed, final text-meaning when they were edited into the Gospels.[5]

In his classic study on the parables of Jesus, Joachim Jeremias distinguishes three moments in their transmission.[6] The parables have a setting in the ministry of Jesus (*Sitz im Leben Jesu*), a setting in the life of the early Church (*Sitz im Leben ecclesiae*), and a setting in the Gospels (*Sitz im Leben evangelii*). In each new setting the parable is given a new form, fulfills a new function and acquires a new meaning. Parables uttered by Jesus to throw light on concrete situations in his ministry were taken up by the early Church and adapted (often by allegorization or by the addition of 'lessons') to new post-Easter contexts very different from the ones in which they were originally spoken. Parables from the oral tradition of the early Church were taken up by the evangelists and re-edited to conform the specific perspectives of their Gospels.

The Parable of the Sower (Mk 4:3-9), spoken by Jesus to encourage his disciples disheartened by the failure of the Galilean ministry (its message being that spectacular success will follow large initial loss), is allegorized by the early Church (Mk 4:13-20) into a description of the dispositions that hinder the fruitful reception of the Word. The Parable of the Wicked Tenants (Mk 12:1-8) used by Jesus to drive home to the Pharisees the enormity of their hard-heartedness (like the wicked tenants they are deliberately deaf to every possible appeal) becomes in Matthew (Mt 21:33-39) an allegory of salvation history, neatly illustrating a key theme of his theology—that the Jews by rejection Jesus have lost their right to the Promise, so that it is the Church, made up of Jew and Gentiles, which is now the true Israel.[7] The Parable of the Dishonest Steward (Lk 16:1-8) through which Jesus summons his listeners to act as decisively as the steward does in crisis

---

[5] George Soares-Prabhu, "Are the Gospels Historical?" *Clergy Monthly* 38 (1974): 112-24, 163-72; Joseph Pathrapankal, *Understanding the Gospels Today* (Bangalore: Dharmaram Publications, 1977).

[6] Joachim Jeremias, *The Parables of Jesus* (London: SCM Press, 1971).

[7] Editor's comment: we see here an unfortunate example of a re-placement theological and anti-Jewish interpretation ("the enormity of their [the Pharisees] hard-heartedness" "Lost the right to the promise.") Cf. the discussion in Amy-Jill Levine, "Lilies of the Field," 331-32. Levine lists the most typical anti-Jewish statements, which she calls "weeds," as they occur in many emancipatory interpretive traditions. See also above, chapter five n. 19.

they are in because of his proclamation of the Kingdom, is turned by Luke, through the addition of a series of lessons (Lk 16:9–13) into an illustration of the right use of riches.

What Does a Parable Mean?
What, then, would be the true meaning of such parables which have undergone considerable reinterpretation in course of transmission in the early Church? Would it be what Jesus meant when he uttered them, or what his hearers understood him to have meant? Is the meaning read out of parable by the early Church, or that given to it by the evangelist when he edits it to express the theology of his Gospel? Or is it the meaning a preacher finds in the parable when he propounds it for an audience today?

For historical criticism the answer is clear. The real meaning of a parable is its 'literal' meaning—that is, its original author—meaning, the meaning intended by Jesus when he first spoke it to his listeners in Palestine. So historical criticism sets out to recover this meaning, working its way back through the layers of interpretation. That may have accumulated round the parable during its oral transmission in the early Church and its integration into a Gospel. Historical criticism, that is, attempts to trace the history to the parable, in order to recover its original form and meaning.

But it is precisely this preoccupation with history that is both historical criticism's strength and its weakness. If close attention to history is a source of the method's objectivity, it is also the source of its ultimate irrelevance. Focusing exclusively on their original author-meaning tends to rob the parable of significance for us today. For since the parables of Jesus were originally spoken in concrete situations very different from those we live in, their original meaning is not likely to say much to us.

But is the original meaning of a parable its true meaning? An increasing number of exegetes would question this. The historical critical method, they would suggest, has misunderstood the parable form. It has failed to perceive that the parable (indeed the Bible as a whole) is a literary work, and like any literary work has a meaning which is not fully exhausted by what the author intended to say. The parables, that is, have a text-meaning which goes beyond their author-meaning, and which can be recovered by subjecting them to the methods used by literary critics for the study of creative literature. This is what rhetorical criticism, a new method that has been developed for the study of the Bible as creative literature, attempt to do.[8]

2. Rhetorical Criticism

Rhetorical criticism treats the parables as autonomous aesthetic objects. Like a painting by Amrit Sher Gil or a poem by Tagore, a parable can be appreciated and understood even if we do not know how and when it came to be. It has a meaning it itself, independent of its origin and its history. Parables, that is, have not only an author-meaning which historical criticism can discover, but a text-meaning which escapes historical criticism. For historical criticism treats a parable as a disposable container in which an original author's message is packaged, whereas in fact the parable is itself the message!

Parable as Metaphor

Rhetorical criticism expresses this by saying that a parable is a metaphor, using the word in the rather special sense it has acquired in modern literary criticism. Grammatically a metaphor is an expression comparing one thing with another in which the element of comparison is omitted. In this it differs from a simile where the comparison is explicitly stated. To say that Ranjit Singh was as brave as lion is to use a simile; to call Ranjit 'the lion of the Punjab' is to use a metaphor.

This apparently trivial difference is fraught with significance. For metaphor and simile function in very different ways. Whereas a simile "sets one thing against another; the less known is clarified by the better known," in a metaphor "we have an image with a certain shock to the imagination which directly conveys a vision of what is signified."[9] A simile, that is, illustrates; a metaphor reveals. A metaphor, then, does not embellish a proposition nor illustrate a truth; it communicates an insight and evokes a new experience—indeed an experience so radically new that it can only be grasped within the metaphor itself.[10] Like a poem a metaphor is "not equal to, but true"!

---

[8] See William Beardslee, *Literary Criticism of the New Testament* (Philadelphia: Fortress Press, 1970); George Petersen, *The Literary Critic and the New Testament* (Philadelphia: Fortress Press, 1978).
[9] Amos Wilder, *Early Christian Rhetoric* (London: SCM Press, 1964), 80.
[10] John Dominic Crossan, *In Parables: The Challenge of the Historical Jesus* (New York: Harper, 1973) 13.

The rhetorical criticism of a parable will concentrate, then, on the parable itself taken as a metaphor, with little interest in its origin (who uttered the parable) or its effect (who was the parable understood by those to whom it was spoken). It will focus, that is, on the text-meaning of the parable, rather than on its author or reader meaning, thus avoiding both the *intentional fallacy* of judging a literary work in terms of the intention of its author, and the *affective fallacy* of judging it in terms of its audience effect.[11] Instead the rhetorical critic will try and 'enter' into the parable itself, and resonate to the curious combination of realism and strangeness ("the disclosure of the extraordinary in the ordinary") through which the parable is able to evoke in us the 'limit-experience' of the Kingdom.[12]

As an extended metaphor evoking such a limit experience a parable obviously cannot be conceptualized. One can never reduce it to a neat set of propositions or lessons. No one interpretation of a parable, not even a historical interpretation which would recover what Jesus meant when he first uttered it, will exhaust its meaning. For like any metaphor a parable is open to the future, and will continue to disclose an indefinite sequence of new meanings (all true!) as it is spoken into a succession of new situations. Each new situation will bring out a new understanding of the parable, because the meaning of a parable is not a fixed given to be unlocked by grammatically or philological keys, but is the actualization of its limitless revelatory potential through the perspective and perceptiveness of the reader/listener, in ever new ways.[13]

Such actualization is always personal, not intellectual. It involves the whole man. Unlike the proposition which is grasped by the mind alone, a parable, because it is an aesthetic object, engages the whole man in the totality of his knowing-feeling, conscious-unconscious response. A parable, therefore, is to be understood not through intellectual abstraction but through imaginative participation. It is through the imagination that one enters into a parable, experience that shock of the "dislocation of the familiar" that its story conveys, and is brought into a fleeting, vertiginous confrontation with the limits of one's world.[14]

---

[11] Dan O. Via, *The Parables: Their Literary and Existential Dimension* (Philadelphia: Fortress Press, 1967), 76–78.

[12] Paul Ricoeur, "Biblical Hermeneutics," *Semeia* 4 (1975): 170–228.

[13] See Susan Witting, "A Theory of Multiple Meanings," *Semeia* 9 (1977): 75–103.

[14] Funk, *Language*, 143.

The evocation of such a limit experience is effected in a parable through the tensions in tis imagery. Parables are "riven with radical comparisons and disjunctions."[15] Such disjunctions are of course the very essence of metaphor, which, until it is deadened by use, shocks the imagination by its juxtaposition of two realities (man and lion) that are not perceived as related until the metaphor joins them. The unexpected juxtaposition jolts the mind into a new insight into the reality compared, so that one moves through the metaphor to a new level of meaning.

3. *Metaphor as 'Dhvani'*
Clearly, then, in interpreting the parables of Jesus as metaphor, rhetorical criticism is relying on *dhvani*—that is on "that use of language which through either the primary or secondary meaning or through both of them takes the reader to a depth meaning which is experienceable but not expressible."[16] Metaphor, that is, functions much as *dhvani* does. Like *dhvani* it does not communicate a lesson, but evokes a limit experience—an experience of the transcendent which is so utterly beyond conceptualization, that it can only be experienced as the limit of our 'world.' The evocation occurs only when the sensitivity of the reader is attuned to and resonates with the symbolic language of the metaphor. And it leads not to a communication of truths but to a communion of realities.

But unlike *dhvani*, which, since it functions through primary as well as secondary meanings, can occur anywhere in a text, interpretation through metaphor would strictly speaking be confined to the explicitly figurative portions of the New Testament. There is however a growing awareness that the metaphorical process can occur beyond the boundaries of metaphor proper, and that the whole New Testament can in fact be treated metaphorically, since it is the story of Jesus who is "par excellence the metaphor of God."[17] The "familiar and mundane" story of Jesus is the way through which one arrives at the experience of God. This insight unfortunately has not been followed up, and we have hardly any examples of a metaphorical or *dhvani* interpretation of non-parabolic New Testament texts. A fruitful field for exploration

---

[15] Sallie Te Selle, *Speaking in Parables* (Philadelphia; Fortress Press, 1975), 32–33.
[16] See the article of Francis X. D'Sa on "Dhvani as a Method of Interpretation," *BiBh* 5 (1979): 276-94.
[17] Te Selle, *Speaking in Parbles*, 37.

lies open here. We shall investigate its potentialities by attempting a *dhvani* interpretation of a Gospel miracle story.

B. *A 'Dhvani' Interpretation of Mark 4:35-41*

The Stilling of the Storm in Mark (Mk 4:35-41) is a convenient subject for such an attempt. The story is compact, well structured (almost a perfect example of the Miracle Story form) and obvious rich in significance. Allusions to the Old Testament and the explicit use of technical exorcism terminology prevent us from reading it as a simple factual report of something which once happened. The story is obviously loaded with symbolism and riven with the tensions which suggest the straining of language called upon the express a limit experience. It thus lends itself admirably to an interpretation through *dhvani*. Before attempting such an interpretation, however, it will be useful to see how traditional historical critical exegesis would go about interpreting it. This will throw our *dhvani* approach into sharper relief.

1. *Historical Critical Analysis*

Historical Criticism takes tensions in the story as indications of the conflation of sources or of the editing of underlying traditions by Mark. It thus sees the *introductions* to the narrative (vv. 35-36) as a largely redactional composition, which serves to integrate the originally independent story of the Stilling of the Storm (which came down to Mark as an isolated unit of tradition) into the context of the Gospel. This is obviously the function of (a) the typically Markan double time indication in v. 35a (cf. Mk 1:35; 14:12), which rounds off the parable discourse of Mk 4:1-34; of (b) the command of Jesus to "cross over to the other side" in v. 35b, which makes the episode part of a series of miracles narrated by Mark as occurring on the shores of the Lake of Gennasareth, repeatedly criss-crossed by Jesus (Mk 4:35; 5:1; 5:21); of (c) the dismissal of the crowds in v. 36a, which refers back to the beginning of the parable discourse when crowds gather round Jesus (Mk 4:1a); and of (d) the curious note that the disciples take Jesus "just as he was in the boat" in v. 36b, which makes sense only when we remember that the parable discourse in Mark is delivered by Jesus from a boat (Mk 4:1b).

The *narrative* itself (vv. 37-41) approaches to have been taken by Mark from his tradition, but incorporates several *redactional* elements. Among these would be (a) the word of Jesus which stills the storm in

v. 39, whose language clearly echoes the exorcism terminology (Jesus "threatens" [epitiman] the wind, and says to the sea "be muzzled" [phimoun]) of Mark's narrative of the healing of the demoniac in the synagogue of Capernaum (Mk 1:25); and (b) Jesus' rebuke in v. 40, which disturbs the flow of the narrative and contains the characteristically Markan theme of the disciples' lack of understanding and faith (cf. Mk 6:51; 8:17–18). The chorus in v. 41 is a natural response not to the rebuke in v. 40 (which is left unanswered and hanging in the air) but to the description of the stilling of the storm in v. 39. Verse 40 thus appears to be an intrusion. Its first half (v. 40a) may have been a secondary addition to the pre-Gospel tradition, occurring originally after v. 38; but v. 40b with its characteristic Markan theme is clearly redactional.

Other elements in the story appear to be *secondary but pre-Markan* additions inserted into the story during its transmission in the oral tradition of the early Church. This may be true (we have said) of the rebuke in v. 40a. It is probably true of the description of Jesus sleeping in v. 38a, which fits in ill with the miracle story form, and unnecessarily delays the denouement of the story. Unless, then, we take it as a vestigial reminiscence of what actually happened (which is unlikely, given the strongly functional and formally stylized character of the Gospel miracle stories), this odd little detail is probably a secondary addition to the primitive narrative.

Taking it as such, Ludger Schenke, in a remarkable thorough study of the narrative, is able to describe three stages in the history of its transmission.[18]

a) In its original form (shorn, that is of all its redactional and secondary elements) the story was formulated in the gentile-oriented mission preaching of diaspora Judaism, where it functioned not indeed as a miracle story highlighting a miraculous event but as the story of an epiphany or manifestation, which focused on the figure of Jesus. Jesus was presented as the one in whom the awesome power of the Old Testament God, who stills the storm,[19] and rescues the just man from threatening waters,[20] is made fully manifest. The story this put

---

[18] Ludger Schenke, *Die Wundererzählungen des Markus Evangeliums* (Stuttgart: Katholisches Bibelwerk, 1975), 1–93; see also Karl Kertelge, *Die Wunder Jesu im Markusevangelium* (Munich: Kösel, 1970), 91–100.
[19] Cf. Job 26:12; 38:8–11; Ps 104:6–9; Jer 5:22.
[20] Cf. Ps 18:16; 32:6; 42:1–3; 69:1–2; 107:23–31; Is 43:2.

Jesus before the gentile world as one superior to all their wonderworking "divine men" (*theioi andre*), and summoned it to a christological decision. That is why its concluding chorus took the form of a striking question ("Who then is this?"), which was meant to be not a catechetical question testing the knowledge of believers but a kerygmatic question inviting unbelievers to faith.

b) With the addition of v. 38a (a secondary but pre-Markan insertion) the story is given a new meaning to respond to a new situation in the early Church. With the Church as an already established but persecuted community, living in imminent expectation of the parousia, concern for mission gives way to need for consolidation. The story now serves not missionary preaching but inner-community exhortation. It invites the community, tossed in the storms of persecution[21] and waiting apparently in vain for the appearance of its saving Lord who never seems to come, to an unconditional trust in Jesus, who even though "sleeping" can and will save them.

c) Markan redaction, and in particular the addition of the rebuke in v. 40, gives the story a new point. Unconditional trust in Jesus could lead to a "divine man" soteriology, which would expect the risen Lord to save his persecuted community through a miraculous intervention. Mark's editing corrects this. The disciples are rebuked not because they are not reassured by the presence of Jesus even though he is sleeping, but because they are not willing to perish with him. They are not willing to, that is, follow him on the way of the cross as true disciples should (Mk 8:34), but look to be delivered by him through a miracle. Salvation, the story teaches us (along with the whole of Mark's Gospel), comes not through miracles but through the cross. For it is the cross rather than his miracles which is the true epiphany of Jesus.

Starting, then, from the many literary tensions in the story, historical criticism is able to detect various strata in it and reconstruct with some plausibility the history of the transmission. It shows us a story that was continuously reinterpreted as it was handed down in the tradition of the early Church, in order to meet the new needs that kept emerging as the Church developed. Such an analysis is obviously enlightening and useful. But it does not take us to the heart of the story—to the "limit experience" which the story as a religious text presumably enshrines. An interpretation through *dhvani* might take us there.

---

[21] Cf. Ps 74:13–14; 89:10; Apoc 13:1.

2. A 'Dhvani' Interpretation

Unlike historical criticism, interpretation through *dhvani* is not interested in the history of a text but takes it as it now stands. As it now stands, the story of the Stilling of the Storm in Mark falls, we have seen, into two parts, each with it own particular finality and meaning. An introduction (vv. 35-36) leads up to a dramatic narrative rounded off by a comment of Jesus and the chorus of the awed disciples (vv. 37-41). Examining each of these in turn with an ear to the limit experience it evokes we find the following.

The Introduction (vv. 35-36)

The introduction in vv. 35-36 prepares for the narrative that follows by disengaging Jesus from the situation in which he has been involved (the parable discourse of Mk 4:1-34) and freeing him for the action to follow. Every element in the introduction contributes to this. The time indication (v. 35a) rounds off the parable discourse by bringing to a close the day on which it was delivered ("when evening had come"). The command of Jesus to cross over to the other side (v. 35b) and the dismissal of the crowds (v. 36a) distances Jesus from the place where he had spoken and the people he had addressed. Only the mention of the "other boats with them" (v. 36b)—boats which subsequently vanish from the story—strikes a discordant note. Their mention serves no useful purpose in the story.

The result of such disengagement is the privatization of the miracle that follows. It is a miracle that is performed away from the crowds and before the disciples alone. The miracle mediates a revelation that is not accessible to public opinion but only to the faith of the believing community.

The Narrative (vv. 37-41)

The narrative that follows is sustained by three oppositions or tensions through which it mediates its meaning.

1) The dominant opposition is that between the "great storm" (*lailaps megalē*) with which it begins and the "great calm" (*galēnē megalē*) in which it ends. The terse announcement: "and there was a great calm" (v. 39) rings out with impressive force after the vivid description of the storm (v. 37) and the clamour of the frightened disciples (v. 38b). One can almost experience physically the depth of the tranquil stillness and quiet it announces. The movement of the story is thus not circular but spiral. The great calm is not simply a return

to a pre-storm quiet, but the attainment of a new depth of stillness, immeasurably greater that that obtaining during the anxious bustle that preceded the storm.

The movement from storm to stillness is effected by the might word of Jesus who "threatens" (*epitiman*) the wind, and commands the sea to "be muzzled" (*phimoun*). The use of such exorcism terminology lights up a new and terrifying dimension to the story. We are suddenly made aware of the fact that the stilling of the storm is not just a spectacular work of wonder, a dazzling display of power over the forces of nature, but a rescue operation in which men are saved from the force of destruction that continually threaten the world we live in. We experience vividly the precariousness of human existence lived out in a world teetering on the edge of chaos. The fragile boat of man's existence can at any moment be overwhelmed by the 'sea,' home of the great primeval monsters in biblical mythology (Gen 1:1; Ps 74:13–14; Is 27:1) and powerful symbol of the forces of destruction that always threaten to life of man (Rev 21:1).

2) Yet even as we resonate to this evocation of the precariousness of human existence, we become aware of another tension in the story: the opposition between Jesus, who is asleep, and the disciples, who panic (v. 38) The significance of this opposition is again brought out by a word of Jesus, this time a word of rebuke: "Why are you afraid? Have you no faith?" (v. 40). Faith is opposed to fear. The peacefully sleeping Jesus (like the Psalmist in Ps 3:5 and 4:8) is a model of trusting faith, whose sleep reveals the ultimate stability that underlies the surface instability of human life. The frightened disciples are too disturbed by their panic to reach this level of awareness. They will experience it only if their fear gives way to faith.

3) The focal point of this faith is revealed to us in the third of the oppositions that make up our story—that between Jesus who is taken almost passively ("just as he was") in the boat (v. 36), and the Lord who evokes the wondering cry: "who then is this that even the wind and the sea obey him?" We move from the Master who teaches in parables to the Lord who commands the wind and the waves. The wondering cry of the disciples evokes a great sense of awe. We experience the awesome yet immensely reassuring presence of the all-powerful Lord who has complete control over the demonic forced that threaten our lives. In his presence the fragility of human existence always threatened by destruction and death. We recover our trust in the ultimate security and meaningfulness of life.

But our trust is not a return to a juvenile confidence in the benevolence of nature, or in the ability of our science to control it. It is only when we have experienced (as our world is beginning to) the terrible frailty of human life, lived out on a tiny planet spinning like a fretful midge in the vast emptiness of space and pulsing with titanic forces that threaten any moment to blow it apart, or when we have looked with terror into the caldron of savage violence and destructiveness that seethes in each human heart—it is only then that we can reach the great calm which recognizes behind the fragile patterns of human existence the unshakable stability of the ground of our being. It is this experience of ultimate stability behind the turmoil of our agitated and threatened existence that the story of the Stilling of the Storm evokes.

9.2 George Zachariah (Gurukul Lutheran Theological College, Chennai, India). The Parable of the not so Prodigal Daughters: A Postcolonial Dalit Womanist Reading[22]

Luke 15:30	
³⁰But when this son of yours came back, who has devoured your property with prostitutes, you killed the fatted calf for him!	[30] ὅτε δὲ ὁ υἱός σου οὗτος ὁ καταφαγών σου τὸν βίον μετὰ πορνῶν ἦλθεν, ἔθυσας αὐτῷ τὸν σιτευτὸν μόσχον.

> ....but when this son of yours came back, who has devoured your property with prostitutes you killed the fatted calf for him. (Luke 15:30)

> Have you heard me today? No sex. No school. That's the choice I face. I know this makes me vulnerable to HIV but many of us can only afford to go to school by allowing our bodies to be used. www.unaids.org

Postcolonial studies is an emerging discipline committed to engage with the cultural and textual articulations of communities affected by colonialism and neo-colonialism. One can identify two major focuses in postcolonial studies; 1) to analyze the strategies by which the colonizer constructed the images of the colonized, and 2) to understand

---

[22] First published in *In God's Image (The Haunts of Pain: Theologizing Dalits)*, Vol. 26 No. 3, September (2007): 65–70.

the ways in which the colonized made use of, and went beyond those strategies for survival and self-representation.

The irruption of hitherto subjugated and marginalized voices into the mainstream discourses in the field of biblical studies paved the way for the use of postcolonial interpretation in biblical hermeneutics. In postcolonial biblical reading, there are two foundational affirmations; 1) the Bible is an imperial text, and 2) the Bible is also a text of resistance to imperialism. As an imperial text, it functions as a hegemonic institution to legitimize and perpetuate imperial interests by subjugating and silencing other voices. At the same time, it becomes a text of resistance when the postcolonial subjects read it from their vantage point of neo-colonialism and globalization.

Any postcolonial reading of the Bible needs to take into consideration the multiple realities of subjugation. The oft-quoted sub-Saharan African experience of the interconnection between the Bible and colonization is relevant here. "When the white man came to our country he had the Bible and we had the land. The white man said to us, 'let us pray.' After the prayer, the white man had the land and we had the Bible."[23] This story is central to postcolonial biblical hermeneutics as it illustrates the multiple layers of imperial invasion. It analyses how scripture has been used to colonize the land and the psyche of a people.

When we examine carefully the complexity of colonialism, we realize how it disrupted and transformed the life of the colonies. The colonizers controlled religion, race economy, culture, and transformed the colonies according to their worldview. Colonialism is not a past epoch in history. It is a contemporary reality. The new world order under globalization is a new manifestation of imperialism. "It is amazing how fast the process has moved from former colonies' struggles for independence to the current phenomenon of these same nations calling for their former colonies to come and do business in their countries in the name of "globalization."[24] Hence, a postcolonial reading of the Bible is of great importance in our times.

---

[23] Musa W. Dube, *Postcolonial Feminist Interpretation of the Bible* (St. Louis: Chalice Press, 2000), 3.
[24] Musa W. Dube, "Postcoloniality, Feminist Spaces, and Religión," in *Postcolonialism, Feminism & Religious Discourse* (eds. Laura E. Donaldson and Kwok Pui-lan; London: Routledge, 2002), 101–2.

As we have seen earlier, postcolonial studies point to the multiplicity of subjugation under imperialism. We always tend to forget about this reality. Women's bodies become the colonies of violence and exploitation in all imperial exercises of power and control. Rape and sexual exploitation are part of the imperial campaign. So this biblical exposition is an attempt to explore how patriarchy is integrally related with imperialism. Further it aims to examine how the process of colonization has excluded women, and more than that, portrayed women as just colonies to be plundered and used without recognition.

The construction of a universal image of the other—the colonized—is the primary strategy of imperialism. The stereotypical portrayal of women in the two-third world is an example here. "Either overtly or covertly, prostitution is still the main if not the only source of work for African women."[25] This kind of representation portrays women as politically and economically dependent and sexually perverted. They are the symbols of sin, immorality and evil. This portrayal indirectly points to the colonizer as the model to be emulated by the colonized. The contemporary attempts to export freedom and democracy to other countries in the form of invasion and occupation also stems from this same imperial strategy.

As we have seen in the above quotation, women in the two-thirds world are positioned in a very complex manner. They are oppressed by patriarchal structures in their societies, the patriarchal structures of their colonizers, as well as the imperial structure of the western men and women. But, their brothers operate with a "first things first" approach where patriarchal oppression is not an issue as it is submerged in the big story of nationalism and freedom. This critique applies to certain sections of the feminist movement who also have ignored the realities of race/caste and class in their projects. This is the context in which the women of color from the two-third world—the colonized readers and writers—have initiated a subversive reading strategy which rejects "the privileging of imperial texts and institutions as the standard of all cultures at all times."[26] They are engaged in a cross-cultural discourse incorporating the cultural resources of both the colonized and the colonizer. Such an engagement will provide a new impetus to the struggles of the Dalit Christian women in India.

---

[25] Maria Rosa Cutrufelli, *Women from Africa: Roots of Oppression* (London: Zed Books, 1983), 13.
[26] Dube, *Postcolonial Feminist Interpretation*, 116.

To put it differently, in the postcolonial Dalit womanist reading the meaning of the text is constructed by the readers, through their engagement with the text, informed by their context of imperialism, casteism and patriarchy. The meaning of the text is not located in the original context, or in the intention of the author or the original audience. The significance of the reading is its relevance for the readers here and now—the Dalit women who are excluded, silenced and objectified.

The primary concern of a postcolonial Dalit womanist reading is to expose the colonial strategies of constructing the image of Dalit women as other, and to recreate imaginatively their history rememorizing Dalit life narratives. Such imagined histories are "*testimonios*, which forge a right to speak both for and beyond the individual and contest explicitly or implicitly the 'official forgetting' of histories of caste oppression, struggles and resistance."[27] For Dalit women, this is more than a hermeneutical method. As Sanal Mohan observes, "if individuals and collectivities have been produced in discourses, it is possible to imagine discourses that will produce 'new selves.'"[28] Said differently, a postcolonial Dalit womanist reading is committed to the creation of 'new selves' coming out of the colonial images inscribed on them.

Having given this introduction to postcolonial Dalit womanist reading let us look at a biblical text using this methodology. This paper attempts to unveil two basic presuppositions of postcolonial hermeneutics; the Bible is an imperial text, and it is also a text of resistance against imperialism. So we need to expose the deliberate imperial attempt in the Bible to make women invisible and voiceless. Also the politics of using women's body as object or property for the advantage of the imperial, male hierarchical powers as a sign of power and control needs to be exposed. At this point, we cannot help but refer to the analogy between "biblical promise" and "the White man's burden." This approach insists that "imperialism is a duty, a burden, a cross that a white man must carry, not for his own sake but for another's profit,

---

[27] Sharmila Rege, *Writing Caste/Writing Gender: Narrating Dalit Women's Testimonios* (New Delhi: Zubaan, 2006), 13.

[28] Sanal Mohan, "Theorising History in the Context of Social Movement: Challenges to the Reigning Paradigms of History," in *The Struggle for the Past: Historiography Today* (ed. Felix Wilfred and Jose D. Maliekal, Chennai; Department of Christian Studies University of Madras, 2002), 103–4.

another's gain."²⁹ This reading will enable us to perceive women's bodies not only as colonies of violence and representation, but also as sites of a new discourse on resistance and self-worth.

The text that we have chosen for our reading is Luke 15:11–32. Our attempt is to re-read this story from the perspective of the invisible characters—the prostituted women—in this story (15:30). Interestingly, these characters are not mentioned in the main plot or by the main characters. They are only casually mentioned by the brother and that too in a stereotyped way. The text is so excited about the *metanoia* of the prodigal son, but it does not analyse and critique the system that dehumanized him and several others. The son, irrespective of his actions, was pardoned and taken back to his father's house. So the task in this paper is to exegete one verse from the text: "but when this son of yours came back, who has devoured your property with prostitutes, you killed the fatted calf for him" (15:30).

Let us begin with narrating this story from the perspective of those prostitutes, whose lives and bodies have been used and exploited by the young and rich men. "Yes, of course we remember this young man. He was part of a group of youngsters who came to this city. They had lots of money. They had real fun in the city. This young man spent several nights with us. Once he spent all his money, he decided to go back to his father. His father accepted him." If we stop this narration at this stage, it can be canonized as part of the scripture. However, these women would like to speak more, and let us enable them to speak out and represent themselves.

> We came here not of our choice. Many of us were sent by our parents to work in the city hoping that our family could survive. The men, who guaranteed us a job, in fact took some money from our parents and imprisoned us in this brothel. It was a shock for us when we realized the truth. But we decided to endure to help our families to survive. It is next to impossible to escape from here as some of our friends who attempted to escape were brutally tortured. More than that, even if we succeed in escaping from here, who is going to accept us? We don't have a father like the father of the young man who is willing to welcome us back to our home. We don't have a society that accepts us as fellow beings. We don't have a religious community that provides us fellowship. We are the outcaste: the socially ostracized. We are not prostitutes; we are the prostituted women; prostituted not only by individual men, but also by

---

²⁹ Dube, *Postcolonial Feminist Interpretation*, 85.

a colonial system of hierarchical power relations and its morality and religiosity.

The parable of "the Prodigal Son" is a very familiar parable to everyone irrespective of age, race, gender or ethnic divisions. It is one of the common texts for preaching and Bible studies. It is quite interesting to explore why this group of prostituted women are made invisible both from the biblical narrative and from the proclamation of the Word. Is the parable's motif just to save the prodigal son? Doesn't it seem that the inclusion of the prostitutes in this story was a deliberate attempt to enhance the sinfulness of the young man, and to portray the intensity of the forgiveness that the father granted to his son? What about the "not-so prodigal daughters" who have been forced into such a situation? Is salvation a rescue operation of young rich men from sinful women? The rich young man had the luxury to come back to his home. He was redeemed. Is there a "Father" who is deeply concerned about the systems that make women prostitutes, and committed to the redemption of those systems and its victims?

> I write to you because I miss you...I am not working as a servant, but as a prostitute. Each day I must serve 7–8 men. I can get diseases like VD, TB, AIDS, etc. They threaten to beat me up if I don't do it. They beat up girls who refused them, until they died. They won't take us to be treated because they are afraid that we will run away. Instead they give us two or three tablets...Being a prostitute is like being a bird in a cage. They can't fly away.[30]

This is not an isolated story. This is the life experience of thousands of poor women and girls in Asia and other third world countries who have been "exported" to different countries thanks to the growing global market economy and the Structural Adjustment Programs. Poor women tend to be the victims of such dehumanizing practices. "The link between prostitution and global economic injustice and the market economy is increasingly recognized, and it was recently said that a poor nation's most marketable commodity is its women."[31]

Religion plays a significant role in perpetuating prostitution as a necessary evil. Prostitution was accepted as a necessary evil from the early period of Christianity. It is a fact that religion plays a significant

---

[30] Aruna Gnanadason, *No Longer a Secret* (Geneva: WCC, 1993), 19.
[31] Gnanadason, *No Longer a Secret*, 17.

role in building social attitudes towards women's body and sex which is translated into legislation.

> Prostitutes were a necessary evil, according to Thomas Aquinas of the thirteenth century, as they were permitted by God to prevent chaotic eruptions of sinful male lust...In other words, prostitutes protected "good" wives from the immoral, lustful demands of their husbands. Prostitutes supposedly exhibited the sexual licentiousness inherent in all women, inherited from Eve, which good women repressed. The most "holy" women, like the most holy men, were supposed to follow a celibate vocation.[32]

Biblical history reveals that the Bible maintained a system of keeping the prostituted women as tricksters, harlots, queens, priestesses and concubines. Tamar, Rahab, Gomer, the woman who anointed Jesus etc. are some among them who came from different empires, cultural backgrounds, languages and cultures. They were the objects of imperial projects operated according to the colonizer. They were not only ignored and made invisible, but their lives were torn and destroyed.

Luke's Gospel is unique in terms of its narrative and theological themes and its presentation of Jesus as a compassionate friend of the outcasts. The heart of Luke's Gospel is a record of mighty acts and teachings of Christ in solidarity with the outcasts. Luke divides the ministry of Jesus into three periods: the ministry in Galilee, the ministry en route to Jerusalem, and the ministry in Jerusalem. This text comes under the travel narrative, the ministry of Jesus on his way to Jerusalem. One of the most emphatic themes of Luke is his affirmation of the universality of the salvation in Christ. When the Pharisees and scribes see the tax collectors and sinners coming to Jesus, they grumble and complain that Jesus welcomes and eats with sinners. The famous collection of parables in chapter 15 is a response to that complaint. The parables of the lost sheep, the lost coin and the prodigal son share the common theme of recovery and return of the lost and the alienated. So it is important to situate this parable along with the other two parables that explain Jesus' solidarity with the last, the least and the lost.

In this parable, the conversation is initiated by the younger son. "Father, give me my share of the estate" (15:12). Without any dialogue or argument, the father gives the younger son the money he wants.

---

[32] Rita Nakashima Brock, "Marriage Troubles." Online: *www.panaawtm.org/images/BROCK_Marriage_Trouble.doc*.

The younger son spends all his money with a group unidentified in the text. He was "dying of hunger," (v17) while his father's servants had enough to spare. Out of hunger and starvation, the younger son decides to go back. He decides to repent to his father and the father accepts him with love and compassion. The elder brother's response clearly shows that he was very angry with the father and the younger son. It is the elder brother who complains that the younger brother was devouring his property with the prostitutes.

No doubt that the father is concerned about the healing and the restoration of both his sons. However, the thrust of the parable is to articulate the reverse priority of the Reign of God. It is the last that matters. It is the insignificant that brings in happiness. It is the silenced and the represented that make the banquet a possibility. Jesus' commitment to bring back to life those who are lost and dead is hence, more than an act of benevolence and paternalism. By affirming the colonized, Jesus opens up the possibility for them to contest the images inscribed on them, and to venture into new journeys creating new selves, rememorizing their life stories. Unfortunately, the biblical narrative and our proclamation of the Word do not even bother to recognize the women who had to sell their bodies for survival. This reality challenges us to analyze critically the various factors that prevented us from hearing the voices of the prostituted women in this parable. When women from debt ridden countries whose bodies are the last colonies read this text, it empowers them to strive for self-worth as they experience a God who is Emmanuel in their midst.

Let us briefly try to analyze this text from a postcolonial Dalit womanist perspective. This text underscores the postcolonial position that the Bible is an imperial text. As we have seen elsewhere, imperialism operates by constructing the other as evil, in order to legitimize and perpetuate a system of domination and hierarchically structured power relations. It is naïve to consider this parable as an innocent and simple story. A simplistic reading of the parable resembles some of the myths that the dominant system and its morality tell us everyday as the reasons for poverty. Why did the younger son have to leave his home? Why did he revolt against the status quo in the family and demand his share? Mary Ann Beavis in her interpretation of this parable points to the possibility of an abusive relationship of the father.[33]

---

[33] Mary Ann Beavis, "'Making up Stories': A Feminist Reading of the Parable of the Prodigal Son (Lk. 15.11b–32)" in *The Lost Coin: Parables of Women, Work and Wisdom* (ed. Mary Ann Beavis; London: Sheffield Academic Press, 2002), 98–122.

Another possibility is the undemocratic and unjust power relations within the household economy. Imperialism and caste system always blame the colonized and the Dalits for their rebellion and resistance against the status quo as the primary reason for their socio-economic and political disempowerment.

From a Dalit womanist perspective, purity-pollution is a dominant motif in this text. As we think disobedience is not the real issue here. The younger son became prodigal through his contact with the "polluted beings": the prostituted women and the pigs. "So he went and hired himself out to one of the citizens of the country, who sent him to his fields to feed the pigs." (15:15) He must have worked with people who were destined to engage in impure and polluting professions because of their race/caste. Again his co-workers are invisible in the text. However, the motif is clear and visible. Contact with the impure and the polluted is sin, and that will alienate us from the earthly father and the heavenly father. They were not just silenced they were also constructed as inherently impure and sinful. This is the context in which a postcolonial Dalit womanist reading affirms the power of rememorizing to rebel against the imperial representations and to construct new selves based on Dalit *testimonios*.

The presence of the prostituted women in this parable can be considered as a layer that is meant to intensify the sinfulness of the younger son. It is the story of a household. Interestingly, we don't find any female characters in this story such as a mother or sisters or daughters or wives or even maids. The very absence of household female characters and the presence of prostitutes underscore that this imperial text considers women as symbols of evil and sin.

Having said this, how do women read this text as a text of resistance against contemporary manifestations of imperialism? The very realization that the Bible is an imperial text is in itself liberative for these women, as it enables them to become suspicious about the way the doctrine of the authority of the Bible has been used to suppress their humanity. It also helps them to realize that a new meaning is constructed when their mutilated and colonized bodies become the sites of a discursive engagement with the biblical text.

A postcolonial Dalit womanist reading of this text will focus on a reading from the perspective of the "not-so prodigal daughters." The bias of God's salvation towards the last, the least and the lost at the expense of the better ones provides new meaning and hope to Dalit women because it affirms their agency. Moreover, the way Jesus did uphold the humanity of the prostituted women (John 8:7) gives them a new meaning of fellowship and community. Unlike the story of the prodigal son, Jesus did not send the prostituted woman back to the patriarchal family; rather, he let her anoint him, and affirmed her self worth and agency in the expansion of the Reign of God. A postcolonial Dalit womanist reading, therefore, has to engage in creating imaginative histories and testimonies that create new selves.

> A certain young woman ran away from her father's house to a new city. She went to college, married, divorced. She became successful, and many people knew her name. But she was full of sadness, anger and shame, and she didn't know why. Sometimes she starved herself, sometimes she ate too much, to punish herself for the pain and emptiness she felt inside.
>
> One day, she came to herself and remembered that her father had abused her. She learned to believe these memories. She realized that she had no reason to be ashamed, and that her father had sinned against her! The evil spell that had possessed her was broken, and now she could be free.
>
> When her father died, she returned to the house that has been his. She told her mother what her father had done to her. Her mother believed her, and apologized for pretending not to see, for not protecting her. She tenderly embraced her daughter, weeping, and from that day on, the daughter and her mother became closer.
>
> I tell you, the angels of God rejoice more over when one innocent person who survives than over the repentance of the sinners who have abused them![34]

---

[34] An alternative parable composed by Mary Beavis loosely based on Sylvia Fraser's autobiographical novel, *My Father's House: A Memoir of Incest and Healing* (New York: Perennial Library, 1989), Beavis. Op. cit., 122.

BIBLIOGRAPHY

Adam, Andrew K. M. *Faithful Interpretation: Reading the Bible in a Postmodern World*. Minneapolis: Fortress Press, 2006.
Adam, Ian and Helen Tiffin, eds. *Past the Last Post: Theorizing Post-Colonialism and Post-Modernism*. Calgary: University Press of Calgary, 1990.
Ahern, Emily M. *The Cult of the Dead in a Chinese Village*. Stanford: Stanford University Press, 1973.
Ahn, Byung-Mu. "Jesus and the Minjung in the Gospel of Mark." Pages 85–104 in *Voices from the Margin: Interpreting the Bible in the Third World*. Edited by R. S. Sugirtharajah. Maryknoll: Orbis Books, 1995.
———. *Minjung Theology: People as the Subject of History*. Maryknoll: Orbis Books, 1981.
Alexander, Donald. "The Concept of T'ien in Early Confucian Thought." *His Dominion* 3 (1985): 11–14.
Alexander, Philip S. "The Demonology of the Dead Sea Scrolls." Pages 331–53 in *The Dead Sea Scrolls After Fifty Years: A Comprehensive Assessment, Vol. 2*. Edited by P. W. Flint and J. C. VanderKam. Leiden: Brill, 1998–1999.
Amaladass, Anand. "'Dhvani' Theory in Sanscrit Poetics." *Bible Bhashyam* 5:1 (1979): 261–75.
———. *Indian Exegesis: Hindu-Buddhist Hermeneutics*. Satya Nilayam Publications: Chennai, 2003.
———. *Philosophical Implications of Dhvani: Experience of Symbol Language in Indian Aesthetics*. Vol. 11. Publications of the De Nobili Research Library. Vienna: Gerold, 1984.
Amore, Roy. *Two Masters, One Message*. Nashville: Abingdon, 1978.
Appiah, Kwame Anthony. "Is the Post- in Postmodernism the Post- in Postcolonial?" in vol 1 of *Postcolonialism: Critical Concepts in Literary and Cultural Studies*. Edited by Diana Brydon. 5 vols. London: Routledge, 2000). Repr. from *Critical Inquiry* 17:2 (1991): 336–57.
"Applied Logic." Pages 279–90 in vol 23 of *Encyclopædia Britannica*. Edited by Robert P. Gwinn, Peter B. Norton, and Philip W. Goetz. 29 vols. Chicago: The University of Chicago, 1991.
Argenti, Father Cyrille. "A Meditation on Mark 5:1–20." *Ecumenical Review* 23 (1971): 398–408.
Ashcroft, Bill. *Post-Colonial Transformation*. London: Routledge, 2001.
Ashcroft, Bill, Gareth Griffiths, and Helen Tiffin. *The Empire Writes Back: Theory and Practice in Post-Colonial Literatures*. London: Routledge, 1989.
———. *Post-Colonial Studies: The Key Concepts*. London: Routledge, 2002.
———. *The Post-Colonial Studies Reader*. London: Routledge & Kegan Paul, 1995.
Attridge, Harold W. "Christianity from the Destruction of Jerusalem to Constantine's Adoption of the New Religion: 70–312 C.E." Pages 151–94, 340–50 in *Christianity and Rabbinic Judaism: A Parallel History of Their Origins and Early Development*. Edited by Hershel Shanks. Washington, DC: Biblical Archaeology Society, 1992.
Augsburger, David W. *Pastoral Counseling Across Cultures*. Philadelphia: Westminster Press, 1986.
Augustine, of Hippo. *The City of God against the Pagans*. Edited and translated by R. W. Dyson. Cambridge Texts in the History of Political Thought. Cambridge: Cambridge University Press, 1998.

Aus, Roger David. *My Name is "Legion": Palestinian Judaic Traditions in Mark 5:1–20 and Other Gospel Texts.* Studies in Judaism. Lanham, Md.: University Press of America, 2003.

Avotri, Solomon K. "The Vernacularization of Scripture and African Beliefs: The Story of the Gerasene Demoniac Among the Ewe of West Africa." Pages 311–25 in *The Bible in Africa: Transaction, Trajectories, and Trends.* Edited by Gerald O. West and Musa W. Dube. Leiden: Brill, 2000.

Baird, William. "History of Biblical Criticism." Pages 726–36 in vol. 1 of the *The Anchor Bible Dictionary.* Edited by David Noel Freedman. 6 vols. New York: Doubleday, 1992.

Beardslee, William. *Literary Criticism of the New Testament.* Philadelphia: Fortress Press, 1970.

Beavis, Mary Ann. "'Making up Stories': A Feminist Reading of the Parable of the Prodigal Son (Lk. 15.11b–32)." Pages 98–122 in *The Lost Coin: Parables of Women, Work and Wisdom.* Editor Mary Ann Beavis. London: Sheffield Academic Press, 2002.

Bhabha, Homi K. "The Commitment to Theory." *New Formations* 5 (1988): 5–23.

——. *The Location of Culture.* London: Routledge, 1994.

——. "Of Mimicry and Man: The Ambivalence of Colonial Discourse." Pages 234–41 in *Modern Literary Theory.* Edited by Philip Rice and Patricia Waugh. London: Edward Arnold, 1989.

Blaser, Mario, Harvey A. Feit, and Glenn McRae, eds. *In the Way of Development: Indigenous Peoples, Life Projects and Globalization.* London: Zed Books, 2004.

Boehmer, Elleke *Colonial and Postcolonial Literature.* Oxford: Oxford University Press, 1995.

Boer, Roland. "Introduction: Vanishing Mediators?" Pages 1–12 in *A Vanishing Mediator? The Presence/Absence of the Bible in Postcolonialism.* Semeia 88. Edited by Roland Boer and Gerald West. Atlanta: The Society of Biblical Literature, 2001.

Boff, Leonardo B. *Global Civilization: Challenges to Society and to Christianity.* Cross Cultural Theologies. London: Equinox Publications, 2005.

Bong-rin, Ro ed. *Consultation on Christian Response to Ancestor Practices, Christian Alternative to Ancestor Practices.* Taichung, Taiwan: Asia Theological Association, 1985.

Borg, Marcus, ed. *Jesus and Buddha: The Parallel Sayings.* London: Duncan Baird Publishers, 2002.

Breton, Stanislas. *The Word and the Cross.* Translated by Jacquelyn. Porter. Perspectives in Continental Philosophy 22. New York: Fordham, 2002.

Brown, John, *Secwana Dictionary: English-Secwana and Secwana-English.* Tiger Kloof: LMS Book Room, 1895.

Brown, Tom J. *Secwana Dictionary: Secwana-English and English-Secwana.* Tiger Kloof: LMS Book Room, 1925.

Bruns, J. Edgar. *The Christian Buddhism of St. John: New Insights into the Fourth Gospel.* New York: Paulist Press, 1971.

Brydon, Diana, ed. *Postcolonialism: Critical Concepts in Literary and Cultural Studies.* London: Routledge, 2000.

Burdon, Christopher. "'To the Other Side': Construction of Evil and Fear of Liberation in Mark 5:1–20." *Journal for the Study of the New Testament* 27 (2004): 149–67.

Byrskog, Samuel. "Nya testamentets forskningshistoria." Pages 33–41 in *Jesus och de första kristna: inledning till Nya testamentet.* Edited by Dieter Mitternacht and Anders Runesson. Stockholm: Verbum, 2006.

Cabral, Amicar. *Unity and Struggle: Speeches and Writings.* London: Heinemann, 1980.

Capel Anderson, Janice, and Stephen D. Moore, eds. *Mark and Method: New Approaches in Biblical Studies.* 2^d ed. Minneapolis: Fortress Press, 2008.

Caputo, John D. *Deconstruction in a Nutshell: A Conversation with Jacques Derrida*. New York: Fordham University Press, 1997.
———. *The Prayers and Tears of Jacques Derrida: Religion without Religion*. The Indiana Series of the Philosophy of Religion. Bloomington: Indiana University Press, 1977.
Carter, Warren, *Matthew and Empire: Initial Explorations*. Harrisburg: Trinity Press, 2001.
Chakkuvarackal, Johnson T. "Translating Bible in the Indian Context." *Bible Bhashyam* 28:4 (2002): 656–71.
Childs, Peter and Patrick Williams. *An Introduction to Post-Colonial Theory*. London: Prentice Hall, 1997.
Chiu, Milton M. *The Tao of Chinese Religion*. Lanham: University Press of America, 1984.
Chung, Hyun Kyung. "Han/Han-puri." Pages 96–97 in *Dictionary of Third World Theologies*. Edited by R. S. Sugirtharajah and Virginia Fabella. Maryknoll: Orbis Books, 2000.
———. *Struggle to be the Sun Again: Introducing Asian Women's Theology*. Maryknoll: Orbis Books, 1990.
Clarke, Sathianathan. *Dalits and Christianity: Subaltern Religion and Liberation Theology in India*. New Delhi: Oxford University Press, 1998.
———. "Dalit Theology." Pages 64–65 in *Dictionary of Third World Theologies*. Edited by Virginia Fabella and R. S. Sugirtharajah. Maryknoll: Orbis Books, 2000.
Comaroff, Jean and John Comaroff, *Of Revelation and Revolution: Christianity, Colonialism and Consciousness in South Africa, I*. Chicago: The University of Chicago Press, 1991.
Cooppan, Vilashini. "The Ruins of Empire: The National and Global Politics of America's Return to Rome." Pages 80–100 in *Postcolonial Studies and Beyond*. Edited by Ania Loomba, Suvir Kaul, Matti Bunzl, Antoinette Burton and Jed Esty. Durham: Duke University Press, 2005.
Cranfield, C. E. B. *The Gospel According to Saint Mark*. Cambridge: Cambridge University Press, 1959.
Crossan, John Dominic. *In Parables: The Challenge of the Historical Jesus*. New York: Harper, 1973.
———. *Jesus: a Revolutionary Biography*. San Francisco: Harper, 1994.
Cutrufelli, Maria Rosa. *Women from Africa: Roots of Oppression*. London: Zed Books, 1983.
D'Sa, Francis X. "'Dhvani' as a Method of Interpretation." *Bible Bhashyam* 5:1 (1979): 276–94.
Davies, W. D. and Dale C. Allison. *A Critical and Exegetical Commentary on the Gospel According to Saint Matthew II, 8–18*. International Critical Commentary. Edinburgh: T&T Clark, 1991.
DeMan, Paul. *The Resistance to Theory*. Manchester: Manchester University Press, 1986.
Derrida, Jacques. "Letter to a Japanese Friend." Pages 1–5 in *Derrida and Difference*. Edited by Wood and Bernasconi. Warwick: Parousia Press, 1985.
De Smet, Richard. "Hindu and Neo-Hindu Exegesis." *Indian Theological Studies* 21:3–4 (1984): 225–40.
———. "Some Characteristics of Buddhist Exegesis." *Indian Theological Studies* 21:3–4 (1984): 241–49.
DeHay, Terry. *What is Postcolonial Studies?* http://www.sou.edu/English/IDTC/Issues/postcol/postdef.htm, 2004 [cited 8 October 2004].
Derrett, J. Duncan M. *The Bible and the Buddhists*. Casa Editrice Sardini, 2000.
———. "Contributions to the Study of the Gerasene Demoniac." *Journal for the Study of the New Testament* 3 (1979): 2–17.

———."Spirit Possession and the Gerasene Demoniac," *Man*, New Series 14/2 (1979): 286–93.
Donahue, John R. and Daniel J. Harrington. *The Gospel of Mark*. Sacra Pagina 2. Collegeville, Minneapolis: Liturgical, 2002.
Donaldson, Laura E. "Gospel Hauntings: The Postcolonial Demons of New Testament Criticism." Pages 97–113 in *Postcolonial Biblical Criticism: Interdisciplinary Intersections*. Edited by Stephen D. Moore and Fernando F. Segovia. London: T&T Clark, 2005.
Donaldson, Laura E. and Kwok Pui-lan, eds. *Postcolonialism, Feminism, and Religious Discourse*. New York: Routledge, 2002.
Donaldson, Laura. E. "Postcolonialism and Biblical Reading: An Introduction." *Semeia* 75:3 (1996): 1–14.
Dube, Musa W. "Divining Ruth for International Relations." Pages 67–79 in *Postmodern Interpretations of the Bible: A Reader*. Edited by Andrew K. M. Adam. St. Louis: Chalice Press, 2001.
———. "Divining the Texts for International Relations (Mt. 15.21–28)." Pages 315–28 in *Transformative Encounters: Jesus and Women Reviewed*. Edited by Ingrid Kirtzberger. Leiden: Brill, 2000.
———. "'Go Therefore and Make Disciples of All Nations' (Matt 28:19a). A Postcolonial Perspective on Biblical Criticism and Pedagogy." Pages 224–46 in *Teaching the Bible: The Discourses and Politics of Biblical Pedagogy*. Edited by Fernando F. Segovia and Mary Ann Tolbert. Maryknoll, New York: Orbis Books, 1998.
———. "Post-Colonial Biblical Interpretations." Pages 299–303 in vol. 2 of *Dictionary of Biblical Interpretation*. 2nd ed. Edited by John H. Hayes. Nashville: Abingdon Press, 1999.
———. *Postcolonial Feminist Interpretation of the Bible*. St. Louis: Chalice Press, 2000.
———. "Postcoloniality, Feminist Spaces, and Religion." Pages 100–22 in *Postcolonialism, Feminism and Religious Discourse*. Edited by Laura E. Donaldson and Kwok Pui-lan. New York: Routledge, 2002.
———. "Rahab Says Hello to Judith: A Decolonizing Feminist Reading." Pages 142–58 in *Postcolonial Biblical Reader*. Edited by R. S. Sugirtharajah. Oxford: Blackwell, 2006.
———. "Readings of Semoya: Batswana Women's Interpretations of Matt. 15.21–28." *Semeia* 73 (1996): 111–29.
DuBois, W. E. Burghardt. *Dusk of Dawn: An Essay Toward an Autobiography of a Race Concept*. 1940. Repr., New York: Schocken Books, 1968.
———. *The Souls of Black Folk: Essays and Sketches*. Chicago: McClurg, 1918.
———. *The Suppression of the African Slave-Trade to the United States of America, 1638–1870*. New York: The Social Science Press, 1954.
———. *The World and Africa: An Inquiry into the Part which Africa has Played in World History*. New York: Viking Press, 1947.
Dutton, Denis. *Philosophy and Literature*. http://aldaily.com/bwc.htm, 1998 [cited 17 March 2005].
Edmunds, Albert Joseph. *Buddhist and Christian Gospels*. 4th ed. Edited by Masaharu Anesaki. 2 vols. Philadelphia: Innes & Sons, 1914.
Eiman, O. Zein-Elbdin, and S. Charusheela, eds. *Postcolonialism Meets Economics*. Economics as Social Theory. London: Routledge, 2003.
Elisha, James. "Liberative Motifs in the Dalit Religion." *Bangalore Theolgical Forum* 34:2 (2002): 78–88.
Elliott, John H. *What is Social-Scientific Criticism?* Edited by D. O. Via. New Testament Series. Minneapolis: Fortress Press, 1993.
"Exegesis." Pages 629 in vol. 4 of *Encyclopædia Britannica*. Edited by Robert P. Gwinn, Peter B. Norton, and Philip W. Goetz. 29 vols. Chicago: The University of Chicago, 1991.

"Exegetik." Pages 1223 in vol. 6 of *Nordisk familjebok: Encyklopedi och konversationslexikon*. Edited by V. Söderberg. Malmö: Nordisk familjebok aktiebolag, 1923-1937.
"Exegetik." Pages 58 vol. 6 of *Nationalencyklopedin*. Edited by K. Marklund. Höganäs: Bokförlaget Bra Böcker, 1991.
Fabella, Virginia and R. S. Sugirtharajah, eds. *Dictionary of Third World Theologies*. Maryknoll, New York: Orbis Books, 2000.
Fanon, Frantz. *Black Skin. White Masks*. New York: Grove Press, 1967.
——. *The Wretched of the Earth*. Translated by C. Farrington. New York: Grove Press, 1968.
Fee, Gordon D. "Εἰδωλόθυτα Once Again: An Interpretation of 1 Corinthians 8-10," *Biblica* 61:2 (1980): 172-197.
Feuchtwang, Stephan. "Domestic and Communal Worship in Taiwan." Pages 105-129 in *Religion and Ritual in Chinese Society*. Edited by Arthur P. Wolf. Stanford: Stanford University Press, 1974.
Fortes, Meyer. "An Introductory Commentary." Pages 1-17 in *Ancestors*. Edited by William H. Newell. Haugue/Paris: Mouton Publishers, 1976. Finns på Hebrew U.
Foskett, Mary F., and Jeffrey Kah-Jin Kuan, eds. *Ways of Being, Ways of Reading: Asian American Biblical Interpretation*. St. Louise: Chalice Press, 2006.
Foucault, Michel. *The Archaeology of Knowledge*. London: Travistock Publications, 1972.
Fraser, Sylvia. *My Father's House: A Memoir of Incest and Healing*. New York: Perennial Library, 1989.
Funk, Robert. *Language, Hermeneutic and the Word of God*. New York: Harper, 1969.
Gairdner, William H. *An Account and Interpretation of the World Missionary Conference*. London: Oliphant & Ferrier, 1910.
Gandhi, Leela. *Postcolonial Theory: A Critical Introduction*. New York: Columbia University Press, 1998.
Geijerstam, Jan af. *Mitt i världen, mitt i tiden*. Stockholm: Ordfront, 1993.
Georgi, Dieter. "The Interest in the Life of Jesus Theology as a Paradigm for the Social History of Biblical Criticism." *Harvard Theological Review* 85:1 (1992): 51-83.
Gnanadason, Aruna. *No Longer a Secret: The Church and Violence Against Women*. Geneva: World Council of Churches Publications, 1993.
Goodmann, Hananya. "Introduction. Judaism and Hinduism: Cultural Resonances." Pages 1-14 in *Between Jerusalem and Benares: Comparative Studies Between Judaism and Hinduism*. Edited by Hananya Goodmann. Delhi: Sri Satguru Publications, 1997.
Groot, Jan Jacob Maria de. *Religion in China*. American Lectures on the History of Religions. New York, London: The Knickerbocker Press, 1912.
Hall, Stuart. "When was 'the Post-Colonial'? Thinking at the Limit" Pages 237-57 in vol 1 of *Postcolonialism: Critical Consepts in Literary and Cultural Studies*. Edited by Diana Brydon. 5 vols. London: Routledge, 2000). Repr. from *The Post-Colonial Question: Common Skies, Divided Horizons*. Edited by Iain Chambers and Lidia Curti. London: Routledge, 1996: 242-60.
Hammar, Anna-Karin. "Globalisering, ekonomi, teologi: ett kristet perspektiv." Pages 70-89 in *Varför ser ni mot himlen? Utmaningar från den kontextuella teologin*. Edited by Thorbjörn Sjöholm and Anders Runesson. Stockholm: Verbum, 2005.
Harasym, Sarah, ed. *The Post-Colonial Critic: Interviews, Strategies, Dialogues*. London: Routledge, 1990.
Hawley, John C., ed. *Postcolonial and Queer Theories: Intersections and Essays*. Westport: Greenwood Press, 2001.
Hayes, John H. and Carl R. Holladay. *Biblical Exegesis: A Beginner's Handbook*. London: SCM Press, 1987.

Hollenbach, Paul W. "Jesus, Demoniacs, and Public Authorities: A Socio-Historical Study." *Journal of the American Academy of Religion* 49 (1981): 567-88.
Holmberg, Bengt. *Sociology and the New Testament: An Appraisal*. Minneapolis: Fortress Press, 1990.
Hooker, Morna D. *The Gospel According to Saint Mark*. Black's New Testament Commentaries 2; Peabody: Hendrickson, 1991.
Horsley, Richard A. "'My Name is Legion': Spirit Possession and Exorcism in Roman Palestine." Pages 41-57 in *Experientia, Volume 1: Inquiry into Religious Experience in Early Judaism and Christianity*. Edited by F. Flannery, C. Shantz, and R. A. Werline. SBL Symposium 40. Leiden: Brill, 2008.
——, ed. *Paul and Empire: Religion and Power in Roman Imperial Society*. Harrisburg: Trinity Press, 1997.
——. "The Struggle Against Roman Rule." Pages 121-48 in *Hearing the Whole Story: The Politics of Plot in Mark's Gospel*. London: Westminster John Knox, 2001.
Hsu, Francis L. K. *Under the Ancestor's Shadow: Kinship, Personality, and Social Mobility in China*. Stanford: Stanford University Press, 1971.
The Interpretation of the Bible in the Church. Indian edition. Vatican Document: The Pontificial Biblical Commision. Bangalore: The National Biblical Catechetical and Liturgical Centre, 1995.
Iverson, Kelly. "First Journey into Gentile Territory." Pages 20-39 in *Gentiles and the Gospel of Mark: "Even the Dogs Under the Table Eat the Children's Crumbs."* London: T&T Clark, 2007.
Jeremias, Joachim. *The Parables of Jesus*. London: SCM Press, 1971.
Jones, Derek. 'Preface.' Page viii in Z. I. Matumo, *Setswana English Setswana Dictionary*. Gaborone: Macmillan, 1993.
Johnson, Barbara. *The Critical Difference: Essays in the Contemporary Rhetoric of Reading*. Baltimore: Johns Hopsins University Press, 1981.
Johnson, Teng Kok Lim. "Historical Critical Paradigm: The Beginning of an End." *Asia Journal of Theology* 14 (2000): 252-71.
——. *A Strategy for Reading Biblical Texts*. New York: Peter Lang Publishing, 2002.
Jussawalla, Feroza and Reed Way Dasenbrock, eds. *Interviews with Writers of the Post-Colonial World*. Jackson: University Press of Mississippi, 1992.
Kim, Sung-Hae. "Silent Heaven Giving Birth to the Multitude of People." *Ching Feng* 31:4D (1988): 195-224.
Käsemann Ernst. "The Problem of the Historical Jesus. " Pages 279-313 *The Historical Jesus Quest: A Foundational Antheology*. Edited by Gregory W. Dawes. Leiden: Deo Publishing. Repr. from "Das Problem des historischen Jesu." Pages 125-53 in *Zeitschrift für Theologie und Kirche* 51 (1954).
Kertelge, Karl. *Die Wunder Jesu im Markusevangelium*. Munich: Kösel, 1970.
Kgasa A. and J. Tsonope. *Tlhanodi ya Setswana*. Gaborone: Longman, 1995.
King, Richard. *Orientalism and Religion: Postcolonial Theory, India and 'The Mystic East.'* London and New York: Routledge, 1999.
Kipling, Rudyard. *The Jungle Book*. London: Macmillan, 1907.
Krentz, Edgar. *The Historical Critical Method*. Philadelphia: Fortress Press, 1975.
Landry, Donna and Gerald MacLean, eds. *The Spivak Reader*. London: Routledge, 1996.
Lausberg, Heinrich. *Handbuch der literarischen Rhetorik: Eine Grundlegung der Literaturwissenschaft*. 2 vols. 2nd ed. Munich: Max Heuber, 1973.
Legrand, Lucien. "Inculturation and Biblical Studies in India." *Indian Theological Studies* 20:1 (1984): 61-70.
Levine, Amy-Jill. "Anti-Judaism and Postcolonial Biblical Interpretation: The Disease of Postcolonial New Testament Studies and the Hermeneutics of Healing—Roundtable Discussion" *Journal of Feminist Studies in Religion* 20 no 1 (2004): 91-99.

———. "Lilies of the Field and Wandering Jews: Biblical Scholarship, Women's Roles, and Social Location." Pages 329–52 in *Transformative Encounters: Jesus and Women Re-Viewed*. Edited by Ingrid Rosa Kitzberger. Leiden: Brill, 2000.
———."Matthew's Advice to a Divided Readership." Pages 22–41 in *The Gospel of Matthew in Current Study*. Edited by David E. Aune. Grand Rapids: Eerdmanns, 2001.
Liddell, Henry George, Robert Scott et al. *A Greek-English Lexicon: Revised Supplement*. Edited by P. G. W. Glare with the assistance of A. A. Tompson. Oxford: Oxford University Press, 1996.
Ling, Amy. "'I' am Here." *Feminisms: Anthology of Literary Theory*. Edited by Robyn R. Warhol and Diane Price Herndl. New Brunswick: Rutgers, 1993.
Longkumar, Limtula. "In Search of a Holistic Educational Ministry in the Churches of Nagaland." *Journal of Tribal Studies* 7 (2003): 177–91.
Loomba, Ania. *Colonialism/Postcolonialism*. London: Routledge, 1998.
———. *Shakespeare, Race, and Colonialism*. Oxford: Oxford University Press, 2002.
Loomba, Ania, Suvir Kaul, Matti Bunzl, Antoinette Burton, and Jed Esty, eds. *Postcolonial Studies and Beyond*. Durham: Duke University Press, 2005.
Lowe, Lisa. *Critical Terrains: French and British Orientalisms*. Ithaca: Cornell University Press, 1991.
Magnusson, John. "Örebro Missionsförenings mission i Brasilien." Pages 321–29 in *Missionen i bild*. Edited by G. Lindeberg. Stockholm: AB Svenska Journalens Förlag, 1948.
Manickam, Thomas. "Cross Cultural Hermeneutics: The Patterns of Jaimini, Bharthari and Sankaracharya." *Indian Theological Studies* 21:3–4 (1984): 250–67.
Martin, Dale B. *The Corinthian Body*. New Haven: Yale University Press, 1995.
Martin, W. A. P. "How Shall We Deal with the Worship of Ancestors?" *Chinese Recorder* 33 (1902): 117–19.
———. "The Worship of Ancestor—A Plea for Tolerance." Pages 619–31 in *Records of the General Conference of the Protestant Missionaries of China Held at Shanghai* (1890).
———. "The Worship of Confucius: is it Idolatry?" *Chinese Recorder* 34 (1904), 92–93.
Martínez-Vázquez, Hjamil A. "Breaking the Established Scaffold: Imagination as a Resource in the Development of Biblical Interpretation" Pages 71–91 in *Her Master's Tools? Feminist and Postcolonial Engagements of Historical-Critical Discourse*. Edited by Todd Penner and Caroline Vander Stichele. Society of Biblical Literature: Atlanta, 2005.
McClintock, Anne. *Imperial Leather: Race, Gender, and Sexuality in the Colonial Contest*. London: Routledge, 1995.
Mchami, R. E. K. "Demon Possession and Exorcism in Mark 1:21–28." *Africa Theological Journal* 24 (2001): 17–37.
McKenzie, Steven L. and Stephen R. Haynes, eds. *To Each Its Own Meaning: An Introduction to Biblical Criticism and Their Application*. Louisville: Westminster John Knox Press, 1999.
Meeks, Wayne A. "The Polyphonic Ethics of the Apostle Paul." *Annual of the Society of Christian Ethics* (1988): 17–29.
Melanchthon, Monica Jyotsna and George Zachariah eds. *Witnessing in Context: Essays in Honor of Eardley Mendis* (Tiruvalla: Christava Sahitya Samithi, 2007).
Metzger, Bruce M. *A Textual Commentary on the Greek New Testament*. London/New York: United Bible Societies, 1971.
Miller, J. Maxwell. "Reading the Bible Historically: The Historian's Approach." Pages 17–34 in *To Each its Own Meaning: An Introduction to Biblical Criticisms and their Application*. Edited by Steven L. McKenzie and Stephen R. Haynes. Louisville: Westminster John Knox Press, 1999.
Misra, Neelesh. "Instincts May have Saved Isolated Tribes." *The Hamilton Spectator*, Canada/World (January 5 2005): A9.

Mishra, Vijay and Bob Hodge. "What is Post(-)colonialism?" *Textual Practice* 5:3 (1991): 399–414.
Mohan, Sanal. "Theorising History in the Context of Social Movement: Challenges to the Reigning Paradigms of History." Pages—in *The Struggle for the Past: Historiography Today*. Edited by Felix Wilfred and Jose D. Maliekal. Chennai: Department of Christian Studies University of Madras, 2002.
Moon, Cyris H. S. "A Korean Minjung Perspective: The Hebrews and the Exodus." Pages 228–43 in *Voices from the Margin: Interpreting the Bible in the Third World*. Edited by R. S. Sugirtharajah. Maryknoll: Orbis Books, 1995.
Moore, Charles A. ed. *The Chinese Mind; Essentials of Chinese Philosophy and Culture*. Honolulu: University of Hawaii, 1971.
Moore, Michael. *Fahrenheit 9/11*. Edited by Michael Moore, 2004.
Moore, Stephen D. *Empire and Apocalypse: Postcolonialism and the New Testament*. The Bible in the Modern World 12. Sheffield: Sheffield Phoenix, 2006.
Moore, Stephen D. and Fernando F. Segovia, eds. *Postcolonial Biblical Criticism: Interdisciplinary Intersections*. Bible and Postcolonialism. London: T&T Clark, 2005.
Morris, Charles W. *Varieties of Human Value*. Chicago: University of Chicago Press, 1956.
Muthuraj, Joseph G. "New Testament and Methodology: An Overview." *Asia Journal of Theology* 10 (1996): 253–77.
Myers, Ched. *Binding the Strong Man: A Political Reading of Mark's Story of Jesus*. Maryknoll, NY: Orbis, 1988.
Nakashima Brock, Rita. "Marriage Troubles." Onine: www.panaawtm.org/images/BROCK_Marriage_Trouble.doc.
Ng, Chae-Woon. "Filial Piety in Confucian Thought." *North-East Asia Journal of Theology* 28 (1982): 13–48.
Ngubane, John B. "Theological Roots of the AICs and their Challenge to Black Theology." Pages 71–100 in *The Unquestionable Right to Be Free: Black Theology from South Africa*. Edited by Itumeleng Mosala and Buti Tlhagale. New York: Orbis Books, 1992.
Nirmal, Arvind P. "A Dialogue with Dalit Literature." Pages 64–82 in *A Reader in Dalit Theology*. Edited by Arvind P. Nirmal. Madras: Gurukul, 1991.
———. "Towards a Christian Dalit Theology." *Asian Journal of Theology* 6:2 (1992): 297–310.
Nkrumah, Kwame. *Africa Must Unite*. New York: International Publishers, 1970.
———. *Neo-Colonialism: The Last Stage of Imperialism*. New York: International Publishers, 1966.
Olsson, Birger. "A Decade of Text-Linguistic Analyses of Biblical Texts at Uppsala." *Studia Theologica* 39 (1985): 107–26.
———. "Ett bidrag till metodfrågan." *Svensk exegetisk årsbok* 45 (1980): 110–21.
———. "Förstår du hur du läser?" Pages 7–22 in *Religio* 11. Edited by René Kieffer and Birger Olsson. Lund: Teologiska institutionen, 1995.
———. "Reflektioner vid konferensens slut." Pages 147–60 in *När religiösa texter blir besvärliga*. Konferenser 64. Edited by Lars Hartman. Stockholm: Kungl. Vitterhets Historie och Antikvitets Akademien, 2007.
———. "Text är arbete att förstå: Om olika textperspektiv i svensk bibelforskning under 1900–talet." *Svensk exegetisk årsbok* 64 (1999): 5–22.
Oosthuizen, Gerhardus C. *The Healer-Prophet in Afro-Christian Churches*. Leiden: Brill, 1992.
Pathrapankal, Joseph. "A Re-reading of John 12:20–27 in the Context of Religious Pluralism." Paper presented at the Studiorum Novi Testamenti Societas 56th General Meeting, Montreal 2001.
———. *Text and Context in Biblical Interpretation*. Bangalore: Dharmaram Publications, 1993.

———. *Understanding the Gospels Today*. Bangalore: Dharmaram Publications, 1977.
Peek, Phillip M. ed. *African Divination Systems: Ways of Knowing*. Indianapolis: Indiana University Press, 1991.
Perelman, Chaïm. *The New Rhetoric and the Humanities: Essays on Rhetoric and its Applications*. Dordrecht: D. Reidel, 1979.
———. *The Realm of Rhetoric*. Notre Dame: University of Notre Dame Press, 1982.
Permer, Karin and Lars Göran Permer. *Klassrummets moraliska ordning: Iscensättningen av lärare och elever som subjekt för ansvarsdiskursen i klassrummet*. Malmö: Malmö Högskola, 2002.
Pesch, Rudolph. "The Markan Version of the Healing of the Gerasene Demoniac." *Ecumenical Review* 23 (1971): 349–76.
Petersen, George. *The Literary Critic and the New Testament*. Philadelphia: Fortress Press, 1978.
Petrella, Ivan. *The Future of Liberation Theology: An Argument and Manifesto*. Aldershot: Ashgate, 2004.
Poythress, Vern. "Analysing a Biblical Text: Some Important Linguistic Distinctions." *Scottish Journal of Theology* 32 (1979): 113–37.
Premnath, Devadasan N. "Biblical Interpretation in India: History and Issues." Pages 1–16 in *Ways of Being, Ways of Reading: Asian American Biblical Interpretation*. Edited by Mary F. Foskett and Jeffrey Kah-Jin Kuan. St. Louis: Chalice Press, 2006.
Pui-lan, Kwok. *Chinese Women and Christianity, 1860–1927*. Atlanta: Scholars Press, 1992.
———. *Discovering the Bible in the Non-Biblical World*. The Bible and Liberation. Maryknoll: Orbis Books, 1995.
———. *Introducing Asian Feminist Theology*. Introductions in Feminist Theology. Sheffield: Sheffield Academic, 2000.
———. "Jesus/The Native: Biblical Studies from a Postcolonial Perspective." Pages 69–85 in *Teaching the Bible: The Discourses and Politics of Biblical Pedagogy*. Edited by Fernando F. Segovia and Mary Ann Tolbert. Maryknoll, New York: Orbis Books, 1998.
———. "Mercy Amba Oduyoye and African Women's theology." *Journal of Feminist Studies in Religion* 20:1 (2004): 7–22.
———. *Postcolonial Imagination and Feminist Theology*. Louisville: Westminster John Knox Press, 2005.
Qian, Zhaoming. *Orientalism and Modernism: The Legacy of China in Pound and Williams*. Durham and London: Duke University Press, 1995.
Radhakrishnan, Sarvepalli. *Eastern Religions and Western Thought*. New York: Oxford University Press, 1959.
Räisänen, Heikki. "Biblical Critics in the Global Village." Pages 9–28 in *Reading the Bible in the Global Village: Helsinki*. Vol. 1. Edited by Heikki Räisänen, Elisabeth Schüssler-Fiorenza, R. S. Sugirtharajah, Krister Stendahl, and James Barr. Atlanta: Society of Biblical Literature, 2000.
Ranajit, Guha, ed. *A Subaltern Studies Reader, 1986–1995*. Minneapolis: University of Minnesota Press, 1997.
Rege, Sharmila. *Writing Caste/Writing Gender: Narrating Dalit Women's Testimonios*. New Delhi: Zubaan, 2006.
Renan, J. Ernest and Henriette Psichari. *Œuvres complètes*. 10 vols. Vol. 8. Paris, 1948: 156.
Riches, John. "Cultural Bias in European and North American Biblical Scholarship." Pages 431–48 in *Ethnicity and the Bible*. Edited by Mark G. Brett. Boston: Brill Academic Publishers, 2002.
Ricoeur, Paul. "Biblical Hermeneutics." *Semeia* 4 (1975): 170–228.

Runesson, Anders. "Vägar till det förflutna." Pages 42–54 in *Jesus och de första kristna: Inledning till Nya testamentet*. Edited by Dieter Mitternacht and Anders Runesson. Verbum: Stockholm, 2006.

Runesson, Anna. "Feministisk exegetik: En undersökning av dess vetenskapliga värde belyst utifrån den feministiska teologin och exemplifierad genom feministisk historisk rekonstruktion och feministisk retorisk analys av 1 Kor 11:2–16." Honours Thesis, Lund Univerity, 1995.

———. "Historisk-kritisk metod i postcolonial kontext: Stötesten eller nödvändighet?" *Svensk kyrkotidning*, 97: 9–10 (2001): 475–79.

———. "Kontextuell exegetik i en postkolonial värld: Bibeltolkning i en postkolonial värld." Pages 122–49 in *Varför ser ni mot himlen? Utmaningar från den kontextuella teologin*. Edited by Anders Runesson and Torbjörn Sjöholm. Stockholm: Verbum, 2005.

———. "'Legion heter jag för vi är många:' En postkolonial läsning av Mark 5:1–20." Pages 475–81 in *Jesus och de första kristna: Inledning till Nya testament*. Edited by Dieter Mitternacht and Anders Runesson. Stockholm: Verbum, 2006.

Said, Edward W. *Culture and Imperialism*. London: Vintage, 1994.

———. *Humanism and Democratic Criticism*. Columbia Themes in Philosophy. New York: Columbia University Press, 2004.

———. *Orientalism*. New York: Vintage Books, 2003.

———. *The World, the Text, and the Critic*. Cambridge: Harvard University Press, 1983.

Sandilands, Alexander. *The History of The Setswana Bible*. Cape Town: Bible Society of South Africa, 1989.

Sandmel, Samuel. "Parallelomania." *Journal of Biblical Literature* 81 (1962): 1–13.

Schenke, Ludger. *Die Wundererzählungen des Markus Evangeliums*. Stuttgart: Katholisches Bibelwerk, 1975.

Schüssler-Fiorenza, Elisabeth. *But She Said: Feminist Practices of Biblical Interpretation*. Boston: Beacon Press, 1992.

———. "Defending the Centre, Trivializing the Margins." Pages 29–48 in *Reading the Bible in the Global Village: Helsinki*. Vol 1. Edited by Heikki Räisänen, Elisabeth Schüssler-Fiorenza, R. S. Sugirtharajah, Krister Stendahl and James Barr. Atlanta: Society of Biblical Literature, 2000.

———. *Rhetoric and Ethic: The Politics of Biblical Studies*. Minneapolis: Fortress Press, 1999.

Schweitzer, Albert. *Von Reimarus zu Wrede: Eine Geschichte der Leben-Jesu Forschung*. Tübingen: Mohr Siebeck, 1906.

Schweizer, Eduard. *The Good News According to Mark*. Translated by D. H. Madvig. Richmond, Va.: John Knox, 1970.

Scott, David. "Construction of Postcolonial Studies." Pages 385–400 in *Postcolonial Studies and Beyond*. Edited by Ania Loomba, Suvir Kaul, Matti Bunzl, Antoinette Burton and Jed Esty. Durham: Duke University Press, 2005.

Sebastian, Mrinalini. "Reading Archives from a Postcolonial Feminist Perspective: "Native" Bible Women and the Missionary Ideal." *Journal of Feminist Studies in Religion* 19:1 (2003): 5–25.

Segovia, Fernando F. and R. S. Sugirtharajah eds. *A Postcolonial Commentary on the New Testament Writings*. London: T&T Clark, 2007.

Segovia, Fernando F. *Decolonizing Biblical Studies: A View from the Margins*. Maryknoll: Orbis Books, 2000.

———. *The Farewell of the Word: The Johannine Call to Abide*. Minneapolis: Eortress Press, 1991.

———. "Introduction: Pedagogical Discourse and Practices in Contemporary Biblical Criticism. Toward a Contextual Biblical Pedagogy." Pages 1–27 in *Teaching*

the Bible: The Discourses and Politics of Biblical Pedagogy. Edited by Fernando F. Segovia and Mary Ann Tolbert. Maryknoll, New York: Orbis Books, 1998.
———. "Mapping the Postcolonial Optic in Biblical Criticism: Meaning and Scope." Pages 23–78 in Postcolonial Biblical Criticism: Interdisciplinary Intersections. Edited by Stephen D. Moore and Fernando F. Segovia. London: T&T Clark, 2005.
———. "Pedagogical Discourse and Practices in Cultural Studies: Toward a Contextual Biblical Pedagogy." Pages 137–67 in Teaching the Bible: The Discourses and Politics of Biblical Pedagogy. Edited by Fernando F. Segovia and Mary Ann Tolbert. Maryknoll, New York: Orbis Books, 1998.
———. "Postcolonial Biblical Criticism." Paper presented at the SNTS, 59th General Meeting, La Salle Bonanova College in Barcelona, Spain, 5–7 August 2004.
———. "Reading Readers of the Fourth Gospel and their Readings: An Exercise in Intercultural Criticism." Pages 237–78 in "What is John?" Readers and Readings of the Fourth Gospel. Edited by Fernando F. Segovia. Atlanta, Georgia: Scholars Press, 1996.
Segovia, Fernando F. and Mary Ann Tolbert, eds. Reading from this Place: Social Location and Biblical Interpretation in Global Perspective. 2 vols. Minneapolis: Fortress Press, 1995.
——— eds. Teaching the Bible: The Discourses and Politics of Biblical Pedagogy. Maryknoll: Orbis Books, 1998.
Småberg, Maria. Ambivalent Friendship: Anglican Conflict Handling and Education for Peace in Jerusalem 1920–1948. Lund: Lund University, 2005.
Smart, Barry. Michel Foucault. London and New York: Routledge, 1985.
Smith, Henry N. "A Typology of Christian Responses to Chinese Ancestor Worship." Journal of Ecumenical Studies 26 (1989): 628–47.
Sneja, Gunew. Haunted Nations: the Colonial Dimensions of Multiculturalisms. Transformations. London: Routledge, 2004.
Soares-Prabhu, George M. "And There Was a Great Calm: A 'Dhvani' Reading of the Stilling of the Storm." Bible Bhashyam 5:1 (1979): 295–308.
———. "Are the Gospels Historical?" Clergy Monthly 38 (1974): 112–24, 163–72.
———. The Dharma of Jesus. An Interpretation of the Sermon on the Mount. Edited by Frances X. D'Sa. Maryknoll, New York: Orbis Books, 2003.
———. "The Historical Critical Method: Reflections on its Relevance for the Study of the Gospels in India Today." Theologizing in India (1981): 314–67.
———. "The Table Fellowship of Jesus: Its Significance for Dalit Christians in India Today." Jeevadhara 22:128 (1992): 140–59.
———. "Two Mission Commands: An Interpretation of Matthew 28:16–20 in the Light of a Buddhist Text." Biblical Interpretation (1994): 264–82.
Spivak, Gayatri Chakravorty. "Can the Subaltern Speak?" Pages 66–111 in Colonial Discourse and Post-Colonial Theory. Edited by Patrick Williams and Laura Chrisman. New York: Colombia University Press, 1994.
———. Conversations. Oxford: Blackwell Publishers, 2004.
———. Death of a Discipline. The Wellek Library Lectures in Critical Theory. New York: Columbia University Press, 2003.
———. "Diasporas Old and New: Women in the Transnational World." Textual Practice (1996): 245–69.
———. "Gayatri Chakravorty Spivak", http://www.english.emory.edu/Bahri/Spivak.html, 2003 [cited 6 May 2005].
———. In Other Worlds: Essays in Cultural Politics. New York: Routledge, 1988.
———. "Moving Devi." Cultural Critique (2001): 120–63.
———. "Neocolonialism and the Secret Agent of Knowledge." Oxford Literary Review 13:1–2 (1991): 220–51.
———. Of Derrida. Oxford: Blackwell Publishers, 2006.
———. Outside in the Teaching Machine. London: Routledge, 1993.

Stählin, Gustav. "Σκάνδαλον." Pages 339–43 in vol. 7 in *Theological Dictionary of the New Testament*. Edited Gerhard Friedrich. Translator and editor Geoffrey W. Bromiley. 10 vols. Grand Rapids: Eerdmans, 1965–1978.

Stendahl, Krister. *Meanings: The Bible as Document and as Guide*. Philadelphia: Fortress Press, 1984.

Stenström, Hanna. "Historical-Critical Approaches and the Emancipations of Women: Unfulfilled Promises and Remaining Possibilities." Pages 31–46 in *Her Master's Tools? Feminist and Postcolonial Engagements of Historical-Critical Discourse*. Edited by Caroline Vander Stichele and Todd Penner. Atlanta: Society of Biblical Literature, 2005.

Stoller, Paul. *Embodying Colonial Memories: Spirit Possession, Power and the Hauka in West Africa*. London: Routledge, 1995.

"Striving for Equity: Voices from Academe: How Far have we come? Where are we Going?" *Academic Matters* (February 2007): 3.

Stower, Stanley K. *The Diatribe and Paul's Letter to the Romans* (Society of Biblical Literature Dissertation Series 57; Chico: Scholars Press, 1981).

Strong, Josiah. "Josiah Strong on the Anglo-Saxon Destiny, 1885." Pages 122–23 in *The Imperialism Reader: Documents and Readings in Modern Expansionism*. Edited by Louis Synder. New York: D. Van Nostrad Company, 1962.

Stuart, Douglas. "Exegesis." *Anchor Bible Dictionary* 2 (1992): 682–88.

Sugirtharajah, R. S. *Asian Biblical Hermeneutics and Postcolonialism: Contesting the Interpretations*. The Biblical Seminar 64. Sheffield: Sheffield Academic Press, 1999.

———. *The Bible and Empire: Postcolonial Explorations*. Cambridge: Cambridge University Press, 2005.

———. *The Bible and the Third World: Precolonial, Colonial and Postcolonial Encounters*. Cambridge: Cambridge University Press, 2001.

———. "Coding and Decoding: Postcolonial Criticism and Biblical Interpretation." Pages 74–102 in *Postcolonial Criticism and Biblical Interpretation*. Oxford: Oxford University Press, 2002.

———. "From Orientalist to Post-Colonial: Notes on Reading Practices." *Asia Journal of Theology* 10 (1996): 20–27.

———. *Postcolonial Criticism and Biblical Interpretation*. New York: Oxford University Press, 2002.

———. *Postcolonial Reconfigurations: An Alternative Way of Reading the Bible and Doing Theology*. London: SCM Press, 2003.

———. *Voices from the Margin: Interpreting the Bible in the Third World*. Edited by R. S. Sugirtharajah. Maryknoll: Orbis Books, 1995. See also the revised and expanded 3[d] edition. Maryknoll: Orbis/Edinburgh: Alban, 2006.

Suh, David Kwang-sun. "Minjung Theology." Pages 143–44 in *Dictionary of Third World Theologies*. Edited by Virginia Fabella and R. S. Sugirtharajah. Maryknoll: Orbis Books, 2000.

Swete, Henry Barclay. *Commentary on Mark*. Grand Rapids, Michigan: Kregel, 1977.

Taussig, Michael. *Shamanism, Colonialism and the Wild Man: A Study in Terror and Healing*. Chicago: University of Chicago Press, 1987.

Te Selle, Sallie. *Speaking in Parables*. Philadelphia; Fortress Press, 1975.

The Bible and Culture Collective, *The Postmodern Bible*. New Haven: Yale University Press, 1995.

Thottakara, Augustine. "An Indian Poet Contemplates on the Life of Jesus Christ: A Critical Appreciation of the Kristu-bhagavata of Prof. P. C. Devassia." Pages 65–92 in *Western Encounter with Indian Philosophy: Festschrift in Honour of Prof. Dr. Thomas Kadankavil*. Edited by Augustine Thottakara. Bangalore: Dharmaram Publications, 2002.

Thundy, Zacharias P. *Buddha and Christ: Nativity Stories and Indian Traditions*. Leiden: Brill, 1993.

Thurén, Torsten. *Vetenskapsteori för nybörjare.* Malmö: Liber, 1991.
Thiongo, Ngugi wa. *Decolonising the Mind: The Politics of Language in African Literature.* London: James Curry, 1986.
Tiffin, Chris and Alan Lawson, eds. *Describing Empire: Post-colonialism and Textuality.* London: Routledge, 1994.
Tolbert, Mary Ann. "A New Teaching with Authority: A Re-evaluation of the Authority of the Bible." Pages 168-89 in *Teaching the Bible: The Discourses and Politics of Biblical Pedagogy.* Edited by Fernando F. Segovia and Mary Ann Tolbert. Maryknoll, NY: Orbis Books, 1998.
Tuckett, Christopher. *Reading the New Testament: Methods of Interpretation.* Philadelphia: Fortress Press, 1987.
Turner, Bryan S. *Orientalism, Postmodernism and Globalism.* London and New York: Routledge, 1997.
Twelftree, Graham. *In the Name of Jesus: Exorcism among Early Christians.* Grand Rapids, Mich: Baker, 2007.
Vandana, Sr. "Water—God's Extravaganza: John 2.1-11." Pages 156-67 in *Voices from the Margin: Interpreting the Bible in the Third World.* Edited by R. S. Sugirtharajah. Maryknoll: Orbis Books, 1995.
Vander Stichele, Caroline, and Todd Penner, eds. *Her Master's Tools? Feminist and Postcolonial Engagements of Historical-Critical Discourse.* Global Perspectives on Biblical Scholarship 9. Atlanta: Society of Biblical Literature, 2005.
Via, Dan O. *The Parables: Their Literary and Existential Dimension.* Philadelphia: Fortress Press, 1967.
Weber, Max. "Science as a Vocation." Pages 129-56 in *From Max Weber: Essays in Sociology.* Edited and translated by H. H. Gerth and C. W. Mills. New York: Oxford University Press, 1946.
Webster, John C. B. *The Dalit Christians: A History.* Delhi: Indian Society for Promoting Christian Knowledge, 1992.
Wei-ming, Tu. "Li as Process of Humanization." *Philosophy East and West* 22 (1972): 179-95.
Westerholm, Stephen. *Understanding Matthew: The Early Christian Worldview of the First Gospel.* Grand Rapids: Baker Academic, 2006.
Wiebe, Phillip H. "Finite Spirits as Theoretical Entities." *Religious Studies* 40 (2004): 341-50.
———. *God and Other Spirits: Intimations of Transcendence in Christian Experience.* Oxford: Oxford University Press, 2004.
Wilder, Amos. *Early Christian Rhetoric.* London: CSM Press, 1964.
Williams, Patrick and Laura Chrisman, eds. *Colonial Discourse and Post-Colonial Theory: A Reader.* New York: Columbia University Press, 1994.
Witting, Susan. "A Theory of Multiple Meanings." *Semeia* 9, (1977): 75-103.
Wolf, Eric Robert. *Europe and the People Without History.* Berkeley: University of California Press, 1982.
Wong, Wai Ching. "Postcolonialism." Pages 169-70 in *Dictionary of the Third World Theologies.* Edited by Virginia Fabella and R. S. Sugirtharajah. Maryknoll, New York: Orbis Books, 2000.
Wookey. Alfred J. *Phuthololo Ea Efangeleo e e Kwadilweng ke Mathaiao.* Tiger Kloof: LMS Book Room, 2nd edn, 1902.
Xavier, A. "John's Gospel in the Indian Context." *Indian Theological Studies* 21:2-4 (1984): 347-64.
Yang, Ching Kun. *Religion in Chinese Society: A Study of Contemporary Social Functions of Religion and Some of Their Historical Factors.* Berkeley: University of California Press, 1967.

Yegenoglu, Meyda. "Sartorial Fabric-action: Enlightenment and Western Feminism." Pages 82–99 in *Postcolonialism, Feminism and Religious Discourse*. Edited by Laura E. Donaldson and Kwok Pui-lan. New York: Routledge, 2002.

Yeo, Khiok-Khng. *Chairman Mao Meets the Apostle Paul: Christianity, Communism, and the hope of China*. Grand Rapids: Brazos Press. 2002.

———. "Li and Law in the Analects and Galations: A Chinese Christian Understanding of Ritual and Property," *Asian Journal of Theology*, 19:2 (2005): 309–332.

———. *Musing with Confucius and Paul: Toward a Chinese Christian*. Eugene, Ore: Cascade Books, 2008.

———. "On Confucian Xin and Pauline Pistis." *Sino-Christian Studies* 2D (2006): 25–51.

———. "Rhetorical Interaction in 1 Corinthians 8 and 10: Potential Implications for a Chinese, Cross-Cultural Hermeneutic." Ph.D. diss., Evanston: Northwestern University, 1992.

———. *What Has Jerusalem to Do with Beijing? Biblical Interpretation from a Chinese Perspective*. Harrisburg: Trinity Press International, 1998.

Young, Robert J. C. *Postcolonialism: An Historical Introduction*. Oxford: Blackwell, 2001.

Yu-lan, Fung. *A History of Chinese Philosophy*. Translated by Derk Bodde. Princeton: Princeton University Press, 1952.

Zachariah, George. *Alternatives Unincorporated: Earth Ethics from the Grassroots*. London: Equinox Press, 2010.

———. "Musings on Climate Justice: A Subaltern Perspective." *Journal of Lutheran Ethics* 9:4 April (2009). No pages. Online: http://www.elca.org/What-We-Believe/Social-Issues/Journal-of-Lutheran-Ethics/Issues/April-2009/Musings-on-Climate-Justice.aspx.

AUTHOR AND SUBJECT INDEX

Adam, Andrew K. M. 89, 90, 136
Adam, Ian 27
Africa 70, 135, 146-147, 149-153, 165-166, 190, 226-227
Ahern, Emily M. 181
Ahn, Byung-Mu 117
Alexander the Great 84
Alexander, Donald 177
Alexander, Philip S. 209
Allison, Dale C. 190
Amaladass, Anand 108-111
Ambivalence 15, 188
Amore, Roy 102
Analects 137, 177, 179-180
Ancestor (incl. spirit) 4, 137, 148, 150, 156, 160, 162, 165, 168-185
Anti-Jewish; anti-Judaism 96, 117, 215
Appiah, Kwame Anthony 30
Argenti, Father Cyrille 189
Aristotle 173
Ashcroft, Bill 13, 17, 18, 21, 27, 142-143
Asia 59, 66, 70, 75-76, 81-82, 86, 89, 91, 101-102, 104-106, 108, 119, 121-122, 135, 136, 169, 230
Asian American 89
Attridge, Harold W. 97
Augsburger, David W. 176
Augustine, of Hippo 210
Aus, Roger David 191, 208-209
Australia 19, 203
Authentic exegesis 127, 132
Authority 69, 73, 83, 173, 183, 209, 212, 233

Badimo 4, 136, 137, 141, 145-152, 155-167
Baird, William 51
Beardslee, William 217
Beavis, Mary Ann 232, 234
Bhabha, Homi K. 15, 17, 20, 30, 188-189
Bhikkus 104
Bible and Culture Collective 30, 34, 40-41, 54
Blaser, Mario 14
Boehmer, Elleke 144
Boer, Roland 25, 29

Boff, Leonardo B. 14
Bong-rin, Ro 169
Borg, Marcus 102, 106
Botswana 135, 137, 141, 145-147, 155, 164, 167
Breton, Stanislas 212
Brown, John and Tom J. 151-162
Bruns, J. Edgar 102
Brydon, Diana 14, 18, 30
Buddhism 12, 102-103
Bunzl, Matti 32
Burdon, Christopher 193
Burton, Antoinette 32
Byrskog, Samuel 107

Cabral, Amicar 29
Canaanite 94, 96, 142, 147
Capel Anderson, Janice 40
Caputo, John D. 39
Carter, Warren 95
Chakkuvarackal, Johnson T. 100-101
Charusheela, S. 14
Childs, Peter 13-15, 20-21
China 13, 25-26, 120-121, 135, 137, 168-169, 181, 183
Chinese Ancestor Worship 4, 137, 168-169
Chiu, Milton M. 179, 182
Chrisman, Laura 13, 15
Christ 185, 172-174, 183-185, 231
Christianity 14, 60, 70, 77, 81, 85, 97, 100, 105-106, 158, 161, 196, 208
Chung, Hyun Kyung 116
Cieng-sin; gods 182
Clarke, Sathianathan 113-114
Climate change,
  academic 73
  weather 2
Colonial power 15, 18, 21, 23-24, 26, 81
Colonisation 8, 13, 18, 20, 27-29, 82, 91, 115, 136-137, 139
  decolonisation 121-122
  political and economical colonisation 22-24
  semicolonisation 120
Comaroff, Jean and John 142, 145, 148, 150, 152-154, 158, 164

Confucianism 177
Confucius 137, 169, 177–180
Constructive; Construction;
  Constructing 7, 10–11, 13–15, 19, 34–36, 40, 50, 52, 57, 68–73, 78, 83, 87–89, 107, 109, 113, 121, 123, 128, 129–130, 132, 144, 152, 157–158, 166–167, 183, 186, 193, 225, 227, 228, 232–233
Context; postcolonial 4, 37, 58, 75, 122–123, 144
Context; theoretical 7
Contextual 3, 32, 43, 61–62, 86, 90–91, 107, 121, 129
Cooppan, Vilashini 22, 122
Cranfield, C. E. B 191
Criticism; postcolonial (critique) 3, 17, 40–41, 45, 49, 52–53, 56–59, 61, 63–64, 67, 71, 74, 87, 128–129, 143, 189
Criticism; postmodern 58, 67, 76, 81, 129
Crossan, Dominic 95, 190–192, 199, 217
Cutrufelli, Maria Rosa 227

D'Sa, Francis X. 58, 109, 111, 138, 219
Dalit 4, 81, 90–91, 107–108, 113–115, 118, 123–125, 130, 138–139, 225, 227–228, 232–233
Dasenbrock, Reed Way 14, 52
Davies, W. D. 190
De Smet, Richard 107
Deconstruction 36, 38–40, 47, 57, 60, 71, 87, 129
DeHay, Terry 18
DeMan, Paul 39
Demon 4, 94–95, 136, 138, 141–142, 145–151, 156–159, 161–163, 165–167, 169, 186–187, 189–212, 221, 224
Demythologisation 188, 192–193, 200, 202–203, 205, 207, 209
Derrett, J. Duncan M. 46, 102, 189, 193–194, 197, 204, 206
Derrida, Jacques 15, 39, 40
Dharmaram Vidya Kshetram 98
Dhvani 4, 90, 107–113, 118, 123–124, 138, 155, 213–214
Dhvani exegesis 101, 108–113, 115, 125, 130, 138, 214, 219–220, 222–223
Dialectic 37, 87, 175–176
Dialogue 11, 45, 72, 87, 96, 103, 113, 121, 123, 173, 197, 200, 231
Diaspora 8, 122–123, 221

Divining (as a method) 136, 164–167
Donahue, John R. 191
Donaldson, Laura E. 11, 14, 18, 27, 69, 189, 192, 226
Dube, Musa W. 4, 9, 11, 58, 63, 82, 90, 136–137, 141, 146, 164, 190, 226, 227, 229
DuBois, W. E. Burghardt 29
Dutton, Denis 30

East; Eastern World 11, 45, 68, 69–70, 97, 103, 121, 124, 131
Edmunds, Albert Joseph 102
Eiman, O. Zein-Elbdin 14
Elisha, James 114
Elliott, John H. 40
Enlightenment; Enlightenment period 23, 41, 43, 51, 53, 55, 57, 64, 68, 73, 74, 78, 84, 85, 92, 138
Episteme 2, 3, 8, 10, 16–17, 23, 32, 33–40, 42, 44, 48–49, 51–53, 56–57, 63, 67–68, 70, 81–83, 85–87, 91, 93, 98–99, 108, 115, 119, 124–125, 127–132
Epistemological 79–80, 82, 87, 95
 – hegemony 16
 – influences 24
 – concepts 33–34
 – paradigm 41
 – presuppositions 43
 – frame 51
 – colonialism 53, 54, 56, 57–59, 61, 67, 74, 77
Esty, Jed 32
Ethnocentric 11, 48, 108
Europe; European 11, 18–19, 21–22, 27, 35, 42–43, 63, 68–69, 81–86, 92, 96–97, 102, 152–155, 157, 159, 166–167

Fabella, Virginia 20
Fanon, Frantz 21, 29, 143–144, 195–199, 201, 206, 210–211
Feminism 42, 52, 59, 75, 96
Feuchtwang, Stephan 182
Filial piety 176–180
First Nations 19
Flesh-and-blood 14, 29, 32, 38, 44, 49, 80, 128, 131
Fortes, Meyer 181
Foskett, Mary F. 89, 90, 100, 136
Foucault, Michel 8, 10, 15–16, 32–35, 42, 48, 82–83, 128
Fraser, Sylvia 234

AUTHOR AND SUBJECT INDEX

Fundamentalism 92
Funk, Robert 214, 218

Gairdner, William H. 161
Galilee 94–95, 197, 231
Gandhi, Leela 22, 24–25
Gandhi, Mahatma 20
Geijerstam, Jan af 28
Gender 8, 10, 14, 39, 42, 72, 135, 196, 230
Gentile 197, 215, 221–222
Geomancy; *Fung shui* 182–183
Georgi, Dieter 65, 84
Gerasa 94
Gerasene demoniac 138, 189–194, 196, 198–201, 204–205, 207–208, 210
Global 7, 9, 15, 18–20, 22, 28, 48, 69, 72, 74–77, 108, 115, 121–122, 127–128, 130, 153, 186, 230
Globalisation 22
Gnanadason, Aruna 230
Gnostic 51, 171, 173–174
Goodmann, Hananya 105
Griffiths, Gareth 13, 18, 21, 27
Groot, Jan Jacob Maria, de 183

Hall, Stuart 18, 24
Hammar, Anna-Karin 26
Harasym, Sarah 26
Harrington, Daniel J. 191
Hawley, John C. 14, 27
Hayes, John H. 41
Haynes, Stephen R. 40, 55
Hegemony 7, 16, 67, 71–77, 80, 82, 84–87, 93, 97, 104, 123, 125, 129, 131, 137, 188
Hermeneutics 4, 54, 66, 76, 80, 99, 141, 176, 226
High Ones, the 136, 148
Historical criticism 42, 45–46, 52, 57, 60–62, 64–67, 72, 74–77, 79, 81, 92, 96, 127–129, 139, 214, 216–217, 220, 223
Historical Jesus 58, 65, 77, 80, 83–86
HIV/AIDS 225, 230
Hodge, Bob 18
Holladay, Carl R. 41
Hollenbach, Paul W. 192, 195–199, 201–202, 205–206, 210
Holmberg, Bengt 37–38
Holy Spirit 104, 165–166
Hooker, Morna D. 191–192, 197, 201, 204
Horsley, Richard A. 95, 192–199, 201–202, 204–207, 210–212

Hsiao 176, 178–180
Hsu, Francis L. K. 181–182
Hybrid; hybridity 8, 12, 15, 20–21, 44, 46, 66, 93–94, 136, 148, 156–157, 161–162

Ideology 56, 61, 71, 84, 128, 145, 150, 152
Immanence 177–178
Imperialism 9, 22, 24, 116, 143, 152, 158, 188, 226–228, 233
India 1, 11, 23, 56, 70, 77–78, 80, 92, 97–98, 100–101, 103–106, 113, 213
Indigenous people 12, 77, 95, 97, 106, 112, 115, 120, 123, 125, 128, 130, 137, 176, 186, 189, 199
Inter-epistemic 37, 39, 49, 128
Inter-textual 46, 91, 102, 104, 137
Interpathic understanding 175–176, 181, 184–185
Interpretation 3–4, 42–43, 47, 49, 53–57, 60–61, 63–66, 75–76, 79, 82, 87, 89–90, 92–96, 104–105, 108, 113, 117, 121–123, 128, 130, 135–136, 139, 145–146, 151, 166, 193, 198–199, 202–204, 206, 214–216, 218–220, 222–223, 226–227, 232
Islam 70
Iverson, Kelly 191, 197

Jen 178–180
Jeremias, Joachim 215
Jew; Jewish 8, 96, 102, 105, 122, 170, 197, 208, 215
Johnson, Barbara 39
Johnson, Teng Kok Lim 46, 58–60, 65, 72–76, 80
Jones, Derek 161
Judaism 221
Jussawalla, Feroza 14, 52

Kah-Jin Kuan, Jeffrey 89–90, 100, 136
Käsemann, Ernst 78
Kertelge, Karl 221
Kgasa A. 154–155, 163
Kim, Sung-Hae 177
King James Version 101, 147
King, Richard 70
Kingdom 95, 191, 198, 216, 218
Kipling, Rudyard 11–12, 159
Knowledge (and hegemony) 13, 16, 24, 33, 35–36, 85, 122, 170
Krentz, Edgar 214
Kui; evil spirit 182

Kwok, Pui-lan 8, 11, 14, 27, 42–44, 58, 63, 69, 75–76, 80–86, 96–97, 107, 115, 118–123, 138, 226

Landry, Donna 15
Lausberg, Heinrich 173
Lawson, Alan 151, 167
Legio X Fretensis 95, 208
Legrand, Lucien 121
Levine, Amy-Jill 31, 96, 215
Li 178–180
Liberation 92, 115, 118, 123, 194, 210–212
 – criticism 11
 – political 24, 31, 45, 59, 81
Liberation theology 27, 39, 114–116
Ling, Amy 45
Longkumar, Limtula 98
Loomba, Ania 12–14, 17–19, 21–22, 25, 32, 70, 72
Lowe, Lisa 70
Luke, Gospel of 145

MacLean, Gerald 15
Magnusson, John 11
Mahabaratha 112
Mahavagga 102, 104
Manickam, Thomas 107
Mark, Gospel of 117
Martin, Dale B. 209
Martin, W. A. P. 169
Marxism 25, 42
Matthew, Gospel of 97, 146
McClintock, Anne 14
Mchami, R. E. K. 190
McKenzie, Steven L. 40, 55
McRae, Glenn 14
Meeks, Wayne A. 175
Melanchthon, Monica Jyotsna 139
Metaphor 36, 52, 87, 95–96, 100, 109–110, 137–138, 207, 214, 217–219
Method 4, 36–40, 52, 60, 65–66, 76–81, 89, 92, 109, 111, 118, 123, 125, 130, 138, 164, 166–167, 214, 217
Metzger, Bruce M. 173
Miller, J. Maxwell 55–56
Mimicry 15
Minjung; minjung exegesis 81, 90–91, 108, 115–118, 121, 123–125
Mishra, Vijay 18
Misra, Neelesh 13
Mission; missionaries; missionary 11, 35, 95–97, 100–101, 104, 106, 120–121, 128, 131, 142, 145, 149, 152–154, 157–159, 164, 166, 169, 174, 183, 197, 222
Mizoram 1, 127, 131
Mohan, Sanal 228
Monotheism 173–174
Moon, Cyris H. S. 117
Moore, Charles A. 179–180
Moore, Michael 25
Moore, Stephen D. 10, 40, 42, 188–189, 192–193, 197, 236
Moral 69, 71, 174, 176–179, 196, 200, 230, 232
Morris, Charles W. 181
Motswana 141, 150, 158, 161, 167
Muthuraj, Joseph G. 92, 106
Myers, Ched 193–195, 207
Myth, mythical, mythological; master 1, 65, 77, 81, 84–86, 98, 120, 128, 181–183, 188, 192, 197, 203, 207, 211, 224, 232

Nakashima Brock, Rita 231
Nationalism 227
Neo-colonialism 13, 115, 192, 193, 225, 226
Ng, Chae-Woon 177–178
Ngaka 145, 155
Ngubane, John B. 149
Nirmal, Arvind P. 113–114
Nkrumah, Kwame 29
North Africa 70
North America 2, 19, 63, 135–136
North, northern 1, 45

Objectivism 61–64, 67, 79, 82, 129
Occident 10, 69–70
Olsson, Birger 41, 66
Oosthuizen, Gerhardus C. 165
Oral; tradition, people, reader, transmission 64, 148, 151, 154, 214, 215, 216, 221
Orientalism 10–13, 67–70, 77, 82, 85–87, 106, 129

Paradigm shift 47–48, 73–74, 88, 119, 129–130
Pathrapankal, Joseph 63, 92–93, 98, 215
Patriarchal, Patriarchy 183, 227–228, 234
Paul, the apostle 4, 135, 137, 169–176, 183–186, 212
Peek, Phillip M. 164
Penner, Todd 42, 52–53, 90, 118, 136

AUTHOR AND SUBJECT INDEX 253

Perceived reality 3, 32–33, 49, 128
Perelman, Chaïm 173
Periphery 11, 14, 26, 69, 72, 119
Permer, Karin and Lars Göran 33
Pesch, Rudolph 201, 202
Petersen, George 217
Petrella, Ivan 14
Poor, the 120, 230
Postcolonial exegesis 4, 7, 16, 63, 89, 96, 124, 129
Postcolonial imagination 107, 118–119, 123, 138
Postcolonial perspective 38, 45, 85, 90, 100, 115, 128–129
Postcolonialism 8, 9, 12, 14–15, 18, 22–25, 27–28, 32, 42–43, 46–48, 59, 67, 71, 89–90, 124, 127, 130, 210
Postcoloniality 2–3, 8, 15, 21–25, 27–28, 31–32, 36, 40, 48, 88, 124, 129–131
Postmodern philosophy 15, 30
Poythress, Vern 214
Premnath, Devadasan N. 100, 103, 114
Prodigal daughter 139, 224, 230, 233
Protestant 100, 169
Psichari, Henriette 43

Qian, Zhaoming 13, 70
Queer 11, 14, 27, 39

Racism 116, 167
Radhakrishnan, Sarvepalli 102
Räisänen, Heikki 45–48
Ranajit, Guha 27
Rege, Sharmila 228
Regionally Colonized 147
Relevance 7, 58, 67, 77–80, 82, 86–87, 93, 98, 107–108, 123, 129, 139, 175, 195, 216, 228
Renan, Ernest J. 43, 84–86
Resurrection 84
Rhetorical Hermeneutic 4, 137, 168
Riches, John 63
Ricoeur, Paul 218
Ritualistic practice 169
Roman Catholic 98, 100, 169
Roman Empire 122, 189
Runesson, Anders 8, 26, 95, 97
Runesson, Anna 10, 49, 95, 97, 104

Said, Edward W. 10, 13, 15, 20, 68–70, 72, 83, 85, 150
Salvation 181, 184, 197, 215, 222, 230–231, 233

Sami population 19
Sandilands, Alexander 145–146
Sandmel, Samuel 102
Schenke, Ludger 221
Schüssler-Fiorenza, Elisabeth 42, 45–47, 81
Schweitzer, Albert 57, 77–78
Schweizer, Eduard 191
Scott, David 32
Scriptures 60, 77, 103, 106, 121, 226, 229
Sebastian, Mrinalini 14
Segovia, Fernando F. 10–11, 17–18, 24, 29–30, 39–44, 48, 58, 60–63, 66, 94, 136, 189
Setswana Bible 4, 136–137, 142, 145, 148–154, 163, 167
Sexism 116
Situative context 63, 92
Småberg, Maria 68
Smart, Barry 34
Smith, Henry N. 169
Sneja, Gunew 14
Soares-Prabhu, George M. 4, 31, 46, 58–59, 61–62, 64–66, 78–80, 92–93, 104, 109, 112, 114, 118, 121, 136, 138, 213, 215
South Africa 146–147, 152, 158
South America 11, 150
South, southern 45, 99, 102, 105
Spirit possession 158, 199, 211
Spivak, Gayatri Chakravorty 14–16, 22, 26, 80
Stählin, Gustav 174
Stendahl, Krister 45–46, 93
Stenström, Hanna 42
Stoller, Paul 148
Stower, Stanley K. 174
Strong, Josiah 157
Stuart, Douglas 54
Sugirtharajah, R. S. 13, 20, 22, 24–25, 27, 32, 44–46, 58, 60–61, 66, 70–71, 76–77, 80–81, 93, 95, 98–101, 109, 117, 122, 136, 189, 193, 198, 211
Suh, David Kwang-sun 115–116
Suvir, Kaul 32
Swete, Henry Barclay 191, 193

T'ien 177–179
Tao Te 176–177
Taussig, Michael 150
Te Selle, Sallie 219
Terror; terrorist 27, 225
Theoretical location 7–8, 16–17, 128, 135
Thiongo, Ngugi wa 143–144, 151

Third World 20, 44, 230
Thottakara, Augustine 46
Thundy, Zacharias P. 46, 102–103, 105–106
Thurén, Torsten 47
Tiffin, Chris 151, 167
Tiffin, Helen 13, 17–18, 21, 27, 142–143
Tolbert, Mary Ann 42–43, 58, 62–64, 136
Trans-cultural 103
Trans-religious 103
Translation; bible and cultural 4, 44, 91, 99–101, 136–137, 142, 145, 148, 150–152, 166, 169
Truth 7, 16, 33, 38, 40, 42–43, 49, 56–57, 64, 71, 75–76, 81, 83, 108, 121, 127–128, 117, 219
Turner, Bryan S. 70
Twelftree, Graham 200
Two-Thirds World 20, 46, 66, 75, 98, 136

Unclean spirit 186–187, 190, 201–204, 207–209, 211–212
United Theological College 1, 99
Untouchables; see dalit

Values; family, conflictual 91, 101, 143, 144, 158, 176–178, 180–181, 184–185, 196
Vandana, Sr. 109, 112
Vander Stichele, Caroline 42, 52–53, 90, 118, 136
Vernacular; translation, poetics 101, 142, 152
Via, Dan O. 40, 218, 238

War; World War, imperial 159, 207, 209
Way Dasenbrock, Reed 14
Weber, Max 200
Webster, John C. B. 113
Wei-ming, Tu 180
Westerholm, Stephen 110
Western academia 15
Western Biblical Studies 3, 51
Western World 10, 78, 83, 108
Wiebe, Gregory David 4, 136, 138, 186
Wiebe, Phillip H. 192, 200–205
Wilder, Amos 217
Williams, Patrick 13–15, 20–21
Witting, Susan 218
Wolf, Eric Robert 36
Womanist 4, 139, 225, 228, 233–234
Women 56, 121, 135, 142, 147, 231, 234
– Asian 75, 76, 110, 136
– Canaanite 96
– Samaritan 94
Wong, Wai Ching 68
Wookey, Alfred J. 148, 151–153, 155

Xavier, A. 46

Yang, Ching Kun 180–181
Yegenoglu, Meyda 69
Yeo, Khiok-Khng 4, 136–137, 168
Young, Robert J. C. 17
Yu-lan, Fung 179

Zachariah, George 4, 136, 225
Zimbabwe 146

www.ingramcontent.com/pod-product-compliance
Lightning Source LLC
Chambersburg PA
CBHW021358290426
44108CB00010B/287